JAMES DILWORTH

JAMES DILWORTH

R C J   S T O N E

Published by the Dilworth Trust Board,
Private Bag 28-904, Remuera, Auckland 5,
New Zealand

© Dilworth Trust Board and R. C. J. Stone 1995

All rights reserved. No part of this publication may be reproduced, stored in a retrieval system, or transmitted, in any form or by any means, without the prior permission in writing of the Dilworth Trust Board. Within New Zealand, exceptions are allowed in respect of any fair dealing for the purpose of research or private study, or criticism or review, as permitted, under the Copyright Act 1962. Enquiries concerning reproduction outside these terms and in other countries should be sent to the Dilworth Trust Board at the address above.

ISBN 0-473-02990-1

Designed by Richard King
Cover designed by Suellen Allen
Cartography by Sandra Parkkali
Production services by Kate Stone
Produced by Egan-Reid Limited
Typeset in Sabon by Egan-Reid Limited
Printed in New Zealand by GP Print Limited

To Bill Cotter

Mr Lely, I desire you would use all your skill to paint my picture truly like me, and not flatter me at all; but remark all these roughness, pimples, warts, and everything as you see me; otherwise I will never pay a farthing for it.

—Oliver Cromwell

CONTENTS

List of Colour Plates		viii
List of Maps		ix
Preface		xi
ONE	Origins	1
TWO	The Young Pioneer: 1841–44	22
THREE	Owners and Sellers of Tamaki-Makau-Rau	34
FOUR	Man of Property: 1844–49	53
FIVE	The Dilworths of Remuera	71
SIX	In the Public Gaze	86
SEVEN	Other Dilworths	96
EIGHT	Dilworth and the Auckland and Drury Railway Company	118
NINE	Graham's Hill	134
TEN	Landed Entrepreneur	148
ELEVEN	Proprietor of City Land	168
TWELVE	Whaiti Kuranui	192
THIRTEEN	Wills and Inheritance	208
FOURTEEN	Last Things	226
APPENDIX A	Summary of the Will of James Dilworth Dated 15 November 1894	235
APPENDIX B	The Dilworth Trust in 1995	239
APPENDIX C	Dilworth School Today	240
References		242
Bibliography		258
Index		264

LIST OF COLOUR PLATES

Mullaghcreevy homestead: the old stone barn and living quarters.

Mullaghcreevy homestead: the 'new' cottage.

Joseph MERRETT, 'View of Newmarket', c.1850, watercolour (355 x 515mm). Auckland City Art Gallery collection, presented anonymously, 1923.

Alfred SHARPE (1836–1908), 'The Environs of Auckland', watercolour. Auckland City Art Gallery collection, purchased 1935.

John Barr Clark HOYTE, 'View of Auckland Harbour from Mount Hobson, Remuera', watercolour (362 x 543 mm). Auckland City Art Gallery collection.

Frederick Rice STACK, 'View from the Waitakere Ranges overlooking entrance to Manukau Harbour', 1862. Alexander Turnbull Library.

Gottfried LINDAUER, 'James Dilworth', 1876, oils. Dilworth Trust Board.

Gottfried LINDAUER, 'Isabella Dilworth', 1876, oils. Dilworth Trust Board.

Gottfried LINDAUER, 'Reverend George MacMurray', 1909, Dilworth Trust Board.

Donaghmore High Cross, estimated c.1000 years old, Donaghmore, County Tyrone, Northern Ireland.

Stephen WOODWARD, Dilworth Centennial Cross, sculpture, erected 1994. Project initiator Staniland West, presented by the Dilworth Old Boys' Association.

The chapel of St Patrick and the Centennial Cross.

Endpapers
Edward ASHWORTH (1814–96), 'Commercial Bay 1843', pen and wash (227 x 378 mm). Auckland City Art Gallery collection, presented by Sir Cecil Leys, 1935.

LIST OF MAPS

1.	James Dilworth's Ulster.	5
2.	Auckland, January 1842.	25
3.	Plan of Dilworth estate 1844–49.	56
4.	Map of Dilworth estate during railway construction, 1860s.	123
5.	Dilworth's main provincial land interests in the 1880s.	203

PREFACE

THIS BOOK is testimony to the conviction of Mr D. F. Cotter, Chairman of the Dilworth Trust Board, that James Dilworth had a life of sufficient intrinsic interest to warrant a full biography. Few would dispute that, in his day, Dilworth was a man of wealth and influence, and is one whose name has endured to the present in the school he founded. For the would-be biographer, the problem has not been one of the importance of his subject. Rather, it has arisen out of the unevenness of the records on which one has had to depend to write Dilworth's life. Some documentary evidence dealing with Dilworth is immensely detailed; one thinks here of the property records preserved in the public domain and available for scrutiny in the Lands and Deeds Registry. Further, because the greater part of Dilworth's residuary estate was made up of property, real estate records of his business affairs are also plentifully available in the Dilworth Trust Board Archives.

Against the abundance of such information, however, must be placed the dearth of personal records. Much of Dilworth's life has remained unrecorded. This inhibits the biographer determined to know what is not immediately obvious, but is essential to the understanding of the inner nature of the one written about, those things which, in G. K. Chesterton's phrase, lie 'on the blind side of the heart'. Little evidence of this kind is immediately available in Dilworth's case. He was a very private man, not demonstrative, and indeed revealed so little of himself that others had little chance to observe and record.

The other impediment to our full understanding of the kind of man that Dilworth was was not of his making. He and his wife Isabella had no children; no sons and daughters to leave reminiscences about what they recall of their parents, to preserve family heirlooms, letters, diaries and photographs; no one acting as custodians of family lore. Further, there have been surprisingly few people, who, from first-hand acquaintance, have been able to say what this childless couple were really like. Some gaps I have been able to fill by drawing upon the reminiscences and oral evidence of collateral descendants—in James's case, the progeny of his sisters in New Zealand and the United States, in Isbabella's, present day members of the Hall family.

To an extent I did not originally envisage, gaps that once seemed daunting have been filled by drawing upon sources of information in

County Tyrone, Northern Ireland. Members of the extended Dilworth family resident today near Dungannon whom I approached proved to be knowledgeable and enthusiastic amateur historians and genealogists. They passed on much valuable information and put me in touch with organizations such as 'Irish World' in Dungannon and the cultural centre in Donaghmore which helped me further in my quest for the historical Dilworth. Ten days spent in Northern Ireland during 1993, and a somewhat longer period in the Republic, served to convince me that traits of personality, idiosyncrasies and convictions, which I had earlier imagined were peculiar to Dilworth, were derived from a broader culture which had shaped him in the first twenty-three years of his life.

I acknowledge with gratitude the grant-in-aid from the Dilworth Trust Board which helped finance my visit to Ireland. The Trust has been constant in its support of this biography, whilst placing no restrictions upon how I have chosen to present James Dilworth. Typing and other facilities were generously placed at my disposal within the Trust Board's office. I would mark out for particular thanks Mr D. F. (Bill) Cotter whose support has been constant, and Mr Clark Thomas, secretary-manager, for his wise counsel. All members of the Trust Board staff, however, have helped by their tolerance of my no doubt disruptive presence over the last three years.

Many other people have helped me in my task but some few must be singled out. In Dungannon three people who assisted me while I was there continued to do so by correspondence and the despatch of photographs and photocopies, even while the last chapters of this book were being written. They are Norman Cardwell of the Royal School, and John and Wilfred Dilworth of Derrybuoy. Anne and Norman Gilpin provided wonderful hospitality and local knowledge while I was in Dungannon. Eionn Kerr of 'Irish World' was very generous with his time and knowledge, as was Bertie McLean of the Donaghmore Historical Society. The insights of William O'Kane have influenced me far more than perhaps he realizes. I thank Paul and Christine Hewitt of the Royal School for their help at a time of pressure.

Two in New Zealand, John Stacpoole and Ian Wilson (senior master at Dilworth School), alerted me to the Irish dimension of Dilworth's life long before I was conscious of it; their intuition was correct. Dr Murray Wilton, principal of Dilworth, went the second mile in helping me. The ideas and researches of Professor Alan Ward and Mr Maurice Alemann with regard to the Maori sale of Tamaki-makau-rau I gratefully acknowledge. Mr J. T. Diamond was of great assistance whenever I was puzzled about some aspect of history touching upon the Waitakeres or west Auckland; he was always knowledgeable and always generous. I acknowledge, too, how much I owe to the researches of almost forty years ago of Mr David Sherratt, no longer resident in this country. Miss Georgina Mossman of Taupo,

xii

her mother Mrs E. D. Mossman and her brother Mr Dilworth Mossman kindly helped with oral history and placed the invaluable Mossman Papers at my disposal. Mr Joe Howard of the same town, Taupo, helped in like manner for which I am grateful.

Institutions which assisted in my researches are the Auckland Public Library whose resources I used constantly, the Auckland Museum Library, the Alexander Turnbull Library and National Archives, Wellington; staff at all these repositories were patient and helpful. I am very proud of the colour transparencies of paintings by Hoyte, Sharpe and others which the Auckland City Art Gallery has given me permission to use. The Catholic diocesan archives and those of the Auckland Anglican diocese have contributed materially to this work. *The Dictionary of New Zealand Biography* staff, and especially Mrs Louise Buckingham, shared their resources most generously.

I thank Barbara Batt for the professionalism of her typing. My friends Mrs Augusta Ford and Dr Dennis McEldowney (particularly) have helped to tidy up the style of my drafts. Kate Stone provided valuable editorial assistance.

I owe most to my wife, Mary, who supported me in all sorts of ways and has been a diligent research assistant in New Zealand and Ireland.

Russell Stone
December 1994

CHAPTER ONE

Origins

IT IS CONSISTENT with the many uncertainties surrounding the life of James Dilworth that even the origins of his surname, found today in a number of countries, should be a matter of conjecture.

An American genealogist, Virginia Bushman, who has made a life-long study of the United States Dilworths, notes that the name, which appears in both medieval England and Flanders, seems to occur in a kindred form in Germany at about the same period.[1] She maintains that the two constituents of the name are Teutonic in origin, with 'dil' at first probably meaning some people in general, later coming to refer to a specific person; and the common suffix 'worth', which occurs in names like Tamworth and Epworth, having the meaning of 'a small estate'. A scholar in linguistics with an interest in how English names began has arrived at a similar conclusion, though following a different path to get there. In his view, 'worth' would have denoted in Old English (the Anglo-Saxon tongue) either a 'homestead' or an 'enclosed place', and 'Dil' or 'Dill' was possibly an abbreviation of a longer name (just as Will is of William).[2] Dilworth would thus have indicated the 'homestead of Dill', presumably a landowner of some prominence. At some later time, descendants of that notable and, often, lesser people living in the vicinity of his estate, may have attached this place name to their Christian name and so begun to use it as a patronymic or surname.

W. J. (Bill) Dilworth of London has another explanation of how the name began in England.[3] It first occurred, he believes, as the name of a place, which he precisely locates—the hamlet of Dilworth in Longridge Fell, near Preston in Lancashire. He is persuaded that this place probably gained its name as 'the place [worth] where the dill grows', the herb being valued in medieval times not only for flavouring food but for treatment of flatulence. Be that as it may, the small hamlet of Dilworth in the form of 'Bileuurde' (which by 1242 had evolved into 'Dilleworth') appears as a place name in the Domesday Survey of 1086.[4]

Once a small hamlet in the Anglo-Saxon capital manor of Prestune (Preston), Dilworth was listed in the Domesday record as one of the sixty-two 'vills'* in that manor which was now 'the land of Roger of Poitu'.

Whatever the name's first meaning, the conflicting versions agree that it is of considerable antiquity, and that the English variant probably derives from the name of a place in the Blackburn Hundred of Lancashire.

Early nineteenth-century Ordnance Survey maps of that part of Lancashire still showed Dilworth as a distinct settlement, also locating a nearby Dilworth House once attached to the village. A building of that name in Dilworth Lane still exists, though now absorbed in the expanded town of Longridge, Lancashire. People taking their surname from this medieval hamlet, Bill Dilworth contends, spread during subsequent centuries through Lancashire, Cheshire and Yorkshire. By the late sixteenth century some were to be found as far afield as London.[5] But it was those concentrated in north-west England who were the main forebears of the world-wandering Dilworths, who migrated to Ireland in the early seventeenth century, and who as a Quaker branch of Lancashire Dilworths went with William Penn to America to found Pennsylvania in the 1680s.

Our James Dilworth belonged to the northern Ireland branch, who were closely associated with the early seventeenth-century Plantations in that part of the country. Under the Tudors, colonists had been introduced into Ireland to consolidate the English expansion which had been taking place there since Anglo-Norman times. The Plantations begun under the Stuart king, James I, were a much more thoroughgoing strategy of subjugation than any carried out before. They were a consequence of the bloody uprising initiated by the Gaelic chieftain, Hugh O'Neill, Earl of Tyrone, in his attempt to expel the hated English from Ulster. After years of struggle he had made his peace in 1603 on promise of a pardon. But the machinations of English officials convinced the Earl that he was being reduced to a mere landlord, and in 1607, accompanied by the Earl of Tyrconnel, he fled the country.

This 'flight of the earls', as the episode has come to be known in history, opened the way to the introduction in 1609–10 of the Plantation system into Ulster. A momentous development, this system was devised to institute English law, and to replace the previous Irish population and culture with British landlords supported by what has been described as a 'privileged labour force' brought in from the British mainland.[6]

On the rather trumpery grounds that because of their flight the earls could be presumed guilty of treason, their vast lands were declared forfeit to the Crown: namely the whole of Tyrone, most of Armagh, most of Donegal and more than half of Fermanagh. The process did

---

* 'Vill' is an old French word meaning a farm or country house. Under feudalism it indicated a feudal township and was the smallest administrative unit.

not stop there.[7] Ultimately six of the nine counties of Ulster were subjected to confiscation.

Under the new order, estates carved out of these lands were as a general rule granted to new English and Scottish owners (invariably men of some substance and position) who were called 'undertakers', or to 'servitors' (senior officials and army officers in Ireland). In a limited number of cases there were re-grants to Irish freeholders.[8] Grants carried certain obligations: payment of an annual rent to the Crown; preparation on each estate of a 'bawn',* a fortified courtyard with a substantial building thereon; and an undertaking to place within three years ten British families for every 1,000 acres held—this last obligation varying, however, according to the kind of grant made. It has been estimated that by 1641 about 100,000 British colonists had been settled in Ulster under this Plantation system.

Present-day Dilworths in County Tyrone are proud of their descent from old Planter stock. As members of the Lancashire branch of the family, they claim to have been part of the first wave of English Planter families introduced between 1610 and 1620 into the fertile lowlands of south-eastern Tyrone centred upon the ancient O'Neill stronghold of Dungannon, a town whose name is said to have been derived from Gaelic, 'the fort of Ceannan'.[9] Almost certainly they would have come by way of Chester, then the major port, apart from London, for trade with Ireland—until the silting up of the Dee Estuary in the eighteenth century robbed that town of the depth of water necessary for its ships.

One account based on family lore precisely locates Dilworths as setting out initially from Lancaster in north-west Lancashire, and speaks of three brothers, weavers, arriving in Tyrone as early as 1612.[10] Mr John Dilworth, historian of the Dungannon branch of the Dilworths, claims that the name first appeared in documentary form in County Tyrone hearth-money rolls, with a seventeenth-century demand for payment of a hearthstone rate for their farmhouse in the townland† of Drumard in the civil parish of Killyman.[11] The author has visited, under John Dilworth's guidance, a cottage which now stands abandoned and in ruins on the site of the cottage so rated, presumably the first Dilworth dwelling in County Tyrone.

Dilworths are said to have slowly built up homes and farms in the Killyman parish, which has a landscape characterized by variously shaped sandy hills, but was, and still is, nevertheless, very good farmland.[12] During the 1641–42 rising, the parish was the scene of a

---

* Bawn is the Anglicization of the Irish term 'badhun' meaning cattle fort. A bawn was usually an earthen enclosure strengthened by timber palisades, and often took in an associated fortified building of coursed stone or brick.

† In the seventeenth century, townlands came into being as the smallest administrative division in the country. They varied in size usually according to productivity. The names given to townlands were often a reused and Anglicized form of the old Gaelic names of 'ballyboes', which themselves measured grazing capacity.

The first known Dilworth cottage at Drumard, near Dungannon.
Norman Cardwell

massacre in which (according to John Dilworth) a number of the family were killed.[13] At this time the old O'Neill fort in the north of Dungannon was destroyed as part of the attempt by Parliamentary forces to reassert their control over the town. Civil disorder, and insecurity for the Planter families of Ulster, did not disappear until 1654, and then only temporarily.[14] In parts of County Tyrone, particularly where lands were less desirable, native Irish still outnumbered British tenants and continued to do so right up to the time James Dilworth emigrated in the 1830s. As Catholic nationalism strengthened in the nineteenth century, Protestants of Planter extraction continued to be looked upon as outsiders. But Dilworth of Auckland always considered himself Irish; identifying passionately with the land which his family had occupied for over two centuries. Nor did he lose his sense of kinship with Protestant Ulstermen. These things gave him his distinct sense of Irish nationhood and were part of the deep folk memories he took with him to New Zealand in 1841.

By the eighteenth century the Dilworths had become more numerous, and were widely dispersed through the undulating countryside of valleys and drumlins—low hillocks made up of glacial deposit—that are a feature of south-eastern Tyrone. Database searches for the name of Dilworth in the pre-Famine period show it on tithe applotment assessments, rating valuations and the like, throughout much of the barony of Dungannon,* for townlands in the parishes of Killyman,

---

* Barony as a territorial unit had a special meaning when it came into use in sixteenth-century Ireland. Baronies seem to have been created as divisions of a county, from the lands of Irish chiefs as they successively submitted to the English Crown.

ORIGINS

Clonfeacle, Donaghmore, Drumglass—some of those euphoniously evocative place-names which, in the image of a Tyrone poet, 'sigh like a pressed melodeon'.[15] By the end of the eighteenth century, eighty Dilworth families were said to be living in the Dungannon area. What is remarkable is the frequency with which certain Christian names recur among these Dilworths from generation to generation, in particular the names of Andrew, John, James and Richard.

Gilbert Pearce in his history of Dilworth School speaks of this tradition as one carried over from Lancashire. He notes that in the parish records of Chipping in that county—Chipping he characterizes as a 'centre of distribution' of the Lancashire Dilworths—the Christian name James appears for thirty-five per cent of the men in the years

James Dilworth's Ulster.

5

between 1559 and 1680.[16] James was equally common as the chosen name of the Irish branch of the family. This creates problems for an historian when an oral reminiscence or written record about, say, a James or a John or an Andrew Dilworth lacks dates or even a generalized time context. Who is the person spoken of, or even the generation to which he belongs?

In my quest for the historical James Dilworth, I became more and more convinced that he has been misunderstood by past commentators because of a failure to put his life in the setting of his family background, and of his Irish experience. The most significant episodes in his life, the decision to leave Ireland and the extraordinary singleness of purpose with which he acquired and developed his landed estate shortly after he came to New Zealand can be understood only in the light of the changing circumstances of the Dilworth family back in County Tyrone during James's formative years before the age of twenty-four.

The Battle of Waterloo, only a few weeks after James Dilworth was born in 1815, not only ended the long French wars but is also generally regarded as marking a watershed in Irish history.[17] Whereas in the half-century before 1815 the Irish economy had expanded, buoyed up by a good market for agricultural produce in England, in the post-war period conditions worsened. Just after the peace, County Tyrone had two bad harvests.[18] Everywhere in Ireland agricultural prices fell, and stayed down; deflationary government policies prevailed. Yet the population grew relentlessly (and most markedly in Ulster, the province with the highest population density), reaching a total of eight millions by 1841. Social tensions were exacerbated by the great structural problem: how could the country continue to support such a mass of people, now dangerously dependent on a single crop, the potato?

Such were (and are) the regional differences in Ireland that conditions in that country overall must not be taken as representative of County Tyrone. Hence the need to study the Dungannon area in rather more detail, for the Dilworths to which James of Auckland belonged were essentially Dungannon people. People bearing that name were listed in the 1820s as tenant farmers in at least one-third of the eighteen parishes making up the barony of Dungannon.[19] The social character of the town of Dungannon itself has also to be taken into account.[20] By the time James Dilworth began at the Royal School there in the mid-1820s, the town had become the market and service centre of south-eastern Tyrone. Manufacturing was also important. Dungannon had a large distillery, two breweries and one of the county's two main flour mills. But, above all else, prosperity, not just for Dungannon itself but for much of the surrounding region, had come to depend on the town's linen market, which disposed of the output of a domestic industry conducted in thousands of country cottages; the 'webs' of linen cloth woven by the families of farming people, some living on the margin of subsistence.[21]

A report of 1802 spoke of the township as 'quite surrounded by bleach-greens'* and as a leader in the linen trade of 'the North of Ireland'.[22] But with the penetration of the Irish market by English factory goods, Dungannon's economy was battered. Whereas the value of linen sold on the Dungannon market each week had once averaged £5,000, by 1834 weekly sales had fallen to about one-fifth of that sum.[23] This lowered living standards among the town's businessmen but was a much more serious matter in the countryside, above all amongst those described at the time as 'farmers of the lowest denomination',[24] for whom the weaving on a hand loom of two or three yards of cloth of a winter evening in cottages lit by tallow candles or rush lights was the means of making both ends meet.

Even before the Great Famine of the 1840s, survival had become a desperate battle for many. With the population constantly increasing, competition among peasants for land was so fierce that when a lease came up for renewal they were prepared to pay rack-rents—rents at extortionate levels bearing little relation either to how productive was the land or to how depressed was the state of agriculture.[25] The strong bargaining position of the landlords when leases fell in made them universally execrated. Those in County Tyrone were no exception. In that county during James Dilworth's youth there were about sixty so-called 'principal proprietors', of whom barely a quarter spent a sufficient portion of the year on their estate to be considered 'resident'.[26] It was commonly believed that those who were 'resident' tended to have a more sympathetic personal relationship with lessees than did the agents of absentees who were prone to apply the letter of law no matter how harsh. So the high level of absenteeism among landlords was a further ground for popular resentment.

In those parts of the barony of Dungannon where James's branch of the Dilworths farmed there were three main landlords: Viscount Powerscourt, at that time as wealthy as he was notoriously absentee;[27] the Verner family, considered by their tenants oppressive and hard; and Lord Northland (later the Earl of Ranfurly), an important proprietor in the town of Dungannon itself as well as in the countryside. The Dilworths had direct dealings with each of these powerful proprietors as tenants and, in the case of Powerscourt, perhaps as rent-collectors as well. When years later James Dilworth became a man of property in New Zealand, he was regarded in the colony on any matter bearing upon land dealing as cautious and secretive and, when he had the upper hand, as decisive, even hard in negotiation.[28] This may well have

---

* Fields where linen cloth could be laid out to be bleached by exposure to sunlight.

reflected the treatment that tenants, especially those belonging to his own family, received at the hands of their landlords back in County Tyrone.

Although when James began farming in Auckland he claimed not to have had first-hand experience of farming, he was always a keen observer of practices pertaining to the land. At the time he lived in Ireland, those parts of the country that were cultivable supported the most intensive farming in western Europe. An 1832 report upon farmland in the neighbourhood of Dungannon, the area he knew best, lauded its 'high state of cultivation' and the improvements taking place in the management of farms, particularly in crop rotation, draining, fencing and manuring. In the opinion of the writer of the report, manure was the key.[29] The fertilizer generally used was what was called a 'mixed manure', a compost which could include animal dung, ashes, rushes and furze, mud and mire from shoughs (drainage ditches), even the 'scrapings of streets and roads'. Farmers who could afford to do so also dressed their land with kiln-fired lime, or even limestone itself if finely crushed, for eastern Tyrone was well endowed with limestone quarries.[30] In later years the enthusiasm of James Dilworth of Auckland for fertilizers and top-dressing became a by-word in the colony. Hailed as an instance of scientific farming, which it certainly was,[31] it was rarely recognized as a habit acquired in Dilworth's youth in Ireland, where manuring had become essential if any farmer were to survive.

Styles of farming in early nineteenth-century Ireland varied from region to region and according to one's grouping within the rural community. The kind of farm of which James Dilworth had first-hand experience in his homeland was that occupied by prosperous tenants. This stood in contrast to the poorer tenants, cottiers and labourers, whose reliance on the potato in the post-1815 years was almost total, and who were often forced to sell all other produce—barley, oats, dairy fat and pigs—to provide for goods such as candles and tobacco which ameliorated an otherwise completely wretched existence. Such was not the lot of the Dungannon Dilworths. They were solid farmers; though, to be sure, their state could suddenly change. On that portion of land which they personally farmed—rather than sublet—they would like most strong tenants follow a rotation which might have potato as a first crop, succeeded by barley and/or oats mainly as cash crops, and perhaps followed by linen flax. Though pasture land was in very short supply, these farmers would also graze stock (horses, cattle, pigs or sheep) where they could, particularly on the damper meadowlands.[32] James's father, John Dilworth, was said to have had pedigree 'blooded stock' on his farm.[33]

The size of a holding, and the kind of farming this allowed, revealed status within Ulster tenant society. Other indicators were farmhouse buildings and the tenurial rights enjoyed by the lessee. In certain parts of northern Ireland, because of the so-called 'Ulster custom', landlords had no responsibility for making capital improvements to leased land. Conversely, under the same legal convention, tenants enjoyed the right to compensation for improvements they had made, often taking the form of landlords conceding long-term leases, or respecting 'tenant-right' (such as giving sitting tenants first right of refusal when a lease fell due for renewal); this in contrast to the tenancies-at-will and annual tenancies characteristic of England and (increasingly) parts of Ireland elsewhere. Two important townland tenancies held by Dilworths in the eighteenth century were 'for ever'* in the case of Mullaghcreevy, and 'for eighteen years' in the case of Garvagh.[34]

The stone barn of a 'strong' tenant farmer of County Tyrone.
Norman Cardwell

Fortified by this security of tenure, prospering farmers in the half-century before 1815 could carry out capital improvements such as draining and fencing, and build substantial houses. These houses of themselves gave a physical expression to the gap between the 'strong' tenants and the poorer farmers and labourers who occupied small cottages built of stone or mud with thatched roofs, one-third of whom in County Tyrone shared their cottages or cabins with cattle or other stock. Both farmhouses James Dilworth lived in as a boy were solid dwellings with four or more bedrooms built of coursed stone or brick and roofed with slate; a circumstance which discredits any idea that his family were struggling tenant farmers living 'generation after generation in little grey stone cottages with thatched roofs'.[35]

The prosperity of the strong tenants during the long period of agricultural boom before 1815 arose out of two related circumstances.[36] First, since most held long-term leases they profited because their rents were static at a time of rising prices for farm produce. Second, secure in the possession of their head leases they were able to sublet (often in the teeth of ineffectual protests from their landlords) at high rents which reflected both the prices of traded farm produce and a general shortage of land. But in the more straitened times that came after the French wars, conditions no longer favoured the tenants. Landlords (often themselves troubled by an erosion of living standards) tried to turn the land hunger arising from the population explosion to their advantage. Gearoid O'Tuathaigh writes of the auctioning of lots repossessed from insolvent tenants. Where the law allowed, landlords increasingly moved to convert long-term leases that had run their course and fallen in, into tenancies-at-will. Old leases were challenged and ejectments common. Hitherto prosperous farmers were forced by inflated rents to tighten their belts. Even before the Great Famine, the larger tenants began to share the sense of vulnerability that had long troubled the lesser rural orders.[37]

During these difficult times, the Dungannon Dilworths, though

---

* Leases 'for ever' were generally granted with great reluctance by landlords, as tantamount to parting with the freehold. In 1792 Lord Northland advertised 'Leases for ever' of certain townlands within the barony, under the following wording: 'A few farms to be let for lives determinable, or for lives renewable for ever'.

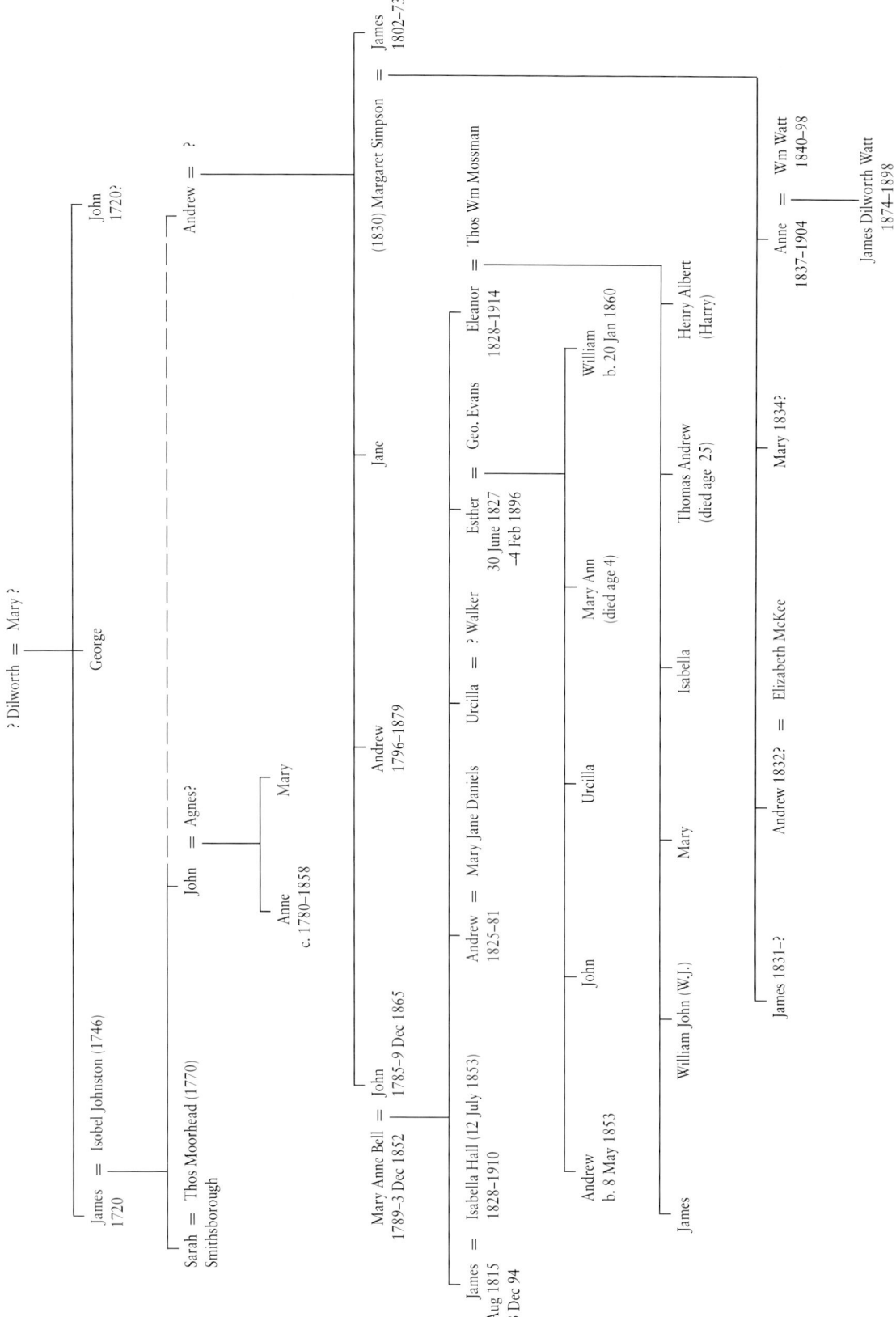

probably uneasy in mind, remained relatively unscathed. Had that not been so, James Dilworth would never have been able to launch himself on his successful land-buying career in colonial New Zealand.

Genealogical research in Ireland, even for a period as recent as the eighteenth and nineteenth centuries, is both difficult and tricky, largely because of the loss of archival records, most notably those public documents destroyed when the Four Courts in Dublin were burnt in 1922 during the civil war. In the case of James Dilworth's immediate relatives, an unchallengeable family tree cannot be put together; probably never could be. But the diagram opposite, based on leases, reports (especially Griffith's 1860 Valuations), tithe applotment lists, copies of marriages, a marriage settlement and wills,[38] is I believe, substantially accurate, except in the case of ambiguities which are clearly indicated.

The people who were most to influence the young James Dilworth were John his father (born 1785), Mary (née Bell) his mother (born 1789) and his father's cousin Anne (born 1780). For convenience we can speak of the Dunseark and the Mullaghcreevy Dilworths, those being the names of townlands on which John's branch of the family and Anne's branch respectively had their homesteads.

Mullaghcreevy, lying some two kilometres south-west of Donaghmore, was always regarded by James of Auckland as the family estate. Family tradition has it that Dilworths first took up land in the Donaghmore parish early in the eighteenth century. The oldest document so far sighted which makes reference to Dilworths as being in possession of Mullaghcreevy is a marriage settlement dated 1777 drawn up by James (born 1720) in favour of his daughter Sarah. In this deed, James, already a farmer of substance, is shown as holding the townland on the best of all titles, a 'lease for ever', from the Archbishop of Armagh.[39] Some years earlier (in or about 1760) Thomas Verner, head of a rising family in the county, had acquired the estate of which Mullaghcreevy was part, but would have been obliged (no doubt grudgingly) by the law of the day to leave intact the favourable contractual terms on which the Dilworths and others held their leases. Seventy years later, Mullaghcreevy was still in Dilworth hands, two sons of Andrew (born 1760), namely Andrew junior (born 1796) and James (born 1802), being the listed tenants. They and their well-to-do unmarried cousin Anne, the heiress of the family, occupied Mullaghcreevy in comfortable circumstances.[40]

Mullaghcreevy (thirty-six acres) was the largest of the townlands in the civil parish of Donaghmore, and considered the most valuable, the tithe paid being £2 5s 9½d, the highest of any in the parish. The brothers were also at one period lessees, presumably on Anne's behalf, of Aghareany, a larger but less fertile townland adjoining their northern

Opposite: *The Dilworth family tree.*

boundary. It is most unlikely they farmed all (perhaps even part) of it themselves. The marriage settlement spoken of earlier spelt out that, as early as 1770, the Dilworths had used their head-lease of Mullaghcreevy to under-lease a twenty-acre portion of it together with proportionate turbary (turf-bog cutting) rights for twenty years. The process continued under Anne Dilworth. Escalating rents, arising out of population-driven competition for cultivable lands, made subletting a more profitable and less burdensome proposition than farming all of one's property oneself.[41] Wilfred Dilworth's view that Anne was a 'woman of substance of the family having considerably property', is confirmed by records of loans she made from 1816 onwards on mortgage secured by land, or sometimes cash advances secured by bond.[42]

Although Mullaghcreevy is still being utilized today for grazing, the collection of buildings once making up the homestead which stood on the high point of the townland now lies disused and derelict. But the number and solidity of the ruined buildings, and the commodiousness of the living quarters, are indicative of their having been occupied for generations by a line of substantial and prosperous tenant farmers. Taken over early in the Plantation period, Mullaghcreevy was long an important part of the parish of Donaghmore. An officer of the Department of the Environment of Northern Ireland, specializing in historic monuments and buildings, recently visited the site. His report, while admitting that 'vernacular farm groups of this type are notoriously difficult to date', assessed the five main buildings as having developed into their present form between about 1700 and the second half of the nineteenth century.[43]

He observed that a distinctive feature of the site was the rath* adjoining the homestead, believing it 'to have been occupied between 500 and 1000 AD'. This rath, approaching half an acre in area and shaped like a very shallow saucer, he characterizes (citing a departmental description) as 'well-preserved' and 'situated on the summit of a low drumlin with fine views all round'. The fine defensive character of this ancient Celtic ring-fort could well have commended it as a site to the first Planter family who established their homestead beside it. The position of certain farm buildings, such as the solid byre adjoining the upper yard (which the summit of the rath in effect became), suggests that they could have been successors to earlier buildings serving as 'flankers' guarding that area. But lacking archeological evidence this remains pure surmise. Certainly the report on the site makes no reference to its ever having been a bawn.

Like the Mullaghcreevy homestead, that at Dunseark stands on one of the ridges of sand and gravel deposited in glacial times in eastern Tyrone, but unlike it, was neither on a site fortified in the past, nor left

---

* A rath is a circular enclosure with an outer earthen wall used in Gaelic times by the chief of the tribe as both a place of residence and a hill fort. There is a number of instances of raths being re-used as bawns in early Plantation Ulster (Robinson, pp.130–31).

derelict in the present. In good repair and currently (1994) occupied, the house at Dunseark remains a roomy, well-constructed, two-storey residence with a solid stable attached.

James's grandfather, Andrew Dilworth (born 1760), in 1797 took up the lease of the sixteen-and-a-half-acre townland on which this house now stands.[44] To do so he had to move from Mullaghcreevy, north-west of Dungannon, to the south of that town, along six miles of winding country roads (reduced by heavy usage to a state of ill-repair) to the parish of Clonfeacle. Dunseark was then part of the 2,000-acre estate which the wealthy Powerscourt family had held in this region since the beginnings of the Plantation.

Andrew Dilworth renewed the lease on 1 July 1805 from Richard, the Viscount Powerscourt, at a high annual rental, £13 5s 1d, but on a reasonably secure tenure, the lease lasting until the date of Andrew's death and for seven years beyond.[45] It has been said that, for some time in the nineteenth century, the Dilworths of Dunseark acted as rent collectors for Viscount Powerscourt, but the author has found no documentary confirmation of that.[46]

Upon the marriage of his eldest son John to Mary Bell in 1814, Andrew Dilworth surrendered the lease of Dunseark to John[47] and returned to Mullaghcreevy with his younger children.

Auckland's James Dilworth was born 15 August 1815 in the impressive farmhouse at Dunseark, the first-born of John and Mary. Three or four succeeding children did not survive infancy. James was eight before a sibling was born (Andrew in 1823) who would live to adulthood. A small window (since enlarged) at the end of the house has been identified by today's Dungannon Dilworths as the one beside which the little boy did his first home lessons.

An extension of the myth of his humble origin describes him as living with a young widowed mother in an Irish cottage. This was supposedly the origin of the sympathy for the plight of deprived boys and widowed mothers which led to his eventual bequest for the support and education of such children. In fact both his parents lived until well after his eventual departure from Ireland, and then Mary died first and was survived by John for thirteen years.

Yet from the age of eight James did not live with his parents. This was not for any reason of poverty: quite the contrary. It was because he was adopted as heir to his father's well-to-do cousin Anne at Mullaghcreevy and went to live with her and his uncles Andrew and James.

It was about 1823 that Anne Dilworth decided on the future disposition of her property that was to have momentous consequences for eight-year-old James.[48] Anne was aged forty-three, unmarried and therefore most unlikely ever to bear children of her own. She

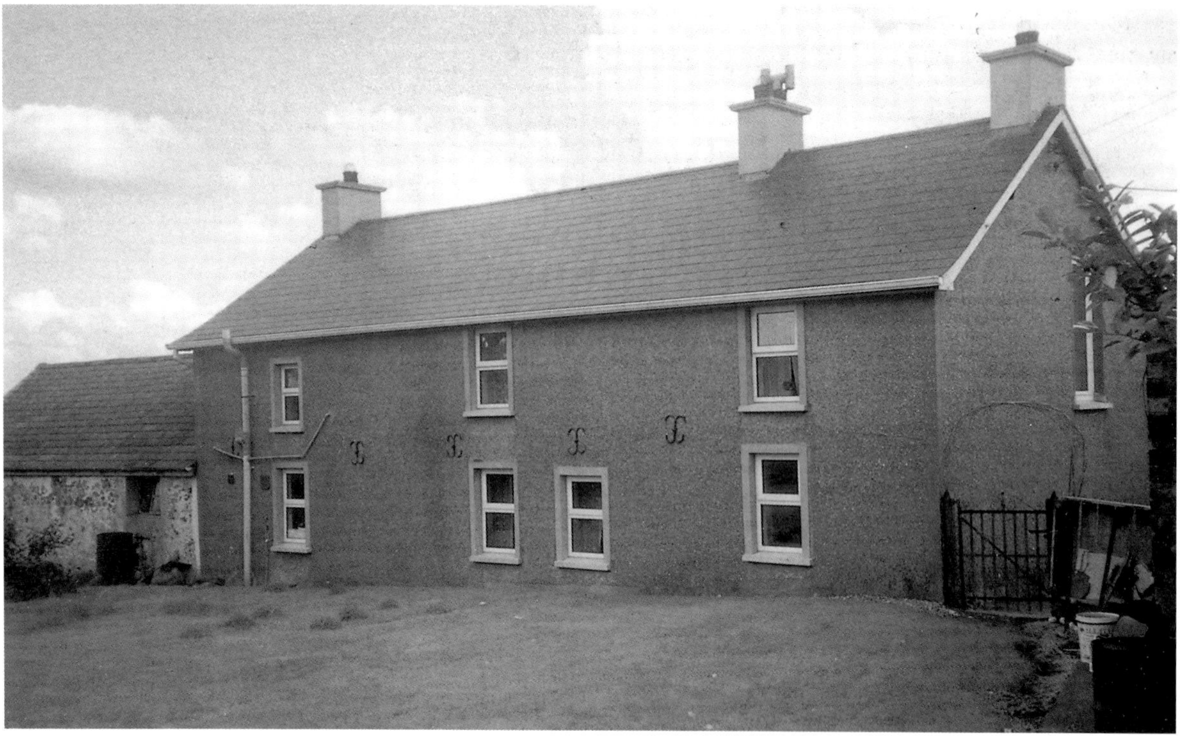

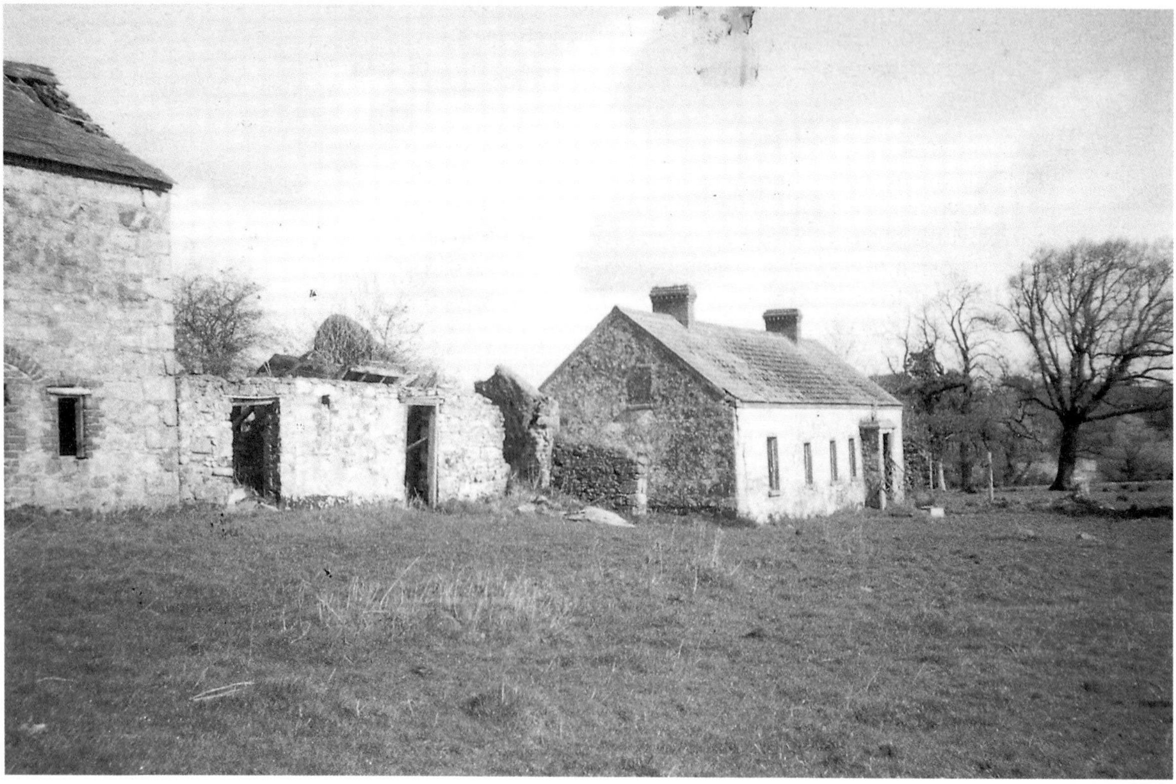

approached the local rector of Donaghmore, the Revd Alexander Staples, to devise a will that would make young James her heir. To call upon the services of the local minister was quite normal because, until the passing of the 1857 Probate Act, testamentary jurisdiction lay with the (Anglican) Church of Ireland and probate was granted by the Consistorial Court of each diocese.[49] The unusual feature of this will lies in its being drawn up while the testatrix was both comparatively youthful and free from infirmity. The tradition in Ireland up to about that time was for most wills to be made within a year of death.[50] (Anne did not in fact die until thirty-five years later.) By making a small boy her heir she was not capriciously singling out a personal favourite who would later enjoy the largesse of an aged relative. Rather was she conferring a future position of responsibility, almost of trusteeship, on someone who would have the duty of husbanding accumulated resources of the family so that they remained intact, or (better still) were increased, in order that the future generations of the family would benefit.

James's becoming the chosen heir explains the readiness of his parents at Dunseark to allow their first-born son to leave the family home and live permanently at Mullaghcreevy. Wilfred Dilworth makes a case for Anne's skipping a generation, so to speak, by ignoring her first cousins John, James and Andrew, the last two of whom in 1823 were both, like Anne herself, still single and without issue. He maintains that 'there was little point in leaving her property to them' since they were more or less of 'the same generation' as herself. The next step was inevitable:

> As was the custom in such cases at the time, the 'nephew' went to live with the 'uncle' or 'aunt' and was reared as their own child. So it was no mere coincidence that James left Dunseark as a boy and went to live at Mullaghcreevy with his uncles, as family tradition has it, but more importantly with Anne. This was the family agreement between Anne and John, and the will thus drawn up remained unchanged until Anne died in 1858.[51]

A number of people in both Dungannon and the Republic of Ireland with whom I have discussed the fostering out of young James Dilworth to older relatives thought it unsurprising. They recalled a number of instances of children, in recent times, being sent to help out on a farm or to act as company for an aged family member such as a grandparent. Some Irish immigrants to New Zealand in the nineteenth century brought the practice with them. In 1900, my great-grandmother, originally from Tullamore, suddenly went blind. My grandfather, her son, whom she had long before brought with her from Ireland, thought it as natural as breathing to send his son as a boy of eight to go to live on a small farm at Birkdale across the harbour from Auckland so that he could help, and be company for, his blind grandmother. There my father remained for six years.

Opposite above: *Dilworth's birthplace at Dunseark. He is said to have done his first home lessons beside the window on the right.*
Norman Cardwell

Opposite below: *Buildings of the Mullaghcreevy homestead (now derelict); Dilworth was reared in the 'new' cottage on right.*
Norman Cardwell

JAMES DILWORTH

As a result of this shift, James had the greater part of his elementary education at the Donaghmore Village School. The Revd George MacMurray, confidant of Dilworth during his last years, recalled how Dilworth used to speak of passing the Donaghmore Cross on his way to school as the most vivid memory of his childhood. This beautiful Celtic high cross, going back perhaps as far as the eleventh century, stands at the head of the village of Donaghmore. Carved in freestone (fine sandstone), it has scriptural scenes on front and back, and geometrical designs on its sides. Eroded by time and possibly defaced when cast down by Puritans in 1641, the cross has sculptured detail that is indistinct and, at sixteen feet, is less than its original height. It is still one of the great crosses of Ireland coming down from medieval times. In the space directly behind the cross was the village school taught by Mr Richard Robinson which James attended.

In 1993 I stood on the site of the old ring-fort, highest point of the Mullaghcreevy townland, trying to visualize the route by which young James, 170 years before, made his barefoot way to school.* Whether by winding country roads or (more likely because more direct) across hilly fields and by swampy streams, the way seemed to me difficult and long. But the president of the local history society standing beside me assured me that a country lad, even a small one, would not have been troubled. 'Och!' he said, 'It's only an Irish mile.'

---

* He could well have carried his brogues to wear at school. Country women coming to Dungannon commonly washed their feet in a little stream on entering that town, 'before putting on the shoes and stockings they had carried so far and which they intended to wear in the town' ('Reminiscences of James Brown').

Donaghmore village school which James began to attend in 1823.
M. Stone

ORIGINS

Left: *The Donaghmore Cross which Dilworth passed daily on his way to school.*
M. Stone

Right: *The Celtic High Cross erected in 1994 at Dilworth School, Auckland; sculptor, Stephen Woodward.*
Kate Stone

Below: *James's journey to Donaghmore School beyond the far tree-topped hill was across boggy fields.*
Norman Cardwell

17

Cousin Anne, who had assumed financial responsibility for the education of James, enrolled him during the mid-1820s at the fee-paying Royal School of Dungannon (RSD). The exact years he was there are not known, the school lists for this period not having survived. Being well-off, Anne would have financed him to be a boarder, as were the majority then attending. It was no small consideration: the first-year costs for a boarder in 1830 were over eighty pounds. Pupils ranged in age from ten to nineteen; but we may assume that James began later and left earlier than those extremes.

The Royal School was an educational institution of very good standing. Founded in 1614 under Royal Charter it was one of the oldest and probably the most famous of Ireland's Public Schools. Prestige had material advantage as its bedfellow; in the early nineteenth century the RSD had an endowment of 3,900 acres which yielded an annual rental income of £1,430.[52] Since 1786 the school had been housed in a fine three-storey stone building with an Italianate tower, standing in some nine acres of grounds beside Northland Row and close to the Dungannon town centre.

In the period during which James was a student—between about 1826 and 1832—the school provided a strongly classical education. But he had the good fortune during his senior years to come under the influence of a talented scholarly headmaster, Dr John Richard Darley, who grafted innovation onto tradition—it was he who introduced school prizes for 'mercantile' subjects. At the end of his term as headmaster (1830–50) Darley was elevated to be Bishop of Kilmore. But it was as a schoolman that his true reputation was made. The reputation of the head dwarfed that of the school. It was not unusual for people to refer to the Dungannon Royal School as 'Dr Darley's school'. During his halcyon years the RSD produced some of the most famous of its old boys: generals, bishops, legal luminaries, and pioneers of Empire.*

Evidence of how effective was the education Dilworth received is provided by the letters he wrote as an adult. He was conspicuously literate, more so than any other member of his family, and with a forceful economical way with words.

Until the later nineteenth century, with the position of headmaster lying in the gift of the Archbishop of Armagh, the Royal School was strongly Anglican in character. It appears (not surprisingly) that while a pupil there James was confirmed according to the rites of the Church of Ireland. A credible family tradition has it that his parents at Dunseark were Presbyterian; however, the adults at Mullaghcreevy were certainly committed to the Church of Ireland. As a colonist in New Zealand James became the staunchest of Anglicans.[53] The dourness and passionate devotion to hard work he came to display were personality

---

* E. W. Stafford, premier heading New Zealand's first stable responsible government (1856–61), was in the Junior School during James Dilworth's last months at the Royal School.

The Royal School of Dungannon in the early nineteenth century.
Royal School of Dungannon Archives

traits supposed by the world at large to be characteristic of Ulster Presbyterian Scots rather than of the Plantation English from whom he had in fact descended. But the more closely one looks at James Dilworth the more one becomes convinced that intimate family experiences rather than broader religious and cultural influences shaped his personality.

There are few hard facts available about what James Dilworth did in his first years after leaving school. The 1830s are the most obscure decade of his life, the most sketchily recorded. But the statement in the posthumous biographical sketch in the *Cyclopedia of New Zealand* that he 'assisted his father in the management of his farm for a few years' is misleading.[54] Shortly after arriving in New Zealand Dilworth was to confess to having little 'practical' experience of farming. Yet he was far from being a tyro. He managed his first farm well enough for us to infer that he had worked part-time on the family farm near Dungannon, and had acquired the awareness of good farming practices that would come to any intelligent person reared in a rural environment. But full-time farm work—no. His uncles, Andrew and James, had the farm work of Mullaghcreevy, which they managed, well under control. James's occupation in Ireland was outside farming.

He told George MacMurray many years later that his first job was in a bank, presumably in the town of Dungannon. Anne's hand can be seen in this: what better training ground could there be for an heir whose future responsibilities would involve the management of landed estate, assessing securities, mortgages, leases, proceeding against defaulters and so on? Mastery of such matters was later to make him a formidable investor in real estate in the colonies. But that had not been Anne's intention when he was first put to banking. Originally the family wanted these skills to be put at its disposal in the conduct of farming and investment affairs in County Tyrone.

No memoirs or family papers survive to explain why, in the mid-1830s, Anne (for the initiative must have been hers) decided to divert the investment of family capital away from south-eastern Tyrone towards the Antipodes, and to send out her designated heir to buy land there. But conditions in Ireland provide the answer. By the 1830s—well before the Famine—rural poverty was deepening, violence and civil disorder becoming endemic.[55] The response of the people was to swell the wave of emigration that had been built up by the agricultural depression following on the Napoleonic Wars. Rory Fitzpatrick speaks of the drain of population from Ireland to America having reached by 1832 an annual figure of 65,000.[56] He makes a distinction, however, between people leaving the province of Ulster and those from other parts of Ireland. Relatively, there were fewer emigrants (he remarks) from the north who were labourers driven by destitution; more highly represented were 'small farmers and skilled artisans'; in the words of a contemporary report, people 'in decent circumstances', who were anxious to maintain living standards perceived to be under threat from deep-seated economic change. This was the group to whom the Dilworths of Dungannon belonged.

A further consequence of the economic uncertainty of the 1830s bears upon the Dilworth story. Recent economic historians have shown that the rural economy was suffering from a dearth of investment. This was not because money capital was not available: it was. The problem was rather that the internal tensions within Irish society, rural depression, and (underlying all) the absence of a secure tenurial system for farmers, built up an extreme reluctance on the part of those with free capital to invest in Irish land.[57]

These were the kinds of considerations that appear to have worked on the mind of Anne and her companions at Mullaghcreevy to persuade them that James's future lay not in Tyrone but in the colonies. The choice of Australia, rather than the more highly favoured destinations of the United States or Canada, could well have been brought about by stories coming back from the Antipodes. One such is recounted by Rory Fitzpatrick, the tale that it was possible for settlers with limited capital to buy land cheaply there and 'carve out a bush empire'.[58]

In 1838 the decision was finally made. James was to go to Australia. In 1839 he arrived in Sydney and took up a position in the post office at Windsor, close to the main settlement. Clerical work was no more than a stopgap. His commission from Anne at home was to look about and ascertain where his capital could most profitably be put into land.

When Dilworth left Ireland at the age of twenty-three, he still had almost six decades of life before him. But in psychological makeup and personality he changed surprisingly little in the years ahead. The stamp of the early formative years spent in his homeland was indelible. People spoke of him at the time of his death as they had spoken of him even as a young colonist: observing a large man with a gruff and somewhat unbending manner which (they said) concealed an innate kindliness; asking how one could be so public spirited yet so reserved, almost to the point of reclusiveness; reminding others that here was one with a stern sense of duty which he expected in others just as he demanded it of himself.

On reflection, it would have been surprising had he been otherwise. Consider these facts. He was taken from his Dunseark home at the age of eight, never to return to live permanently with parents, his brother or three sisters. At Mullaghcreevy he was attached to a household of three unmarried adults, with no children about, but with talk, no doubt, of the privileges and responsibilities that were later to be his lot; just the kind of environment to produce a serious-minded 'old-fashioned' child. Later, by being put to commercial work in a town he was further distanced from his relatives immersed in that farming life which was the family's cultural milieu.

If Dilworth became an unusual personality, it was his family background in County Tyrone which made him so.

CHAPTER TWO

The Young Pioneer 1841–44

It is not known exactly when Dilworth left Sydney or when he arrived in Auckland. But we do know the ship he came on. It was the schooner *Planter*,* 130 tons, master Captain Morrison, operating out of Leith, Scotland; in 1841 plying the southern seas.[1] The *New Zealand Gazette*, London, in its edition of 17 July 1841, reprinted an undated article taken from the *Sydney Morning Herald* reporting that the *Planter* had left Sydney for Auckland with twenty-seven passengers.[2] James Dilworth was named as one of the eleven emigrants on that ship sufficiently well-off to be cabin passengers. Since it would have taken about three months for the Sydney paper to get to London and its information to be published there, it can be assumed that Dilworth left for New Zealand probably sometime in April. Dilworth, like a number of his friends from New South Wales who had gone before him to New Zealand,[3] seems to have had an open mind about whether he would stay on in the new colony, or (if he did) just where he would settle.

There is even conjecture about his motives for leaving Sydney. Many years later, at the time of his death, it was said that James decided to go to New Zealand in 1841 because he found 'the excessive heat of the Australian climate somewhat trying to his health'.[4] This explanation is even more unconvincing than the one published rather later which had him leaving 'Windsor, near Sydney' because he did not like 'the monotony of life there'.[5] Neither the vagaries of climate nor the intrinsic interest of his work would have counted for much with that shrewd young business head. Ambition alone drove him. Like so many who migrated to New Zealand in the early 1840s, Dilworth came to the young colony to buy land while it was still cheap.

Little that he observed during his first year in Auckland would have

---

* There were seven *Planter*s listed in *Lloyd's Register*, 1840, of which the one Dilworth sailed on was the smallest. Most of the others, barques and brigs, were, not surprisingly in view of their name, involved in the West Indian sugar trade.

Auckland in 1841 when Dilworth arrived.
Auckland Public Library

encouraged him to revise that plan. The speculators who bought lots at the first Crown auctions in the capital on 19 April and 8 September 1841 made huge killings. Dilworth personally witnessed how those who traded in land were able to make quick profits after the second Crown land auction at which 'suburban' and 'small farm' sections in the area to the east and south of Mechanics' Bay were put up for sale. Allotments intended to be market gardens and small farms supplying produce for Auckland were 'greedily bought up' by speculators (some still in New South Wales but bidding through local agents), who immediately subdivided them into small residential allotments in paper towns which they created, calling them 'Parnell', 'Windsor Terrace', 'Anna', 'Epsom' and so on.[6] Within three days of the Crown sale the auction rooms of Auckland were full of such subdivisions.[7] Here is the beginning of the speculative taint which was to cling to the founding of Auckland, and of the reputation of its citizens (by no means lost today) for being more concerned with making money than with creating true wealth.

The fact that government officials were among speculative buyers at these Crown auctions angered genuine settlers. One official who did well out of the 'land monomania'[8]—as Auckland's first newspaper branded the fevered speculation and jobbing arising out of the September auction—was the government works engineer George Graham, later in the decade to be the owner of a Remuera farm which adjoined Dilworth's own. Graham noted in his diary that on

23

3 September he bought a nine-acre farm allotment for £31 1s 3d.[9] Immediately he 'devided [sic] it again', and four days later sold this subdivision 'by public auction and it fetched £210'. Lessons such as these were not lost on James Dilworth.

But it must also be said (anticipating somewhat) that when Dilworth himself began serious land buying it was rarely with the thought of quick speculative resale. His was the long-term view. Particularly was this so when he bought those lands in 1844–45 which became his Remuera farm and ultimately the heart of his propertied wealth. He informed the colonial secretary in 1846 that he was 'not actuated to' this particular purchase by 'any speculative motive or other motive than to reside on [it] and make it my home'.[10] Dilworth was quick to grasp, as few settlers were, that if he was patient and kept his suburban land intact, the community, enlarged by continuing immigration, would inevitably push up the value of his farm to a fabulous level.

George MacMurray, Dilworth's confidant during the last years of his life, recalled Dilworth telling him that as the *Planter* sailed into the Waitemata Harbour in 1841 he noticed how the extinct volcanic cone known as Mount Eden (Maungawhau) dominated the isthmus. Dilworth decided this would be an ideal vantage point from which (in MacMurray's phrase) he would 'view the landscape o'er'.[11] While still on shipboard he made up his mind to climb Mount Eden as soon as he could, and from its summit appraise the surrounding country.

The journey he made on foot was not an easy one. Dilworth told MacMurray 'there were no roads, and the intervening country was covered with dense scrub'.[12] The swamp near Newmarket—one wonders whether this lanky young Irishman thought of it as a bog—was particularly difficult to negotiate; while the approaches to the hill itself had ramparts of huge, craggy blocks of basalt rock over which he must scramble.[13] The final ascent had to be made through dense scrub and tea tree, some standing above the height of his head, for the volcanic cone had been undergoing bush regeneration since changes in the modes of Maori warfare over the last century had led to the abandonment of Maungawhau as a fortress. It took him 'many hours of effort', said Dilworth, to reach the summit. His ascent remarkably paralleled that which his fellow pioneer, John Logan Campbell, had made of Remuera (Mount Hobson) the year before. In his classic, *Poenamo*, Campbell recalled how from the summit he 'gazed on the wonderful panorama' with 'gratified amazement'.[14] At that moment Campbell became aware of 'the wonderful capabilities of the Isthmus' and was convinced that somewhere on its eastern shore the capital must eventually be fixed.[15] Dilworth reacted similarly when he viewed 'the glorious landscape' revealed from his hilltop. According to MacMurray, he decided there and then, 'this country will do for me!'.[16]

But if Dilworth had cast the die for the colony, that did not mean

THE YOUNG PIONEER

he had decided to stay in Auckland. Deep caution was already an ingrained trait in this young man. Other avenues must be explored. He spent some weeks after arrival visiting various areas in the northern part of the North Island, 'looking out for land, travelling along the East Coast as far as Opotiki'.[17]

He returned to Auckland. The place he had seen first appealed most. He settled in the capital. But he delayed buying his land.

Much imagination is needed to see in the mind's eye what Auckland was actually like when Dilworth made it his home in the winter of 1841. We must forget entirely modern Auckland with its one million people, large buildings and massive harbour reclamations. Visualize if you can a tiny settlement clinging to a small part of the southern shoreline (now long since disappeared) of the Waitemata Harbour. Lacking statistics for 1841 we can only guess how many European people were there; almost certainly the total would have been under one thousand. These people were concentrated in three pockets of settlement in three adjacent bays. Commercial Bay was where Auckland began. Further east, beyond Point Britomart (on which in mid-1841 the barracks of the 80th Regiment were being constructed) was Official Bay—roughly lower Anzac Avenue of today—already the picturesque residential area favoured by senior government officials.

Auckland as it stood in January 1842.
Auckland City Council

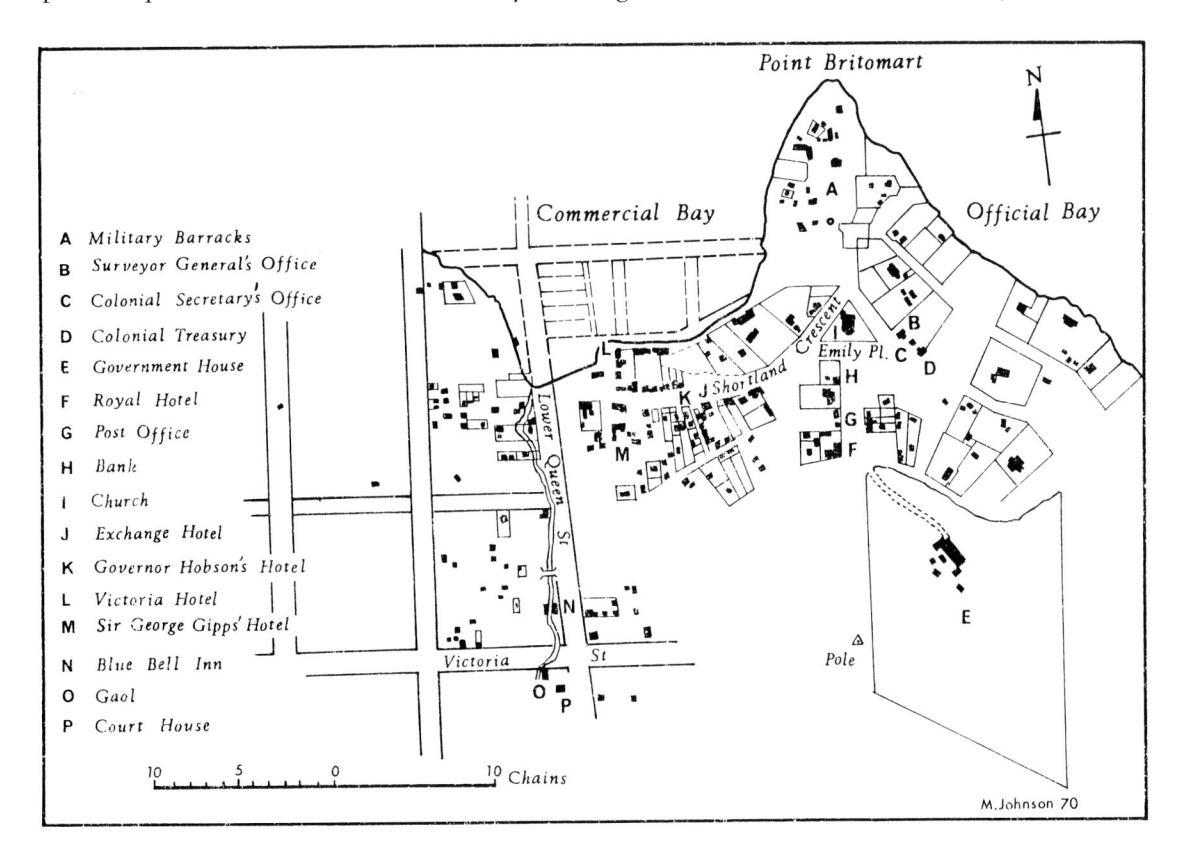

JAMES DILWORTH

Beyond that was lowly Mechanics' Bay with its small collection of raupo huts, housing the families of government artisans and labourers, strung in a line just back from the beach front. This bay was also a favoured resort of Maori people while trading their produce in Auckland, for beaching canoes or establishing overnight encampments.

The land behind Commercial Bay, the bowed shoreline of which more or less follows the course of modern Fort Street, was the centre of settlement. There was, in those early days, a great shortage of flat land for immediate use. With Queen Street, at that time little better than a water-course, swampy and prone to flood, the main business thoroughfare was Shortland Crescent in which a collection of stores, hotels and shops straggled up the hill as far as Princes Street where the main government offices were located.

Move a few hundred yards back from these bays and you were in a wilderness. William Swainson, like Dilworth an 1841 arrival, spoke of 'the land on the outskirts of town' as 'a morass overgrown with tall tea trees. Beyond again for about one and a half miles was a dense thicket, through which to find the way it was necessary to take the bearing of some of the loftier trees'. In just such a fashion, we may assume, Dilworth plotted his course to Mount Eden.

Commercial Bay viewed from Point Britomart, 1841.
Drawn on stone and printed by P. Gauci

THE YOUNG PIONEER

Captain William Crush Daldy, who came on his schooner the *Shamrock* to settle in Auckland on 1 July 1841, a few weeks after Dilworth, said that on arrival he saw only three wooden cottages in the town (one of which would certainly have been Acacia Cottage* into which Logan Campbell's partner William Brown had shifted the week before). According to Daldy, most people were still housed in tents or '*raupo whares*', large and quite comfortable examples of which could be put up by Maoris for ten pounds or less.[18]

Daldy seemed to have exaggerated, however, the primitiveness of the Auckland he first encountered. Contemporary diaries and journals, and drawings of the period as well, indicate more weatherboard structures in 1841 than he implied. The Police Census of 1842 recorded that by then there were 331 wooden buildings in the capital, outnumbering raupo whares by over three to one.† And before we are overwhelmed by talk of the crudity of housing in pioneer Auckland, we should also call to mind that many of the young single, male adults, the settlement's main demographic component, were accommodated in tenements or in the back rooms of hotels, stores, shops and offices in which they worked.[19]

It is likely that when Dilworth first settled in Auckland he stayed in one of the many boarding houses catering for groups of bachelors like himself. But if we do not know where he first lived, the job at which he first worked is recorded clearly. On 27 May 1841 he was appointed as an 'Extra Clerk to the Governor's Councils',[20] a position almost certainly created when Captain Hobson became full governor of the colony, which on 3 May had been proclaimed as fully independent of New South Wales.[21] This post Dilworth held, at an annual salary of £91 5s 0d, for just over two months until he decided to take up banking once again.[22]

When the New Zealand Banking Company opened a new branch in Auckland on 4 August 1841 it confirmed the appointment of James Dilworth as clerk. No doubt his previous clerical experience in banks and post offices had made him very appointable.

Something must be said about this bank and Dilworth's work in it, for the great skill he displayed in land buying and property management in his subsequent life was rooted in his early experience of banking.

The New Zealand Banking Company, New Zealand's first bank, was promoted by settlers in the Bay of Islands during 1839, some months before the country became a colony.[23] It was created to overcome two shortages, in credit and in currency. Like their counterparts

W. C. Daldy.
Auckland Public Library

---

* Acacia Cottage is the oldest surviving Auckland house, since 1920 located in Cornwall Park. It was built by John Logan Campbell, 'Father of Auckland'.

† The enumerations contained in the censuses 1842–45 were carried out late in the year (from November on) to which they applied.

in Australia, from where so many of them had come, early settlers were inconvenienced by the scarcity of legal tender. In 1840 the bank began business in Kororareka (Russell). With the shift of the capital to Auckland and the surge of business associated with the first Crown land auction there, the banking company decided to open a branch in Auckland.

On 4 August 1841 the directors met at the two-storeyed, weatherboarded, public house of Samuel A. ('Rakau') Wood, the Royal Hotel, standing diagonally opposite Government House, at that corner of Princes Street where the Northern Club is located today. Each of the directors, Matthew Richmond, Frederick Whitaker, W. F. Porter, Dr John Johnson and W. C. Symonds, had held, or was currently holding, some official position, confirming the general view that the Auckland branch of the bank 'enjoyed a measure of government patronage'.[24] Consequently, according to another source, government transactions were to become a feature of the business of this pioneer bank, 'both by way of purchase of bills on Sydney, and by way of overdraft', with the rate of interest charged the government going as high as fifteen per cent.[25]

It was at this inaugural directors' meeting that James Dilworth was appointed clerk, and Alexander Kennedy (former accountant for the Union Bank in Sydney) manager both of the bank and of its new branch in Auckland. The minutebook recorded that they, and the directors, signed the customary declarations of secrecy at that meeting.[26] The Auckland branch commenced business on 20 August 1841 at Bank House, a small wooden building which stood at the corner of Princes Street and Shortland Crescent.* According to an advertisement in Auckland's first newspaper, the *New Zealand Herald and Auckland Gazette*, the chief business of the bank was accepting deposits and providing short-term credit (defined as under one hundred days) by discounting trade bills.[27]

Increasingly, commercial activity in the Bay of Islands languished in the shadow cast by Auckland, the new capital. In response to Auckland's growing importance, the Banking Company shifted its headquarters there. As accountant in the colony's only bank, James became a minor public figure. In April 1842 he won mention in the Police Court news reported by the local press in the case of A. Scott who was charged with 'obtaining goods under false pretences' from David Nathan's store in lower Shortland Crescent.[28] After making a large purchase of blankets, Scott attempted to pay by presenting a cheque for fifteen pounds drawn on the New Zealand Banking Company. His suspicion aroused, David Nathan immediately sent the cheque up the street to the bank for Dilworth to scrutinize. The evidence

---

* The allotment on which the bank stood fell steeply away to a small street on its western boundary which became known as Bank Street (today Bankside Street).

Dilworth gave subsequently in Court, that Scott had no funds in the bank, was decisive in the man's conviction.

Shortly after, Dilworth, together with his superior A. Kennedy, was mentioned in the press once again. He was one of twenty-seven 'Landholders and other Inhabitants of this Colony' who called upon the high sheriff of Auckland to convene a public meeting 'for the purpose of considering and adopting petitions to the Queen, and both Houses of Parliament, praying for those representative institutions this Colony is justly entitled to'.[29] An inspection of the names of these advocates of self-government shows that Dilworth had aligned himself with the 'Senate', a local business group who were scathing critics of Governor Hobson and his officials. More than that, its members were citizens of standing: Dudley Sinclair, son of a Scottish baronet; William Brown and Logan Campbell, proprietors of Auckland's most successful merchant house; Dr S. M. D. Martin, a redoubtable journalist; J. I. Montefiore, the land agent; and a number of others. James Dilworth may have been only twenty-six years of age but he was quickly earning acceptance as a man of some consequence within the commercial community.

And yet by the end of 1842 he must have wondered whether he had chosen wisely in selecting New Zealand as the colony where he could make his private fortune, and repair that of his family back in County Tyrone. The bottom had fallen out of the Auckland property market and the returns of the bank confirmed that it was not holding its own in either of its two main spheres of activity, Auckland and the Bay of Islands.

When in October 1842 the *Jane Gifford* and the *Duchess of Argyle*, the first two ships to bring assisted immigrants to Auckland, arrived at the capital they found it deep in gloom. Edward Ashworth, the artist, who had come about the same time, recorded in his journal that farming

Princes Street, Auckland, c.1843. Beyond the lamp-post and to the left of St Paul's Church is the office of the New Zealand Banking Co. In the building at the immediate left, Wood's Royal Hotel, the bank directors held their inaugural meeting in Auckland, 1841.
Pen and wash by Edward Ashworth, Auckland City Art Gallery

in the neighbourhood of the settlement was 'at a standstill'.[30] Elsewhere in his journal he spoke of these new arrivals from Scotland as 'poor deluded wretches', who had been brought to 'semi-starvation on a desolate shore'.[31]

At the Jubilee Reunion of these old colonists in October 1892 Logan Campbell recalled how forbidding the settlement must have seemed to those newcomers:

> Auckland was still in a very primitive state. We had not quite discarded the tents and raupo huts in which we first lived and were quite proud of the few scattered weather boarded houses which began to mark out the lines of the streets. As for the streets, they were literally in a state of nature, and that state of nature in wet weather was ankle deep at least in mud.[32]

More disheartening for these would-be settlers was the prospect of unemployment. The local labour market Campbell described as 'glutted'.[33] In the coming months the government had to provide low-paid relief work for these Scottish labourers on such jobs as levelling Shortland Crescent, and starting the formation of a new road to Newmarket (Khyber Pass).

Dilworth's reaction to this slump in the economy was remarkable, however. He began buying land. It has often been said that if you wish to make money in property you should 'buy in gloom and sell in boom'. Probably Dilworth did not know of this maxim; at least not in those precise words. But he applied its principles throughout his long life. He made his first land purchase in Auckland on 24 December 1842, a time when many prudent people would have thought it particularly inopportune to invest in property. At a Crown auction of suburban land, he succeeded with a bid of £53 8s 9d for a four-and-a-quarter-acre block in the suburb we would now think of as Parnell but was then referred to as Windsor Terrace, after a subdivision of that name which had taken place nearby.[34] Dilworth's allotment, which adjoined the land upon which the colony's first Anglican Bishop, G. A. Selwyn, during the latter years of his episcopate built Bishopscourt, lay at the top end of St Stephens Avenue. Dilworth enlarged this property some three years later by buying two further acres on his northern boundary.[35] In the meantime he had erected a wooden residence on his original block of Parnell land. By the time of the 1845 Police Census, Dilworth (who, significantly, returned his occupation at this juncture as 'farmer') was listed as the owner occupying this house in which there also lived two adult male tenants.[36]

We can assume that when Dilworth bought his Parnell property he imagined he had before him a career at the bank which was both permanent and full of promise. The home he built was within a mile of Princes Street. Admittedly it was outside the main settlement: W. B. White, who in 1846 recorded his journey from Onehunga to Auckland, remarked that on the Newmarket side of the Windsor Castle

Inn, standing just beyond Parnell Hill (now Parnell Rise), there was no settlement to speak of; just 'one or two houses scattered about'.[37] But Dilworth's house was within easy walking distance of his bank office and this no doubt was a reason why he bought land where he did.

An unfavourable turn in the bank's affairs during 1843 forced Dilworth to reconsider whether banking was the best way to make his living in the colony. A disturbing resolution appeared in the minutes of the meeting of directors on 3 March 1843.

> Contemplating with alarm the frightful amount of overdue paper exhibited by the late returns from the Branch at Kororareka, equal indeed to the whole paid-up capital of the Bank (£8,278), and observing at the same time with great pain that apparently little or no exertion is made to reduce that amount, the consequence of which state of affairs cannot but prove most disastrous, more than ordinary stringent measures must be adopted to remedy if possible this unhealthy state of affairs.[38]

This 'unhealthy state of affairs', according to a history of early banking in the colony, had arisen from the practice of 'discounting further bills for parties whose previous bills were still unpaid', and from assuming that, in the words of the minutes, 'the mere deposit of title deeds constituted security'.[39] The condition of the Russell branch continued to deteriorate. At the end of the 1843 financial year, Dilworth was instructed, as the banking company's accountant, to carry out an inspection audit of the troublesome branch. The report he presented to the bank's directors has not survived. Their alarmed response has. Dilworth was told to take over as manager at Russell, dismiss the current incumbent (Mr Dixon) and arrange for the assistant clerk to return to Auckland. The letter of instructions to Dilworth is full of the atmosphere of crisis.

> James Dilworth Esq.   23 April 1844
> Sir,
>   I am desired by the Directors to acknowledge the receipt of your letter to them of the 18th inst. and to state in reply that they approve of your conduct, and that you are at once to take charge of the [Russell] Bank and to carry out the instructions contained in the Minute of the Board dated the 8th. You will also detain Mr Hanley with you as long as you require him, then forward him here. You will be good enough to pay Mr Dixon his salary to the date of his leaving the Bank, if there are no overdrawn accounts, but if this is an obstacle in the way of getting possession, to pay him in full then let it stand over. At all events to get possession.
> I am Sir etc,
> A. Kennedy, Manager.[40]

The position of the bank as a whole continued to worsen, and by no means solely because of present or past mismanagement. Stabilising its affairs during 1844, after the arrival of the new governor Robert FitzRoy, was extremely difficult because as the merchant Logan Campbell bluntly remarked in his memoirs, 'the colony had become bankrupt', with the salaries of some officials months in arrears.[41] Referring to FitzRoy's financial predicament, the governor's wife wrote in a mood of 'deepest anxiety' to a relative: 'you may imagine the singularly embarrassed position in which Robert finds himself'.[42]

The course FitzRoy took to extricate himself damaged both the economy and the government's standing, and destroyed his reputation as the governor. Flagrantly disregarding earlier instructions from the Colonial Office, on 1 May 1844 he issued debentures to pay his bills, a shift Campbell described as 'making money by medium of the printing press'.[43] When these debentures were submitted to public auction a week later they fetched as little as seventeen shillings in the pound.[44] This created a run on the small bank in Princes Street. It would surely have fallen had not the governor rushed through, overnight, a notice in the *Gazette* that his debentures were now to be regarded as legal tender. Thereafter, the bank was not obliged to pay its clients in coin of the realm, but could use debentures or other paper. The consequence was, however, as the editor of the *Southern Cross* had earlier predicted, 'the banishment of gold and silver', and a further loss of confidence in the credit-worthiness of the colony.[45] As well, in the opinion of one member of the governor's council, the position of the small, struggling New Zealand Banking Company had been further undermined.[46]

Meanwhile, Dilworth was still at Russell, remaining until the end of May with his commission to restore order as best he could in the

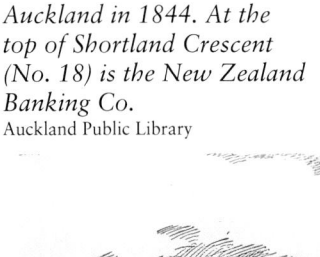

Auckland in 1844. At the top of Shortland Crescent (No. 18) is the New Zealand Banking Co.
Auckland Public Library

business of the branch. For the rest of 1844 he seems to have been rather more intermittently there, holding simultaneously the post of bank accountant in Auckland and branch manager at Russell. His dual responsibility involved regular travel by small ship to and from the Bay of Islands.[47] With the closing of the Russell branch in December 1844 he returned to Auckland as sole passenger on the schooner *Aurora*.[48] But the bank in Auckland itself was by now on its last legs. Overwhelmed by the inadequately secured indebtedness of its past clients, the New Zealand Banking Company was forced to cease its operations during February 1845.[49] Dilworth's career as banker was at an end. But the financial experience he had picked up in the bank remained a valuable part of his mental stock-in-trade for the rest of his life.

More than a year before the bank closed its doors, Dilworth had begun preparing for an alternative career. By the beginning of 1844, bad accounts in Russell and the downturn of business in Auckland already made his prospects at the bank uncertain. From the moment he set foot in Auckland he had the fixed plan of becoming a man of property. There had been no hurry at that stage; his thinking in 1841 was that he would work out his plan in his own good time. Once the bank fell into difficulty he re-ordered his timetable. There was no soul-searching. The political situation was opportune; the governor seemed ready to allow direct dealing between Maori landowners and Pakeha buyers. So there was every incentive for Dilworth to buy his suburban farmland sooner rather than later.

Early in 1844 he began buying farmland from Maori landowners south of Tamaki (later Remuera) Road. By mid-year, in order to continue these operations, he began to draw on capital. In July 1844 the manager of the Bank of Australasia in Sydney responded to a request from Dilworth by sending him two drafts amounting to £525.[50] We do not know whether this sum represented past savings, or funds provided by the Dilworth family back in Ireland; probably the latter. But no doubt need attach itself to the way James used the money: he bought land or he developed what he had. By the close of 1844 he had spent over £200 in this way. And this was just the beginning of his career as a man of property.

CHAPTER THREE

Owners and Sellers of Tamaki-Makau-Rau

JAMES DILWORTH became in time Auckland's very model of a man of property. During his life, property gave him wealth, and gave him status. After his death it was the means of his fabled munificence. So close are the connections between the man and his land that it is impossible to capture the essence of the one without speaking of the acquisition of the other.

At the heart of Dilworth's landed estate was to be his Remuera farm. The story of how he bought this farm and certain other valuable properties in Auckland during the 1840s is by no means straightforward. Not that his was an unusual case. The same could equally be said of much Pakeha land buying in the same decade. The problem has been complicated because, as yet, little has been written, and less published, about the progressive sale of the Tamaki isthmus by the Maori.[1] One thing is certain, it is very unlikely that Dilworth would have elected to make his way in Auckland had not Captain Hobson decided to establish his seat of government there. Hobson's emphatic selection of the south bank of the Waitemata Harbour as the site of his capital after exploring a number of alternatives, Maori readiness to sell that portion of the isthmus which the governor wanted, and Dilworth's early land purchases—three apparently disparate historical phenomena—have one thing in common. Each can be understood only when placed in a broad historical setting that goes far back in time.

The isthmus between the Waitemata and Manukau Harbours (at its narrowest near Otahuhu no more than a kilometre across) has been for time out of mind highly prized.[2] It is today the most densely settled part of New Zealand. Before the white man came, it was also that for long periods under the 'people of the land'. So desirable did contending Maori tribes consider this unique land-bridge that they gave as its name an image of earthly passion: 'Tamaki-makau-rau'—'Tamaki (the maiden) contested for by innumerable lovers'. Rich, easily tilled volcanic soils, surrounding seas teeming with fish and volcanic hills which served as formidable natural fortresses made this isthmus a treasure for those who possessed her, giving rise to the proverb 'Te pai me te whai rawa o Tamaki' (the luxury and wealth of Tamaki).³ But Tamaki was also a dangerous place to live in. It became a natural centre of war, a frontier of convergence for those bent on possessing the isthmus—and a magnet for those needing to cross it with the object of raiding or trading further afield. Inevitably, interests clashed and blood-feud (utu) accounts were created. Boundaries tended to be fluid, therefore, and periods of prolonged, unchallenged dominance rare.

Constantly fought over for generations, Tamaki-makau-rau enjoyed a measure of peace and stability for much of the second half of the eighteenth century. About 1750, a branch of the Ngati Whatua, a tribe entrenched on the Kaipara, completely defeated the then occupants of the isthmus, mainly Wai-o-hua under the paramount chief, Kiwi Tamaki. The victors, sometimes called Orakei Ngati Whatua after the main settlement they set up on the shores of the Waitemata, thereafter claimed rightful ownership (mana whenua) of the land of the isthmus on the grounds of conquest, and of immemorial ancestral descent—having intermarried with remnants of ancient tribes resident in Tamaki. It was with the paramount chief of the Waitemata branch of Ngati Whatua, Te Kawau, that the governor and his officials negotiated for the land which became the site of the capital in 1840.

Apihai Te Kawau, Ngati Whatua chief.
Lithograph by P. Gauci after J. J. Merrett, in Terry's *New Zealand*

Yet it would be altogether too pat to refer to Te Kawau's tribe (in Judge Fenton's later phrase, when speaking of Orakei) as 'dominant lords of the soil'⁴ for the whole of Tamaki-makau-rau. Two hard realities must modify such a claim. The first was the incursion into the region of vigorous intruders, most notably Ngati Paoa, that set in during the late eighteenth century. The second was the new balance of power that emerged in the region during the musket wars of the 1820s and 1830s when Waikato iwi (citing Fenton's phraseology once again) 'assumed a military position which entitled them to be considered the dominant people in this part of New Zealand [Auckland]'.⁵ The extent to which Waikato had become the arbiters of peace and war on the isthmus was demonstrated in 1835 when their redoubtable leader Te Wherowhero, with missionary backing, exploited his power and mana to bring about a peace settlement that enabled refugee Ngati Whatua, Ngati Paoa, Akitai and others (whom Waikato had earlier protected), to resettle once more at Tamaki and about its two surrounding harbours, permanently free from Nga Puhi attack. According to Judge Fenton, Te Wherowhero settled some of his own people at Awhitu (south of the Manukau Heads) as a guarantee to the rest of the protection of Waikato.⁶ But the return of tribal remnants was slow and tentative. In the later 1830s settlement remained sparse on the isthmus; the morale of its inhabitants there low. That was why 1840 was a good time for Governor Hobson to buy land for his new capital at Tamaki.

Powerful though the Waikato tribes had become, no doubt attaches itself to the right of Ngati Whatua to sell to the governor in July 1840 the 3,000-acre wedge of land on the south shore of 'the River Waitemata'.[7]* This block, the most valuable single piece of real estate in New Zealand today, was sold for a ridiculously low figure. What was paid in gold and goods is estimated as totalling £281 sterling. Putting to one side the issue of whether Maori owners were precisely told just what it was they were actually signing away—which modern historians much doubt—we can nevertheless understand why Te Kawau and his fellow chiefs imagined they had struck a fair bargain on behalf of their tribe. As patron of the capital, with the governor (the most powerful man in the colony) as his Pakeha-Maori, Te Kawau would have his mana immeasurably strengthened—so he thought. The governor's presence, moreover, would help tighten the Ngati Whatua grip on the isthmus in the face of any future Waikato or Nga Puhi challenge.

Two even larger purchases of Tamaki land were made by the Crown within the next twelve months. The first of these was the Kohimarama Block, about 6,000 acres, which Hobson's official agent, George Clarke, bought on 28 May 1841 from twenty-four Ngati Paoa chiefs for £200: £100 in cash, and £100 in the form of goods, of which the main items were 'Two Horses, one large Boat, and all its sails and 100 pairs Trousers'.[8] This block took in the greater part of what has been traditionally called Auckland's eastern suburbs. Simplifying considerably, the boundary ran from 'Kohimarama' (modern Mission Bay) along the coastline to the Tamaki River, up its west bank as far as Panmure, across to Lake Waiatarua and north to the starting point at Kohimarama.

Even more spectacular in extent was the sale to the Crown on 29 June 1841 by Te Kawau and four Ngati Whatua chiefs of the 'Waitemata to Manukau Block', estimated to contain over 8,000 acres.[9] Contained within this large block are some of the more important of today's suburbs of the central isthmus, such as Mount Eden, Epsom and Three Kings, and the whole of pre-World War II western suburbs lying beyond Cox's Creek as far as the Whau portage. For this huge area the Crown paid £200 in money, and the remainder of the consideration in goods: 'Four Horses, thirty blankets, ten cloaks, one tent' and, in addition, an item ambiguous in translation, probably a desk.

Two further purchases of isthmus land made by the Crown before the FitzRoy proclamations waiving pre-emption, under which Dilworth

---

* The deed of purchase, executed on behalf of the Crown by George Clarke, chief protector of aborigines, on 20 October 1840, called the area 'Mataharehare, Opou, and Whau', and defined the boundaries as follows: on the north, the Waitemata River between Mataharehare and Opou (Cox's Creek); on the east following the course of stream, Te Ruareoreo, from the shoreline at Mataharehare as far as its headwater (waka matenga) and thence in a straight line to Maungawhau (Mount Eden); on the west, similarly, to the headwater of Cox's Creek and thence in a straight line to Maungawhau.

bought his Remuera land—the main concern of this chapter—were of limited acreage, though in today's terms very great value.[10]

It is also worthy of note what Ngati Whatua chose *not* to sell. Not available to the Pakeha were those lands which lay behind the shoreline between the Kohimarama block and western Waitemata (Hobson Bay) extending back to the ridge along which the first Tamaki Road (today's Remuera Road) ran. Here were the slopes that Logan Campbell and his party had so much admired when they had visited the Tamaki isthmus in May 1840. In *Poenamo*, Campbell contrasted the quiet wilderness of fern, scrub, manuka and tupakihi so typical of most of the isthmus (where the few remnants of mature native bush were to be found only in steep gullies) with the warm slopes of Remuera which had the song of birds echoing through stretches of thick woodland: 'palm tree fern', karaka, puriri, 'evergreen shrubs of every shade'; above, 'lovely flowing creepers'; and 'underfoot . . . a profusion of ferns'.[11]* As Campbell recalled things, to his party's request that they might be allowed to buy some of this wonderful north Remuera land, Te Kawau had given an emphatic 'Kahore! Kahore!' (No). At that time, Ngati Whatua chiefs left Campbell in no doubt, as they did governors subsequently, that this land was untouchable. Remuera was the Ngati Whatua planting ground. Together with the home territory of Orakei, this was ancestral land held in trust, a nest-egg for generations to come.[12]

Settlers continued to cast covetous eyes at Remuera, but for the time being the Crown respected this Ngati Whatua proscription. Certainly at the time of the first annual report of the local Agricultural and Horticultural Society (May 1843) there was land enough for the fewer than 3,000 Pakeha who lived on or near the isthmus. The report stated that of the 36,000 acres surveyed and laid out in country sections of 100 acres in 'the district of Auckland . . . as yet only 4,096 acres have been sold'[13] (almost entirely valuable land in the main settlement or close to it).

These statistics indicate, however, a breakdown in Crown land policy, a policy which had antagonized white settlers not just in Auckland but from one end of the colony to the other. The root of the trouble was that the Colonial Office in London had placed before the local administration two contradictory objectives. The governor was expected on the one hand to protect the Maori people (which surely meant paying a fair price for their land), yet on the other to develop a self-financing administration relying on a sufficiently high margin of profit upon Crown resale price for land bought from Maori to fund not only services and public works, but also future immigration. The

---

* As early as 1845 there was talk in the *Southern Cross* of the need to stop the destruction of Remuera woods in the vicinity of the stream, Te Ruareoreo, by Maori owners who were said to be selling off timber for fencing and firewood (*SC*, 8 Feb. 1845, cit. Ryburn, pp. 10–11).

speculative bidding at Crown land auctions in Auckland in 1841 encouraged local officials to believe for a few months that such a flawed land-sale policy could work.[14] But the high prices of the delusory first auctions were not repeated, while the real damage they inflicted lingered on. Disgruntled Auckland settlers, who had overreached themselves to buy during the early auctions, were stripped of capital needed to develop their landed investment. Nor did profits from subsequent land sales go any distance towards meeting the financial requirements of the administration. In Auckland during 1842–43 land auctions had dismal results. Governor FitzRoy later held that government land policy in the first years caused great mischief. The collapse of property values setting in by 1842 diminished public revenue and had brought about, he wrote in despatches, 'great stagnation in the colony'.[15]* (He was referring here, of course, to the depression of 1842–44 which brought down the New Zealand Banking Company and thereby ended Dilworth's career as a banking accountant in Auckland.)

The trials and disappointments of the capital's first citizens put them at furious odds with Captain Hobson and, after his death, with Willoughby Shortland, the acting governor. For these estranged settlers, cheap, abundant land became the panacea. Crown pre-emption must end. Attacking the Crown's land-buying monopoly had a peculiar advantage. Here was an issue giving a common cause to three influential aggrieved groups in or around Auckland. It appealed to adventurers and land speculators who considered the upset price (reserve) at Crown auctions (ranging from one to five pounds an acre) far too high.† It appealed to Old Land Claimants who came to believe that such a change could speed up a full validation of their pre-1840 (and usually irregular) purchases. The third dissatisfied group was Maori landowners. Partly because funds were not available, partly because government was preoccupied with sorting out New Zealand Company land claims in the Cook Strait settlements, Crown land buying had fallen away. Government payments to Maori owners for land purchases in 1843 fell to a meagre £130, less than six per cent of the previous year's figures.[16] Maori wanting to sell land to get money to buy Pakeha goods became angry. European malcontents stirred them up further

---

* During the Crown Colony period, 1840–53, land sales never achieved their hoped-for financial goals. As a source of revenue for the New Zealand administration they were a bad third. Looking at total net revenue over these years (£822,356), major contributors were customs duties (£319,219) and grants-in-aid from the British and New South Wales governments (£307,831). Receipts from land sales provided less than eleven per cent of the revenue (£86,461). However, this sum represented a return to the government of 360 per cent on what Maori had been originally paid. Nor does the figure take into account *future* income from land already acquired, which had become part of the reserve of land but was as yet unsold (*Statistics of New Zealand for the Crown Colony Period, 1840–52*, Table 47, Auckland, 1954).

† The *New Zealand Government Gazette* listed upset prices at Crown auctions at that time: suburban lots (3–7 acres) in Suburbs of Auckland £5 per acre; allotments in Town of Auckland £100 per acre (13 Jan 1844); suburban farms in Parish of Takapuna (approx. 25 acres) £2 per acre (27 Jan 1844). Most of these transactions were in scrip in lieu of Old Land Claims.

by telling them that they had not been paid enough for the land they had already sold.

On 23 April 1843 the *Southern Cross* newspaper was founded to champion the cause of the 'unhappy original settlers' whose properties (said the editor) had been 'confiscated' by inept colonial administrators knowing as little about organising settlement 'as they do of the domestic economy of the Emperor of China, or the Grand Turk'.[17] It began to badger the government of the day without mercy. In editorials and articles, alternating self-pity with aggression, it pressed for the ending of Crown pre-emption. Maori should be freed from their 'state of demi-slavery' and given 'the full rights of Englishmen' so that they could sell their land to whomsoever they wished. Speaking for the settler faction, this paper assured humanitarians 'at Home' and colonists with tender consciences that they need not be alarmed. Maori landowners would not be bested in direct land dealings. They were astute enough to drive a hard bargain. After disposing of unwanted, surplus lands, they would still be left with 'princely domains' of their own.[18]

This was essentially what certain self-seeking Pakeha felt. The truth was almost certainly different. Whether tribes should sell, and where and how much, whether through the Crown or privately, were land matters on which Maori spoke with misgivings and with a divided voice. With such divisions in mind, Major Thomas Bunbury, senior military officer in the colony at the time, recalled that throughout 1843–44, 'the tribes in the vicinity of Auckland, and indeed all over the country were in an unsettled state', so much so that in July 1843 Ngati Whatua and Waikato, 'two tribes who are located in the suburbs of Auckland', were threatening to 'go to war' over the right to sell land to Pakeha.[19] He probably exaggerated the danger of war, but the tension between tribes near Auckland was real enough.

The source of the trouble was the occupation by Waikato of certain lands on the isthmus over the whole of which Ngati Whatua claimed title according to Maori customary rights. Waikato people were established at Mangere where Takewaru Kati, younger brother of Te Wherowhero, lived with his Nga Puhi wife Toha.* Kati and members of his tribe also occupied land in a block which became known as Pukapuka No. 1, located in today's Upland Road area, extending down from Remuera Road to the Orakei Basin; the gift being originally made by Uruamo of Ngati Whatua to Te Wherowhero.[20] Another block in Waikato's lands was made up of about 400 acres in Hillsborough.[21] But the most valuable of the isthmus land Waikato laid claim to was a block of upwards of 1,000 acres in Remuera, said to have been gifted to Wiremu Wetere (William Wesley) Te Kauae and other Waikato chiefs requiting them for services to Ngati Whatua.[22]

---

* Te Kati married his wife Matire Toha in about 1824 to place a diplomatic seal, it has been said, upon a pledge for Waikato and Nga Puhi to remain at peace. The Ihumatao block (Mangere area) of 1,100 acres was taken from Waikato by confiscation in 1865.

JAMES DILWORTH

The initial merit which the Waikato tribes saw in these lands once Auckland became the capital was the access to trade with Europeans that they provided. They lived on the land, cultivated it, sold its produce to the Pakeha. But by 1843 they wanted to sell it. Conscious of the erosion of the Ngati Whatua power base, they became arrogant, claimed the land as theirs, 'by right of conquest' in the opinion of one official, to keep or to dispose of as they chose.[23]* Ngati Whatua were outraged. Any land on the isthmus occupied by Waikato was held (in their opinion) as a tuku or gift to the tribe invited to be there, a gesture of

---
* After the musket wars there was a saying that the boundaries claimed by Waikato were 'Tamaki ki runga Mokau ki raro' (from Tamaki in the north to Mokau in the south). Such pretensions were said to have set the teeth of other iwi on edge.

Te Wherowhero, the principal chief of all Waikato.
Lithograph 1847 after G. F. Angas, Alexander Turnbull Library

40

goodwill, a payback to allies for services rendered during the musket wars. But the gift was not to be thought of as outright. Ngati Whatua considered it gave only conditional rights of residence and cultivation. When the land was no longer needed for those things, ownership must revert to themselves as holding the mana whenua. However, Ngati Whatua were equally agitated by the prospect that, if Waikato sold, wellnigh irresistible pressure would also go on to Ngati Whatua to sell the Remuera-Orakei lands they wanted to retain for their children.

This then was the issue that Major Bunbury claimed to believe held the threat of intertribal war in mid-1843. Through the mediation of others, differences were patched up. But only temporarily. Waikato were determined to settle, once for all, their right to sell. In an October 1843 issue of the *Southern Cross* it was reported that the subject of land sales

> is at the present moment canvassed by all natives over the length and breadth of New Zealand and a Congress of Native Chiefs amounting to the number of 6,000 is to be held in January or February [1844] for the purpose of discussing and deciding upon this point. This Assembly of Natives is to be held in the vicinity of Auckland. Many of our readers are doubtless aware that a considerable body of the natives have been employed some months ago [probably in late July or August] cultivating land and planting potatoes near Mount Hobson: this has been done with the view of providing provisions for the ensuing native congress.[24]

For reasons that are not entirely clear, this Maori gathering was postponed for three to four months, and when held in May 1844 had rather fewer attending than had been expected. But it was to be, nevertheless, still spectacularly large, a dramatic emdodiment of the mana and political power of the Waikato (Tainui) people who convened it.

Interestingly, the venue of the congress was the site of James Dilworth's future farm, within whose boundaries also lay many of the potato cultivations spoken of in the newspaper account. The hui was summoned, not just to thrash out the question of Crown pre-emption—as the somewhat self-interested article in the *Cross* stated was its primary purpose—but also to settle the much weightier issue of whether Maori should sell land at all; and, in some cases, whether those claiming rights of ownership even had the right to sell. It was no coincidence that Waikato chiefs convened the hui. In 1843, they were anxious to assert their right to sell, just as in the later 1850s leaders of those same tribes were the most resolute among Maori in opposing sale of land to Pakeha.

The site of the congress had been deliberately chosen, and not just because it was a locality where Waikato hapu presently lived and

---

* This western boundary also took in the small 'Manukau Road Block' of 200 acres bought by the Crown on 14 September 1842 (Turton's Deeds, No. 209).

cultivated. It was also at the heart of a particularly sensitive area where feelings among Maori for and against land sales were at their most intense, the most valuable portion of the 'huge corridor' (so described by Maurice Alemann) of unsold Maori land on the central isthmus.[25] This corridor lay between the two great Crown land purchases of 1841, on the east the 'Kohimarama Block', on the west the 'Waitemata to Manukau Block',* running north to south from Tamaki Road to the upper Manukau Harbour.

Over the greater part of this as yet unsold corridor Ngati Whatua held the mana whenua, an indisputable title based on Maori custom and the then Native Land Law. But it so happened that the northwestern part of this block, lying, in today's terms, between Cornwall Park and Remuera Road, was a kind of upland valley, some of which was occupied by Ngati Whatua, and the remainder by Waikato. This valley had fertile soil of fine tilth, enriched by tuff and other airfall which had been ejected from surrounding volcanoes, but, unlike the land around some cones such as Mount Eden, Owairaka (Mount Albert) and Rarotonga (Mount Smart), lacked a troublesome litter of rock debris, and so could be immediately farmed. The area had a particularly rich inner portion adjacent to the little villages of Newmarket and Epsom and close to the capital's three main access routes for that part of the isthmus: Manukau Road, Papakura (Great South) Road and Tamaki Road—which by late 1843 were either under construction or likely to be improved. Its potential as farmland had already been demonstrated by a few settlers who had established fine market gardens nearby on a subdivision of the village of Epsom.[26]* On the inner portion itself there were flourishing native cultivations. Here was the prime target of Pakeha speculators who wanted to end Crown pre-emption so that they could buy directly from Maori. And not because of its possibilities as farmland alone. It happened to be occupied by those Waikato subtribes—Ngati Te Ata, Ngati Maoho and Ngati Mahuta—who were particularly bent on exchanging it for white man's goods temptingly for sale in the township.

This agitation over land sales, building up among Maori and Pakeha in the district of Auckland, must now be put in a colony-wide setting. When the new governor Captain Robert FitzRoy, arrived at the end of 1843, not just Auckland but the whole colony was in turmoil. He was welcomed by a barrage of 'complaints and lamentations' from almost every settlement.[27]

The treasury was empty. Race relations were dangerously strained. Twenty-two Europeans had been killed in an armed clash in the Wairau Valley in June 1843 and Cook Strait settlers, still seething, were calling

---

* Epsom was originally a suburban allotment bought by a New South Wales speculator who created the artificial township of Epsom, subdividing the land as villa sites some of which became market gardens (Sherrin and Wallace, p. 553).

out for vengeance. The economic downturn in the Bay of Islands—reflected in the dishonoured bills that had imperilled the branch of Dilworth's bank there—threatened to lead to race war. Daunting problems were made worse because, as Ian Wards puts it, 'the government in England was not prepared to provide funds, troops or a warship, or to give the governor any liberty of action'.[28]

We can appreciate in the setting of these very general difficulties why FitzRoy's response to an address presented by 'the Inhabitants of Auckland' at his inaugural levee was muted. But he obviously thought of himself as a new broom. (His wife Mary, no doubt repeating pillow talk, confided to a relative at the time that, 'The indolent mismanagement of our predecessor is quite wonderful'.[29]) To the 'Inhabitants'' plea that 'the Natives of New Zealand' should have 'the full-rights of British subjects so that they could buy and sell their own land', the new governor gave an answer leaving land-hungry buyers not without hope: 'The power of selling their land to whom they pleased was withheld from [the Natives] by the Crown for their own benefit. I am authorised to prepare for other arrangements more suitable to their improved, and daily improving condition'.[30] Having more pressing matters to look to, however, he did not change the land regulations before he left for the south to attempt to lower racial tensions in the Cook Strait settlements of the New Zealand Company. But he had said enough to convince a number of Auckland settlers that the ending of the Crown monopoly of land sales was at hand.

After that, many land buyers in Auckland concentrated their efforts on the area near Mount Hobson and Mount St John, later to designated 'Sections 11 and 12 Suburbs of Auckland', which Bunbury described as 'now [early 1844] by far the most valuable [suburban] land in New Zealand'.[31] Unscrupulous speculators, knowing there would be fierce competition for this rich volcanic land, decided to anticipate the change in the law which would allow direct dealing with Maori. They began to negotiate by stealth with Wetere (sometimes described in deeds as being of the Ngati Maoho hapu, sometimes as of Ngati Te Ata) rumoured to be ready to sell for about five shillings an acre, in contrast to the prevailing upset price of one pound for land much inferior to this sold at Crown auctions.[32] These clandestine transactions, which involved paying deposits as low as twenty per cent of the agreed price, effectively shut out potential buyers who were prepared scrupulously to observe the law.[33]

An instance of the profits that could come by anticipating in this way the change in the law is provided by Charles Henry Moffitt, a dentist (like many early Aucklanders he was practising land speculation as a sideline) whose surgery was almost opposite the bank where Dilworth then worked. On 26 February 1844 he put down three double-barrelled guns as 'part payment' to Wetere for sixty acres of Remuera land which was going for one pound an acre.[34] The size of

Governor FitzRoy, n.d. (mid-1840s?).
Auckland Museum Library

the block available to Moffitt was progressively reduced to a little under thirty-one-and-a-quarter acres; but the asking price per acre remained the same. An inventory of the payments which Wetere provided for the court of the land commissioner in February 1847 makes interesting reading. 'Wetere testified', say the notes in the Old Land Claims archives,

> He received £5 in cash and the articles enumerated:
>
> | | |
> |---|---:|
> | '1 Superior double-barrelled gun | £9-0-0 |
> | 2 Double-barrelled guns | 8-0-0 |
> | Medicines from 14 May to 29 August [1844?] | 1-3-0 |
> | Large Meerschaum pipe | 5-0-0 |
> | Bag of shot | 12-0 |
> | Shot Pouch | 16-8 |
> | Cloth Cap | 10-0 |
> | Cash | 5-0-0 |
> | Ream Paper | 1-5-0 |
> | | £31-6-8 |
>
> This was the consideration agreed upon.'[35]

Te Hiahia, drawn by H. G. Robley. Double-barrelled guns were often used as consideration in the purchase of Maori lands.
Alexander Turnbull Library

Because he had envisaged this particular allotment adjoining Manukau Road as part of his own future farm, Dilworth was probably aggrieved that Moffitt had so stolen a march on him. However, when FitzRoy's waiver of Crown pre-emption placed Wetere's conveyance to Moffitt within the law, Dilworth negotiated with Moffitt a provisional transfer of this land to him, depending on an exchange with another Remuera property.[36] The deal fell through, but when Moffitt received the Crown grant for his allotment on 1 November 1847 Dilworth persisted and bought one quarter of it for exactly ten pounds an acre.[37] In less than four years Moffitt had made a profit of 900 per cent on his speculation.

The first recorded example of these illicit deals was not Moffitt's but another which, untypically, was based on full payment and not a deposit. This deal was struck, once again with Wetere, on 17 February 1844 by Henry Hayr, surveyor (but in later years an innkeeper in town). Turton's Deed No. 14 reads:

> Epsom Feby. 17th, 1844
>
> I this day agree to give to Henry Hayr a piece of land on the East side of Mount St John containing 7 acres more or less marked out by myself in exchange for 1 double barrelled Gun, 1 Single Barrelled Pocket Pistol and Maogany [sic] Case, 4 Double Barrelled Guns, 1 Powder Flask, 1 Shot Pouch.
>
> Witness W. Sansom
>
> Signed W. Wetere[38]*

We know from the reminiscences of Major Bunbury, acting governor for about five weeks over January–February 1844 while FitzRoy was away from Auckland, that a number of these transactions were taking place before the date given on the deed above.

When news of these underhand sales came to the ears of neighbouring Ngati Whatua they were dismayed. A deputation from the tribe called on Wetere and asked him to desist. He refused. Two letters of complaint written by Ngati Whatua chiefs the following week to George Clarke, as chief protector of aborigines, express eloquently the tribe's resentment. The first was from Paora Tuhaere, son of Aterete, Te Kawau's sister, who though not yet twenty already spoke with the authority which was to stay with him over a long life.

> 10th February 1844.
>
> Paul to Clarke,
> This is what I say to you. Our land is taken by Te Wetere. This taking of our land has no foundation or root (of equity). This is the ground or foundation. A word from our parent since deceased [Tarahawaiki?]. . . . He said to them (Wetere and his people), here

---

* Wetere and a fellow chief, Apera, subsequently sold two adjoining lots totalling seven acres as well for five pounds cash. In 1847 Hayr was awarded a Crown grant (No. 1168a) for ten acres (4G: 13).

reside and cultivate food for yourselves, in order that you may be near the Europeans. This was his speech which we all agree [upon], that they should settle by sufferance, on . . . our land.

Mr Clarke—on Friday, Kawau went to Remuera, when Wetere got up, and said the land was [his]. His speech was very obstinate, or determined . . . ; Kawau then arose, when Edward Meurant* said to Kawau, your speech is wrong, sit down.

This is Kawau's speech for us. . . . This is our speech also . . . that this is our land as long as we live, when we leave it to our children.[39]

Te Kawau's letter to Clarke, on the other hand, combined anger with a threat—towards whom is not clear.

> Friend, Mr Clarke
>
> Saluting you. Listen to what I have to say about Remuera. Wetere has sold it to the Europeans; but I say, I will not let my land go for him. If Wetere persists I shall be mischievous; that is all. This is to let you know, that I shall be mischievous.
>
> From Kawau.[40]

Paora Tuhaere, nephew of Te Kawau.
Lithograph by P. Gauci, in Terry's *New Zealand*

How Te Kawau proposed to 'be mischievous' he never made clear. Bunbury considered that this threat lay behind the confrontation shortly afterwards between the government and Ngati Whatua arising out of the arrest and conviction of a minor chief of the tribe. Just as the prisoner was about to begin a term of imprisonment for stealing a forage cap from an Auckland store, sympathisers rushed the dock of the court and spirited him away to sanctuary at Orakei.[41] Soon after, a senior military officer with a few redcoats arrived at the village in pursuit. Te Kawau then intervened to defuse the situation by persuading the refugee to return peacefully to Auckland to serve out his sentence. This was a trivial riot expressing little more than Ngati Whatua disillusionment with what they had once imagined was to be their mutually supportive partnership with the Crown. Te Kawau's enduring anger was, in fact, directed less at the Crown than at Waikato chiefs living (as Paora had expressed it) on sufferance upon his Tamaki land. But the truth of the matter was that he lacked the power to do anything other than to give vent to frustration. Waikato were, in FitzRoy's view, 'one of the most powerful as well as numerous tribes in New Zealand', having in Te Wherowhero 'probably the greatest chief'.[42] So, undeterred, Waikato went their own way, selling off Tamaki land; and preparing for their hui which obliquely was an assertion of their right to sell. 'Ostensibly . . . a return feast to other tribes',[43] this gathering had developed another and more important purpose of demonstrating

---

* Edward Meurant, formerly a lay agent of the Wesleyan Mission, was hired by Wetere to act as interpreter for his land deals. By 1845 he was also a government interpreter. His Maori wife of Waikato stock, Kenehuru (later christened Eliya), was given twenty-five acres of Remuera land near Newmarket by Waikato for the support of herself and her children— during her and their lifetime (CG in 16D: 770).

'the extent of Te Wherowhero's . . . influence and alliances' and of his rangatiratanga (commanding influence and status) in this centre of Pakeha government.[44]

After FitzRoy's return from the south he looked once more at the local Maori land problem. Lacking the money to buy on behalf of the Crown himself, he decided to placate Maori opinion by allowing private sales of land in a limited number of places approved of by the government. On 26 March 1844 he issued a proclamation waiving Crown pre-emption in these specified areas, provided that a certificate was obtained by the Pakeha buyer that would cost ten shillings for each acre bought (the sum to be paid in two stages), and provided that a Crown grant would be issued later only when there was verification that the land had been properly surveyed and legally purchased. On the day following the waiver proclamation, FitzRoy, wittingly or not, carried out a transaction which could be regarded as giving a kind of vice-regal sanction to the Waikato claim of the right to sell. He signed a deed on which he was the sole listed 'witness' with the Ngati Maoho chief, Epiha Putini,* who on payment of fifty pounds surrendered all rights to property north of Tamaki Road to which he might have a putative claim.[45]

Despite the complaint of some local settlers that an impost of ten shillings for each acre bought under the proclamation was 'much too dear',[46] this sum was trivial when placed, say, beside the potential value of the rich Epsom and Remuera lands opened up by the waiver. One should also look sceptically at the reiteration of older texts that 'relatively few purchases were made under this proclamation',[47] causing Maori to become resentful and forcing the governor six months later to drop the charge to one penny an acre. However true this may have been for distant or inferior lands, it was not so for those of the Tamaki isthmus. Of the 250 pre-emption waivers issued by FitzRoy, sixty-four were for the central isthmus lands, the great majority of which were bought under ten-shilling certificates.[48] For Auckland speculators (however much they complained) the first FitzRoy waiver, in setting a tax of ten shillings an acre, was not too expensive, and was most effective where it counted. Indeed, the 26 March proclamation led to a stampede among Pakeha buyers. Those who had already negotiated underhand purchases hastened to regularize them by getting 'Pre-emption Certificates' and by completing down-payments. Those who (like Dilworth) had waited upon the governor's proclamation, scrambled from the day it was gazetted to buy those inner volcanic lands of the isthmus which were still available.

---

* Epiha Putini is the English version of the name Jabez Bunting (one-time secretary of the Church Missionary Society (Anglican)) which was the name given to Te Rangia Tane by Anglican missionaries on his conversion. Subsequently he became a Wesleyan. The son of the powerful Waikato chief Wetere, he resided during 1844 at Pehiakura near the Manukau.

By the end of 1844, Waikato chiefs had sold almost 1,500 acres, virtually all of their Auckland lands. Fears expressed earlier by Ngati Whatua leaders that direct sales between Maori and Pakeha would have adverse consequences for their tribe proved to be only too well founded. Chiefs became exposed to the pressure of land-selling elements from within tribal ranks. Even more insidious (in Alan Ward's phrase) 'in inflaming the tendency to sell'[49] was the competition between tribes and subtribes over certain territories for which the precise boundaries did not exist, at least in white man's terms. To Ngati Whatua it sometimes seemed that only by clinching a sale could they assert ownership. The alternative might be to have the land sold from beneath the tribe's feet.

The problem of overlapping boundaries could be compounded by intertribal marriages in the past, and therefore multiple ancestry of claimants. Thus, the Waikato tribes Ngati Te Ata and Ngati Maoho had links with Nga Oho/Wai-o-hua, inhabitants of Tamaki-makau-rau extending centuries back.[50] An area of considerable overlap—and possibly chosen by Waikato as the venue of their 1844 hui for that reason—was the part of Remuera which Dilworth set about buying after the ten-shillings proclamation, particularly that part of his future farm lying to the east of Mount Hobson. In a small but critical part of this area three groups—Mahuta, Maoho and Ngati Whatua—had rival claims. Settling who were to be regarded as the accredited owners necessitated the intervention, in one case, of the protector of aborigines, and in another of the governor himself, who required representatives of the three tribes to meet on the disputed land and draw on the ground a boundary line agreeable to all.[51] Once again the FitzRoy proclamation served Ngati Whatua ill. Such contests over, and sales of, land south of the Tamaki Road, in the long run weakened the tribe's resolve not to sell land north of it.

The only feature of these direct sales between Maori and European which could be construed as an improvement for Maori on the system of Crown purchase was the rate per acre paid by private buyers in extinguishing Maori titles. This was higher than that previously paid by the government, although, it must be said, not dramatically so.[52] Where payment was in goods, the real price paid is not always easy to estimate. Obviously prices could vary widely, from as low as two shillings an acre to more than twenty times that sum. Alemann has estimated that Ngati Whatua parted with their lands on the central isthmus at this time for about five shillings an acre.[53] However, the good volcanic land between and around Mount Hobson and Mount St John was sold by Waikato subtribes for about one pound an acre, whilst in certain choice acres in that district (usually small blocks) commanded prices of over two pounds an acre.[54]

During 1845 FitzRoy was replaced as governor by Captain George Grey, who shortly after arrival restored Crown pre-emption. But the

FitzRoy waiver proclamations had done their work. Virtually all of the isthmus save for the Ngati Whatua nest-egg lands of Orakei and Remuera north of Tamaki Road (still intact but by now much under threat) were in Pakeha hands. Grey looked on the waiver sales as little short of disastrous. He deplored the 'reckless spirit of bargaining for lands'.[55] Reporting to his ministerial head in London about the 'various complicated disputes' which he had inherited, he admitted he feared that 'a series of new land claims have arisen which are likely to prove more troublesome than those [Old Land Claims] which have already been so perplexing to the Government'.[56] But the clock could not be turned back. Grey was instructed that purchases made during the waiving of Crown pre-emption, if found on investigation to have been transacted according to the regulations of the time, must receive a Crown grant.

In the will of James Dilworth, made six weeks before his death in 1894, there was an unusual provision. To the customary bequest that a dutiful husband makes to his 'beloved wife' for 'her own absolute use and benefit' of all household effects, ornaments, jewellery and the like, Dilworth listed four exceptions: portaits of himself and Isabella painted by Gottfried Lindauer, a water colour sketch of early Auckland and 'the lithograph of a Maori Feast framed with New Zealand Woods'. The will directed that on Mrs Dilworth's death these pictures would revert to the executors of the estate who would then cause them to 'be hung in a conspicuous place in the principal building of the [Dilworth Ulster] Institute'.[57]

The lithograph of the Maori feast, often refered to as 'The Remuera Feast', within its hand-carved frame of native woods, hangs today in the foyer of Dilworth School beside the main entrance to the Hall. Made from a drawing of J. J. Merrett,* it is a valuable record of the meeting of seventeen tribes which Waikato called during May 1844. Merrett was well qualified to make such a record. He spoke Maori, had travelled extensively through Northland and the Waikato, and was sensitive to Maori customs.[58] The drawing, moreover, combines a landscape artist's sense of perspective with a draughtsman's concern for detail. Merrett drew from more than one vantage point. The orientation of the volcanic cones indicates that the landscape features were sketched from a distant promontory in eastern Remuera— probably from the summit of Little Rangitoto which was beside today's Upland Road.† The very precise detail such as tattoo on bodies, on the other hand, came from personal encounter; while the more general view of the land between Mount Hobson and Mount St John was what

---

* Joseph Jenner Merrett, 1816–54; artist, surveyor and interpreter. His drawing, executed in 1844 in Auckland where he then lived, was converted into a lithograph in the following year.

† Little Rangitoto was the name given by Europeans to the volcanic cone called by Maori 'Maunga Rahiri'. The cone was quarried away and the land is now a council reserve.

Remuera Feast of 1844; arrival of Governor FitzRoy.
Left: *In the left foreground note the seasonal lake at the south-east boundary of what was to be Dilworth's estate. The hills on the left horizon are the volcanic cones known as the Three Kings.*

Right: *The hill on the left is Mount Hobson, to its right is Mount Eden. FitzRoy, mounted on a black horse, is being welcomed by members of Ngati Mahuta, a Waikato tribe. In the distance are rows of blankets and dried shark to be distributed among guests.*
Lithograph after J. J. Merrett, Alexander Turnbull Library

would have registered with a close observer who placed himself about where the junior Dilworth School now stands, but who then used a generous artistic licence in his placements so that the whole dramatic record of the occasion was captured.

This one may surmise; no more. What is not conjectural is the site of the feast. The huge encampment of tribes lasting for a week or more was located, in FitzRoy's wording, within that 'picturesque . . . natural amphitheatre' which Dilworth was in the process of buying at the very time Merrett made his drawing.[59] We can easily understand therefore why Dilworth, fifty years later, should have been anxious that this record of the appearance of the land, as it was just before it came into his hands, be preserved for posterity.

At the time, the feast aroused great interest. It was widely written about. FitzRoy was so much taken with the gathering that he wrote a long despatch about it to his minister in London. But despite all the narrative there was then and has been since, there has been surprisingly little discussion about what the feast actually portended.

The facts are clear enough and easily accessible. Only those which signify historically are recounted here. Being a paremata (a return feast for one previously given—sometimes with presents for guests) its ostensible purpose was to enable the hosts, Te Wherowhero and Wetere, on behalf of Waikato, to reciprocate other tribes, notably Ngati Haua, for past hospitality. Three-and-a-half-thousand attended, visitors on some days swelling the number to over 4,000. Only eighty Ngati Whatua were there; a deliberately subdued presence, one imagines.

The feast came to a climax on Saturday, 10 May, the day FitzRoy and an official party had been formally invited by Wetere's son, Putini. On horseback, Putini met the governor shortly after he left town and escorted him over the greater part of his three-mile journey. FitzRoy and the many Pakeha sightseers (almost certainly including Dilworth)* who went to the hui that day saw two spectacular events. The first was an awesome mock battle between 800 (mainly) Waikato men and 800 warriors drawn from visiting tribes. After chanting defiant haka and brandishing muskets and other weapons from the hilltop, the two rival units alternately rushed down, though in well-drilled fashion, the slopes of Mount Hobson and Mount St John upon which each had positioned itself, to confront their rival at a mid-point on the plain. After further haka the 'battle' ended. The other spectacle was the ritual distribution of gifts to guests—over 1,000 blankets, thousands of sharks and thousands of kits of potatoes. And this was not the sum of the largesse of the Waikato hosts who during the week had plied guests with food to a point of seeming self-impoverishment. Ann Parsonson has reminded us this was not mindless generosity but a display of power that no other tribe could hope to equal in the future.[60]

This palpable demonstration of Waikato mana and power was not lost on the governor. It was no coincidence that two days later, at the reception given to 200 chiefs in Government House, Te Wherowhero

---

* Dilworth would surely have been there, if only because he had already made a down-payment to Wetere to buy the land on which much of the paremata was taking place.

stood at FitzRoy's right hand. If we look ahead we can see why it was a comfort to FitzRoy as it was to his successor Grey that during the Northern War of 1845–46 the Waikato tribes stood aside, considering Heke's rising (as the great Tainui historian Lesley Kelly has put it) 'no business of theirs'.[61] Later still, Grey recognised 'the powerful position of Waikato [by making] overtures to Te Wherowhero to place [Auckland] under his mana'.[62]

It has been pointed out that, having the advantage of hindsight (and the reflective informed research that this can bring in its wake), historians can sometimes discern in certain past events a deeper import than did those who actually took part. This is true of the Remuera feast. Regarded by Pakeha observers as a bizarre spectacle, it was in fact a striking demonstration of the extent to which, in Maori terms, Waikato had become the power-brokers of Tamaki-makau-rau.

And so, in seeking to preserve a copy of Merrett's 'Remuera Feast' for posterity, Dilworth acted more wisely than he knew. At the feast Waikato showed, in effect, that regardless of any customary claims Ngati Whatua may have had over the isthmus land on which Waikato subtribes were currently residing, considerations of power allowed Wetere and his fellow chiefs to sell with impunity. Waikato dominance illustrated in the 'Remuera Feast' provided, by one or two removes, the means by which Dilworth could buy his land. The Merrett lithograph symbolised much more than Dilworth thought.

CHAPTER FOUR

Man of Property 1844–49

Between 1844 and 1849 Dilworth bought and began to farm the Remuera land which with little change he kept intact for the rest of his life. Even today this suburban estate remains at the financial heart of the Dilworth Trust.

The land claims commissioner, F. Dillon Bell, said in 1862 that in his opinion those people who had bought land 'within the City of Auckland' at Crown auctions during 1844 and had then hung on to it had seen the value of their investment increase at least tenfold.[1] Dilworth's investment in suburban land did much better than that.

A number of things contributed to this turn of events. It helped that the farm he owned was close to the growing town. And the peculiar circumstances of FitzRoy's governorship played their part, too; above all, his decision to throw open the central isthmus to private Maori-Pakeha land dealings. Further, having a moderate stock of capital at his disposal gave Dilworth a distinct advantage over most of his competitors. Yet the most important ingredient in his success was his skill as an investor; in selecting the land, and in financing its management once it came into his hands. In choosing his land he thoroughly assessed its long-term rather than its immediate worth. Hence his determination, once he had bought land, not to part with it except on very favourable terms. Even more important was his shrewdness as a financial manager, remarkably developed in a man who, it must be remembered, was only twenty-eight. This was to stand him in good stead in a colonial settlement where so many in the nineteenth century lost all by overreaching themselves in the property market on borrowed money.

During 1844 Dilworth followed two callings concurrently: banking and land buying. Though he continued to work diligently at the former, he had begun to think of it as a phase of his life about to end. It was to the latter he now looked for his future career.

For a settler wanting to buy suburban land cheaply, 1844 was a good year. Whereas the property market had stagnated over 1842–43,

53

events during 1844 conduced to move large parts of the isthmus into Pakeha hands. The waiving of Crown pre-emption is part of the explanation, but not all of it. Also significant, though little written about since, was the widespread use of government land scrip originally designed to allow settlers with old land claims in remote districts, generally in the North Auckland peninsula, to exchange them for land close to the capital. Dilworth took full advantage of both the waiving of pre-emption and the use of land scrip.

Upon the issue of the 26 March 1844 proclamation waiving Crown pre-emption, Dilworth set about negotiating with Wetere for that part of the chief's land lying between Mount Hobson and Mount St John which was as yet unsold. Purchasing there the kind of compact suburban estate Dilworth had set his heart on would, he knew, not be easy. Already before the governor's waiver, desirable property fronting the Onehunga Road between Newmarket and Epsom had been sold by Waikato chiefs. Competition among buyers was keen. Almost to a man, Dilworth's rivals were speculators. He was not. Two years later he was to explain in a letter to the government, pointedly addressed as from his residence on his new farm, why he should get an immediate Crown grant for his land. After pointing out that he intended his purchase to be a long-term investment in farm land, he continued:

> I was not actuated to the purchase of the small portion of land I claim by any speculative or other motive than to reside on and make it my home (which is proved, if proof be wanting by the fact that I now hold every acre I bought, and now have more than 40 of it under crop). Consequently I took the greatest trouble and care to find out and entirely extinguish all Native claims which I believe to be effectually done by large payments to them in cash, I may say the largest in proportion to the extent in acres of any purchase made under the Proclamation and therefore, as is clear, the Government would run no risk in ensuring a title . . .[2]

If the case Dilworth argued here, that he was no fly-by-night land jobber, was sincere—and I think it was, though subdivision and sale were never entirely dismissed from his mind—one can understand why in the years ahead he was so reluctant to part with any section of his Remuera farm.

How Dilworth proceeded to buy his land is recorded in the Old Land Claims files at National Archives, Wellington. That he behaved in much the same way as others who used pre-emption waiver certificates (PCs) is confirmed by comparing the evidence given by witnesses testifying during the hearing of his claim in 1847 with that of witnesses for other claims which came before the land claims commissioner. The almost universal practice (quite contrary, let it be said, to the intention of the waiver proclamations) was for the Pakeha buyer, before obtaining his pre-emption certificate, to go out with a surveyor and an interpreter to the land he wanted to buy and there negotiate with

Mullaghcreevy homestead (1993): the old stone barn and living quarters.

Mullaghcreevy homestead (1993): the 'new' cottage.

View of Newmarket, by Joseph Merrett. c. 1850. This view is from the vicinity of Carlton Gore Road looking south-west; with Khyber Pass centre to right foreground; Broadway left to right across centre, and Hobson bridge on left. Tamaki (Remuera) Road is centre middle distance; Mount Hobson centre background; Mount St John right background.

Environs of Auckland by Alfred Sharpe. This is a view looking south-east from the grounds of today's Auckland Grammar School, showing Mount Hobson (left centre) and part of Remuera. The building in the centre is Rockwood, home of the Richmond family, that on the more distant right is Harewood, home of the Lascelles family, later incorporated into the Mater (today's Mercy) Hospital.

View of Auckland Harbour from Mount Hobson by John Barr Clark Hoyte. 'A wonderful panorama . . . of infinite beauty, . . . pre-eminent, unequalled unsurpassed' (John Logan Campbell). The northward-facing summit of Mount Hobson was a favourite vantage point for nineteenth-century artists.

View from the Ranges by Frederick Rice Stack. This picture conveys the broken nature of the Waitakere Ranges and the rugged, indented nature of the Manukau Harbour shoreline. This area, well known to both Dilworths, was close to the scene of Joseph Howard's milling operations in the 1870s.

James Dilworth *by Gottfried Lindauer. 1876.*

Isabella Dilworth *by Gottfried Lindauer. 1876.*

Reverend George MacMurray
by Gottfried Lindauer. 1909.

Above: *The limestone of the Centennial Cross and the volcanic stone of its surrounds actualise the Irish and New Zealand existences of James Dilworth.*
Below: *The chapel of St Patrick (1958) and the Centennial High Cross (1994): the Christian faith lies at the heart of the school.*

the assumed owners a deal which would be clinched by paying part or whole of the consideration money agreed upon. The next step was for the buyer to write to the governor (in practice to his colonial secretary, Dr Andrew Sinclair) requesting a PC, specifying the block for which it was required with boundaries precisely described, sometimes to the extent of providing an accompanying sketch plan. Dr Sinclair would then refer the application to the protector of aborigines, George Clarke. If he saw no problem as to the mana whenua of the sellers, the certificate would be issued by the governor as a matter of routine.

The speed with which Dilworth moved once direct purchase from Maori became legal on 26 March showed that he had already made up his mind where he wanted his farm to be. His eye was on the sixty-acre block which straddled the then crudely formed Papakura Road (later to be called Great South Road) just after it branched from the Onehunga Road (Manukau Road) a few hundred yards beyond Newmarket. The Papakura Road divided this block of land into two unequal portions: about two-thirds lay on its Mount Hobson or northern side, the remainder was on the south side of the road roughly according with the position of the senior Dilworth School and its grounds today. This southern portion, the best land of the estate, ultimately became the home farm.

Dilworth succeeded in making his purchase by way of three transactions requiring three separate PCs. Two of the waiver certificates were to cover fifty acres bought from Wetere alone, at the price of one pound an acre. The third transaction concerned an area of eleven acres bought by James Dilworth, 'Accountant of the New Zealand Banking Company', for seventeen pounds from Wetere and Aperahama (Abraham), 'Native Chiefs of the Tribe of Ngati te Ata of Waikato'.[3] A deed covering the lesser amount was signed—with Joseph Merrett, the artist, acting as interpreter—on 18 September 1844. The deed covering the larger purchase was not executed until 31 January 1845.[4] But the execution of the deeds was just a formality. There is solid evidence that this estate was effectively Dilworth's before April 1844 was out. In that month the young banker hired labourers to begin to fence off thirty acres and sow there a crop of winter wheat.

Dilworth then contrived to buy an even more substantial block of land adjacent to this farm; one lying east of Mount Hobson and (in today's terms) running roughly southwards from Remuera Road towards St Cuthbert's College. Other Pakeha buyers would surely have snapped up this area earlier had it not been a politically sensitive one with overlapping tribal boundaries. At particular issue were two questions: at what point east of Mount Hobson did Ngati Maoho rights of ownership give way to those of Ngati Mahuta; and where south of Tamaki Road did undisputed Ngati Whatua mana whenua resume? Dilworth instructed his agent to deal with the Ngati Mahuta chief Kati Takewaru, foremost land claimant and younger brother of

JAMES DILWORTH

Te Wherowhero (no doubt encouraged in this course by the display of power Te Wherowhero had laid out for all to see at the Remuera feast). Kati agreed to sell him a block of about 107 acres for £112.

On 6 June 1844 Dilworth wrote to the colonial secretary, applying for a pre-emption waiver certificate for this block 'that I have bought from the Native Chief Ekati'.[5] When the application was passed on to

Plan of Dilworth estate, 1844–49.

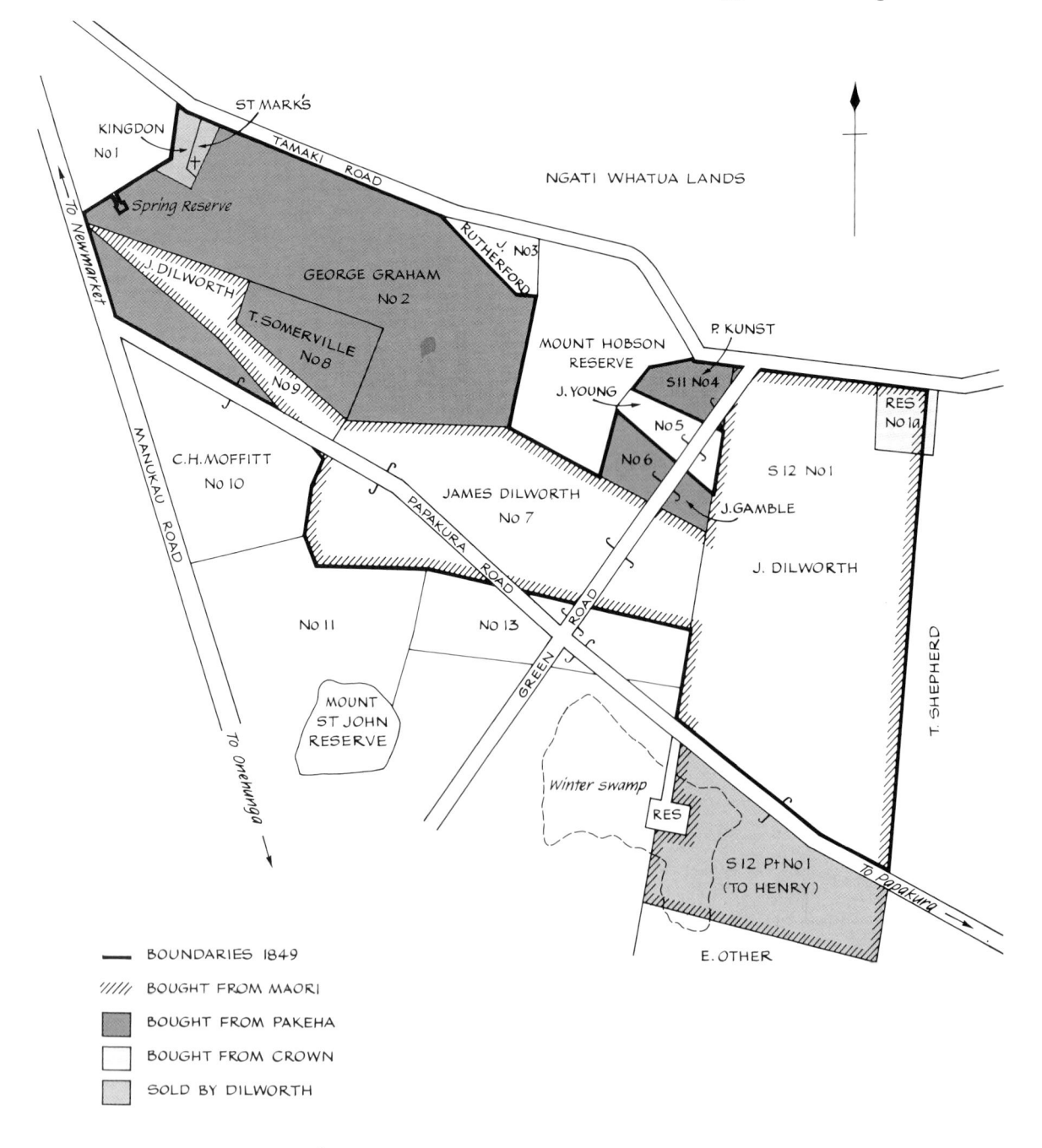

George Clarke he refused to recommend a certificate. Sensitive to Ngati Whatua rights over this land, he minuted the letter thus: 'Inform Mr Dilworth that he should procure the consent of Kawau'. This Dilworth did.[6] But unwilling to add to his present mountain of troubles, FitzRoy still would not issue a certificate. He asked the government interpreter Edward Meurant to call together a meeting of chiefs affected by the sale—a meeting which in the opinion of Apera (Abel), who was there, took the 'colour of a 'ceremony'—in order (as Meurant recalled it)

> To assist the Natives in marking out the Boundary line between the Tribes. I went to the Ngati Whatua tribe and told them the Governor wished to lay down a line of Boundary between the three tribes. On the west of the line . . . [the land] belonged to Wetere, on the east to E Kati and on the south of E Kati to the tribe of Ngati Whatua. Several of each tribe met at the Tamaki Road, drove in a peg which is still [1847] remaining as placed by them.* A straight line was marked out as the boundary leaving One Tree Hill on the left.† There was no curve in the line at all. The Natives themselves marked out the line and drove pegs into the ground. . . . The whole of the Native tribes were perfectly satisfied with the line laid down as the true boundary.[7]

The governor was reassured. He issued the required certificate (PC 36). The sale was completed months before a formal deed of conveyance was signed on 31 January 1845.[8]

The end of January 1845 is to be seen as characteristic in the evolution of the Remuera estate. Apart from one further purchase and one further sale it remained for the next fifty years substantially within the boundaries of the land as purchased by that time.

By that date Dilworth had bought from Maori owners in three separate deeds of conveyance an estate of 169½ acres for £176. However, F. Dillon Bell later warned, after scrutinizing many hundreds of early deeds of sale between Pakeha and Maori, that the sum on such deeds 'by no means represents the whole amount which was paid away'.[9] That is why the return Dilworth gave in November 1845, in response to an enquiry of the colonial secretary into the expenses incurred by each buyer under the pre-emption waiver scheme, is so valuable.[10] The following summarizes what Dilworth stated he paid in the purchase (but not development) of his estate:

---

* Early in the proceedings Te Keene Tangaroa of Ngati Whatua drove in pegs to show the southern boundary of Kati's block by indicating where Ngati Whatua land began. No one questioned his decision. He had considerable mana and claimed direct ancestral descent from both Ngati Whatua and Wai-o-hua. S. Percy Smith said that he 'represented both conquerors and conquered' (1897, p. 69); but in speaking of his 'very pure blood' Fenton was probably stressing Keene's Wai-o-hua descent (Fenton, p. 82).

† The line ran in a south-south-west direction from the western side of the junction of Market Road and Remuera Road to about the location of the Observatory today in the One Tree Hill Domain.

	£ s p
Payment in coin and colonial debentures	185 0 0
A Superior Gun . . . Manton*	15 0 0
Sundry articles of clothing	No price put
Expenses for Interpreting, Conveyancing, Surveying	30 12 11
Payment of first instalment of 10s waiver	42 0 0
	272 12 11

Dilworth's purchase of his Remuera estate was part of a long-term strategy of investment. Not so his venture into the property market on the North Shore of the Waitemata Harbour during 1844. This was an unvarnished speculation which he would not have entertained had he not been able to get hold of land scrip very cheaply.

During 1844 there was a Crown auction of 'farm lots' near Lake Pupuke, then known as Lake Takapuna. Dilworth bought two of the 104 lots which were auctioned in a subdivision of a portion of the huge Mahurangi block running from the Waitemata as far north as Te Arai.[11†] Those who bought this Takapuna land over 1844–45 included Robert Hunt, W. S. Grahame, James O'Neill and Hastings Atkins, men who notoriously made multiple purchases in separate localities within the parish of Takapuna. Willy-nilly, Dilworth was in the company of speculators. The sections knocked down to Dilworth were a narrow allotment of twenty acres with an attractive lake frontage[12] and a larger one of sixty acres not far from a tidal reach of Shoal Bay.[13] The lakeside section he sold within a year for sixty pounds to Thomas E. Conry, at that time the main conveyancing lawyer of Auckland and himself a very active dealer in land.[14] The Shoal Bay section Dilworth held on to for ten years and then sold it, still in an undeveloped condition, to the Catholic Bishop J. B. F. Pompallier for £78 17s 6d.[15] (For all his Ulster Protestant background, young Dilworth seemed free from sectarian rancour, and quite untroubled about making such a sale.)

While the total sum Dilworth received when he resold these two properties may seem modest, he probably made money on the transactions. The Crown grants record that he paid for his Takapuna lots not in legal tender but in land scrip. Little has been written about land scrip, important though it was in the buying up of Auckland and its suburbs. Its origins are to be found in the instruction despatched by Lord Stanley, secretary of state for colonies, to allow those claimants to land 'in the more remote positions', whose titles had been

---

* Joseph Manton, a famous gunsmith, was the manufacturer of a variety of firearms including first-rate flintlock double-barrelled sporting guns of which this was a likely example (C. Blair, *Pollard's History of Firearms*, 1983, p. 533).

† The highly dubious purchase of the Mahurangi block initiated on 12 April 1841 on behalf of the Crown by George Clarke contradicted both his title and function as chief protector of the aborigines.

'established', to have the option of 'exchanging their lands . . . for grants nearer the Town of Auckland'.[16] Because this remote land was generally overvalued, the credit available to claimants who decided to exchange it for Auckland property (town, suburban and 'country' allotments) had the effect of forcing up prices at Auckland sales and driving cash buyers out of the market. Not untypical was a report of a December 1843 Crown auction where 1,000 acres of land were exchanged but not one acre was actually bought.[17] In a proclamation of 26 March 1844 Governor FitzRoy announced that no further exchanges of land would be permitted after the end of June, but that at large auctions of Crown lands to be held in June, September and December transferable Treasury notes (which became known as scrip) could be used by claimants wishing to bid, which would be equivalent in value to their surrendered land.

There was a rush of scrip onto the market. Dillon Bell estimated that 'in Hokianga claims alone, the scrip issued was upwards of £32,000'.[18] Those awarded scrip, usually preferring ready money to Auckland land, would then attempt to discount their 'paper' (of which there was soon a glut) by selling it through merchants or auctioneers. These in turn would sell the scrip to speculators who would use it at Crown land sales, forcing up prices to the face value of scrip they had bought at only a fraction of the figure at which they were now bidding. The exchange value of scrip further plummeted when the governor announced that the 30 December land sale was the last at which scrip could be used.[19]

It was such scrip, originally granted to Hokianga land claimants like the legendary Baron de Thierry, that Dilworth used at the Takapuna auction.* So although he bought one lot with scrip carrying a face value of £236 12s 6d, and another with scrip marked £126 15s 3d, his real outlay in cash was probably between one-quarter and one-tenth of those sums. Exactly what he did pay will probably never be known.

Dilworth was not exceptional in buying land with scrip. What he did in 1844 was simply standard business practice. The whole of modern Grey Lynn was bought with scrip at Crown auctions in 1844 by speculators who resold cheaply to Dilworth's neighbours in Epsom, the partners James Williamson and Thomas Crummer.[20] In that way Williamson and Crummer picked up for a song the 314-acre Surrey Hills Estate (Grey Lynn) which forty years later was valued at over £100,000.[21] Looking back from 1862, Dillon Bell claimed that 'very valuable portions of the city and suburban lands in Auckland [were] given away in 1844 for scrip which represented nothing tangible at the time'.[22] Heaphy's famous 'Plan of the Town of Auckland, 1851', which shows individual owners of each of the town allotments and

---

* The scrip used by Dilworth came from Thomas Cassidy, Henry Pearson and Baron de Thierry.

the means by which those allotments were acquired, confirms Bell's statement. One-half of 'Heaphy's Town' was bought by scrip given for surrendered land claims.[23] If we are unaware of the role of land scrip in the movement of Crown lands into Pakeha hands, our understanding of early Auckland remains a stunted one.

Two government initiatives in 1844, therefore, accelerated Pakeha land buying on the Tamaki isthmus: the introduction of pre-emption waiver certificates and land scrip. Dilworth used both, confirming once again that his life provides in microcosm, an unusual instance of how much of the land in pioneer Auckland came to be bought and sold.

As Dilworth's career at the New Zealand Banking Company came to its close early in 1845 his working life became bound up in developing his new suburban farm. He perceived himself to have become 'farmer' or 'settler'. By 1846 he gave that as his occupation on all official returns, and 'Remuera' as his place of residence. Nonetheless he was never simply a farmer. His interest in land was broader than that. And the habit of attending land auctions was hard to shake off. Dilworth never could. Almost to his life's end he continued to buy land and (more rarely) to sell it.

Even in the mid-1840s he seems to have concluded that careful buying in the city or inner suburbs could not fail. He made two revealing purchases then, though the sums involved were modest enough. At a Crown auction in August 1846 he bought for £22 1s 1d a two-acre allotment adjacent to his Parnell property which was now no longer the site of his permanent home.[24] Although he had obviously decided to sell up his old property, he also seems to have calculated that he would get a higher price for it if it were enlarged and given a frontage on St Georges Bay Road as well as its existing one on St Stephens Avenue. The substantial figure for which he sold the combined properties two years after showed how shrewdly he had summed up the short-term market in residential property.[25]

But it is skill in long-term property investment that marks off the master from the tyro. The master has to assess, perhaps decades ahead, what the trend in values will be, and then, his decision made, have the resolve, come what may, to back that judgement over many years. Among the pioneers David Nathan, Logan Campbell, Edward Costley, Thomas Henderson (probably) had such a gift: very few others. By the late nineteenth century Auckland became, so to speak, a graveyard for property speculators. Dilworth was not of their number. He was masterful when it came to property. Even he, in old age, stumbled; but he never fell.

Investment in city property which Dilworth entered into at the age of thirty-two became a great money-spinner for him in later years. At an 1847 Crown auction he bought for £231 a quarter-acre allotment of reclaimed land on the corner of the newly-formed Customhouse Street East and lower Queen Street.[26] Shortly after his purchase he was able to sell off the eastern (and less valuable) third of this allotment for £125.[27] At the time it probably seemed an unprepossessing piece of real estate, untidy with an odoriferous foreshore nearby. Appearances deceived; not for the last time his investment in property bordered on the prophetic. He realized he need be in no hurry to build. If he held to his purchase, in time he would have within his hands the gateway between the port and the city of the future. It is a comment on his farsightedness that in effect he bought for £106 the allotment on which the Dilworth Buildings now stand.

But these developments lay far in the future. In 1844 Dilworth's ambitions centred upon his newly-acquired Remuera land; developing it as a farm and securing for it an indefeasible title. These two objectives were of a piece. It was government policy to make issuing a Crown grant conditional on the land in question being resided upon and productive. Consequently, less as a matter of making a profit and more in order to cement his title to the land he had just bought, he began cropping as early as the winter of 1844. We know how he set about this because of a letter he wrote in typically concise style to his friend William Brown, partner of Logan Campbell, and owner of the *Southern Cross*. About to return briefly to Britain where he planned to publish a book which would encourage immigrants to Auckland, Brown solicited letters from Dilworth and his neighbour George Graham. This was Dilworth's response:

The foot of Queen Street, 1852. Dilworth's Queen Street purchase in 1847 was not far from where Maori canoes are being beached.
Engraving by W. S. Hatton after P. J. Hogan, Alexander Turnbull Library

JAMES DILWORTH

Auckland, 19th December, 1844.

Dear Sir,—Knowing as I do the interest you take in all matters connected with the produce of the country, I beg to give you the result of an experiment I made to grow wheat upon the lands I bought from the natives in April last.

You may rely with confidence upon this statement as correct, because I had everything to pay for, and all moneys that I paid I charged to the wheat.

I selected thirty acres as a suitable extent to try the experiment upon, which cost . . .	£30 0 0
Pre-emption fee to Government	6 0 0
Pre-emption fee still to pay	9 0 0
Paid fencing in thirty acres	19 9 0
Paid for seed wheat	19 12 5
Paid for preparing the ground, and putting in the seed	20 4 7
Paid for building a house for overseer	3 8 9
His pay until wheat is reaped	12 0 0
Total cost	£119 14 9
Sold the produce as it now stands on the ground at £5 2s. 6d. per acre	153 15 0
Which shows a clear profit of	£34 0 3

After paying all expenses, and leaving the ground fenced in, and a house upon it. I may add, that a practical man could have done it much cheaper, and, of course, would have a greater profit. . . .

I remain, dear Sir, yours very truly,

J. Dilworth.[28]

William Brown, owner of the Southern Cross, *to whom Dilworth sent a description of his farm in 1844.*
Auckland Public Library

Dilworth, following the pattern of the early improving farmers in Ireland no less than in the colony, rated fencing as essential. He had neither timber freely available, nor rock-strewn fields (for which latter he was no doubt grateful), so post-and-rail fencing and dry-stone walling were at this stage both precluded. He employed ditch and single rail (or hurdle) fencing, for which the going rate of construction was about two shillings per perch (five metres).[29]* We may assume that Maori labour built the house of the 'overseer'; the cost of £3 8s 9d implying a raupo whare of moderately good standard, with European-style windows and door, and with two rooms.[30] Such a whare would last for about three years. The overseer would have been European and the labour force used for 'preparing the ground' probably a mixture of European day-labourers and a Maori team paid at a lower rate.

---

* The contractor would dig a ditch three to four feet deep, tapering slightly from top to bottom. Beside it he would erect his 'fence', posts of puriri or similar timber charred to give extra durability, and rail from timber cleared on the estate or land nearby.

The somewhat lengthier report on his Mount Hobson farm which Graham passed on to Brown tells us indirectly about what was happening on Dilworth's farm as well. Similarities between the two properties abound. They were side by side. Both had wheat for their first cash crop, grown during the same period and cultivated over a roughly comparable area—although Graham also planted a little oats, Irish flax, and barley. The similarities go even further. What Graham earned from his first harvest (£152 10s 7d) was within a few shillings of Dilworth's earnings. It is not unreasonable, therefore, to infer that information provided by Graham can also be generally applied to Dilworth's farm.

Graham was able to explain why it was that the land which he and Dilworth took over could go into immediate production. That land, far from being in a state of nature, had been used very recently by Waikato Maori to cultivate potatoes in readiness for their Remuera feast. They had prepared the ground, wrote Graham, in their own traditional way.

> This land was not cleared, the wood having been cut and burned down, and the potatoes sown between the stumps, in the usual way that they cultivate their land.*
>
> I sowed my wheat on this land after merely clearing the potato haulms, and chipped in the seed with hoes. This work was performed with native and European labourers, and cost 10s per acre, and I paid £1 additional to the man that sowed the wheat. The crop is very fine; I think it will average forty bushels per acre.[31]

Later events were to confirm that Graham's good opinion of Remuera land was well justified, but they were also to reveal that his confidence in the future of wheat farming in the neighbourhood of Auckland was misplaced.

Dilworth was able further to strengthen his claim to a Crown title to his Remuera land because of steps he took to erect 'permanent buildings' upon it and to be a permanent resident there. Sometime during 1845 or early 1846 he put up his first house, which he called Ivy Cottage, on a part of his land near the corner of today's Mount Hobson and Market Roads. Of unpretentious construction, this weatherboard house was built in the first instance for Dilworth's farm manager and wife. In 1846 Dilworth shifted in, presumably as owner-lodger, to overlook work on the estate. From that time he gave 'Ivy Cottage, Remuera' as his home address, though he did not dispose of his Parnell residence until two years later. In the 1850s Dilworth moved into the cottage, enlarged it and planted further trees and shrubs.

---

* Taking over Maori cultivations probably saved a year's preparatory work: 'two deep ploughings in the autumn and letting [the land] remain fallow during the winter, and in spring, putting in a crop of potatoes and oats, then giving it the following autumn a good crossploughing and harrowing [and] it will then be prepared for a crop of wheat or barley' (*Report of Ak. Ag. Soc. 1843*, p. 12).

Like a number of claimants who had bought with pre-emption waiver certificates, Dilworth waited fretfully over 1845–46 to have his validating title confirmed. Uncertainty came to an end when in 1846 the Home government, albeit reluctantly, agreed to look into and give a ruling upon all pre-emption certificate claims. On 15 June 1846 Governor Grey instructed all claimants to send in copies of deeds, plans and other documents relevant to their purchase.[32] This Dilworth promptly did. Within a few days of the enactment by the governor-in-council on 18 November 1846 of a Land Claims Ordinance setting up a commissioner's court to inquire into PC purchases, he wrote directly to the governor.

> As a land claimant under the proclamation of the 26th March 1844 I have been waiting for a title for several months past, but after what has fallen from the Governor in Council there is reason to believe that Titles shall be given to actual settlers in a short time: and as it is my intention to go to England as soon as I get my title and leave again if possible before the winter sets in. Were I to await the ordinary course of things I would in all probability lose the season and would thereby be delayed another year in carrying out my views which would be a sacrifice of time as well as money that I hope the Government will not oblige me to make. I do therefore most respectfully solicit His Excellency's favourable consideration of my case with a view to the issue of a confirmatory Grant at the earliest period practicable.[33]

Grey passed on this request to the commissioner whom he appointed, Major Henry Matson of the 58th Regiment.

The note of urgency Dilworth conveyed in his application would seem to explain why he was the first of the sixty-two 'ten-shillings-an-acre' PC claimants to be called by the commissioner when he began his sittings on 1 February 1847.[34] The procedure adopted by Matson with Dilworth became routine for all later claimants. Dilworth was asked to outline how he had fulfilled the conditions upon which the issue of his pre-emption certificate had depended: had he paid the required fees? was the purchase properly made?—for instance, were the sellers the true owners of the land they had undertaken to sell? was there a proper survey? and were qualified interpreters present? Dilworth then went on at the hearing to establish that he was indeed a genuine settler by testifying that he had permanently resided on the property for some time and that he had fenced and developed it. As a claimant, Dilworth was obliged to bring the Maori sellers to the court for cross-examination. Two of these, Kati and Wetere, were questioned as to whether they understood the terms and conditions of the deed of conveyance, and whether it had been fully explained to them at the time by the interpreter. Edward Meurant the interpreter also testified at length on Dilworth's behalf.

Dilworth's was one of the forty-nine ten-shillings-an-acre claims upheld by Matson after he had examined witnesses. Because the formula which he used in his judgment (really a recommendation to the governor) upon Dilworth's claim was the one he also applied to the others, the wording merits citing:

> having maturely considered the whole of the evidence, taking into consideration the Claimant having been in undisputed possession of the Land since the Purchase . . . [and] having a large portion of the Land in cultivation, and Buildings erected thereon, and having paid the pre-emption fees on the same to the amount of £30 12s. 11d., I recommend that a confirmatory Crown Grant be issued to the said James Dilworth including the Reserve tenths in compliance with the 14th clause of the Land Claims Ordinance.[35]*

Eight months later Dilworth received his Crown grants.[36] How he had fared is best shown in a table.

DILWORTH'S PRE-EMPTIVE LAND CLAIMS, OLC 1055–58

Area claimed	No. of PCs	Area awarded	Final payment required	Title of Crown grant
63a 0r 14p	5, 37, 46	56a 1r 3p	£33 2s 11d	11 Nos 7, 9
107a 0r 26p	36	103a 1r 16p	£58 18s 9d	12 No. 1
170a 1r –		159a 2r 19p	£92 1s 8d	

These grants issued on 6 November 1847 show that the 160 acres approximately which he was awarded were something less than the 170 acres which he had claimed; the main reduction coming from land which would become dedicated public roads. Nor was he given all of the reserved tenths for which he had hoped. The sums he was required to pay prior to the issue of grants were: the remaining payment of four shillings per acre for his waiver certificate, one pound an acre for the 'tenths' he had been allowed, and registration fees; in all £92 1s 8d. If this sum is added to Dilworth's own estimate of the costs he had incurred in buying the land up to 4 November 1845 (£272 17s 11d), the total cost to him of the undeveloped land which became the farm would be just on £365.

Dilworth was delighted to have his Crown grants at last. But much remained to be done if the farm was to become a going concern. It was still largely undeveloped; the boundaries, in his opinion, were far

---

* Under Section 14 of the Act, it became lawful for the Crown to effect the sale to private persons at the rate of one pound an acre, the one-tenth part of the land purchased under the waiver proclamations that had been 'set apart for public purposes'. Dilworth applied to be allowed to purchase those lands of his claim which had 'been reserved for the Natives and Publick purposes', but some only were ultimately released to him.

from ideal. Remedying these things required money, increasingly becoming a scarce commodity for the young Irishman. And his former self, the banker, stayed with him as a kind of alter ego, never to be quite shaken off, always peering prudentially over his shoulder. On the one hand he must build up pasture, buy equipment and provide boundaries that would make the estate cohere. On the other hand, his ingrained experience as a banker kept reminding him that plans for his farm, however justifiable, must be moderated by the need to keep his borrowing within sustainable bounds.

Yet buy further land he must. The angularly irregular boundaries of the estate to which he had title reflected the helter-skelter conditions under which ten-shilling waiver sales had been conducted. They bore little relationship to Dilworth's ideal of systematic farming. In consequence he was always on the alert for an opportunity to buy a neighbouring property, however small, that would round off his estate. Just before Matson summoned him to his commission court in February 1847, Dilworth was able to buy for sixty pounds a small (nine-acre) block which separated his farm from that of George Graham.[37] The chance to buy dropped out of the blue when a city merchant Samuel Brown foreclosed on the mortgage which he had over this block and certain other landed securities upon the default of the mortgagor Edward Constable.* Dilworth agreed to buy, contingent upon Constable, the previous owner, and the mortgagee both using all 'due diligence' to secure the title before the commissioner.

This they did successfully; and an otherwise intrusive pocket of alien land came into Dilworth's hands. Although small, it was a good property on which 'a considerable sum' had been spent, some of which had already been recouped by the past owner through successful harvests.

Later in the same year Dilworth acquired what he had long sought, a property that would give his estate a Manukau Road frontage.[38] He had been much put out, back in 1844, when Charles Moffitt the dentist had stolen a march on him by clandestinely buying as a 'spec' a sixty-acre block beside Manukau Road; for some at least of that land Dilworth had intended for himself. Shortly after, he and Moffitt made a tentative deal, but this fell through. Upon Moffitt receiving, in November 1847, the title to his original purchase—though much reduced in area (twenty-nine-and-a-half acres)—he revived the transaction in a modified form and sold a quarter of the property to Dilworth for seventy-three pounds and the remainder to Dilworth's

---

* This property, which became Sect. 11 No. 8 Suburbs of Auck., was bought by Edward Constable, 'farmer', from the first Pakeha owner Thomas Somerville in January 1846 for £150 (forty pounds down), the price including a crop on the point of harvest. On 7 October 1846 Constable used it as part-security for a mortgage advance for £245 from Samuel Brown, merchant. Constable's failure to pay the first instalment led to immediate sale of the security, the standard remedy for default used by mortgagees in that era.

Mount St John from Mount Hobson, 1863, said to be the earliest known photograph of this area.
Dilworth Trust Board Archives

neighbours Williamson and Crummer for £220.[39] Admittedly Dilworth got only a small section, and the price was high; but his stock were now close to the only perennial well in the area, his boundary was extended further along Papakura (Great South) Road and best of all he had his Manukau Road frontage at last.

However, no acquisition of a neighbour's land was ever to delight Dilworth so much as buying George Graham's farm in 1848. Just as One Tree Hill was for Sir John Logan Campbell the embodiment of his enduring stake in Auckland, so Mount Hobson was for James Dilworth. So integral a part of Dilworth's life is 'Graham's Hill' (as Mount Hobson and its farm were already known in 1848) that it has a special place in this book as a topic in its own right. What needs to be said here is that the sixty-acre farm and the hill on which it was found were particularly picturesque, and that Graham at the time of sale had already spent a considerable sum in developing the land. Graham placed a premium price upon it: £800. Nevertheless, Dilworth jumped at the opportunity to buy, even though to take it up meant leaving £500 of the consideration money on a five-year mortgage carrying interest of ten per cent.[41]

Dilworth had subjected himself for the first time in his life to what he would have considered a heavy burden of debt repayment. This also drove him towards the unpleasing expedient of having to sell off some of his own land.[42] He decided to put on the market twenty-six-and-a-half acres on the south side of the Papakura Road, across which it was troublesome to move stock, a portion of which contained the winter swamp to the east of Mount St John. A willing buyer was at hand, neighbour and fellow-Irishman, Thomas Henry, a man (it must be said) with grandiose ideas but little capital. Henry, who had recently enlarged his One Tree Hill farm (which he called Mount Prospect) by buying a fifty-acre block from Edward Other, saw in Dilworth's offer a chance to roll the boundary of his farm as far north as the Papakura Road. In August 1848 he paid Dilworth £316 10s, thereby pushing himself further into the mire of debt, which was to be his ultimate undoing.*

Lopping off this outer land provided Dilworth with further money to continue to buy up small parcels that would help consolidate the heart of his farm. A fortnight after his sale to Henry, Dilworth bought a small parcel of land (three-and-a-half acres) on the eastern side of Mount Hobson from Philip Kunst, a printer of German extraction who had been in Auckland since 1841.[43] Kunst had purchased this land in 1844 from Wetere of Ngati Maoho, probably as a speculation, though later in life he was to be a serious full-time farmer at Maraetai.[44] Kunst paid eight guineas: four pounds in cash; the remainder in goods—a double-barrelled gun worth four pounds, a box of percussion caps (two shillings) and two regatta shirts (six shillings). This little farm, though developed and briefly occupied, had suffered some neglect. Kunst admitted as much to Commissioner Matson: 'Cattle have destroyed part of [my] fencing', he said.[45] But the price Dilworth paid (forty-eight pounds) on 16 September 1848 was not high, and there was an additional strategic benefit arising out of the sale. For he now owned the corner sections on either side of the junction of (today's) Market Road with Remuera Road.

Dilworth needed to make two further purchases to round off the north-eastern section off his farm. On the day that he settled with Kunst he made a successful bid for a three-and-three-quarter-acre public reserve which the Crown put up for auction.[46] This reserve lay across the boundary between Dilworth's eastern block and the land of his neighbour, Thomas Shepherd.[47]

Because the two owners had obviously arranged for Dilworth to bid on their joint behalf, Dilworth had the section knocked down to himself at the upset price of fifty pounds. The sixth of the former reserve that was within Shepherd's land, Dilworth passed on to him for £8 6s 8d.[48] The rest he kept.

His final purchase was a five-acre block (Sect. 11 No. 6) running parallel to Kunst's, and adjoining his own farm.[49] Bought originally in 1844 from Wetere and Apera (Abel) by James Gamble for thirteen pounds, it had passed through four sets of hands before being conveyed to 'James Dilworth, gentleman' on 30 July 1849. Evidence provided

---

* Thomas Henry, who had a background in the Auckland retail trade, was unusually sanguine. He went too far and too fast in his attempts to build up Mount Prospect farm, borrowing from local capitalists like Barbara Burnett, or from holders of trust funds like Revd Walter Lawry, to do so. By 1853 he had overreached himself and was forced to put his farm on the market. Brown and Campbell bought it for £16,500.

for the commissioner's court in 1847 points to its development as having been limited, and buildings upon it as being rudimentary. But the premium price of £100 which Dilworth paid indicates that it served his purposes well.[50] By that date only two properties,[51] totalling less than seven acres, intruded upon the boundaries of what had become (excepting them) the rounded, self-contained estate that Dilworth with patience and persistence had built up over five years.

Before the 1840s were out Dilworth had virtually all the Remuera land he wanted—or perhaps, expressed more accurately, could at that stage afford. But to get to this position, like so many settlers, he had used up his limited store of money capital. If he was going to survive and keep his lands intact, he must go further and convert this estate into a going concern generating income. He must spend more; and borrow more—though to do both simultaneously went against the grain. But how else could he build up the assets of his farm? He needed money to buy more machinery, livestock and seed; to install fencing and drains; and to tide him over until the farm was fully productive and yielding an adequate return. That was why running parallel to his policy of land buying over 1848–49 were concomitant policies of rationalizing landholding and, above all, of reorganizing his finances.

At the time he purchased Graham's Hill, Dilworth's spare capital had run out. But Graham's farm aside, the rest of his estate was debt-free; and his credit-worthiness seemed not open to question. His cash flow in the next few years was increasingly going to depend on three supplementary sources of income: leasing out parts of the Remuera estate, selling off surplus property and raising loans.

Precisely how much of his Remuera land Dilworth leased in the 1840s is not known. By 1852 he was prepared to put out virtually the whole of his farm on lease.[52] It seems that in the last thirty years of his life, the greater part of the farm was continually leased. Running a home farm and having tenants on the rest of one's property was entirely congruent with his Irish background. And leasing substantial portions of large suburban farms for dairy paddocks and market gardens was the norm in early Auckland: George Graham did it before 1848, Williamson and Crummer practised it on Surrey Hills, Brown and Campbell at One Tree Hill, and William Potter at Epsom. Dilworth followed a general trend.

Nonetheless, Dilworth was aware that more money than could ever come from farm rents was needed. After he had bought Graham's land, he felt the time had come to realize on his Parnell property. In November 1848 he reached an informal agreement with Henry Figg, a local surveyor, later executed in a deed on 9 April 1849, by which he agreed to convey to Figg for £450 his six-and-a-half-acre property 'together with all the houses and buildings thereon erected'.[53] It was a measure of Dilworth's anxiety to be quit of this Parnell property that he acted as a guarantor of mortgage loans given to Figg, who needed to use the property as collateral; and that, in the 1850s, he was prepared to take over this mortgage himself, while insisting that Figg add certain of his city land as an extra charge. Final release of Figg by Dilworth did not come until 10 October 1856.[54]

But of course Dilworth's real need at this juncture was to borrow rather than lend. Obviously regarded by those with capital as a good mark, he had no difficulty in securing before 1848 was out an advance of £350 for three years from the Revd Walter Lawry, 'General Superintendent of the Wesleyan Missions in New Zealand'.[55] The charge imposed by the Wesleyans was heavy—the developed part of the Dilworth estate lying between Mount Hobson and Mount St John—while the interest rate of twelve-and-a-half per cent was rather high. But Dilworth was fortunate to have, during a critical stage of his affairs, loan money behind him. He continued his borrowing into the 1850s. Although when the Graham and Wesleyan Mission mortgages fell due in July 1853 Dilworth paid both off,[56] he was able to do so only because two solicitors, Frederick Whitaker and Thomas Shayle George, raised a new advance (£800) on his behalf from a wealthy widow, Mrs Agnes Jackson.[57] This mortgage Dilworth discharged four years later.[58]

The borrowing of these years was decisive in ensuring Dilworth's survival.

CHAPTER FIVE

The Dilworths of Remuera

DILWORTH HAS BEEN described as 'a strange self-centred man and something of a recluse' who was nevertheless a 'capable and progressive farmer' for whom 'land was his chief interest'.[1] To see him as an able farmer alone, and as a man of strange habits and preferences, is, however, reductionist and misleading. The misconception has arisen, I believe, because the two great influences upon him before he came to New Zealand have not been taken sufficiently into account: his family and northern Ireland. His solitary upbringing as family heir had much to do with the reserve, the inflexible sense of duty, and the stern work ethic so conspicuous in his adult years. Nor was he a stereotypical stolid farmer. His was a complex personality, not easily explained. His aloofness which can be too simply equated with harshness, could equally be construed as a shy man's attempt at decorous behaviour. However we seek to interpret his inner nature, his early life in Dungannon provides the clues.

Even the Remuera estate itself, as it took shape under Dilworth's hand, was in many ways a replication of County Tyrone. As long as he lived, his homeland kept a peculiar resonance for him. The name he gave to his first home on the estate, Ivy Cottage, is a name common in northern Ireland, and the name of a well-known house in Donaghmore. The unformed road running north to south across his farm (today's Market Road) he called his 'Green Road',[2] a term unknown in colonial nomenclature but in universal use in the Ireland Dilworth had left, depicting a dirt thoroughfare or a partly formed road where grass grew on the ridge between ruts formed by wheel tracks.

It is because of this Irish rural background that one pauses before accepting Dilworth's disclaimer to being 'a practical man' on farming matters when he first took over Remuera in 1844.[3] F. W. Weston, who knew the pioneer scene well, spoke of Dilworth as arriving in Auckland 'already skilled in farm-management'.[4] Recent first-hand experience Dilworth might not have had, but his family had been farmers for more than two centuries. With James, respect for the land had been bred in the bone. It was no coincidence that he became in time one of Auckland's most progressive and successful farmers, and a pillar of

A Green Road towards Donaghmore taken from a windowframe of Mullaghcreevy homestead.
Norman Cardwell

71

the Auckland Agricultural Society.

But if by 'progressive' farmer is meant one guided by science, better to describe him as an 'efficient' farmer. From the hard experience of his family in Ireland he knew that survival depended on efficiency, above all on feeding the land. He, and later his brother Andrew, became renowned among colonial farmers for the attention they paid to top-dressing by fertilizer. The lesson that the overcrowded Ireland of their youth had drummed into them was that only by manuring would otherwise unyielding soil give its increase.

Moreover, his need to invest in land in a way that would benefit himself and ultimately his family back in Dungannon gave a further Irish flavour to his holding of land in New Zealand. No sooner had he been granted his indefeasible title to his Remuera land in 1847 than he began subletting,[5] just as his 'strong tenant' forebears had previously done in the barony of Dungannon. The great extent of his landholding in later life confirms his conception of himself not as a simple farmer but as a landlord for whom leasing or (less commonly) selling to others could be a better way to invest than farming the land oneself.[6] In Ireland, being a landlord could be a source of profit; even more surely it was a symbol of status. There is little doubt that this was just how Dilworth regarded the estate he built up in the colony.

When in 1852 Dilworth happened to advertise his Remuera farm as being available for lease he made much of the point that most of it had been 'inclosed [sic] and divided into paddocks by a sheep-proof fence'.[7] Fencing was already a feature of this farm, his perimeter hedge of hawthorn especially so. Undiscerned, this was yet another Irish dimension to his estate. At an early stage of Auckland's settlement, hawthorn (or whitethorn, or quickthorn, as it was often then called) became very popular, most markedly in Remuera and Parnell.[8] In the mild climate of the isthmus, whitethorns grew prolifically, and, as was noted at the time, 'contrary to their habits in Europe grew easily from cuttings'.[9] Bishop Selwyn hedged the road boundaries of his new St John's College with it: for a century that hedge remained a feature of the approaches to the College. For his part, James Dilworth needed no persuading to plant a hawthorn hedge. His affection for things Irish never far below the surface, he seems to have been emotionally drawn to this kind of hedge, which had been introduced by improving farmers through much of the early nineteenth-century Ulster he had not long since left, transforming the bleak landscape of strips there 'into a pattern of small sheltered fields'.[10] But Dilworth did not keep his hedges as close-cut thickets impassable to cattle, Ulster fashion. Bowing to the realities of a lusher climate he let them grow rampant. Thus many an early settler, quite unmindful of the Irish provenance of Dilworth's tall hawthorn hedges (through which dog-roses and other old English roses climbed), fondly remembered them into old age as the very epitome of the fine colonial farm they enclosed.[11] One charming reminiscence of an elderly shepherd tells how the scent of Dilworth's hawthorn blossom would waft, of a spring, to the upper slopes of One Tree Hill where he was among his flock.[12]

The earliest panoramic photographs of the Epsom area taken from vantage points like Mount Eden show not only hedges ringing the Dilworth estate but a number of internal post-and-rail fences as well.[13] Ditch-and-hurdle fences, which do not show up on landscape photographs, were Dilworth's first fences: post-and-rail came later. Ditches were cheaper, and served, Irish style, both to enclose and to drain.

Flooding troubled the early European farmers in Remuera and Epsom. Mid-century Newmarket was notoriously swampy. 'Broadway during a rainy season', a local historian has written, 'degenerated into elongated bogs of mud.'[14] An old-time resident recalled stormwater coming from the One Tree Hill area and forming two 'sizeable lakes' near Dilworth's farm.

> In very wet weather these lakes overflowed, the water rushing down to the junction of Manukau and Great South Roads. The ditches were rapidly choked with debris and the properties in the vicinity became flooded, the water eventually finding its way to a swamp where the Captain Cook brewery now stands.[15]

For one who had been raised on a farm in Tyrone, there was a time-honoured way to deal with surplus water or unwanted bog—dig a shough (the Irish name for a drainage ditch), generally with a ridge of soil alongside, progressively added to by the clearing of the watercourse. Whereas in Ireland a quickthorn or other small hedge often went on the ridge, upon those of his Remuera farm Dilworth placed a hurdle. A simple fence, but effective.

In any event, getting rid of surplus water was not to be for Dilworth the problem it was for many of his neighbours. Straddling a gentle saddle between Mount Hobson and Mount St John, his Remuera land was well drained, and became better so once he had adopted his system of internal fencing by ditches and hurdles. And, like many who in 1844 bought isthmus land containing porous volcanic soils, he found after a single year's farming experience that more to be feared than winter flood was summer drought. So ditches originally designed to fence, and to dispose of water, developed the additional function of feeding an irrigation system. At the Auckland end of his property, Dilworth had a large 'dry pond' dug—so called to differentiate it from the 'perennial well' nearby. He 'puddled' it* and diverted as many as possible of his downward-sloping ditches in that direction so that the pond could be used in the dry season as a watering hole for stock.[16]

---

* To 'puddle' a pond after it had been dug to the wanted depth, a farmer would attach to the pond's sides and bottom a layer of loose silty clay, and then mix straw and water into it so that it became puddled and provided an impermeable covering. It would remain watertight until the pond emptied, dried out and the clay covering cracked.

'S. Mark's Remuera & Mt Eden 1859'. Painting by J. Kinder from the boundary of Dilworth's estate looking south-west toward Mt Eden. The large wooden building in the middle distance is Clovernook.
Auckland Public Library

Dilworth's system of conserving water by a network of dirt drains was in reality much more characteristic of an Australian farm[17] than one in nineteenth-century New Zealand where constant rainfall generally made shortage of water far less of a problem.

It was said around the time that Dilworth took over his Remuera land that the two main difficulties standing in the way of any Auckland farmer were 'the want of good public roads, and of materials for fencing'.[18] The second of these he had overcome admirably. He was not too concerned about the first. The farms of Dilworth and his Epsom-Remuera neighbours were, in the 1840s, close enough to the town of Auckland, their main market, not to be greatly hindered by the still primitive roads which gave access to it. But the prudent traveller avoided Khyber Pass until the later 1850s, in spite of the attempts by Captain Rough,* working with destitute immigrant labour in 1843 to blast an adequate road through rocky spurs and fill the 'almost insatiable swamp' near Newmarket.[19] In effect, there was still only one tolerable route out of town: the Onehunga (Manukau) Road which came up through Parnell and passed south through Newmarket. Beyond Newmarket almost all roads were unsatisfactory. Not until the later 1850s did military imperatives arising out of threatening race war lead to an upgrading of the Papakura Road which ran through the Dilworth estate so that it became what its name said it was, the Great South Road. Travelling from Newmarket along the tortuous Tamaki (Remuera) Road (which in those days dipped down to a lower level, to a terrace on Mount Hobson along which a former Maori track ran) could be so difficult and tedious that other routes were often chosen.[20] Bishop Selwyn preferred to go by boat up the Purewa Estuary

---

* During 1842–43 David Rough combined the duties of harbour-master with those of temporary official in charge of public works.

to 'the bleak, ferny hillside' at Meadowbank where in August 1844 he relocated St John's College.[21] Others moving in the direction of Tamaki would for many years avoid today's Remuera Road by descending from Parnell to Hobson Bay, taking Shore Road—which was then literally that—before striking inland at the Ohinerau Creek (by Portland Road) or at some point beyond. But shortcomings of transport were a pinprick to Dilworth. They simply delayed the possibility of his being able to convert his farm (should he so choose) into an extraordinarily valuable subdivision of villa sites.

Yet the trial of three soldiers charged with armed robbery was to reveal, shortly after Dilworth shifted into Ivy Cottage as the lodger of his farm manager and wife, Mr and Mrs Charles Wann,* that the isolation of the Remuera estate gave an element of insecurity to life there that Dilworth could scarcely have anticipated.[22] During the 1840s the *New Zealand Government Gazette* made frequent reference to soldiers deserting from regiments successively stationed in Auckland: the 80th, the 42nd and the 58th.[23] The *Gazette* in its public notices often described deserters in a way that not only gave distinctive personal details about them but also provided reasons why they had deserted. A surprising number—reflecting no doubt the composition of the British army of that time—were (like Dilworth himself) Irish; they were often about twenty-four years of age, and some were said to bear on their bodies 'the mark of corporeal punishment received in New Zealand'. Discipline was extraordinarily harsh for the private soldier; a feature of the Fort Britomart grounds was a triangle to which the insubordinate were tied and flogged.† This could explain some desertions. But motives varied. In one public notice there was a warning that the deserter was 'supposed to be endeavouring to get to America'. For the civilian population, punishment of those who 'concealed', or 'harboured', or even employed a deserter was particularly severe.[24]

Just after three o'clock in the morning of 26 July 1847, three deserters from the garrison at Auckland, Michael Maguire, William Hughes and Charles Curson, burst into Ivy Cottage fully armed, and rounded up the three occupants.[25] According to one newspaper account, 'the armed ruffians' with their 'threats and violence' extending over a long period caused Dilworth and the Wanns 'great anxiety and fear'.[26] The soldiers pillaged the house, stealing among other items a watch and a sporting rifle from Wann, and from Dilworth (according to the report of his testimony in Court) 'several items of wearing apparel, the property of Mr James Dilworth, who resided in a room in the same house'. The men decamped with their loot to move on to

---

* The going rate of pay for a man and wife 'with rations' and accommodation found was twenty-seven pounds a year. But as a manager and a gentleman (so described) Mr Wann would have been paid more.

† An officer in the 58th Regiment, notorious for the harsh punishment he meted out to soldiers in the 1850s, was nicknamed 'Triangles'.

JAMES DILWORTH

raid two other local farms, discharging a musket as they left in the direction of Wann whom they suspected of spying on them.

The band next raided the homestead of Thomas Henry at Mount Prospect (One Tree Hill) where with cool audacity they gained entry by claiming to be a detachment of soldiers in search of deserters. This house they also pillaged.

The three men were caught later that day. Ten weeks later they were arraigned in the Supreme Court on charges of armed robbery.[27] During the trial Dilworth was called on to give evidence. The wretched soldiers raised no defence, and with great speed the jury found them guilty. Two of the convicted men were sentenced by William Martin, the chief justice, to seventeen years' transportation to Tasmania; the third man to ten years. These were terrible punishments; little better than a living death.

Dilworth was a typical man of property of that era, stern and unbending on matters of crime and punishment. His treatment at the hands of the deserted soldiers seared him, giving him yet another reason to distrust criminals. And so, when in the year following the trial, Earl Grey, the colonial secretary, proposed that ticket-of-leave men from Australian convict settlements should be introduced into New Zealand as a step in their rehabilitation, Dilworth was up in arms. His sense of outrage was shared by others. He was one of a group of twelve prominent citizens, including leading merchants like David Nathan and

Fort and barracks at Point Britomart from which three deserters came to terrorize Ivy Cottage on Dilworth's Farm.
Lithograph by P Gauci, c. 1841–42, from Terry's *New Zealand*

J. I. Montefiore, and two men who were later to be colonial premiers, T. S. Forsaith and Frederick Whitaker, who convened a public protest meeting at the Exchange Hotel in Shortland Street.[28] The crowded gathering resolved to send to the Queen a petition which the action group of twelve had prepared. After expressing 'regret that such a measure has ever been contemplated', the petitioners went on to declare 'distinctly and solemnly' that they

> entertain the most decided and insuperable objection to the introduction of convicts. . . . That although this Northern Province is suffering most severely from the want of an adequate supply of labour, and your Majesty's petitioners would gladly welcome to their shores the poor but honest subjects of your Majesty, who are starving in their native land . . . [yet they] can never consent to sacrifice the character of their adopted country . . . by voluntarily admitting amongst them those [against whose names stand] a conviction.[29]

For a settlement which had 'already been subjected to an experiment with the Parkhurst boys',[30]* the advantage of cheap labour would be more than counterbalanced in the judgement of the petitioners, by 'the loss of character to the colony . . . and degradation and crime'. The Home government did not go ahead with the proposal, and Dilworth's interest in political questions subsided for another four years.

All who knew Dilworth agreed that he was single-minded to an extraordinary degree, that having decided on a line of action he was not easily diverted from it.[31] Political entanglements he avoided as a distraction from the true focus of his new life, his private business affairs. His aim above all, in the early years, was to ensure that the Remuera estate was developed. Yet this had to be done without building up an undue burden of debt. But what capital inputs should he make? His Irish background gave little guide as to how Remuera could be best farmed. How could it, with conditions of climate, soil, land tenure and market outlets so different? But he succeeded, turning to account his native shrewdness, financial know-how and a readiness to respond swiftly to changing circumstances.

He and George Graham had grown wheat as their first cash crop on Remuera land,[32] but Auckland's humid climate showed itself ill suited to this kind of arable farming. In any event the grain needs of the colonists in the nearby capital were soon being adequately met by suppliers from outside the district, usually by Maori farmers. Through the 1840s and early 1850s Pakeha observers continued to praise the extent and high quality of Maori wheat farming in the Waikato and elsewhere.[33]

---

* In 1843, ninety-two boys who had been serving sentences in Parkhurst Prison in England had been sent to Auckland as part of a scheme of rehabilitation.

Auckland's suburban pioneer farms moved towards a pastoral emphasis. The *New-Zealander* reported in November 1847 that 'the hay harvest has already commenced at Epsom; the soil of that district appears particularly suitable for the cultivation of the grasses'.[34] The area under sown grasses in Auckland, which was 202 acres in 1844, by the end of the Crown Colony period (1852) had lifted to 11,627.[35] By 1850 only 243 acres were used for growing wheat in the Auckland district. Arable land was now being used in other ways, the two major field crops being oats (795 acres) and potatoes (1,067).[36]

Auckland's livestock population for the same year shows why pasture had become the remunerative crop: the figures for horned cattle were 7,003; sheep 3,341; horses 726.[37]* In his handbook on Auckland published in 1853, William Swainson observed as 'the most noticeable feature of the country' in the neighbourhood of Auckland, 'the large quantity of cattle to be seen grazing'.[38] He explained why this was so: by 1853, 'nearly one-third of the European population of New Zealand are settled within sight of Auckland'.[39]

Dilworth shrewdly allowed the growth of population in the capital to set his pattern of farming. The European population of Auckland in 1844, the year he took possession of Remuera, was 2,754; within eight years that number had grown to over 9,000.[40] As the settlement expanded, so did the demands of its people for meat and dairy produce, and for hay to feed their horses, at a rate to keep the production of Dilworth and other suburban farmers at full stretch. A newspaper item of 1851 indicates the emphasis that Dilworth's farm had developed. 'We are informed', reported the *New-Zealander*, 'that the Commissariat Contract for meat (from the first of August ensuing) has been taken at $4^{15}/_{16}$d. per 1b. by a company of respectable farmers in our neighbourhood—Messrs Dilworth, Donovan, Henry etc.'.[41] The three respectable farmers named were Irish. But so was the editor of the *New-Zealander*!

Just what kind of inputs Dilworth had made to raise the productivity of his farm so that he had become a 'respectable farmer', able to win commissariat contracts, can be learned from two main sources. First, there are the Old Land Claims files in National Archives in Wellington which contain the evidence of claimants before the commissioner in 1847, with regard to improvements they had made since their purchase from Maori under the FitzRoy waiver proclamations three years before. Second, there are certain newspaper advertisements of the early 1850s which describe the Dilworth estate in detail.

In February 1847, Dilworth testified to Commissioner Matson as to the nature of the changes he had brought about on his farm which

---

* The comparable totals for livestock in Auckland in 1843, the first year for which statistics are available: horned cattle 494; sheep 712; horses 91.

he had hedged and enclosed. 'A considerable proportion of the land', he said, 'is now and has been in cultivation there in my possession, and several buildings are erected on the property.'[42] Dilworth did not spell out the laborious and costly preparatory work which had been needed to make the land productive. After initial clearing, deep ploughing with a team of bullocks and then harrowing were essential.[43] (Thereafter, ploughing could be carried out by a pair of horses.) From other sources we can gather the nature of the 'cultivation' Dilworth testified to in 1847; it probably involved the sowing of mixed grasses (which would have included perennial rye) for the depasturing of sheep and cattle (some dairy).[44] It appears he also grew cash crops: grass for hay, and potatoes. By the end of the 1840s he had invested substantially in horses, cattle and sheep, and farm machinery. Early in 1852 Dilworth placed an advertisement in the local press that is informative and revealing: informative in the precise detail of improvements to the farm since 1847; revealing (since the advertisement came from Dilworth's own hand) as an indication that he no longer looked upon himself as a farmer pursuing a lifelong vocation, but as a landed entrepreneur.[45]

> TO LET, for a term of years, as a Sheep Farm only, about 200 Acres of Land at Remuera,—and in March, 1854, a considerable addition shall be made in land at present under lease. The whole is inclosed and divided into paddocks by a Sheep-proof fence. The paddocks have a good sole of mixed grasses, every requisite for sheep farming, indeed their many advantages are too well known to require being put forth in an advertisement. 1000 Ewes will be to let with the place, if required,—and to an eligible person who can give security, no other need apply, the rent will be moderate, and an interest taken by the Proprietor, if thought desirable.
>
> ALSO FOR SALE
>
> A considerable number of Choice Dairy Cattle; two truly good Farming Mares in Foal, and one of them has a fine Filly at her feet; with single and double mould-board ploughs, harrow, trees, and harness complete; A Stock Horse, two good Saddle Horses, a quantity of Potatoes, a Stack of Hay, and a variety of things useful and requisite to settlers.
>
> Apply to
>
> J. Dilworth
>
> Remuera, 23rd February 1852.

This attempt by Dilworth to lease his whole estate and sell off much of its live- and dead-stock failed. A year later, he tried to rationalize his farming activities in another way. This scheme he outlined in an advertisement directed 'TO CAPITALISTS' which he put in the *New-Zealander*.[46] He offered for outright sale that portion of his estate lying to the east of Mount Hobson, describing it as 'a beautiful property . . .

known to be one of his best in the district—the land of the richest description, and abundantly wooded and watered'. In spite of an offer to help with loans 'on liberal terms', investors in land were not attracted. At that point Dilworth gave up any short-term plans for subdivision.

By the later 1850s the Remuera estate had a stable pattern of land use. Dilworth seems to have reconciled himself to farming a substantial portion of it himself for the indefinite future. On those parts which he farmed he usually ran cattle.[47] As cash crops, he grew grass for hay, and oats and potatoes.[48] He kept his options open. When any opportunity offered to lease land which he was currently farming, he was rarely averse to doing that.

The farm could be regarded by the later 1850s as falling into three parts, differentiated by value rather than any natural feature such as soil or configuration.[49] Number 1, or the western farm of sixty acres, lay (in today's terms) west of Mount Hobson and roughly north of the modern motorway. South of the motorway and extending across Great South Road to include the grounds of today's Dilworth School was Number 2 farm of about fifty acres. To the east of Mount Hobson and Market Road was Number 3, the so-called 'Dairy Farm' of ninety acres; the name was often a misnomer as lessees who almost invariably farmed it as often as not grazed stock, beef cattle or sheep upon it. Dilworth generally farmed Numbers 1 and 2 farms himself, apart from two valuable portions, about ten acres in all, which he put out on long-term lease to market gardeners. Providing the rental was right, however, there was no part of these farms which he was not prepared to lease. There was one exception: an area of about twenty acres lying south-west of, and adjoining, Great South Road which after his marriage in 1853 he regarded as the homestead farm. On those parts of the estate which he personally farmed he was an assiduous fertilizer of land and a diligent uprooter of weeds. A 1958 biography of Dilworth, which utilized reminiscences of those who had actually worked for him as farm labourers, records the tale that 'Mr Dilworth invented, or caused to be made, a weapon against the dock weed [with its] long tuber-like roots which grow deeply into the soil; against this, the tool had a long blade and a spade-like handle, so that the operator rammed the spike into the earth, turned it and the weed came out root and all'.[50] This tool, it was said, 'proved very effective'.

Dilworth was also an ardent arborist, leaving intact, where he could contrive it, clumps of native trees, planting scattershot through the fields elsewhere native and exotic trees alike. Trees were planted around homesteads, too. And as a good 'improving' Irish landowner, he established a four-acre plantation of mixed trees on Remuera Road,[51] probably on the site of an orchard which George Graham had planted when he owned the land.[52]

*

Within ten years of being confirmed in his title to Remuera, Dilworth had become the owner of a very valuable suburban farm. But it would be mistaken to give sole credit for his success to his skill in the purchase and development of the land. His astuteness and industry are undoubted. But much more important was the fact that he had bought the land when Auckland was in its infancy.[53] This allowed his farm to be enriched by what nineteenth-century land reformers called the 'unearned increment'—the value added to one's property when the growth of population made land a scarce commodity.[54] We have a reasonably firm measure of the increase in value of Dilworth's land. At an arbitration hearing held in the Supreme Court in 1866 a number of land valuers estimated what would have been the going price for the three sections of the Dilworth farm had the whole estate been put up for sale in February 1865.[55] The average figures were: for the western section (No. 1) £350 per acre; for the southern (No. 2) £250; for the eastern or 'Dairy Farm' (No. 3) £150. On the basis of these figures the value of the land alone would have been over £42,000, a great sum in colonial New Zealand. It had become the most valuable suburban farm land in Auckland.

Being wealthy in a society where material possessions tended to determine status, Dilworth was now a local notable. He had been that for some time; in 1853 he was elected to the first provincial council. That year was a turning point in Dilworth's life for another reason. In 1853 he married. Time was to prove he had begun the closest and most enduring relationship in the forty-one years of life he had yet before him.

On 12 July 1853, James Dilworth, 'a farmer of Epsom' and a bachelor of thirty-eight, married Isabella Hall, a spinster of Otahuhu aged twenty-four.[56] The ceremony was a private one conducted by the Revd Thomas Buddle, a Wesleyan minister, in the Otahuhu home of the bride's brother, John Hall. Isabella was, like James, descended from an Ulster Protestant farming family.[57] With a sister and five brothers she grew up at Aghalee, a village twelve miles south-west of Belfast. It appears that on 7 March 1848, when she was nineteen, she arrived in Auckland on the *Elora* in the company of two of her younger brothers, William (eighteen) and Robert (sixteen).[58]* The oldest brother, John (twenty-four), who had apparently preceded them by two years, was working at that time as a shopman in Shortland Street.[59] Shortly after, John conducted the family group to Otahuhu which had been designated as the site of one of the four garrison towns, manned by imperial army pensioners, that the government had decided to set up to guard the southern approaches to Auckland. On 15 May 1848 the first detachment of Royal New Zealand Fencibles destined for Otahuhu

---

* Passenger lists in the Auckland Public Library do not record the arrival of Isabella or John Hall. A 'Mr Hall' was reported by the *New-Zealander* as a passenger on the *Terror*, which berthed in Auckland 6 January 1846.

Left: *Isabella Dilworth, at the age of 46.*
Gottfried Lindauer, Dilworth Trust Board.

Right: *James Dilworth, earliest known photograph, n.d. (mid-1860s?).*
Dilworth Trust Board

arrived in Auckland on the barque *Ann*.[60]* When the seventy-three pensioner soldiers and their wives and families from that vessel reached Otahuhu a few days later, the Halls were already resident there. John Hall was in possession of the only store in the district, having bought the building and the thirty-acre block on which it stood from the previous owner, S. H. Andrews, for £600. This block became known in time as the Hall Estate. The Halls soon rose to be Otahuhu people of consequence.

Until her marriage, Isabella was housekeeper at the family home.[61] But not long after their arrival at Otahuhu, William and Robert moved on and took up farming in the Mangere district, probably at first living and working together on the same farm. They proved to be splendid farmers, anxious to develop their skills. They were early members of the Agricultural and Pastoral (A&P) Association, and competed at shows. William won one of the first ploughing matches to be held in Auckland, at a fair at Epsom in August 1850.[62]† Robert Hall was considered by Logan Campbell as the best farm manager he knew over a long life.[63] These two brothers James Dilworth befriended. Always reserved, Dilworth was much more comfortable in the company of those who, like the Halls, had the same kind of Ulster background as

---

* The Royal New Zealand Fencible settlements were set up by Governor Grey at Onehunga, Otahuhu, Panmure and Howick. The Fencibles were recruited as retired imperial army soldiers, under forty-eight years of age, of proven good character, who were granted a cottage and an acre of land in exchange for light military duties (pay 1s 3d per day).

† Ploughing matches were encouraged at shows, being seen as beneficial in attempts to raise 'standards of excellence' among agricultural labourers (*SC*, 9 Oct. 1860, p. 2).

himself. It is most likely that he met his young compatriots initially through a shared A&P interest. We can only surmise that it was through them that he in turn was introduced to Isabella.

How deeply the Dilworths felt towards each other, and whether theirs was a love match, are unknown. But at least there was a partnership of minds. In a letter written shortly after James's death Isabella affirmed that she was privy to most of her husband's views on vital matters, because he 'very frequently expressed to me his earnest wishes . . . in the event of his predeceasing me'.[64] There is other evidence, too, that they confided in each other during their life together, and that she exercised much influence over his affairs.[65] This being so, it is frustrating for a biographer to have to accept that so little is known about Isabella. Primarily this has come about because she (and James) had no direct descendants, no keepers of reminiscence and family lore. But not entirely. It was part of the pre-twentieth-century mentality that women should be self-effacing, invisible. Able women like Isabella have tended to remain unrecognized and unrecorded.

One stares at the few pictures of Isabella which remain to see what secrets can be teased from them. In a portrait painted by Lindauer in 1876, Isabella as a forty-seven-year-old gazes unblinkingly back at the viewer, her strong jaw-line set. Like her brothers she was big-framed. Here was a woman who looked as though she both knew her mind and would stand by her opinions. (On this she was at one with her husband.) Isabella was literate. Those few of her letters which have survived are written in an elegant cursive hand, and are expressed in a clear businesslike manner. She was a capable organizer, in whom James had full confidence—in his will he made her one of the trustees of his estate. Trust Board minutes show that James had chosen shrewdly; at meetings, fellow trustees listened to her with deference and with a tinge (one suspects) of trepidation as well. Among nieces and nephews she inspired respect, sometimes fear, rarely affection.[66] That they should have called her Aunt Dilworth and not Aunt Isabella is telling.

Though the Dilworths were not reclusive, they did not often entertain. When they did, Isabella was a significant presiding presence. It is recalled she baked excellent sponge cakes. On such feats did the reputation of able colonial helpmeets often depend.

Marriage forced upon James two changes within his establishment; as a married couple of consequence the Dilworths must have an appropriate home; and Isabella must be provided with transport. While he had been a bachelor answerable only to himself, James had generally travelled outside his farm on horseback. He was a good horseman, a careful horse-breeder and, as long as he continued to ride, always fastidious about his mounts. One of his nephews, Harry Mossman, recalled James Dilworth at the age of fifty-four turning up at the Mossman home in Ellerslie at five in the morning, astride 'his magnificent hack'.[67] A newspaper account of an A&P Show held at

83

JAMES DILWORTH

Buckland's Yards, Newmarket, in 1862 reported that Dilworth's pedigree 'grey colt by Invincible' paraded on the road outside.[68]

In 1856 Dilworth provided his wife with a conveyance with an equal appeal to himself. His choice was an Irish jaunting car, a light, low-set, two-wheeled vehicle which can carry four passengers sitting back-to-back, facing sideways with a seat in front for a driver. Only one other Aucklander at this time owned a jaunting car: Captain William Powditch, a venerable and well-off early settler, by this time living in Onehunga, and like Dilworth a member of the Auckland Provincial Council.[69] Pearce, the school historian, spoke warmly of Dilworth's purchase as:

> A vehicle of some consequence . . . specially ordered from the makers in Belfast, it attracted much interest when it arrived; its blue cushions were trimmed with lace, it had mountings of plated German silver for the harness and its glossy paintwork had been carefully wrapped in oiled paper and hay to protect it during the long voyage out.

Immediately after the marriage James and Isabella shifted into the first farmhouse at Remuera, Ivy Cottage, by that time somewhat enlarged.[70] How long they continued there is not certain. It would appear that in the later 1850s the Dilworths shifted to a new residence, a farmhouse put up on a knoll of volcanic origin on the south farm. This house at a later date was dismantled to be erected on another site closer to Mount St John, and its original site used for the construction of the

The Dilworth homestead, 'a mansion-farmhouse'; undated photograph.
Dilworth Trust Board Archives

large two-storey wooden building that became known as the old Dilworth homestead.[71] This was the homestead which was converted into the first Dilworth school in 1906 and which continued to be used for school activities until it was demolished in 1962 to make way for the new administrative block of the school.[72] A school historian claimed that the old homestead was erected by 1863.[73] On that issue, however, the jury is still out, and the final verdict is likely to be 'not proven'. What is not open to question is that Dilworth had already planted by this date a fine avenue of trees leading up to a south-farm homestead.

Because of its size and solidity of construction the old Dilworth residence, built of finest native timber, mainly kauri, cannot be considered other than 'imposing'. But architecturally it was undistinguished. In design and function it was, like A. K. Taylor's original Alberton, essentially a large farmhouse. The Dilworth homestead never had that later imaginative embellishment which gave the final Alberton its character and architectural distinction. Within, the Dilworth homestead was more impressive than it was without; the large rooms with high studs gave a sense of pleasing spaciousness, offsetting the sombreness which the substantial exposed timbers, darkly stained in the fashion of the time, would otherwise have imparted. The house was furnished without ostentation. It suited James and Isabella well enough, and they ended their days together there.

CHAPTER SIX

In the Public Gaze

DILWORTH'S PERFORMANCE in public affairs has been consistently underestimated. The man himself was largely responsible for that. An unobtrusive manner, combined with a seeming preoccupation with his own business affairs to the exclusion of all else, ensured that he was rarely in the public gaze. If he happened to be caught there, a native reserve caused him to recede Cheshire-cat-like until he disappeared once again. Yet those who knew him best, worked with him on community matters touching banking or farming, or on committees and boards concerned with diocesan trusts and education, highly valued his ability and respected his contribution. Dilworth's salutary caution and his wide practical and managerial skills guaranteed that.

His first foray into the public arena came about with the founding of a savings bank in Auckland in 1847. With his background of commercial banking in Dungannon and Auckland—and probably Sydney too—it was not surprising that he should support the formation of a body that set out to encourage the 'poor and improvident' to be self-reliant by teaching them how to save. He was no stranger to trustee savings banks. At the time of his emigration, Ulster had six such banks in various regional centres, including one at Dungannon.[1] It is very likely, therefore, that he knew at first hand just how the trustee savings bank system worked.

As early as 1842, settlers in Auckland began speaking of the need to have a savings bank for ordinary working people. Encouraging regular saving was in keeping with the mood of the time, particularly among local Scots who came from communities which already had savings banks.[2] On 3 December 1846 Dilworth and his former bank manager, Alexander Kennedy, went with ten other settlers to the office of Brown and Campbell, merchants, in Shortland Street to discuss setting up a bank.[3] Those present felt that there was enough interest to take the scheme further. They were also confident that the other precondition for forming a savings bank had been met, namely that they had assembled sufficient local capitalists of standing to guarantee repayment of sums entrusted to them. Dr J. Logan Campbell was appointed to draw up a set of 'Rules and Regulations' for the conduct of the bank,[4] and shortly after was empowered to purchase from Sydney an iron fire-proof safe and the various kinds of ledgers needed to make the bank a going concern.[5]

By May 1847 all was ready. Governor Grey had given his blessing; Campbell had drawn up the rules and regulations;[6] the merchant J. I. Montefiore had agreed to have the safe lodged in his brick store in Queen Street; and James Dilworth, Campbell and Montefiore had volunteered to act as accountants. An approach could now be made to the public. A publicity campaign was mounted as a prelude to the opening of the bank.[7] In the local press thrift was presented as much more than a social virtue; it was said to be a safeguard against excessive drinking. In a special leader the *New-Zealander* spelt out the moral benefits of savings banks:

> their peculiar influence in checking not only waste and unthrift but also intemperance, and the crapulous manner of life induced by what is called 'living from hand to mouth'; their power in raising that feeling of self-respect, that consciousness of a position in the world, to be maintained and bettered, which generally follows upon the acquisition of property.[8]

J. I. Montefiore, ASB President, 1847.
Auckland Public Library

However, settlers of the humble sort in Auckland did not seem to share at first the enthusiasm for thrift of their propertied betters.[9] On two successive Saturdays after the bank had officially opened on 5 June 1847, a pair of trustees sat in rotation at Montefiore's store between seven and eight in the evening waiting for depositors to appear. None came. The drought was broken on the third Saturday, 19 June, when Dilworth was duty trustee with John MacDougall, a customhouse agent of Fore (Fort) Street. In came a carpenter from Fields Lane, one Matthew Fleming, with ten pounds to deposit. As Campbell later told the story, after Fleming left Montefiore's store erupted: the two trustees 'jumped up and made quite a noise' shouting out, 'THE BANK EXISTS!'[10] Staid young Mr Dilworth doing the equivalent of a war dance after accepting the first deposit must have been an unusual sight.

Progress was tardy in the bank's early years. Not until the stimulus of the Thames goldfields did the bank gain general support among the artisan classes. Even after that there were times of testing, in the 1880s and 1890s.[11]* Yet working-class depositors in Auckland remained loyal. By the turn of the century the bank had three-quarters of a million pounds in deposits distributed through branches in several suburbs.[12] James Dilworth had been a founder of what later became regarded as a great Auckland institution.

---

* The most notable 'time of testing' was the panic run on the bank on 1 September 1893 when an absurd rumour swept the city that the bank had insufficient funds to meet all the demands of depositors. A display of resolution by trustees and support by trading banks quickly quelled the panic. (See chapter 14.)

In 1884 the bank opened a new head-office building in Queen Street. At the celebratory function presided over by Governor Jervois, Logan Campbell remarked, as guest speaker, that of the seventeen original trustees 'only two are now here—myself and my old friend, Mr James Dilworth'.[13] It was singularly appropriate that these two survivors should have been together on that platform, for they probably more than any of the others who had banded together in 1847 would have regarded (as would few of us today) saving money as a supreme social virtue. Each in his own life was committed to the nineteenth-century ideals of financial prudence and self-help which men of property wanted to inculcate in the lower orders; each had that blend of philanthropy and business acumen needed by trustees that had enabled the infant savings bank to survive. But if Campbell in old age became known as the Father of Auckland, Dilworth is more entitled to the minor honour of being regarded as father of Auckland's first savings bank. Holding office as he did 1847–66 and 1886–94, he was (when he took over in 1886 from W. C. Daldy as senior trustee) the longest serving of the original trustees.[14]

While Dilworth's well-developed sense of duty lay behind his support of the cause of trustee savings banks in the 1840s, no such moral compulsion was needed to induce him to link up with the early agricultural associations. Support there was spontaneous; fostering agriculture was a cause close to his heart. The first association of this kind in Auckland was the short-lived Agricultural and Horticultural Society of Auckland formed in 1843.[15] What is remarkable about this society is how many of its members were merchants, officials, bankers and professional men and other town dwellers rather than farmers. This characteristic continued in successor societies. Erik Olssen has reminded us that, right up to the beginning of the twentieth century, Agricultural and Pastoral Associations in New Zealand 'were largely city-based'.[16] Since they were often booster organisations formed to encourage further settlement this was not surprising. The town's élite was expected to participate in the association as an act of local patriotism. Dilworth had no difficulty in embracing that position. In the Auckland Provincial Council he was to become an ardent advocate of backblocks settlement. But as a practising farmer and landowner he warmed to any organisation which was a clearing-house for ideas on farming, and raised standards of husbandry through emulation and competition.

The first society held shows at the Exchange Hotel (Shortland Street) in 1843, and in the following year at the Royal Hotel (Princes Street).[17] But in spite of a particularly high-powered executive of senior officials and prominent settlers, by 1845 the society had faded away. The *New-Zealander*'s explanation was that the depression of

1844–46 and 'the departure for England of Dr Johnson [Colonial Surgeon], who was both President and mainspring, caused it to fall into a state of lethargy'.[18] Dilworth was one of the fifty-four Auckland settlers who convened on 21 March 1848 to resuscitate the moribund society, and who donated one pound each for that purpose. A provisional committee which had been set up to reform the organisation reconvened a meeting of the original subscribers at the Masonic Hotel on 9 December.[19] Those attending agreed to reconstitute themselves as the Auckland and New Ulster Agricultural and Horticultural Society under the patronage of 'His Excellency, Sir George Grey'. Dilworth was elected to the committee of nine appointed to run this new society.

The committee wasted no time in mounting a show which was held on 6 March 1849 at Robertson's Rope Walk, Mechanics' Bay, a venue which would be located today at about the foot of Parnell Rise. Kalaugher cites the press as reporting that 'Sir George and Lady Grey and almost all the elite of Auckland were present'.[20] The standard of stock on show was said to have been 'particularly good'. It was further reported that Dr Courtenay (presumably in proud innocence of consequences) 'exhibited a remarkably fine pair of rabbits'.

Dilworth retired from the committee after its first year, but he and his Hall brothers-in-law continued to support the society during the 1850s and 1860s at its shows, usually in Buckland's Yards, Newmarket, and at its ploughing matches held at various farms in Epsom, Mount Albert, Otahuhu and Mangere. For some time, in imitation of an old English custom, the society also held, on the first Saturday of each month, what it called 'market dinners', but it is not known whether James attended these.[21] Probably not.

A measure of the high standing in the community of the New Zealand Agricultural Society, as the Auckland group became known after 1862, was the repute of its leadership. Presidents between 1868 and 1874 included two provincial superintendents, John Williamson and T. B. Gillies. Gillies was followed in 1875 by a past governor and now local hero, Sir George Grey, with William Goodfellow (an early settler and self-made man) as his vice-president. So it was a signal honour for Dr J. Logan Campbell and Dilworth to be elected as president and vice-president of the society when it reformed in 1877 as the Auckland Agricultural and Pastoral Association.[22] The association was now on a sound footing. The recent completion of the Auckland-Onehunga railway had made available as a fine showground that part of the Ellerslie estate which was within easy reach of the Greenlane station. Soon after, an opportunity arose for the association to buy from Robert Graham, owner of the Ellerslie estate, this seventeen-acre block as its own permanent site for shows and functions. Under the leadership of Campbell and Dilworth the society clinched the deal for a figure of £425. This was a coup enabling the association, says Sherratt, 'to have a definite venue for its functions' and to establish it 'as an integral part of farming life in the community'.[23] Campbell, Dilworth and W. I. Taylor of Tamaki, the three most substantial suburban farmers in the Auckland area, were appointed the trustees of this new A&P property.

After having served for two years as Campbell's deputy, Dilworth himself became president in 1881.[24] In the year before, he had presided over the annual luncheon of the association held in the upper storey of the covered showroom built on the new grounds during the Campbell-Dilworth regime.

At the end of his presidential year Dilworth dropped out of the society's affairs, almost certainly because of family tragedy. Being now aged sixty-five he had no need for qualms over his sudden withdrawal. Others could take over the reins. Although he did not formally hold office in the A&P society during his last years, he remained a kind of elder statesman in Auckland's agricultural affairs.

J. Logan Campbell, Dilworth's associate in many public affairs.
Auckland Public Library

Some people are by nature political animals who embrace party politics and the pursuit of office with zest. Most are not. To this latter group Dilworth belonged. At an early date he advocated colonial self-government,[25] but he gave no hint that he himself had political aspirations. It was something of a surprise, therefore, that when representative institutions were introduced in 1853 he became one of the twenty-four members of the first provincial council in Auckland. He served continuously for eight years during what was probably the most eventful period in the affairs of Auckland's provincial government.

Almost coincidental with the date of Dilworth's marriage, three prominent citizens, following, as was then general practice, the conventions of the British political system organized a petition calling on him to stand for the council. The requisition was published in the press.[26]

TO J. MACKY, T. HENRY AND J. DILWORTH, ESQRS

We, the undersigned, Electors of the Southern Division request that you will permit us to put you in nomination to represent our interests in the forthcoming Provincial Council in Auckland.

Your long residence in the Colony, and the important position you have achieved by your own enterprise and industry, afford the best guarantee for your future exertions for the benefit of the Province and consequent furtherance of our mutual prosperity.

Thomas Crummer
W. S. Graham
Joseph Greenwood

[Here follow the other signatures]

Dilworth and the two others called upon in the requisition published an equally florid but coyly submissive acceptance.

Auckland, 19th July 1853

Gentlemen,—Were we to consult our personal convenience or private feelings we should decline; but a sense of public duty and the manner in which it has been pressed upon us, makes us feel that we can no longer resist your invitation, and, if elected we shall be the advocates of every measure that will tend to advance our adopted country,

We have the honour to be,
Gentlemen,
Your most obedient servants

James Macky
T. Henry
J. Dilworth

To the Gentleman signing the Requisition

Dilworth won his seat in the ensuing election as one of the four representatives for the southern division;* and this seat he successfully defended in the next two elections in 1855 and 1857.[27]

Those who were elected to the first council had little idea of what their duties would be. Almost all were (like Dilworth) men of means, making a social rather than a political statement. By successfully offering themselves as ostensibly selfless legislators working for the public good, they in effect legitimized their status within the settler community. The reality was that it was also to the personal advantage of landowners, merchants, professional and other propertied people to serve. In the council they could protect the interests of their own sectional group or local area. For Dilworth, who by 1853 had extensive landed interests,[28] being present at provincial decision-making was a distinct advantage. Ensuring that constituents had their fair share of roads and bridges meant that he retained their electoral support, while inflating the value of his own properties in the region. Constant speechmaking and political posturing were not required. His was a watching brief; keeping a hawk's eye on expenditure and works, promoting husbandry and shielding farms from diseases like sheep scab and noxious weeds like the thistle, insisting that Crown land be cheap and freely available for settlement.[29] Like most councillors, he conveniently believed there was a happy coincidence between his own self-interest and the progress of the Auckland province.

Dilworth's career as a provincial councillor was to be neither leisurely nor gentlemanly. The sedate character of the official records (*Votes and Proceedings of the Auckland Provincial Council*) gives no true sense of the turbulent and bitter spirit of Auckland's factional politics between 1853 and 1857. There were two opposing parties, calling themselves, respectively, Progress and Constitutional.[30] Progress was led by William Brown, proprietor of the *Southern Cross*; Constitutional by John Williamson, editor of the *New-Zealander*.† The clash between these two ambitious men was less one of principle than of personality. At first they fought one another using as weapons of war the papers which they controlled. Conflict entered the council chamber in March 1855 when Brown, after a notoriously corrupt contest, won a special election for the superintendency. Most of the council including Dilworth were followers of Williamson.[31] This hostile majority refused to grant Brown supply and the new superintendent was forced to expend money without authority.

---

* The successful candidates for the southern division with votes polled were: Joseph Newman 246, James Dilworth 222, W. I. Taylor 209, and James Macky 189. There were three unsuccessful candidates.

† John Williamson (1815–75) was born in Newry, County Down, northern Ireland. He arrived in Auckland in the same year (1841) and at the same age (twenty-five) as Dilworth, and with a fellow-Wesleyan, W. C. Wilson, founded the *New-Zealander* in 1845. Superintendent of Auckland, 1856–62, 1867–69, 1873–75, he has been called 'Auckland's first professional politician'.

The deadlock seemed to be ended by fresh elections in October 1855 for superintendent and council, once again fiercely fought and with the perpetration, by both sides, of scandalous instances of bribery, intimidation and personation—there were instances of men voting in the name of electors long dead.[32] During the fifth session of the council (28 January to 23 April 1856) a Progress superintendent (J. Logan Campbell), supported by a narrow majority of councillors, was able to ensure that government could proceed. But respite was only temporary. The dog fight resumed in December 1856 when, on the retirement of Campbell, Williamson became superintendent. A quarrel between Williamson and his council which flared up over the result of a disputed by-election was said to have

> culminated in one of the most disgraceful scenes, which ever occurred even in the Auckland Provincial Council. . . . In connection with this squabble, the whole Council was locked up for a night and a day. During the night, the rowdy crowd [outside] hurled stones at the building, and even passed through an open window a cat with a tin of turpentine tied to its tail.[33]

As a result of this episode the superintendent prorogued the council. Order could be restored within the council only after legislation purifying electoral practices was passed in the General Assembly and fresh elections held in Auckland. Only then could a session be convened

The Provincial Council and General Assembly Buildings, nicknamed the 'Shedifice'.
Alexander Turnbull Library

in October 1857 with council and superintendent in sufficient harmony at last to allow a resumption of normal constitutional life.[34] This council was to be the first in Auckland to continue for a full four-year term. But the unconstitutional antics of superintendents over the 1855–57 period disgusted Dilworth and, in his opinion, had resulted in 'serious injury to the Province'. During the ninth session of the council, on 8 October 1858, he moved that the system of responsible government should be introduced into the Auckland province to bring to an end the 'hitherto irresponsible management of its affairs'.[35]*

It is not easy to discern a simple pattern in Dilworth's political performance during a provincial council career which extended over eight years and twelve sessions, and covered what was for Auckland a period of dramatic change. Between 1853 and 1861 the remarkable increase in the province's Pakeha population from just over 10,000 to 24,420 of itself quite revolutionized the nature of Auckland political life.[36] But certain features in Dilworth's conduct stand out. First, and this was most marked in the early sessions, he regarded himself as spokesman of the farming-settler interest to which his southern division constituency belonged. Measures to eradicate thistle or 'to prevent the extension amongst sheep of the diseases called Scab and Influenza' had his full support.[37]† Above all he pressed for better roads for country settlers. (In one case he urged on behalf of Patumahoe settlers that a road be put through to their district, willy-nilly, passing across lands still in Maori hands.)[38]

Yet he was no narrow 'roads and bridges' man, taking part in a pork-barrel scramble for a lion's share of public works. His range of legislative concerns was much wider than that. This became most marked by 1858 when, with the wastage of councillors after three elections, he became one of a small nucleus of members who had seen continuous service since 1853. The value of experience was enhanced by his background of banking and accounting, enabling him to speak authoritatively, for instance, on matters of audit, or how to make debenture issues. The special committees onto which he was voted during the sixth session show the breadth of his interests: audit, fencing and impounding, the Sheep Act, exchange of properties, ordinances, library, the eight-hour [day] system—predictably, as a farmer and employer he was opposed to the last.

The cause he was most interested in, however, was the opening up of the waste lands of the Auckland province to settlers of modest means who demonstrated a capacity for self-help. This was the underlying

F. A. Whitaker, Dilworth's political ally in the Provincial Council.
Alexander Turnbull Library

---

* By responsible government Dilworth meant not simply making the executive (the superintendent and his committee) responsible to the council. He wanted the council itself to be more effective, representative and accountable. Hence his motion also advocated an increase in numbers of councillors.

† In 1864 he was one of nineteen honorary inspectors appointed to halt the spread of pleuro-pneumonia among cattle in Auckland (Kalaugher, p. 42).

principle embodied in the 1858 Waste Lands Act which provided that land orders in the province would be granted free of cost to immigrants from the northern hemisphere who were prepared to finance their own passage out to Auckland. So strongly did Dilworth believe in this measure that, when it was rumoured that the General Assembly was likely to disallow it, he was prepared to advocate that Auckland break free from the rest of the colony. As a result he was voted onto a select committee set up by the council to 'prepare a Petition to the Queen and both Houses of Parliament [of the United Kingdom] praying for a separate Government and Legislation for the Province of Auckland'.[39] Dilworth had no need to so agitate himself. The Act was approved by the General Assembly and the governor. A most important measure, it was built into the 1859 Auckland Land Regulations, and remained the foundation of much 'special' and military settlement in the province for years to come.

After 1858, Dilworth's attendance at the council became increasingly irregular. During the last (thirteenth) session of the council, which was prorogued on 27 February 1861, he did not attend at all. Nowhere did he ever explain why he had abdicated his political role. But some reasons strongly suggest themselves. Logan Campbell reflecting on the riotous nature of politics in the mid-1850s maintained that, what he branded 'the madness of party', had disillusioned many serious-minded colonists.[40] Comments made by Dilworth in the council, and the indication of his mood in motions put to the vote, confirm that he became sickened by Auckland factionalism. The affairs of the council, moreover, consumed a great deal of time. Sittings lengthened; during its eleventh session (11 July–1 November 1859) the council met on forty-four separate occasions. Each attendance meant for Dilworth a two-mile ride by horse to town over barely tolerable roads. Extensive private business affairs, too, in town and country were now demanding more of his attention. Dilworth could ill afford to spend precious time listening to the drawn-out palaver of professional politicians like Hugh Carleton, Reader Wood, Captain I. R. Cooper and James Busby into whose hands the council seemed to have fallen.

But probably more important than these considerations in persuading Dilworth that his political day was done were matters of family. During 1858 a new turn of events in Ireland reawakened in James a sense of his duty toward his close Dilworth relatives. To this revived responsibility he devoted a major share of his time and thought over the next few years.

CHAPTER SEVEN

Other Dilworths

IN THE MODERN WORLD, families and communities have often transplanted themselves by what is called chain migration.[1] In its simplest form this has begun with a young adult male leaving his homeland to travel far in search of employment, or earnings, or status, perhaps all three. The chain process itself really begins when the migrant, having successfully established himself, encourages others from his home family network or home district to join him, often helping them on arrival to find jobs and housing.

James Dilworth initiated such a chain movement among his own kinsfolk back in County Tyrone. And although his summons to others to join him in New Zealand was somewhat delayed, the prospect that they would be able to do so had never been in doubt, not least among those who, as far back as 1838, had taken part in the family discussion and debate that preceded the decision to send him as representative of the Dilworth family interest to the far side of the world.

It is tempting to see James's (by now) ingrained caution as causing this delay in the 1840s and 1850s. But that was only part of the explanation. The journey from Ireland to the Antipodes, taking three months or more, was the ultimate in mid-nineteenth-century, long-distance migration, something which was, 'with the exception of birth and death', in David Fitzpatrick's opinion, 'the most mobile act which most nineteenth-century Irish men and women could be expected to accomplish'.[2] For some years there was little economic need driving James's relations back in County Tyrone to contemplate that momentous step. No family member was a refugee from the Great Famine.

By the late 1850s, however, the scales had tipped in favour of emigration. James had become a substantial Auckland landowner. His strong sense of responsibility towards family was well known to relatives back home, even if the severity of his adult personality was not. The Dungannon Dilworths felt sure they had a champion in New Zealand on whom they could rely. Furthermore, between 1859 and 1866, the years of chain migration of the Dilworths, there were other, more general inducements. By the mid-century, ocean transport was 'cheap and abundant', while in the Australasian colonies hunger for labour had become a byword.³ In the more precise instance of the Auckland province over these years, there was the added incentive of assisted passages provided by the provincial and general governments,⁴ and the prospect of cheap, even free farms, some of it upon land confiscated from 'rebel' Maori.⁵

Changes in the private family circumstances of the Dilworths in County Tyrone also bore on James's decision to invite relatives to Auckland. He was deeply attached to his mother Mary Ann Dilworth, in spite of, or perhaps even because of, his having been separated from her at the impressionable age of eight. Unlike his father who was of English Planter extraction, his mother was the grandchild of a Scot, one John Bell who had immigrated into the Belfast region in the early eighteenth century. Her being Scottish in her ways (or so it was said) could well explain how the dour, single-minded drive associated with the Ulster Scots became part of the personal makeup of her older son James.

In the mid-1840s Mrs Dilworth fell into what her children later spoke of as a 'delicate' state of health.⁶ It is probable that anxiety over his mother's health was the reason why James seriously proposed to make a hurried return to Ireland over the summer of 1846–47, even though negotiations with the government to get a secure title to his Remuera lands had reached a critical juncture demanding his continued presence in Auckland.⁷

In the event he stayed put. Circumstances in Dunseark had taken a reassuring turn. Mrs Dilworth had prevailed upon her middle (and ablest) daughter, Esther Ann, to promise to 'stay home' and take care of her until she died.⁸ This was no small sacrifice, obliging Esther to break off her recently-contracted engagement to a widower, Thomas Mossman, who was farming the nearby townland of Mullaghboy. Believing time not to be on his side, the forty-seven-year-old Mr Mossman thereupon paid court to Esther's younger sister Eleanor and married her within a year (28 November 1847).⁹ Esther continued to take care of her mother who died in December 1852 at the age of sixty-three. In the same year Esther married a local farmer George Evans. Shortly after, this young couple crossed the Atlantic for the Californian goldfields.

It is part of the Dilworth family tradition that, some time after his mother's death, James of Auckland fell out with his father.¹⁰ In spite of persistent research in modern Dungannon, the full cause of the quarrel has not been determined, perhaps never will be. However, family historians there seem agreed on one point: that one major difference of opinion between father and son was over which member of the immediate family should succeed as tenant of Dunseark once the father died.¹¹ Matters came to a head when the lease expired in 1858, and ready money was needed to ensure that on renewal it would remain in his hands. The father wrote to James in Auckland appealing

JAMES DILWORTH

for help. Because a letter from Ireland and a reply from Auckland took a minimum of six months, the son did not respond in time. John Dilworth at the age of seventy-three was ejected from Dunseark, with some feeling on his part, substantially unjustified, that James when called upon had refused to come to his rescue. Although the lease was not lost to the wider family, since John's younger brother James took it over, James Dilworth and his father remained at odds. Nor were they reconciled by the time John died seven years later, to be buried beside his wife Mary in the family plot, at the Benburb churchyard in the parish of Clonfeacle. In 1873, James Dilworth, with Isabella as companion, made the traditional 'journey Home' of the successful colonist. A special feature of his stay was an excursion made to County Tyrone where he stayed with his Dilworth cousin Mrs Mary Nelson of Alton Lodge, Pomeroy. After a visit to the family plot at Benburb, James arranged for a commemorative headstone to be erected there. Moss covered, it remains legible today:

1873
In Memory of
Mary Dilworth
Dunsirk
Who died 3rd Dec. 1852
Aged 63 years

This stone was erected by
her devoted son
James Dilworth
of Auckland, New Zealand

The Dilworth family graveyard, Benburb, County Tyrone.
M. Stone

The exclusion of the father from the commemoration could scarcely have been more obvious.

John's ejectment from Dunseark was part of a wider crisis which overtook the whole family when his well-to-do cousin, Anne Dilworth of Mullaghcreevy, died on 2 February 1858.[12] Following on her death there was a delay in the proving of her will which, it has been suggested, was related to the time taken over the return of accounts from New Zealand, where Anne Dilworth had helped finance the more important of the early land purchases of her protégé James. This was another example of the time taken for two-way correspondence. Probate was not finally granted until November 1858.[13]

By an unfortunate coincidence, 1858 not only saw the death of Anne, the one 'who held the purse strings at Mullaghcreevy', but was also the year when the two main family leases, Dunseark and Mullaghcreevy, fell in. Renewal depended on ready money. Anne was no longer there to supply it, and no one in County Tyrone could take her place. Certainly James Dilworth, James of Auckland's uncle, was secure in his tenancy of Lissan. But in the hard times of the 1850s he could not offer monetary help to others. And the Auckland James, now comfortably off and with the means and the willingness to assist, was powerless to act in time, thwarted by the 'tyranny of distance' under which, as Geoffrey Blainey has reminded us, all in the Antipodes then lived.[14] So Dunseark was lost by John. More seriously, Mullaghcreevy was also lost. The financial straits of the Dilworths gave the agent of the Verner estate the opportunity he needed to convert the tenure of the Mullaghcreevy townland into a much-preferred short-term lease. Wilfred Dilworth remarks that the agent could now 'terminate the lease, evict the family there, and install another on a yearly rental'.[15] And he did.

James Dilworth never got over his feeling of remorse at the loss of the family farm to which he, however unwittingly, had contributed.[16] In the mid-1880s, when he was just on seventy and making his last visit to Tyrone, he went with a small family group to visit Mullaghcreevy. A ten-year-old Irish boy who was one of the party, a son of James's cousin Mrs Anne (née Dilworth) Watt, and himself a James, recalled in later years his astonishment at the spectacle of his heavily-bearded old relative from Auckland reduced to tears at the sight of the farm on which he had grown up, but which was now irredeemably lost to the family and in other hands.

Dramatizing as they did the shrinking economic opportunities for the family in northern Ireland, the Mullaghcreevy and Dunseark evictions speeded up both James Dilworth's readiness to invite his kinsfolk to Auckland and their willingness to accept. The first to respond was his brother Andrew. Unfortunately for the historian, Andrew has left no personal papers to tell us exactly how and when he went to New Zealand. But family lore, newspapers and certain legal records allow some likely inferences to be drawn. It is almost certain that he travelled to the colony by way of the United States and that, while there, he encountered his American wife-to-be, Mary Jane Daniels,[17] though whether he married her during 1859 in San Fransisco where they met, or in Sydney (the other possibility) in 1860, existing records do not tell. We may confidently assume, however, that he went to California chiefly to visit his sister Esther and her husband George Evans, and to meet for the first time their four young children. This reforging of the family link between Andrew and Esther was later to be a factor in her going to New Zealand herself, and that under circumstances bearing significantly on this life story of James Dilworth.

Late in 1859 Andrew moved on from California to Sydney. There he joined twenty-seven other passengers who travelled on a small trans-Tasman sailing vessel, the *Airedale*, which arrived in Auckland on 24 November 1859.[18]

Though there was much in the way of family 'bars'* to be exchanged between James and Andrew, who were meeting for the first time in over twenty years, Andrew did not stay long on his brother's Remuera farm. After all, he had been induced to come out by the promise that he would have a farm of his own. And James had land at hand to give.

In later life, James Dilworth owned numerous parcels of land scattered through the Waitakere Ranges, which lie just north-west of Auckland, a region of limited agricultural worth, but one where he continued to buy and sell land as long as he lived. Most of the allotments he bought there were small,[19] but the block he called his 'Waitakere estate' was an exception. With an area of 1,977 acres, it was the largest single piece of land anywhere that he owned at the time Andrew arrived, having bought it for £909 10s 0d at a Crown land sale on 30 June 1855.[20] This block changed little in shape over the next forty years. A small bit was sold off here to some settler or miller or gumdigger, or a small parcel was acquired there to straighten out a boundary line;[21] but on Dilworth's death it was much the same size as when he first got it, being just over 2,000 acres.[22] The estate extended westwards from the valley flats formed by small tributaries of the Kumeu River, rising through foothills (some deeply broken) to the main divide. Within its boundaries was the 366-metre peak of Maungatoetoe, one of the three highest in the ranges.† The upper reaches of the block commanded views of both east and west coasts, and provided a superb prospect of the infant settlement of Auckland.

---

* 'Bars: All the news and gossip that has to be caught up with' (O'Kane ed., *You Don't Say*, p. 7).

† Mount Eden (196 metres) and One Tree Hill (183 metres)—half the height of Maungatoetoe —provide a useful comparison.

OTHER DILWORTHS

Years later, Bishop W. G. Cowie recalled his delight in viewing from Dilworth's farm the spire of the Church of the Holy Sepulchre in Khyber Pass, twenty miles away to the south-east.[23] Those wishing to locate the estate today can do so by moving from the Waitakere railway station westward up the Te Henga Road which, within a kilometre or so, cuts through the site of the old Dilworth farm, the chief part of which lay to the left of this road.

In 1860, James offered to place his brother Andrew on one of the more accessible and less infertile parts of this block, although accessibility and fertility are relative terms when applied to the nineteenth-century Waitakeres. The soil was mainly compacted clay, in summer drought unyieldingly hard, but with winter rain transformed into a quagmire. At that time, the region was virtually roadless, apart from Maori tracks and primitive clay mill roads.[24] Access from Auckland was by boat, which would sail up the Waitemata Harbour, round Te Atatu Point, move up the Henderson Estuary (Taikata) as far as its junction with the Huruhuru Creek. Journey's end was a tidal lagoon marking the headwater of the Huruhuru, beside which was Prior's Landing, so named after the pioneer bush-contractor who had constructed it.[25]* Movement to Dilworth's from there was usually by

---

* The site of Prior's Landing with its associated buildings and garden—now long gone—can be viewed today at Helena Park, Henderson.

Prior's Landing in Huruhuru Creek which provided access to the Waitakere farm.
M. Stone

horse and dray. The direct westerly route taken by today's Swanson Road would have involved negotiating the dangerously steep Tunnel Hill Road; instead, travellers took a longer, circuitous route which climbed from the foot of Crows Road, then moved along successive ridges until Waitakere was reached.*

Disregarding both the remoteness of this proffered land and its undeveloped state—for it was substantially covered in bracken and tea tree—Andrew did not hesitate over accepting. He was delighted to become, at the age of thirty-seven, a landowner for the first time in his life. It appears that, before beginning to break in the land, he moved to Sydney to collect Mary Jane whom he had summoned from California. On 23 August 1860 Andrew and his wife returned to Auckland.[26] He then set about establishing what local historians agree was the first substantial Pakeha farm in Waitakere. He never regretted his decision. In the years ahead he became a very successful and much admired Waitakere identity.

An 1867 map of the northern Waitakere region shows an area designated as 'Dilworth's Farm'.[27] But which Dilworth—whether James or Andrew—the map of course does not say. Two stories were current in this period. The first had James still as owner, having placed Andrew on the farm as salaried manager. The second version spoke of Andrew as outright owner of the whole block. Each story was partly true. The key to actual ownership is contained in the Auckland Land Registry where a deed of conveyance dated 19 January 1861 records that James had 'made an absolute sale' to his brother 'for the sum of £5,500' of approximately 140 acres.[28] Whilst James retained legal ownership of the remainder of the estate, in practice Andrew had full use of that too, cleared and fenced it in part, and grazed his stock there.† Andrew seems not to have been paid a salary but, like any other family member invited to the colony, was given by James financial support in making a start, and was probably paid an annual allowance as well. Nor is there any doubt that in the early breaking-in stage of the farm, James helped finance the building of his brother's house, the fencing and fertilizing of the land, and the sowing of pasture.

James's true generosity, however, lay in the fact that in spite of the wording of the deed of conveyance, he did not sell the farm to Andrew but gave it to him. A consideration figure went on the deed, no doubt, to give the transaction enforceability in law. But why, we must ask, did James specify an astronomic figure of thousands—many times the market value of the land—when a peppercorn payment of one pound

---

* Winding ridge roads were used to save the laborious work of 'cut and fill' involved in putting straight roads through steep-sided gullies. Descent from ridge roads into valleys was often by way of zigzags to ease the strain on the horses (Diamond, *Once the Wilderness*, pp. 17, 164–71).

† The 1868–69 electoral roll for the provincial council (northern division) has Andrew Dilworth 'in occupation of 1000 acres'.

would have served equally well? Perhaps he was making an effort to remind Andrew how generous had been the gift. Or perhaps this was his way of 'writing up' the value of the land, in case Andrew wished to use it in the future as a security upon which to raise a loan. What his real motive was we can only guess.

What is beyond doubt is that Andrew remained grateful as long as he lived. In the will which he signed a week before his death he acknowledged that his brother James had 'gratuitously presented me with my property at Waitakere which was the foundation of my success in life'.[29]

James's confidence in his younger brother had not been misplaced. Andrew adapted easily and successfully to colonial life. His Waitakere farm won local renown as the first effective farming venture in the Waitakere region. Like James, he saw fertilizing the land well as a precondition of success. Jack Diamond, historian of the Waitakeres, writes of Andrew as a pioneer of the practice of top-dressing by artificial fertilizer, preparing his land first with a heavy dressing of lime—shades of County Tyrone!—followed up by treatment with bonedust. Ledgers covering the late nineteenth century, in the Dilworth Trust archives, record fertilizer going each year into this farm by the ton. One Henderson pioneer recalled Dilworth's paddocks being whitened with bonedust. Supplies, including fertilizer, were brought into the farm from Prior's Landing by an employee on the Dilworth farm called 'Old Luke'* who scorned the roundabout ridge route, taking his bullock team and dray by way of Swanson's mill-camp to mount the steep mud track up and over today's Tunnel Hill to drop directly onto Dilworth's farm.[30]

Andrew specialized in fattening cattle and sheep: Old Luke maintained 'the farm contained the fattest sheep he ever saw'.[31] Stock was sent down to Buckland's auction yards in Remuera for disposal in the Auckland market but, increasingly, meat from the farm butchery was sold locally to encampments of mill-hands, gumdiggers and railway navvies.[32] Old timers have recalled how R. J. Vercoe of Henderson, who was in the business of revictualling and cooking for the navvies, used to send packhorses every Saturday to the farm to bring back loads of meat for the camps of men working on the railway line.[33]

In his skill as a farmer, his passion for manuring and his readiness to apply Ulster farming practices to colonial land, Andrew was a mirror image of James. Yet although they shared certain attitudes—both could be strict, both were demanding in their expectations of others—and although they got on well together, they had contrasting personalities. James had the better brain and the wider business competence, Andrew

---

* Luke was the man's surname: efforts to ascertain his first name have been unsuccessful. He was said to be the father of Samuel Luke, a prominent Otahuhu citizen and chairman of the Auckland Education Board.

A bullock team with a load of provisions for a nineteenth-century timber mill in the Waitakere Ranges.
Auckland Public Library

the greater sociability. Relatives recognized differences. One spoke of Andrew as 'not the same kind of man at all';[34] another regarded him as 'a much more humane and likeable person'.[35] Certainly Andrew lacked his brother's reserve, and appeared relaxed in the company of others. James himself seemed to recognize this and sent friends and business acquaintances to stay with Andrew and Mary Jane at Waitakere. Beside the Huruhuru landing Andrew was said to have put up a shed both to store goods and to shelter guests (his and James's) while they waited to be taken by horse and cart to the farm. Once there they would while away a holiday weekend that could include riding, hunting, bush walks, perhaps an excursion to one of the west coast surf beaches.[36]

Andrew entered fully into district affairs. It was in character that, although he and his wife had no children, he should have been elected to the committee of the first Henderson school which was set up by the provincial council in May 1873.[37] Out of a mixture of principle and self-interest, he also joined the action committee that advocated an Auckland-Kaipara rail link.[38] In lighter vein, he was one of the founders of the Henderson's Mill Turf Club, which between 1879 and 1888 held annual race meetings on a course located in the general area where the Henderson High School stands today.[39] The community's goodwill towards Andrew is conveyed in the newspaper account of the annual race meeting held on St Patrick's Day, 1879: 'Mr A. Dilworth', it said, 'officiated as judge in his usual satisfactory and impartial manner'.[40] Given his popularity, it was a matter of little surprise that, after the abolition of the provinces, he was elected as representative of the Waitakere riding to the newly formed Waitemata County Council.[41] He had become a local notable. Back in Auckland James had every reason to be satisfied with the success of his scheme of bringing out Andrew, a brother of whom he was genuinely fond.

*

The occasion of Andrew's migration had been a falling away of the family's prospects in Ireland. A private crisis within James's little family circle in Remuera itself gave rise to his next attempt to settle a relative in the colony.

In writing about that relative, James Dilworth Mossman, there is a responsibility to warn readers that what follows is not primarily based on the documents and published works upon which the critical historian customarily relies. The chief source has been oral evidence passed down by Dilworth relatives by blood or marriage. Fortunately, some of that family lore was committed to paper in correspondence between American and New Zealand branches of the family over fifty years ago. Nevertheless it is in essence hearsay. Where possible, corroboration has been sought from newspapers, official papers and published works. Where such checks have been available, some instances of apparently doubtful family gossip have been confirmed in surprising detail. For all that, the reader must recognize that much of what follows about J. D. Mossman lacks corroboration provided by independent sources and is open therefore to all those shortcomings to which oral testimony is subject. Yet believing that a biography of James Dilworth must include the life story of J. D. Mossman, I have presented this as the family have told it except where their version has been contradicted by other evidence.

After eight years of marriage, Isabella and James Dilworth had to reconcile themselves to the possibility that their union would be childless. One of the family descendants has testified that 'it was a great grief to James Dilworth that he had no children'.[42] There was more to this than just frustrated parental longings. As the designated heir of the family who had, by the 1860s, accumulated broad acres, James seems to have felt that the time had come to select a relative who, on his death, would carry on in his stead. Characteristically taking his Irish experience as a guide, he decided to overlook his brother Andrew (whom he had generously provided for in 1861, or so James believed), and to skip a generation, just as his cousin Anne had done forty years before in selecting him. His choice fell on a nephew whom he had never seen, James Dilworth Mossman, eldest son of his favourite sister Eleanor and her husband Thomas Mossman.

In or about 1853 the Mossmans had migrated to Canada with their infant sons, James and William John.[43] During the next thirteen years passed by the family in Canada and the United States, two further sons and two daughters were born. Family lore does not tell how James Dilworth in Auckland set about persuading his sister Eleanor in Canada to give up her eldest boy, James Dilworth Mossman, so that he could be reared by a faraway uncle in Auckland as heir to the Dilworth wealth. Eleanor had the reputation of being very possessive towards her children: in later years her daughter-in-law remarked that she 'couldn't let any of them get away from her'.[44] But Eleanor was somehow won over to the scheme, and it was arranged for her son to be sent back to Ireland from Canada to await a passage to the colony by ship.

Much is known about the boy's journey to New Zealand, because its somewhat dramatic beginnings were observed and recorded by a member of the large Bradley family (husband and wife, twelve children and a son-in-law) who set out from Ulster for the port of London in October 1862. Catherine Bradley later recalled that

> soon after leaving Belfast, at another place, a boat hailed our ship. The passengers were greatly thrilled. In that boat was a very big Irishman, a boatswain, and a little boy of ten or eleven years. He was left aboard [and the other two] went to shore again. [One of the Bradleys asked] 'What is your name little man?' He replied 'James Dilworth Mossman' 'And who will meet you?' 'A rich uncle in New Zealand'.[45]

At London, young Mossman and the Bradleys boarded the 1,300-ton sailing ship the *Gertrude*, which was the fourth vessel to go to the colony under the non-conformist Albertland special settlement scheme that was to be so prominent in the peopling of the Auckland province. Under this scheme the provincial government provided for land beside the Kaipara Harbour in North Auckland to immigrants who could provide their own modestly priced passage money.

The loneliness of this boy sundered from his family in Canada had not been eased by travelling arrangements made for him in that crowded passenger ship. The 'rich uncle in New Zealand' had paid for Master Mossman to be one of the thirteen passengers with separate cabin accommodation, thereby physically isolating him from the 134 emigrants who had been squeezed into second class and steerage. But the large Bradley family took this solitary boy under its wing. Mrs Bradley who, like many on the *Gertrude*, 'wondered at a little chap like that sent alone' to the Antipodes, was said to have virtually mothered him.[46] The Bradley boys called him 'Jimmy'; made him one of their set. Perhaps he was one of the 'number of boys on board' who according to the commemorative account of the voyage 'used to gather in the shelter of one of the [life] boats and tell wonderful tales of pirates and robbers'.[47]

The seventy-day passage out was uneventful, though the ship was overcrowded, provisions scarce, and many passengers downcast. It was a bewildering society that unfolded before the lonely boy; some passengers organizing prayer-meetings; others (according to a lay-preacher's diary) 'casting off all restraint' to become 'leaders of frolic and much shameless wickedness', while the worst were 'like returned convicts ready for any wickedness or villainy'.[48]

The *Gertrude* arrived in Auckland on 9 February 1863[49] to find the town devastated by the news that, two days before, a steamer corvette, the HMS *Orpheus*, had foundered on the bar of the Manukau

Harbour with a heavy loss of life.[50]* James was immediately taken by carriage to his new home, the Remuera farm of Uncle James and Aunt Isabella Dilworth. Shortly after, they secured a governess for their nephew by advertising in the local press. When he reached his teens, Jimmy was sent to a boarding school, the name of which is not known, where it is said he showed a flair for languages. His education completed, he returned to Remuera to be under his uncle's eye, and there to learn how to be a farmer. It was also intended that he be progressively inducted into the Dilworth property business.

By all accounts, Jimmy Mossman grew into a talented and personable young man. According to his sister-in-law, Marion Mossman, he 'was a great musician (no other Mossman was), was six feet, had very dark hair and eyes, and very good looking'.[51] By the time he left school, things appeared to be moving in his favour. Late in 1866 his isolation had been seemingly broken: his parents had come from Canada to Auckland, with his brothers and sisters, to settle permanently in the colony. For some months they stayed on the Remuera estate and Jimmy lived with them. But it is significant that he chose not to establish close relations with any of his family. Beneath a surface of indifference he had become emotionally vulnerable. Perhaps he felt that having been cast adrift by his family once before he must never again expose himself to the possibility of having that hurt repeated. (He never would or could, throughout his life, establish close relationships with people. He died alone and unmarried.)

It was Jimmy's psychic state that caused James Dilworth's schemes for his designated heir to go awry. The young man became restless, could not settle on the farm. In an odd way, Jimmy's abiding sense of his own loneliness, his anomie, alienated him from those about him. Moreover, although he knew he was heir to James Dilworth's wealth, he (using Marion Mossman's words) 'detested the dead man's shoes business . . . and in the end he cleared out'.

How long it was before Jimmy's place of concealment was discovered, the family traditions of the Mossmans—scorning chronology—do not specify. The received version within the family is that, some time later, word came through to James Dilworth that his nephew had been found working on a sheep station in Hawke's Bay.[52]† Dilworth then commissioned Willie John, Jimmy's brother, to go to the station and persuade the runaway to come back. Jimmy's response was to remove himself yet again, and to migrate to Australia, shipping out under the newly assumed surname of Lorraine. He joined the Melbourne police force as a detective.

---

* The loss of life on the *Orpheus*, which had been wrecked in clear weather, though known to be heavy, was in fact underestimated at first: in the final death toll 189 (including the master) of the ship's complement of 259 were drowned.

† Mrs E. D. Mossman, W. J. Mossman's daughter-in-law, in 1994 was providing oral evidence with great clarity at the age of ninety-nine.

Once again James Dilworth ultimately discovered his nephew's whereabouts, but decided this time to go himself to persuade his heir to come back. In spite of being offered a financial inducement to return and resume the relationship afresh, Mossman spurned the offer. Dilworth, it is said, came back from Melbourne 'a very disappointed man'.[53] Revised will-making which took place during 1873 makes it obvious that Jimmy Mossman was no longer the heir-apparent, and was expressly excluded from any share in the Dilworth estate upon his uncle's death.

When he was about fifty years of age, Detective Lorraine (for so the *Melbourne Argus* described him) committed suicide on the steps of the city's police office. Marion Mossman, whose family recollections have informed much that has been written here about James Dilworth Mossman-Lorraine, should have the last word. Having been up to the time of his death, she wrote, 'a great gambler, Jimmy had no money and few possessions. And what he had (including a gold watch and chain) were sold & paid [the] expenses of burial. A wasted life & sad!'.[54]

With that final sentiment James Dilworth would have agreed, though perhaps not the Dilworth Trustees who in 1894 became the beneficiaries of the Dilworth fortune which could have been J. D. Mossman's had he so chosen.

Over 1865–66, fourteen more people with Dilworth family connections came to Auckland. The first to arrive was a young man of twenty-one with the same name as Dilworth himself.[55] This James Dilworth came from Portadown, a town to the east of Dungannon in the adjoining County of Armagh. It has been claimed that these eponymous Auckland colonists were cousins.[56] The family connection was in fact much more tenuous than that. Neither had previously known of the other: indeed, the young Irishman carried a letter of introduction to present to James of Remuera should they ever happen to meet. To be sure, they had forebears in common—the seventeenth-century Dilworths of Killyman, County Tyrone. But as early as 1717 some of these Dilworths had moved to County Armagh to live in Seagoe, just north-east of Portadown, where sometimes they continued under the name of Dilworth, sometimes under 'Dillard', a corrupted form of the original name.* The younger James Dilworth, born 10 April 1843, was a descendant of this branch, and so was at best a very remote relative of the subject of this biography.

He emigrated to New Zealand quite independently of James of Remuera, having been recruited in late 1864 by agents of the New

---

* The process of 'folk etymology' was almost certainly at work here. Perhaps people in County Armagh found Dillard easier to say because it was closer in form to the familiar Irish name of Dillon.

Zealand Government Emigration Board, W. S. Grahame and John Morrison, who were providing free passages to colonists from Britain prepared to go out and settle on land confiscated from Maori in the Pukekohe-Tuakau area.[57] In their attempt to fill one particular vessel, the *Ganges*, due to leave Queenstown,* County Cork, in early November, the agents had confined their efforts 'almost exclusively' to the northern counties of Ireland.[58†] At the time of his selection as an assisted emigrant James was a bachelor. In very quick order he became a family man. On 12 October 1864, just before leaving Portadown, he married Sarah Whitten of Seagoe, a spinster aged nineteen. And when the young couple embarked at Queenstown three weeks later, they were accompanied by a four-year-old boy, listed as their son Christopher Dilworth. Whose child he really was is not clear. Perhaps he was a child born out of wedlock to one or both parents; possibly, and much more likely, he was the son of Sarah's recently widowed brother, Robert. At this distance in time it is difficult to determine where precisely he came from, or indeed his true age. Perhaps the boy's size led James to put up his own age on the passenger list by one year and that of his wife by two (to twenty-one).[59**]

The journey of the 1,211-ton clipper, the *Ganges*, was to become notorious in the annals of nineteenth-century New Zealand immigration. On the eve of the vessel's departure, the *Cork Herald* had declared that it had accommodation which was 'roomy and judiciously arranged', with standards of 'the utmost cleanliness', and 'sanitary precautions well attended to'. The reality was that the *Ganges* was overcrowded, grossly unhygienic and short of food, some of which turned putrid during the passage out. Further, shortly after the ship left Queenstown an epidemic of bronchitis and whooping cough swept through the 125 children on board. Over the voyage of 100 days, fifty-four out of a complement of 474 government immigrants died—entirely children under the age of five.[60‡] Shortly after the ship berthed at Queen's Wharf, Auckland, on 14 February 1865, conditions aboard became the subject of two successive inquiries launched by the provincial government. Little wonder the *Ganges* has come down in history as 'the Death Ship'.[61]

So debilitated were the passengers on arrival that the authorities decided not to send them directly to their allotments, but to hold them for some weeks in the former military barracks at Onehunga so that

---

* Queenstown, today Cobh (pronounced Cove), was usually a departure point in the nineteenth century for emigrants crossing the Atlantic to North America.

† All but five of the 289 adult passengers on the *Ganges* were Irish, principally farmers and farm labourers.

** Each assisted immigrant and his whole family were provided with a free passage to Auckland and thence to the place of settlement (Morris, *Early Days in Franklin*, p. 136).

‡ There were two adult deaths, both members of the crew, sailors who fell from the mainyard into the sea and were drowned.

The barque Ganges, *'the Death Ship' on which 54 children died on the journey out from Ireland, 1864–65.*
Dickie Collection, Alexander Turnbull Library

they could recuperate.[62] Over this time, James, formerly of Portadown, made no approach to Dilworth of Remuera. There was no point in his doing so. The young man had not come to New Zealand to work as a farm labourer. The prospect of being a landowner had been the bait attracting him. And he could be that only by going straight to his allotted ten-acre section and occupying it for three years, thereby earning the Crown grant that would make it his.

In the winter of 1865 James and his family went to his ten-acre block in the Pukekohe district.[63] Like all who settled under this scheme, he endured great privation.[64] Hurriedly, the settlers had to put up slab whares or huts, usually with earthen floors, and roofs thatched with nikau fronds. Rations promised by the government were in short supply, and public works were not regular enough to provide an income to tide these poor settlers over the pioneering stage. The result was destitution and despair. Some settlers turned from farming to gumdigging. Others, upon the discovery of gold in the Thames, went to the fields leaving behind wives to keep farm, home and family together. There is an unconfirmed story that, in 1868, Dilworth of Remuera sent for James of Pukekohe offering work on his farm, which the young man turned down.[65] By staying put he received, in December 1868, the Crown grant for his original allotment. This land he enlarged. Next year he was paying rates for a holding of thirty acres.[66]

Like a number of Pukekohe settlers, during the 1870s James finally gave up the struggle and shifted to Auckland, although others of his family remained to become farmers and storekeepers in Franklin County.[67] James became a carter in the city, living with Sarah and their large family in humble circumstances in a rented house in Alexander (today Airedale) Street. Theirs was an existence with its share of tragedy. During December 1882, within the space of four weeks, three of their children died during a scarlatina epidemic.[68]

Thus it came about that after 1878 there were two James Dilworths in Auckland. Though for sixteen years they lived within two miles of one another, their paths, it has been said, never once crossed. Inevitably it became a matter of some curiosity among Aucklanders, both before and after the death of Dilworth of Remuera, why it should be that two men who bore the same name, lived in the same town, and were reputed to be first cousins, had no dealings with one another, and further, why the wealthy landowner should give the humble carter no financial assistance while he lived, nor leave him a legacy upon death. The explanation was simple. Beyond a shared name, the men had little in common. And that little—no more than a remote family link—James senior would have disregarded if, as seems likely, he felt some disrepute was attached to the one-time Pukekohe settler.[69]

At the very time the *Ganges* brought James Dilworth of Portadown to the colony, his Auckland namesake had much on his mind. Within two days, on 16 February 1865, the Auckland and Drury Railway Company was scheduled to begin the construction of its line across his Remuera farm in such a way as to sever it entirely, a momentous development. As well, Dilworth was preoccupied on a personal level with a scheme which meant much to him, the impending arrival of his sister and her sons to settle in Auckland.

After her marriage to George Evans in 1852, Dilworth's sister Esther Ann had migrated with him to California.[70] Over the next ten years the couple had led a transient existence in that State, as George turned his hand initially to goldmining in the north at Shasta, and thereafter to farming, mostly in the southern region about Los Angeles.[71] Shortly after the birth of their last child, George died.* When news began to come through to New Zealand that Esther was both in poor health and struggling to support four children, James and Andrew united to write urging their thirty-seven-year-old sister to come out to New Zealand where they could support her and educate her family.[72] Esther had misgivings; but the arguments of her brothers prevailed. She decided to leave behind in the States, however, her only surviving

---

* One family source recorded, somewhat enigmatically, that Esther and George had simply parted permanently.

daughter Urcilla, to be raised by Esther's older sister (herself an Urcilla) who, though married, was childless.

Andrew travelled to Sydney to await the arrival of Esther and her three sons from San Francisco. Thence he conducted them to Auckland on the trans-Tasman passenger ship, the *Alfred*.[73] (The boys no doubt were delighted to have as fellow passengers from Sydney the 'unique troupe' of the entertainment entrepreneur Mr Foley, returning yet again to the colony with his 'ten first-class performers, fourteen horses, two African zebras, one pony, and also his celebrated troupe of performing dogs and monkeys'.)

Shortly after Esther arrived with her sons—Andrew Thomas aged twelve, John James five, and William three—they went with Uncle Andrew to his Waitakere farm.[74] They were content enough there not least because they got on well with Andrew's American wife, Mary Jane. But the Dilworth uncles had brought the boys to the colony to be educated, and that could be properly done only if they lived in town. (The school nearest to Waitakere was located at Ponsonby: until 1873 children in the Henderson region, if taught locally, had to be instructed by parents at home.) So the two older boys, Andrew and John, were sent to Remuera to live with James and Isabella, and to be enrolled at the local school. Accustomed to a light rein, they were shattered by the harsh discipline of their new colonial school.

Nor was there relief in the solemn big Dilworth home. As the Evans children reported it in later years, all the Dilworth relatives in New Zealand, Uncle Andrew included, 'were very strict in an Old Country

Market Square, Dungannon, in the late nineteenth century.
Royal School of Dungannon Archives

way'. But Uncle James was particularly so, being a stern severe person who thought children should obey adults without question. This galled his nephew Andrew, now thirteen, and a 'high-strung fiery boy' who, it was said, had been accustomed, since the death of his father, to be the 'man of the family'. Before long he was 'in constant rebellion' at James Dilworth's attempts to discipline him.

Esther, by all accounts a woman of independence and ability, who was 'equal to holding her ground with [her brother] James', ended the deadlock. The venture of coming out had failed, she declared. Rather than leave her family 'under James's domination and tutelage', she would return to America and bring them up herself. Dilworth was bitterly disappointed and, according to the version passed down within the Evans family in later years, presented his sister with the ultimatum that 'if she left, she could never expect any further help from him or his estate'. But Esther seems to have been as strong-minded as her brother. She would not budge. But tension eased before she left. She agreed to leave behind with Dilworth and Isabella her middle boy John, regarded within the family as 'kindly, gentle lad'. Yet Dilworth could not forgo a parting shot just before Esther left. The only cure for young Andrew's rebellious nature, he informed her, was to have him enlist on an American man-o-war when they got back to the States.[75] (He never did.)

After her return to America, Esther Evans lived in California and Oregon, before finally settling permanently in Idaho. She supported her family by becoming in turn an art-teacher, a bespoke seamstress and a nurse. Her later life also demonstrated that she had the ability as a parent on her own to raise her family to be honourable, independent adults.

The experiment of leaving John Evans in Auckland failed. After some years* Dilworth returned him to his mother with a letter saying that unfortunately he too was 'rebellious'.[76] The boy seems in fact to have been homesick, and fretful for his family. It is tragic that the shy, severe and (one suspects) lonely uncle and aunt had become so set in their ways that were unable to win the heart of the lad who had been committed to their charge.

The last members of his family whom Dilworth succeeded in bringing to New Zealand were the Mossmans. According to Mossman descendants, James wrote to his sister Eleanor in Canada 'begging her' to migrate with her children.[77] After 'repeated requests', Eleanor and her husband Thomas agreed,[78] doubtless influenced by the prospect of being reunited with their oldest son Jimmy whom they had not seen for four years, although James Dilworth held out financial and career

---
* Two sets of reminiscences specify an actual time for John Evans's life in Auckland: one says three years, the other six.

Eleanor Mossman, James Dilworth's favourite sister; photograph taken 1894.
Mossman family

inducements as well to persuade the family to come. The Mossmans went to London to board the *Winterthur* of the Shaw Savill line, the first available passenger ship for New Zealand. The family group arrived in Auckland on 19 October 1866, a party made up of two parents, two girls and three boys, one of whom was the baby boy Henry A. (Harry).[79] Dilworth installed them in the first house he had had built on his estate, Ivy Cottage, which adjoined the Green (Market) Road. There reunited with their son Jimmy, the Mossmans stayed for some months.

Late in 1866 was not an auspicious time to begin life in the new colony. Auckland was enveloped in a business depression. But at least there was cheap land available in the Waikato. Some was being offered, it was said, 'for a mere trifle' by military settlers abandoning their allotments.[80] And then there was land put to the hammer at Crown auctions in Auckland in early 1867 at upset prices of ten to fifteen shillings an acre. Thomas Mossman, though sixty-six years of age, elected to take up farming once again by buying at ten shillings an acre a fifty-acre block near Hamilton, a settlement not inappropriately described by P. J. Gibbons as being at that time 'stuck out in the middle of nowhere'.[81] A five-pound deposit paid in May 1867 gave him access to this block which he paid off within a year.[82] It remained undeveloped, however, until the Mossman family shifted there in the mid-1870s.

In the meantime the Mossmans, apart from Jimmy, remained in Auckland. In 1868 Dilworth was able to relocate them, moving them on from Remuera where they had been living since arrival, to a farm he had taken possession of in that year as a result of a mortgagee sale.[83] This new farm was close to the Harp of Erin Hotel in the Penrose-Ellerslie area. Thomas and Eleanor worked on this farm, assisted by their three boys, Willie John, Thomas Andrew (usually called Tom) and Harry. The boys also spent part of their time, as they grew older, with their uncle working on the Remuera estate. Willie John in particular is said to have worked there for 'some years'.[84] (Willie John, or 'W. J.' as Dilworth called him, was the nephew who, it will be recalled, was sent by Dilworth to Hawke's Bay to retrieve his runaway elder brother.) Upon the failure of W. J. and later of Dilworth himself to persuade Jimmy to return, W. J. became Jimmy's replacement as worker at Remuera, but not as heir to the Dilworth fortune. Many years later, as an old man, Willie John would recollect ploughing, and planting trees, at Remuera. An easy-going fellow, he got on tolerably well with Dilworth, perhaps because his uncle did not have high expectations of him. Willie John had had little regular schooling in Canada and was devoid of business ability.[85] But to the end Dilworth lived in hope that if his nephew got the right instruction he might just learn to abandon his feckless ways.

Letters written by Dilworth to Willie John in the 1890s bristle with commonsense business advice alternating with the ironic observations

OTHER DILWORTHS

of an adept resigned to the likelihood that his guidance will be disregarded anyway. 'If you ever again complicate yourself or act so thoughtlessly or so foolishly I will positively give you up.'[86] 'I have not said a word to [the land agent] about your or my intentions, *so keep your own counsel*.'[87] Or again, '[Don't] build castles in the air, without saying how you would occupy or maintain them, in fact leaving out the vital parts'.[88] 'There is no use in [my] making remarks. I see you are still "yourself" and will carry out your own views.'[89]

These comments late in their relationship both illuminate Dilworth's personality and explain why, after the final departure of Jimmy Mossman to Australia, Willie John (though next in age to Jimmy) was never regarded by Dilworth as his replacement as sole heir to the Dilworth estate. Nevertheless, while bitterly angry at Jimmy's failure to answer up to what Dilworth considered his family responsibilities (to the point of treating him as if he were dead), Dilworth continued, after 1872, to look on his other Mossman nephews as those who would be his main beneficiaries when he died.

Thomas Russell, who advised Dilworth on the making of his 1873 will.
Russell family

During his visit to England in 1873, Dilworth, acting upon the advice, it seems, of the legendary Thomas Russell* who was then temporarily resident in England, arranged for a firm of London solicitors, Bridger and Collins of King William Street, London Bridge, to draw up a will.[90] Made when Dilworth was fifty-eight, this is the earliest of his wills to survive to the present day. After making a number of bequests and providing for his widow, Dilworth set up a trust whose responsibilities he carefully outlined. The Trust was instructed to:

- secure and administer certain annuities, chief of which were those for Isabella, £350, and Eleanor, £250;
- pay off as soon as possible the £10,000 mortgage on his city properties;
- sell off certain of his Queen Street properties in order to develop the others; and
- generally administer his deceased estate until his Mossman nephews 'excluding the said James Dilworth Mossman for ever' had attained twenty-one years.

His real property was divided in this will into three unequal sections. To the eldest nephew, Willie John, were to go the Ellerslie farms and certain Papakura and Maramarua lands. The portion provided for Tom, the next eldest, was the least valuable, namely land in Mount Eden and on the North Shore, and those Waitakere lands not in the name of Andrew (Uncle James's brother). All other property was to

---

* The Hon. Thomas Russell, lawyer and property entrepreneur, and a man of great persuasiveness, was the dominating figure in Auckland business for much of the second half of the nineteenth century. He shared with Dilworth interests in banking and swamp development. It was he who nominated Dilworth in 1871 for membership in the newly-formed gentlemen's club in Auckland, the Northern Club.

115

go to the youngest nephew, Harry; he, as the designated heir of the residuary estate, was to receive the lion's share of the land, including the Remuera estate, the other farms of the isthmus (called the 'Scoria farms') and the city properties.

This 1873 will was lengthy (over 3,000 words) in its provisions. Certain distinctive features stand out, however. First, Isabella, who was both able in business and much in James's confidence, was nominated as an executor and a trustee, together with her brother Robert Hall and F. C. Lewis, a settler of East Tamaki. Hall, now just over forty, was a most able estate manager—he had been entrusted by Dilworth with the control of his farm lands on a salary of £250 a year. An unusual provision of the will was that sister Eleanor was to 'occupy . . . the House now occupied by me at Remuera [the new homestead?], for the term of her natural life', whereas Isabella 'would enjoy my old House' and all the land 'on the southwest side' of 'Great South Road' (that is, the twenty-two-acre homestead farm); she like Eleanor was to be a life tenant only. Furthermore, to ensure that the lands he had so laboriously accumulated over thirty years of pioneer life would not be dissipated by any nephew neglectful of his oligations to the family, Dilworth had the principle of 'heir in tail' written into his will. As a result, the line of succession to the properties he had 'devised' or passed on was clearly prescribed through certain male members of the Mossman family, the effect of which, 'in default of male issue' among the brothers, was to consolidate the propertied position of Harry Mossman or of the senior male of his branch of the family.

This was not a normal entail will, however, where succession moves to the senior male. The mere selection of Eleanor's youngest son as heir of the residuary estate nullified that principle. A further curious feature of the will was that, at the time it was made, Harry was eight years old, about the same age as James Dilworth had been fifty years before when Anne Dilworth had chosen him as her heir and taken him to live at Mullaghcreevy. And just as Anne had paid for James to be educated at the Royal School of Dungannon, so Dilworth instructed his trustees to set aside during Harry's legal 'infancy' £100 a year for his education.* But the condition that Dilworth attached to H. A. Mossman's succession was the most remarkable feature of all. He declared that within twelve months of Harry's 'attaining the age of twenty-one years' he must drop the name of Mossman and 'assume the surname of "Dilworth" '. Should 'he fail to comply with [this] direction', the will declared, his rights as heir 'shall wholly close . . . as if he were then dead' and succession 'go over to the person next entitled'.

Superficially it would seem that Dilworth chose Harry as heir because, whereas the older brothers Willie John and Tom were almost

---

* At that time, £100 a year was no inconsiderable sum. An adult clerk in a commercial office was paid about that; an artisan was paid only slightly more.

grown men, he was young and therefore malleable. But Dilworth must also be given credit for a deliberate choice; he was a shrewd judge of people. The oral history of the Mossmans speaks of Willie John disqualifying himself from getting on later in life because of his inefficiency and lack of ambition.[91]

Nor did Tom show himself to be particularly able, before he died of a fever at the age of twenty-five. The fact remains that Dilworth could discern in a boy of eight a man of promise. The Mossman oral tradition is that when Harry reached adult years he developed into a tall well-set man revealing the self-same shrewdness and business drive as his very successful uncle. But by then he was no longer the heir. James Dilworth had written another will.

That lay ahead, in an impenetrable future. On the return of Uncle and Aunt Dilworth from England at the end of 1873 the Mossman family could justifiably entertain great expectations.

In or about 1875 Thomas and Eleanor Mossman moved to their Waikato holding, leaving behind Willie John on the Dilworth farm at Remuera. In 1879 they sold up their Waikato farm and went to live in retirement in Hawke's Bay.

CHAPTER EIGHT

Dilworth and the Auckland and Drury Railway Company

FARM PROPERTIES customarily increase in value when traversed by a railway. To this phenomenon Dilworth's farm was an exception. Once severed by the southern railway, the Remuera estate was damaged both as an existing farm and as a future residential subdivision. Yet it cannot be denied that the compensation paid to Dilworth for land lost to, or injured by, the railway company, though less than the amount he had hoped for, greatly strengthened his financial position.

As late as the 1860s there was no shortage of cheap land in the Auckland province. Land-hungry settlers did not rush to buy it up simply because they did not have the money to do so. The banking system was rudimentary. Mortgage money, which was mainly provided by individual capitalists, was never sufficient to meet the demand. Consequently, that minority of settlers who did command funds—whether from past profits as pioneers, or through family wealth, or through the backing of British capitalists—were very well placed to build up a landed estate. Aucklanders (to give a sample only) able to use such a position of advantage were: Frederick Whitaker and Thomas Russell, partners in a very profitable law practice; the Taylor family, farmers in East Tamaki and Mount Albert; James Williamson and Dr John Logan Campbell, merchants; and Edward Costley, a city landlord with tenements all over the place.

Property made the man; and not just because, as in Britain so in the colony, broad acres were considered a badge of social worth. In a very practical way property helped you get on. Providing your real estate was relatively debt-free, it could be a source of continuing income through lease or sale or, if used as security, could become the means of generating loans to develop your estate further, or to strike out in other investment directions. That is how Dilworth used his property over the years. The amount the railway company paid James Dilworth as compensation in 1866 was £6,343. By the standards of the time, this was a considerable sum. It made him one of the substantial debt-free landowners of the settlement, and that at a time when the province was gripped by a slump. But to think of the payments as undeserved good fortune is to forget with what care he went about selecting the location of his farm in 1844.

The scheme to build a southern railway initially arose out of the discovery in 1858 of an economically significant deposit of coal at Waihoihoi, just east of Drury and about twenty-two miles south of Auckland.[1] The find was made on the property of James Farmer, a Scot who speculated in country land while acting as manager of Brown and Campbell's One Tree Hill, the large suburban farm which virtually adjoined Dilworth's Remuera estate.[2]

The possibilities of the field excited interest at all levels in the colony. On 22 December 1858, not long after the mine's discovery, the Austrian frigate *Novara* called in at Auckland on its world tour of goodwill and scientific exploration. At the time of the official reception, Governor Gore Browne successfully urged the expedition's leader to release temporarily his talented young geologist, Ferdinand von Hochstetter, so that he could visit and evaluate the Drury field.[3] Hochstetter's report proved so thorough that the Auckland Provincial Council (of which Dilworth was a member) prevailed on him to stay and carry out further geological surveys. Amongst those was his classical study of the volcanoes of the Auckland region, which included the area of Dilworth's own farm. This geological classification of the two volcanoes which flanked the farm (Mount Hobson and Mount St John) stands well in the light of twentieth-century research, although he seems not to have recognized how much the rich soil cover of the farm, and of its neighbours such as Campbell's One Tree Hill estate, owed to the air-borne deposit from the volcanoes of the Three Kings group.[4]*

Auckland capitalists continued to have high hopes for the Drury coalfield, in spite of Hochstetter's guarded assessment of it. Early in 1861 some of them promoted the Waihoihoi Coal Company, the first company registered in New Zealand under the recently passed Joint Stock Companies Act 1860.[5]

Since the coalfield could be profitably worked only if linked by rail with Auckland, it is not surprising that shortly after the discovery of the deposit in 1858 the construction of a railway had been proposed.[6] But although planning and surveys continued, the scheme was held back by a greater concern—the building up of racial tension that erupted to become the Anglo-Maori Wars of the 1860s. With the

---

* It would have been astonishing had Hochstetter been aware of this. He had to carry out his survey of the volcanic region of the isthmus in a very limited time, with no opportunity for thorough digging or sampling.

Broadway, Newmarket, in the 1860s, showing the encampment of the 40th Regiment (South Lancs). The two large houses are Clovernook (Stitchbury's) on the left, and Highwic (Buckland's) on the right.
Auckland Public Library

beginning of the Waikato campaign in 1863, however, the earlier economic argument for building a railway south from Auckland became reinforced by military considerations. Influential members of the war-time cabinet like the lawyer Thomas Russell, anticipating a swift victory in the field, proposed establishing military settlements at strategic locations within the middle Waikato valley, such as Kirikiriroa (Hamilton) and Horotiu (Cambridge). The advocates of the railway saw therefore an added advantage in constructing it quickly, and extending it well beyond Drury to some point on the lower Waikato River such as Meremere where it could act as a base to service, economically and militarily, the whole Waikato River Valley region.[7] These kinds of arguments influenced the decision of members of the General Assembly to consider favourably a petition of the Auckland Provincial Council for a railway, and to pass, on 14 December 1863, the Auckland Drury Railway Bill.[8]

Under this legislation, the superintendent of Auckland was constituted a corporation for the purposes of the Act, with power to purchase lands compulsorily, and to appoint a board of commissioners as a managing body for the railway company.[9]

In the following year the superintendent was empowered under an amendment to the Act to 'borrow money for the completion and maintenance of the Railway'.[10] Five commissioners, appointed in 1864, chaired by Provincial Councillor Thomas Cheeseman, set about their task of preparing to construct a railway 'commencing on the seabeach, at or near the easterly end of Customhouse Street, in the City of Auckland'. Although the precise route of the line was not settled for some time, it was intended that the railway would cross two tidal bays on the foreshore of the Waitemata Harbour, before passing by tunnel under the Parnell Hill to Newmarket, to pass thence to Drury.[11] Inevitably the railway would pass through James Dilworth's estate. No alternative route out of Newmarket was contemplated.

THE AUCKLAND-DRURY RAILWAY

By early 1865, when the commissioners were ready to authorize construction, Auckland settlers had built up grandiose expectations of the proposed railway. The *Daily Southern Cross* caught the new mood. Its editor told readers that the label 'Auckland and Drury Railway' had become a misnomer. The line to Drury should be looked upon as simply the first stage of a main trunk route to Wellington. The Auckland Provincial Council had already decided, off its own bat, to continue the survey of the line beyond Drury to the Waikato River. Only by extending the railway in that direction, remarked the editor of the *Cross*, would it be possible to divert the present 'tide of immigration' away from the South Island 'towards the fertile lands of Waikato hitherto lying waste'.[12]

On a fine mid-February afternoon in 1866 about 200 people went to James Dilworth's farm to gather on a field bordering Manukau Road midway between Newmarket and the Junction Hotel at the corner of Great South Road. As the landowner to be most affected by early line formation, Dilworth had put his paddock at the disposal of the railway commissioners for the ceremony of turning the first sod.[13] This was carried out by the superintendent Robert Graham who, after using his spade 'in a workmanlike manner' according to the reporter there, announced 'amid the acclamations of the assemblage' that the railway was 'now commenced'. Guests then withdrew for a special luncheon provided in three interconnected marquees standing nearby. The provincial council had voted £200 for the celebrations. We can assume the whole allocation was spent. Over the next four hours 'an excellent and sumptuous collection . . . of viands' was washed down by 'wines and varied liquors' rated by one guest as 'of a superior class'. There was much speechmaking, and something like twenty toasts were drunk, each accompanied by a different tune played by a band stationed outside the main marquee. The toasts and speeches tended to catch the ardently patriotic tone of Auckland at that time, and particularly honoured the army and navy. Nor was the Auckland volunteer militia forgotten. Though these part-time soldiers had never heard a shot fired in anger, yet—in the opinion of the chairman of the commissioners—they 'had stood nobly in the way of danger for the purpose of the defending their homes and hearths from the invasion of savages'.

The politicians who spoke at the luncheon were optimistic. Even though they were prepared to admit that the Bill had been hastily prepared and (in the words of one speaker) 'passed in a very crude and imperfect state', yet costs of construction, they were sure, would be low. Thomas Cheeseman believed that the first section of the railway would be completed very cheaply; 'something less than £2,000 per mile'. (This was in contrast to the comparable stretch of Great South Road nearby which had cost £6,000 per mile.) Cheeseman miscalculated badly. He failed to anticipate engineering problems. Nor did he reckon upon the extent of the claims for compensation by owners

Robert Graham, provincial superintendent 1862–65, and Dilworth's near neighbour at Ellerslie.
Alexander Turnbull Library

121

through whose property the railway had to pass—above all, Dilworth's claim, which he was at that very time preparing.

Two days after the ceremony, the Auckland superintendent notified Dilworth that he intended to use his powers of compulsory purchase to take for purposes of railway construction a strip of land eight-and-three-quarter acres in area* and ninety chains in length, running from one end of Dilworth's Remuera estate to the other.[14] The letter also informed Dilworth just how he and any other landowner could go about satisfying any claim 'for purchase price and payment for loss, damage, or injury arising out of taking of land or construction work thereon'. Neither the extent of land taken nor the timing of the forced sale was a surprise to Dilworth. Provincial surveyors had been measuring up his estate for months and purchase had been in the air much longer than that. As far back as 1862 he and certain other neighbouring landowners had been approached by a select committee of the provincial council which had been planning a railway route. Committee members, we are told, were taken aback at that time when they learned how much landowners proposed to claim in compensation.[15]

By 1865 Dilworth's claim was easily the largest of those confronting the railway commissioners. Yet the Remuera landowner was not out to make money. He later claimed that he 'took no steps whatever to oppose the passing of the Railway Bill through the House'.[16] But he clearly would have preferred the line not to have run through his estate, whatever the level of compensation. He well knew that once his farm was completely severed it would be much more difficult to run. And that was the lesser part of the long-term damage to his interests. A local auctioneer and land agent, George Sibbins, said of the Remuera farm at the time: 'I know of hardly a piece of land as good for cutting up as that land'.[17] Dilworth agreed. He was convinced that, once the railway line had gone through, the value of his remaining land would be much lower. A recent subdivision almost on Dilworth's doorstep, so to speak, would have alerted him to how profitable it could be for him to cut up his own farm into housing sites.[18] A fellow Ulsterman, James Williamson[19]—whose Irish origins are commemorated in the name Erin Street—had formerly owned a block of land bordering on what is now the site of the main buildings and grounds of the senior Dilworth School.† Between 1848 and 1855, Williamson, who made a fortune in early Auckland mainly through the sale of alcohol, spent upwards of £2,000 in buying up for speculative purposes about seventy acres of land lying between Mount St John and the Junction Hotel

---

* The area of land ultimately taken was somewhat reduced, but the damage did not much abate.

† Williamson, an ardent land speculator, subsequently became a very wealthy man and in the 1870s built the finest house in Auckland, The Pah. He was penniless at the time of his death in 1888, however. (See Chapter Fourteen.)

THE AUCKLAND-DRURY RAILWAY

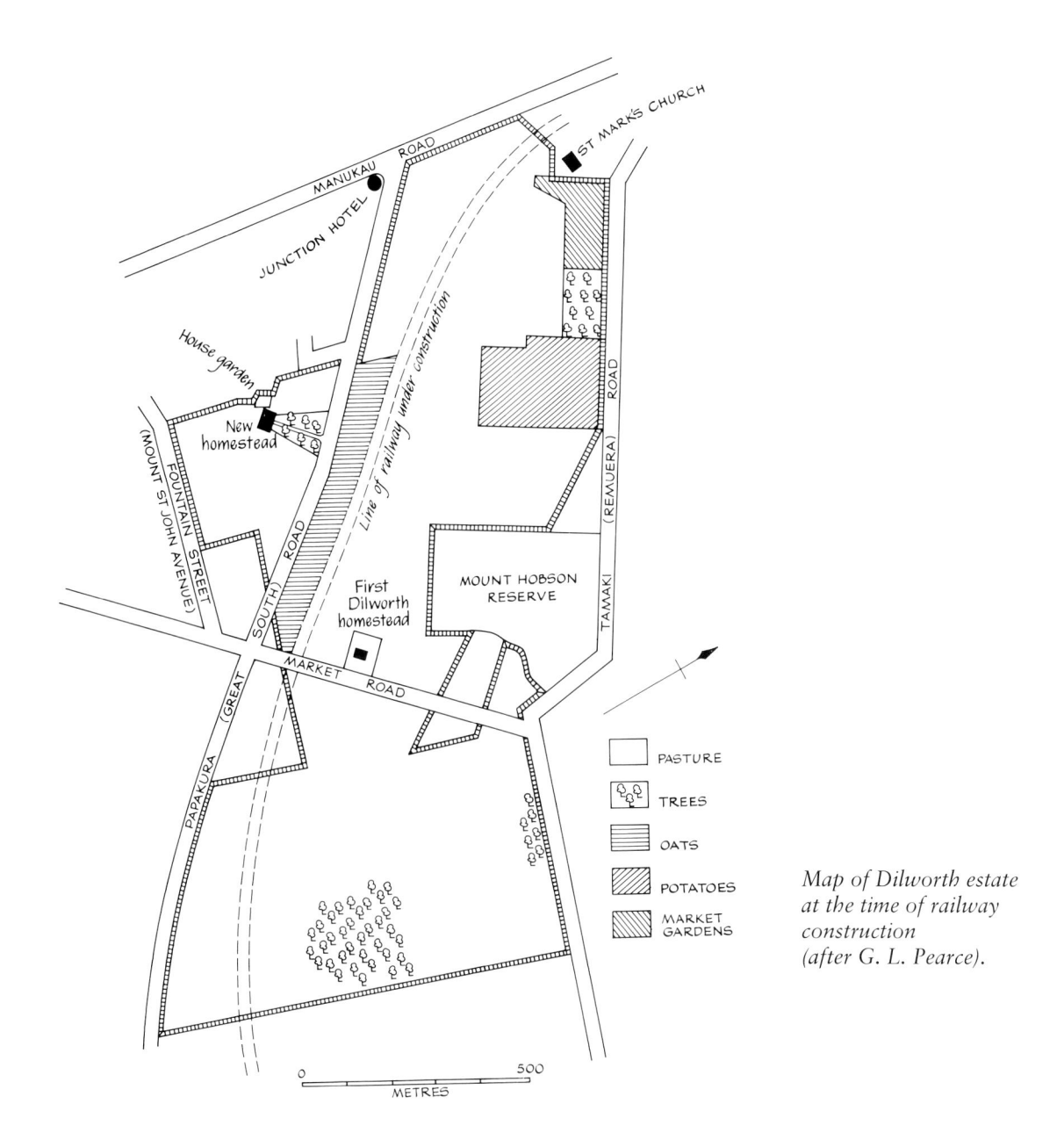

Map of Dilworth estate at the time of railway construction (after G. L. Pearce).

Captain Henry Hardington, who auctioned the Village of Mount St John in 1859.
Auckland Public Library

located at the corner of Manukau and Great South Roads. This was just one of the many parcels of land Williamson owned, scattered over the city and province.

On 22 July 1859 Williamson sold for £7,500 the seventy-acre block to one Henry Hardington, an auctioneer and commission agent.[20] Hardington, with the financial backing of Captain Gladwin Wynyard,* quickly subdivided the block, put in dedicated roads and held a public auction for what he called the Village of Mount St John. Bidding was keen. A deed of conveyance dated 3 September 1859 records that Hardington sold allotments 'to many and diverse persons', one of whom was James Dilworth himself.[21] Dilworth took the opportunity to buy eight adjacent sections, each about one-and-a-quarter acres, to round off the homestead part of his farm standing on the south side of Great South Road so that it continued as far back as Fountain Street (today's Mount St John Avenue), giving him a 400-foot street frontage there.

He paid £1,175 for the sections: about £118 per acre.† How well financially, each in his different way, Williamson, Hardington and Wynyard did out of the speculation, would not have been lost on so astute a property investor as Dilworth. And what happened with Mount St John became a distinct trend in the early 1860s. Between 1862 and 1864, such was the rush onto the market of suburban farms, in areas as diverse as Remuera, Epsom and Avondale, to be cut up into villa sites and farmlets (usually ten acres or less) that newspapers were full of talk of the prevailing 'land mania'.[22]

After the obligatory twenty-one days' notice to landowners, railway contractors began construction.[23] Work went on simultaneously in two separate sections: on the Auckland shoreline, and on the stretch between Newmarket and today's Greenlane railway station. In both sections the contractors ran into serious though quite unconnected engineering problems. As navvies began excavating the Dilworth estate to create a line of even gradient between Newmarket and a high point near Market Road—then called the Green Road—they struck, unexpectedly, two large beds of solidified lava. This was particularly bad luck. Unlike neighbouring Mount Eden, which in its eruptive phase had been a 'great lava-producer', Mount Hobson and Mount St John, between which Dilworth's farm lay, were primarily (as E. J. Searle the vulcanologist has categorized them) 'effusive scoria cones' with but 'minor flows', and those few in number.[24] What was not known until

---

* Captain Gladwin John Richard Wynyard was the son of Col. R. H. Wynyard, senior military officer in the colony 1851–58. When Wynyard's regiment, the 58th, returned to England, he elected to remain in the colony. Advancing money on landed security was a favoured investment for well-to-do officers in Auckland while it was the capital, 1840–65.

† Because Dilworth paid in cash the sections would have cost him less than if sold to normal buyers who would make at most a down-payment of one-third and leave the remainder as a mortgage advance from the subdividers.

construction work began in 1865 was that two lava outflows—the only two of consequence in the whole region—had breached the south wall of the cone of Mount Hobson to lie perversely hidden beneath a mantle of weathered tuff and ash along the route of the line.[25] Consequently, the railway constructors had to blast their way laboriously through large beds of solidified basaltic rock. The railway commissioners reported in the first year of construction that there was already a cost overrun of £5,000 in 'the excavation of rock in Mr Dilworth's paddocks'.[26] Steep rock cuttings, which caused costly delays to the work of the railway company, reinforced Dilworth's conviction that, so injurious was the severance of his estate proving, only a high compensation would satisfy him. He also decided to ask the railway commissioners to build no fewer than twelve bridges to allow free movements of stock between the two now-separated parts of his farm.[27]

In August 1865 the railway commissioners offered Dilworth as compensation the sum of £4,361 18s 7½d.[28] They also pointed out that if he was dissatisfied with this sum, he could elect to have a final figure set by arbitrators. Dilworth rejected the initial offer and made a counter-claim of £13,426, writing that he 'regretted exceedingly' having to nominate any amount at all—better left entirely, in his opinion, to the deliberation of the arbitrators—but that he did so only because he was thus obliged under the provisions of the Act.[29] He nominated as his arbitrator 'James Macky of Papatoitoi' to whom he was related by marriage through his wife Isabella.[30] The superintendent's arbitrator was Alfred Buckland of Newmarket, a near-neighbour of Dilworth and a highly-regarded judge of rural land values.[31] But these two men, after hearing the evidence of a number of witnesses, could not agree.[32] At that point the dispute was referred to the Supreme Court.

Dilworth took five months over the preparation of the case to be presented there. He commissioned ten experts, most of them land agents but also some civil engineers, to provide reports on how the construction of the railway would adversely affect the operation of his estate and depreciate its value. A team of expert witnesses of a comparable number, but overall, it seems, of somewhat lesser professional weight, was gathered together by the railway commissioners to oppose Dilworth's claim. It had earlier been the opinion of the superintendent's legal advisers that the Dilworth claim 'will probably be better disposed of by a Jury';[33] but the hearing ultimately took place before a single umpire, Auckland's senior magistrate Thomas Beckham, in the Banco division of the Supreme Court. Though vain and inclined to be pompous, Beckham was a good choice, for he had a fine record for adjudicating fairly between contending parties in difficult cases such as this. F. M. P. Brookfield, with R. W. Wynn as junior counsel, appeared for Dilworth. T. B. Gillies, a combative barrister recently arrived from Otago, represented the railway commissioners. There was no love lost between counsel. Brookfield, a restrained punctilious man, complained during the hearing of Gillies's 'somewhat coarse invective and assertions' in his attempt to asperse some of the witnesses testifying in Dilworth's cause.[34]

The Court sat for many hours in intermittent hearings held between 15 January and 10 February 1866. Both lawyers looked on the case as a landmark one. Brookfield remarked:

> In this province public works of this character are in their infancy. . . . It is of the utmost importance that the true principle for ascertaining the value of lands taken compulsorily, should be fully investigated and laid down.

Gillies also saw the case as important, and 'not only in regard to the large amount of money involved', but as 'especially important' in establishing 'definite principles' which would 'extend far beyond this special use' and would act as a precedent in future instances where a balance must be struck between private property rights and public advantage.

> We, in this colony, are but in the infancy of great public works of various kinds, which will necessitate the taking of private property for public welfare; it will be a sad thing for the province, if, by the grasping greed of proprietors, backed by the inflated ignorance of land-jobbers, the progress of such great works would be arrested or retarded.[35]

That Dilworth had a strong case for substantial damages was never in dispute. Because his estate of 195 acres was long and narrow, it was particularly injured by a railway line which traversed it from end to end. Admittedly, the actual area of land forcibly purchased, just over seven acres, was not great.

But the strip which was taken varied in width—according to whether it was needed for line alone, or cutting or siding—in a fashion that the architect Reader Wood, one of Dilworth's expert witnesses, considered 'inconvenient, ugly and awkward'. Slopes and undulations on the estate necessitated cuttings as deep as eight metres yet often shading away to nothing. The major cuttings at either end of the estate (the one near Newmarket and the other near Market Road) had the effect, in Brookfield's opinion, of 'dividing Mr Dilworth's property in its entire length by two great ditches or moats'.[36]

For their part, the railway commissioners did not dispute the three broad grounds on which Dilworth made his claim:

1. the quantity of land taken for railway purposes, its value being assessed on how much it could have sold for, to the best possible advantage, in February 1865, the date of compulsory purchase;
2. compensation for being subject to forced sale; and
3. compensation for severance of the estate.

But it was on this third issue, as to how far the estate was really damaged once it was severed by the railway, that the views of the contending parties diametrically diverged.

Both parties agreed (though Dilworth and his counsel with great reluctance) that the law as it stood did not allow for 'prospective damages'.[37] Gillies construed this restriction as meaning that the only value that could be attached to land taken or damaged was what it would have realized pro rata had the estate been sold on the open market for cash in February 1865 for farming purposes, either as one lot or as separate fields, 'according to the then subdivision'.[38]

Whenever hearings took place, Dilworth's counsel contested this interpretation. Even though consideration of 'prospective damages', as Brookfield admitted, was out of court, it was impossible not to take into account how adversely railway severance had affected the future 'carving up into building sites' of 'Mr Dilworth's beautiful estate'.[39] Before the railway was put through, the farm was generally regarded as the Auckland suburban real estate with the greatest potential for residential subdivision. Land agents said it had everything in its favour.[40] Close to the city, with superior soil and gentle slopes, long and narrow and lying between two almost parallel main roads, this was a farm ideally suited for dividing into villa lots of two acres or less, as had been done for Mount St John Village, or into 'fancy farms' (as they were sometimes called) of up to ten acres, which were becoming common in Epsom. In Epsom and Mount Eden the aspiring gentry of the city were beginning to build in a semi-rural setting, to plant orchards and groves of trees, and to graze horses or run a few stock. Epsom was just the place, enthused a local almanac, 'to be inhabited by those who are in a position to keep up carriages', or 'whose business does not require their constant presence in Auckland [city]'.[41]

Edwin Davy, a land agent and a witness in Dilworth's cause, informed Mr Beckham that during the recent land boom Mount St John land which was a mere stone's throw from Dilworth's land had sold for between £350 and £400 per acre.[42] Dilworth himself deposed in court that his new neighbour David Limond Murdoch, the bank manager, had told him he had paid £470 to £480 an acre for land there—presumably to round off the grounds on which his recently built mansion Prospect now stood. Dilworth's view was that Murdoch had got this land for under its true value. 'I would not [have sold] the piece of land for that money, if I had had it', he informed the umpire.[43]

The idea was to gain general currency in the twentieth century that, during his lifetime, Dilworth was essentially an 'improving farmer', with no interest whatsoever in subdividing his lands near the city. This view is a misconception, understandable however in the light of the obstacles that he, beyond the grave as it were, placed in the path of trustees of his estate who (he feared) would be tempted to realize quickly on his most valuable property, by cutting up the Remuera farm into farmlets or residential allotments. Yet as Brookfield informed the

T. B. Gillies, robed as a judge in the later 1870s.
As an advocate of the Railway Company in 1866 he opposed Dilworth's compensation claim.
Auckland Museum Library

umpire in 1866 such a scheme had been in the Irish settler's mind from the time he first began building up his Remuera landed estate. An important aspect of Dilworth's claim for compensation had to be, therefore, the 'permanent injury' inflicted, because he was now

> totally prevented from doing that which, for a long course of years, Mr Dilworth has had the fixed intention of doing. I can scarcely believe that you, sir, would allow a dream of upwards of twenty years duration be suddenly broken in upon by the Auckland and Drury Railway.[44]

Witnesses called before the umpire on Dilworth's behalf spoke of 'blind alleys having been caused by the railway', of back allotments 'rendered useless'. The severance brought about by the line made the subdivision into small farms difficult and the creation of through roads from Remuera Road to Great South Road impossible.[45] An English expert reported that the property had been destroyed for 'superior building purposes', and its overall value had been depreciated overnight by 'at least twenty percent'.[46]

Such arguments cut little ice with Gillies. 'Extravagant estimates and fanciful claims' (he said) should have no place in this hearing. 'The public should pay only for injured realities', not for the 'shattered dreams' of a would-be subdivider.[47] By all means let there be 'full justice' in payment to Mr Dilworth for that part of his land which was lost or injured, but not at the cost of forgetting that this railway was 'a great public work which made his remaining land more valuable'. The principle at stake was that 'a private individual should not reap the greatest advantage from the forced sale of his property' since 'he himself, being one of the general public, reaps advantage as one of the public'.[48]

Beckham seems to have agreed with the position taken by Gillies for the railway commissioners that, in assessing compensation, the value of Dilworth's land must be determined on the basis of its 1865 character *as a farm*. Yet even on that limited interpretation Dilworth could still have hoped for liberal damages. Severance had seriously injured the estate, and that in ways which bridges and crossings, be they ever so many, could only partially put right. Henceforward, routine farming practice, above all ploughing fields, moving stock and safely fencing them in, must become much more difficult. The greatest damage to the farm *qua* farm, however, was the way in which the line, almost immediately after entering the estate at the Newmarket end, shut off the great bulk of the estate from its only perennial source of water, the well which was fed by subterranean springs at that point.*

---

* This well was one of a group found in the Newmarket area whose underground supplies of water usually came from higher land by means of lava caves. It originally overflowed to cross what is now Remuera Road to become the wakamatenga or headwater of Te Ruareoreo, the steam which was the eastern boundary of the 3,000-acre block of land sold to Hobson by the Ngatiwhatua in 1840 to become Auckland, the colony's capital.

Samuel Cochrane, the land agent, remarked that at one stroke 'the head of the estate had been severed from the body'. Before 1866 stock could roam at will to the water. Thereafter in times of drought farm-workers would have to drive cattle over bridges or gated level-crossings to the pond, two to three times a day.

After a lengthy hearing the umpire awarded Dilworth compensation money of £6,343, to be regarded as being 'in full satisfaction of the purchase money of the land [7 acres, 2 roods, 25 perches] and of the damage sustained by him by reason of the severance of the said land'.[49] It was decided that the extent of 'accommodation works'—bridges and crossings over the line—would be separately determined by two justices of the peace. Beckham then formed an arbitration board made up of himself and D. B. Thornton, JP, a local miller. After hearing representations on behalf of the railway commissioners and of Dilworth, the arbitrators directed 'that the said James Dilworth shall be accommodated with Three Crossings by Bridges sufficient for the traffic of Carts, and Two Level Crossings, which accommodation works shall be completed within a term of six calendar months from this date [2 May 1866]'.[50]

Both arbitration awards fell well short of what Dilworth had wanted. Valuators and skilled witnesses who appeared on his side during the Banco hearing had recommended a compensation award either around Dilworth's figure £13,426 or a figure considerably in excess of that. They were, admittedly, Dilworth's witnesses; but a number of witnesses called by the railway company made estimates of what they thought was appropriate compensation which were well above the £6,343 awarded by the umpire. In making so moderate an award Beckham obviously refused to attach to the estate a hypothetical value it could have had as a future residential subdivision. He may well have been influenced, also, by the well-publicized financial problems of the railway commissioners who had already badly exceeded their budget.[51]

Yet it would be wrong to conclude that Dilworth had had a financial setback. He was fortunate that the valuation placed on the farm was tied to February 1865, just before Auckland's so-called 'land mania' came to an end, and not to February 1866 when Auckland was in the midst of a depression, and suburban land had become a drug on the market.[52] And though severance by rail made his farm harder to work in the years ahead, the strengthening of his financial position by a capital inflow in 1866, a time when most settlers were having serious liquidity problems, not only served him well then, but also equipped him for the property forays he was to make in the 1870s.

Once the award was made, Dilworth, who had an unquestioning respect for strict legality (which others took for hard-fistedness on those occasions when legality seemed to work to his advantage), accepted its terms without protest or obvious bitterness. That could not be said

JAMES DILWORTH

of his reaction to the more trifling JPs' award which had given him three bridges not the twelve for which he had asked. Over the next year or so he kept up a running battle with the railway commissioners over the three bridges and two level-crossings they had been obliged to provide.

Relations with regard to these construction works began peaceably. A week after Beckham and Thornton had made their award, Dilworth proposed to the provincial government that if it would pay directly to him the money set aside for the bridges and level-crossings, he would undertake to construct them himself.[53] Vexed with problems enough over the railway, the commissioners were happy to agree, providing that expenditure on each bridge did not exceed £300, and on each crossing twenty-five pounds.[54] The commissioners would have been less prompt in taking up Dilworth's offer had they appreciated that his main motive in making it had been to ensure that the works would be placed just where he considered they would least disrupt his farm's operations, and not where the railway engineer, for structural reasons, wanted them to be.

Mechanics' Bay viewed from Constitutional Hill during the construction of the Auckland-Drury railway. At the foot of the hill, shaped as a hollow square, is the Maori hostel.
Alexander Turnbull Library

Shortly after, Dilworth wrote to the superintendent claiming 'the right of fixing the localities where the bridges should be placed, providing that if placed in such positions they will not interfere with the working of the Railway'.[55] He then nominated sites for his five crossings which were different from, and involved a more costly construction than, those already fixed upon by engineer, James Stewart of the railway company. A rumpus ensued. This, the superintendent peremptorily brought to an end when he informed Dilworth that, acting on the advice of the provincial solicitor, he believed he had no option but to return the matter to arbitration.[56]

The mere threat was enough to bring Dilworth round. He wrote to His Excellency in conciliatory fashion, assuring him it was 'not necessary to appoint an arbitrator. If you will cause an unprejudiced calculation to be made, I will accept it, or make an offer myself on favourable terms'.[57] He followed this up with another letter suggesting that 'the Provincial Treasurer and Provincial Accountant' be 'appointed to adjust matters between us', assuring the superintendent that he would yield to their revised figure.[58] He introduced one new provision which the government promptly conceded as reasonable: that this final figure should incorporate a sum which, capitalized, would provide an annual income for the upkeep of the crossings. (For some years prior to this date, Dilworth had granted to residents of Epsom and beyond, right of way over his estate to go to services at Saint Mark's, or on business to Newmarket. Inevitably, the bridges and other crossings would also be used by the public and subject therefore to additional wear and tear.) Consequently, the sum of £2,050 offered to Dilworth to construct the works included a payment of £242 12s to be an interest-bearing fund to finance annual maintenance.[59] But, that figure fixed, Dilworth and the commissioners continued to bicker about these crossings until the middle of 1867 when work on the Auckland-Drury line was abandoned for lack of finance.[60]

For a few years the scheme went into a kind of limbo. The provincial council sold off some miles of unutilized rail, and items of rolling stock, to the Bay of Islands Coal Company formed in 1868 to operate a mine out of Kawakawa, in Northland.[61] Vogel's great public works scheme, however, resurrected Auckland's southern railway, and in a much more ambitious form. Section 12 of the Railways Act 1870 authorized the resumed construction of a line from Auckland to Tuakau (but as part of a trunk scheme which would open up the Waikato and beyond), and also provided for a branch line from Penrose to Onehunga.[62] Both of these lines were ultimately to be to Dilworth's financial advantage: in the 1870s he acquired extensive lands in the Taupiri region, in the 1880s in the upper Thames Valley—both blocks opened up and increased in value by this Waikato railway. The small branch line to Onehunga acted similarly. It ran close to two of his outer suburban farms, as yet largely undeveloped, one near Penrose station

JAMES DILWORTH

and the other between Te Papapa and the Manukau Harbour. It also passed through another property, close to Mount Smart, which fell into his hands in the early 1880s.

In January 1872, Brogden and Sons, the English firm under contract to the general government to carry out much of its new programme of railway construction, resumed work on the Auckland railway left incomplete by the commissioners. Whereas the commissioners had been dilatory, Brogden's was decisive. Deploying large numbers of workers, the contractors put through the job speedily. On 17 November 1873, as a goodwill gesture, Brogden's allowed the railway line which they had just completed, but not yet officially handed over to the government, to be used by a train which brought about 250 passengers from Auckland to Ellerslie to take part in the opening of the cricket

Parnell tunnel on the Auckland-Drury Line c. 1873. The locomotive is of the type used in drawing the first passenger-carriages to Onehunga.
Alexander Turnbull Library

season on the playing fields of the entrepreneur Robert Graham, another of Dilworth's near neighbours.[63]

The Auckland to Onehunga line was officially opened on 20 December 1873 when, at one o'clock in the afternoon, the first train left the Point Britomart terminus in Auckland.[64] We can well imagine how a few minutes later on that Saturday afternoon, James and Isabella Dilworth viewed, from the front of their home, the sturdy little locomotive named Ada hauling four carriages with 200 passengers up the incline of the Dilworth estate en route to Onehunga. The train took a bare twenty minutes to cross the narrow landbridge linking the Pacific Ocean and the Tasman Sea; the first crossing of the Tamaki isthmus made by a modern mode of transport. It was a memorable occasion, celebrated at Onehunga with bunting, a banquet and enthusiastic speeches.

On Christmas Eve 1873 the regular train service between Auckland and Onehunga began. The journey could be made by passengers for as little as one shilling 'without the jogging and jolting that' (in the view of a contemporary reporter) 'makes bus travel almost unbearable'. Thereafter trains crossing and re-crossing Dilworth's farm several times a day became an unremarked feature of life for those who lived nearby.

CHAPTER NINE

Graham's Hill

THREE EXTINCT volcanic tuff cones dominate the skyline of the central Auckland isthmus. The Maori of old gave to these hills the names of Maungawhau, Maungakiekie and Remuwera (now universally misspelt 'Remuera'). Each is splendid in its own way. Maungawhau (Mount Eden) was and is a superb look-out, commanding views of the whole isthmus and of the enclosing waterways which give access to it: little wonder it was a key to the defence system of the ancient Maori tribes possessing Tamaki-makau-rau. Maungakiekie (One Tree Hill) is the most beautiful of the hills; its shape, the harmonious relationship of its features and its superb earthworks ensure that. Remuera (Mount Hobson), more modestly proportioned, conceals its greatest attraction except to those who make the effort to climb to its top; a northward view of warm slopes falling away to the Waitemata Harbour, of islands of the Hauraki Gulf—Rangitoto above all—and, far off, the Cape Colville Range. Logan Campbell, the most blasé of travellers when he published his classic *Poenamo* in 1881,

View from Mount Hobson towards Orakei Basin, (north-east), late nineteenth century.
Dilworth Trust Board Archives

described this panorama as one 'of infinite beauty ... pre-eminent, unequalled, unsurpassed'. This explains why, among nineteenth-century artists such as Merrett, Kinder, Hoyte, Kennett Watkins and others, the summit of Mount Hobson was so popular a vantage point.

Remuera came into being over 20,000 years ago when the earth's surface in this unstable region was pierced by an explosive eruption, which built up by airfall around its crater a conical hill of ash, and frothed-up lava called scoria.[1] Later, the wall of the cone was breached on its southern side by two flows of molten rock, the first to the south-east as far as Farmer's Hill near where Omahu Road now meets Great South Road; the second and narrower flow, in a westerly direction almost as far as modern Newmarket. It was the second of these solidified outflows through which contractors for both the nineteenth-century railway and the twentieth-century motorway had to blast their path.

The pre-European Maori people altered the regular slopes of Remuwera by terracing it, especially on the steeper eastern side, for defence and habitation.[2] But the pa they created was of more modest proportions than those say on Maungakiekie, Maungawhau, Maungarei (Mount Wellington) or Mangere Mountain.

Like a number of Maori place-names, Remuwera can be variously translated. It means literally the burnt edge (of a skirt). Some students of Maori lore have considered the name to be a metaphorical reference to the killing and subsequent cooking in a hangi (oven) of a high-born Maori woman. But in the view of one modern expert on the place names of Tamaki-makau-rau, no one interpretation of Remuwera (hereafter Remuera or Mount Hobson) is 'really convincing'.[3]

The talented young Austrian geologist, Ferdinand von Hochstetter, who in 1859 made a descriptive study of the volcanic region of Auckland, praised the 'excellence' and 'richness' of the soils derived from the volcanoes. He went on to remark that:

> It is curious to observe how the shrewder among the settlers, without any geological knowledge, have picked out the tuff craters for themselves, while those with less acute powers of observation have quietly sat down upon the cold [and by implication] less fertile tertiary clays.[4]

By 1844 James Dilworth had shown he had a good business head. In his purchase of land between Mount Hobson and Mount St John, covered by a mantle of rich brown-red soil derived from volcanic ash, Dilworth had also demonstrated he was one of those shrewd judges of farming land spoken of by Hochstetter.[5] Dilworth would dearly have loved to have bought from the aboriginal owners the summit of Mount Hobson and its warm northern slopes as well. That he did not is simply explained. Wily George Graham beat him in the race to get it, probably because Graham beat the gun in the first place. In time Dilworth was able to persuade Graham to sell that farm to him; but he never became the owner of the main part of the hill itself. Why, is the concern of what now follows.

A story told over the years has become an entrenched part of Dilworth mythology. One day in the early 1860s (the story runs) as Dilworth gazed from the front door of his home it dawned on him that all the land he could see before him was his—save for the summit of Mount Hobson, a Crown reserve. From that day began his quest for this land. Certainly, Dilworth's persistent pursuit of Graham's Hill bordered almost on obsession. But he was no latter-day version of Ahab in pursuit of Naboth's vineyard.[6] Acquisitiveness, to be sure, was part of his nature; covetousness not. Why then this infatuation with a hill of little economic worth? Perhaps County Tyrone has its answer. No one who has mounted the low drumlin at Mullaghcreevy and trodden the soil of the rath beside which the old Dilworth homestead once stood could fail to see the similarity between it and the terraced hill fort at Remuera. One wonders whether in Dilworth's mind the Maori pa had become the Celtic ring-fort and its associated townland of which he had been deprived by unkind fate. If this were so then by winning Mount Remuera he was in a sense reclaiming a heritage that had been lost. We can suspect this; but we will never know. Of one thing there is no doubt: that he came to believe sincerely the land was his as of right. It is equally certain that his decision to try to get the hill did not arise out of any revelation of the moment. Even before he bought the land adjoining Mount Hobson in the 1840s it had been his intention to lay claim to the summit as well.

In the early days of European settlement, Mount Hobson was popularly known as Graham's Hill, after George Graham, its original buyer. It continued to have that name for many years, and is so called in Dilworth's 1894 will. Graham was a man of consequence in the pioneer capital. After training in England as a clerk of works in the Board of Ordnance (Royal Engineers), he ended up in New Zealand after five years' service in Australia, being one of the official party Captain Hobson brought with him to found the new colony. He was present at the Waitangi meeting when the treaty was first signed. He came to Auckland on 27 November 1840, on the ship *Diana*, in the company of a detachment of British troops. For some time he lived in a bell-tent just above the shoreline in Commercial Bay, probably until 14 April 1841 when the first Crown sale of town allotments took place. He made a successful bid of £270 for a three-eighths of an acre allotment in Shortland Crescent on which he put up a residence he called Frogmore Cottage. During the early days of the capital there were few settlers busier than he. It was under his supervision that skilled Maori stone-masons put up the massive stone wall, with flanking bastions and loopholes for rifles, which enclosed the twenty-one-acre barracks complex on the site of what is now Albert Park and the

University's Old Arts Building.* In later years Graham became a philo-Maori. He opposed the Government of the day over the Waikato war of the 1860s, and the confiscations which followed it.

Already by 1844 a seasoned land speculator, Graham was one of the first Pakeha settlers to take advantage of FitzRoy's proclamation of 26 March 1844 waiving Crown pre-emption to buy some of the most highly prized volcanic land in the central isthmus. His later claim that within a week of the proclamation he had effective control of an eighty-acre block, made up of Mount Hobson and its lower slopes adjoining Tamaki Road, suggests he had been very quick off the mark.[7] So quick, it may be assumed that, like a number of shrewd Pakeha buyers, Graham had approached Maori owners and paid a deposit to secure land in advance of the waiver. The completed payment of £79 10s to the owners, Epiha Putini, Aperahama and Te Hene, of the Ngati Maoho and Ngati Te Ata tribes, was not written into a deed until 14 October 1844.[8†] But as early as 2 April Graham had so little doubt that the land, recently the site of Maori cultivations, had become incontestably his, that he began to develop a European-style farm upon it. By the end of 1844, Maori and Pakeha labourers, housed in three whares which Graham had had put up to accommodate them, had sown twenty-five acres in wheat and enclosed almost two-thirds of the property by a fencing system involving a ditch, and bank with a hurdle top.[9]

Development continued. During Commissioner Matson's investigation of the claim beginning on 27 March 1847, Graham testified that by then he had 'a considerable portion under cultivation and fenced, and two European servants living [permanently] on the same'. He added that he 'frequently employed . . . several natives' and now had in place 'a barn and stockyard'.[10]

After hearing the evidence, Major Matson recommended that a confirmatory grant be made to Graham based on the eighty-one acres he had purchased. But later in the year Graham heard by way of tittle-tattle from the surveyor-general's office that the upper part of the hill, some of which was covered with fine native trees, was to be withheld from him, presumably for later use as a scoria quarry. Graham protested to the colonial secretary, claiming that as a bona fide settler who had 'spent nearly four hundred pounds upon this property' he was entitled to the whole eighty-one acres. 'I need scarcely point out what a nuisance it will be to have a portion of the mountain left for Natives or others to squat upon and overlook my orchards and other grounds.'[11]

---

* Within the barracks wall Graham was responsible for the construction of the soldiers' quarters, military hospital, magazines and stores.

† There were two payments, both in cash: on 17 June 1844, £67 10s; on 14 October 1844, ten pounds; these were the dates payment was noted in the deeds. Payment probably was made earlier.

Governor Grey turned down the application with a not untypical mixture of high-handedness and self-righteousness. In a minute to his colonial secretary he explained that as the land was 'required for public purposes' (which he did not specify) it 'must then be necessarily reserved. At the same time the Government will neither permit the trees to be destroyed, nor the Natives to squat upon the Land'.[12]

The Crown grant issued on 15 November 1847 fell far short, therefore, of the area Graham once imagined would be his. He was given fifty-nine-and-a-quarter acres, reservation being made not only of Mount Hobson, but also, without warning, of a perpetual spring on the eastern side of the property, with an access right-of-way leading to it from Manukau Road.[13] Though obviously much put out by the loss of this land, Graham made no formal protest (a damaging omission in point of law) probably because in the meantime he had decided to sell it anyway. He placed his property in the hands of Connell and Ridings, the town's main land agents. Dilworth moved swiftly to buy. This adjoining land would neatly round off his own farm and give it a lengthy Tamaki (Remuera) Road frontage. By 13 May 1848 the terms were settled.* Dilworth paid £800, a large sum given that the block was encumbered by a lease with four years still to run (at sixty pounds per annum); £300 was to be paid in cash and £500 to remain as a five-year mortgage bearing ten per cent interest.[14] Specifically exempted from the land sold was an area of 'one acre or thereabouts' which Graham had gifted the year before to Bishop G. A. Selwyn and on which the 'little unpretending chapel of wood and thatch' named St Mark's now stood.[15]† Dilworth did not begrudge that gift of land; from first to last he tended to regard himself as the patron of St Mark's Anglican Church.

He was not prepared to surrender, however, any scintilla of right to the reserves which the Crown had cut out of Graham's purchase from the Maori chiefs in 1844. He arranged for a special deed of conveyance to be drawn up whereby Graham agreed to transfer to Dilworth 'any right or claim he may have to the Mount Hobson reserve',[16] and to place in Dilworth's hands 'all documents required for his establishing his claim to the 23 acres above mentioned'.[17] In the following year, the new owner applied, unsuccessfully, to have the spring reserve off Manukau Road returned to him.

---

* Dilworth was effective owner of the farm some time before the deed of conveyance was executed. On 12 March 1848 he had cut out for sale from Graham's former land a one-and-a-half-acre allotment adjoining the St Mark's property to Revd G. T. B. Kingdon for £116 11s 8d. On this allotment Kingdon put up a house he called The Priory. Despite the ecclesiastical-sounding name, the property was owned by Kingdon, not the Anglican Church.

† Gifts of land to the churches on which to erect chapels by well-to-do settlers—like the owners of the land in England of old, remarked Bishop W. G. Cowie, Selwyn's successor—were common in colonial times. A. K. Taylor of 'Alberton' later gave the site on which St Luke's, Mount Albert, was erected, and Thomas Morrin provided an allotment for an Anglican Church in his subdivision which became Morrinsville.

Mount Hobson viewed from Mount Eden in the 1880s. The Dilworth homestead in the centre background may be identified by the avenue of trees which leads to it.
Dilworth Trust Board Archives

For sixteen years Dilworth allowed his claim for Graham's Hill to sleep. Then, on 24 August 1865, just after the capital of the colony had been shifted to Wellington, he approached the newly-appointed agent of the general government in Auckland, Dr Daniel Pollen, an Irishman like himself, and a politician whom he seemed to respect.* (Pollen he knew from way back. The doctor had been a founder of the New Zealand Banking Company which had once employed Dilworth, and they had been fellow-residents of early Parnell when it was just a tiny suburb on the outskirts of Auckland.) The purpose of his letter, Dilworth informed Pollen was 'to protest most strongly against . . . a gross wrong [done] to me'. He had found out that the provincial government intended 'to survey and sell off a part, if not the whole, of the Reserve of Mount Hobson'.[18] Dilworth complained that some time previously he had been informed, by whom he did not say, that this reserve could never be his because it had been set aside as 'the site of an observatory'.† Pollen investigated the rumour. The provincial

---

* Daniel Pollen, born in Dublin in 1813, came to New Zealand via New South Wales after qualifying as a doctor. He practised medicine in Auckland, then took up mining on Kawau Island, but ultimately made his mark as a politician and administrator. He was premier for some months 1875–76. He was decisive and shrewd in administration, particularly on matters touching land. Opponents thought he was indulgent towards some Auckland businessmen.

† No documentary proof of whether this was ever intended has survived. It is interesting that the lower slope of another volcanic cone, One Tree Hill, has been used as the site of an astronomical observatory since 1967. Mount St John had been the site of an observatory before that.

secretary, whom he consulted, assured him that the Auckland superintendent had no plans at all to sell off the land. And so (Pollen reassured Dilworth) 'you have been needlessly alarmed'.

In private, however, Pollen was more uneasy than he let on. He had come to see that, by this protest, Dilworth had raised a tricky problem of a far more general nature than had first appeared to be the case: namely, what was to be done about reserves which had been set apart by governors in days gone by, but which were now being eyed by impecunious provincial governments? After drawing the attention of the colonial secretary, Alfred Domett, to the fact that Mount Hobson land had 'become of very great value', he went on to speak of the great need to preserve reserves in towns where suburban expansion had led to accelerating land prices.[19]

> I venture to recommend that this reserve and all the others still remaining in the neighbourhood of Auckland should be retained by the General Government. The local government, for purposes of revenue, has denuded itself of every available rood of land in the suburbs, and I think that the public interest requires that a further alienation of land in the neighbourhood of the city should be as far as possible put an end to.

Domett agreed. (Regardless of any shortcomings he may have had as a minister, he was a shrewd and knowledgeable administrator of Crown lands.) 'Better', he remarked in a minute to Pollen, 'not to grant reserves to Provincial Councils' and thereby 'lead them into temptation' when the central government was by no means prepared 'to forgive their trespasses'.[20]

Although officials in Wellington had done their best to persuade Dilworth that he had nothing to worry about, he remained unconvinced. In June 1867 he decided to tackle the government head-on by making a full-scale resurrection of his claim to Graham's Hill.[21] The administration of the day was embarrassed. As the attorney-general later explained to his colleagues, because no indication had been given as to the purpose for which this reserve had been originally dedicated, Mount Hobson 'represented a difficult problem. Under existing legislation the Governor could not lease or lend it'.[22] One can understand why there seemed good political reasons to let the sleeping dog lie. The secretary of the cabinet, William Gisborne, wrote notifying Dilworth that after inquiry he could not see 'any reason for reopening this claim'.[23]

Dilworth was awkward, refusing to give up. Perhaps his recent contest with the Auckland-Drury railway commissioners had whetted his appetite for litigation. Whatever the reason, during July 1868, while the Assembly was in session, he wrote to the colonial secretary reopening his claim yet again. Documents which he enclosed, some dating as far back as 1847, he assured the secretary, would put his case 'in a very different light'.[24] He contended that neither he nor Graham had ever been reconciled to the loss of the twenty-three acres. Further, the land was clearly not needed as a Crown reserve; this was 'proved' by the failure of the general government over a twenty-year period ever to utilize it 'for public purposes'. The danger he feared was that his case would be lost by default: two provincial superintendents in succession, Robert Graham and Frederick Whitaker, he complained, would surely have sold off the reserve to raise revenue 'only for my protest to the General Government Agent'.

The somewhat curt, single-page letter which the colonial secretary sent four months later informing Dilworth that 'the Government is advised that it has no power to comply with your request' conceals the great thoroughness with which it had in fact investigated the legality of his claim.[25] The Old Land Claims files in National Archives, Wellington, show that Dilworth's letter had passed through a number of hands including those of Daniel Pollen, Domett as land claims commissioner, and the new attorney-general James Prendergast. It would appear that the opinions of the two latter scrawled on departmental files as minutes or marginalia were decisive. Domett held that Graham's failure to protest in November 1847 at the withholding by the Crown of the twenty-three-acre reserve indicated that he had 'taken his Grant in full satisfaction of his claim'. Likewise, the absence of an appeal by Dilworth, to whom Graham's 'shadow of claim had been made over', against the schedule of all claims (which included Graham's Hill) published in 1863 by Commissioner F. Dillon Bell as 'having been settled', excluded a new hearing.[26] Even more decisive, in the government's view, had been the passage of the Land Claims Settlement Act 1856, whose Section 15, subsection 2, 'expressly shut out by law' any revision of Crown grants which had been accepted by owners. For this reason alone (Prendergast concluded) 'this request even if it were founded on an indisputably equitable claim' could not be considered.[27] It was the government's obvious hope that their ruling marked the end of the claim.

The suspicion remains that, in spite of repeated assertions that the law did not allow the kind of revision Dilworth sought, it was not his precise case at which the government jibbed but rather the fear of a precedent created by any overturning of the Crown reserves provisions of the 1856 Act. Domett was in no doubt that if Dilworth's claim were 're-opened in these circumstances, other claims must be re-opened too'.[28] Pollen was of like mind on the matter:

> Personally I should be glad to see the land restored to Mr Dilworth because he is a good farmer and would make it profitable which it certainly is not now. But this is one of a series of reserves for public purposes made as part of the conditions under which the pre-emption claims were settled by Governor Grey and it cannot be treated exceptionally without opening the door to other claims of like

character which it would be difficult to resist and yet more difficult to satisfy.[29]

By 1868 Dilworth had developed the conviction (which others, unaware of how dogged on matters of principle this Ulsterman could be, must surely have thought an obsession) that while the Crown dawdled, the province was likely to step in and appropriate land 'rightfully' his. Nor was the suspicion entirely without foundation. Even before the government had written refusing his request, the superintendent of Auckland gave notice of his intention of converting, under a recent Act of his provincial council, many pieces of Crown land into provincial reserves.[30] Amongst these was Mount Hobson. Pollen forwarded this *Gazette* notice to the colonial secretary drawing his attention by ticks to Mount Hobson and three other highly valuable Crown reserves in the neighbourhood of Auckland that had been included in the schedule.* Pollen's comment was pointed: 'Several attempts have been made by the Provincial Government to get hold [of] and dispose of this lot. I think the Governor should be advised to reserve [them]'.[31] For his part, Dilworth was galled by an attempt by the third superintendent in succession to lay hands on *his* Mount Hobson (which was not to be the end of it; the next superintendent, T. B. Gillies, also laid claim to the reserve on behalf of his government).

In the same *Gazette*, Williamson put up Mount Hobson for lease for one year in order to eradicate thistles which had become a 'nuisance'. When Dilworth protested,[32] the offer was withdrawn, and he, as the owner of the adjoining property, was given permission, for which he had asked, to occupy it in order to get the thistles down, it

---

* The reserves were: the Rifle Range, Great North Road (127 acres); Mount Hobson (23 acres 1 rood); One Tree Hill (123 acres); Mount Victoria Flagstaff Reserve.

The view towards the south-west from the summit of Mount Hobson in the late 1870s. The foreground, which is reserve land, shows signs of infestation by thistles.
Dilworth Trust Board Archives

being understood that this concession was 'to have no bearing on his impending claim'.[33]

In the meantime the provincial council reserved the land for educational purposes. Nor did a change in superintendent augur well for Dilworth. After a hard-fought and exciting election, T. B. Gillies won office from John Williamson in November 1868 to begin a four-year term.[34] As someone who had clashed with Dilworth's counsel over the railway arbitration case, Gillies was unlikely to be indulgent towards the Remuera landowner. But, to be fair, Gillies's determination to keep the hill out of Dilworth's reach was based on principle rather than prejudice. What he wrote shortly after attaining office was nevertheless ominous:

> It seems clear that Mr Dilworth has no claim in reference to this reserve. Nor does it seem that this piece has been legally made a reserve, though some steps were taken towards that object. In my opinion these volcanic hills ought to be granted to the Superintendent as reserves for the purposes of public recreation grounds, and of scoria ash pits for road purposes, and rendered inalienable either way by lease or sale.[35]

In articulating the need for local authorities to set aside volcanic cones in their keeping as recreational reserves for the use of the community as a whole, Gillies was voicing more than a personal viewpoint. Many settlers were also now of the same mind. Fearful that in this new climate of opinion his claim to the hill would be lost forever, Dilworth instructed his solicitors, Jackson and Russell, to prepare a petition to the House of Representatives for the session of 1872.[36] The essence of his argument was that since no irregularities in the original purchase of the eighty-two-acre block had been found by Commissioner Matson in 1847, the withholding of twenty-three acres as a reserve—when by law 'the only equitable reservation, if any, which the Government of New Zealand were empowered to make was one tenth of the area'—meant that he had 'been wrongfully deprived of a large portion'.[37]

The select committee heard the evidence, amongst that of others, of F. Dillon Bell,* land claims commissioner in the critical 1856–62 period, who submitted that he had 'no recollection of any claim being raised before me by Mr Dilworth, his being one of those claims which were excluded by the Act of 1856'. He went on to observe that at the time he made a point of looking at the Mount Hobson file.

> I was struck with [sic] this reserve of Mount Hobson Hill which used to be a favourite spot of mine to sketch from in the very earliest days and I always wondered why it had been excepted from the Dilworth

---

* Because Dillon Bell as land claims commissioner had had special responsibility for clearing up, after 1856, unresolved old land, pre-emptive 'and other claims', his views carried particular weight in official circles. His report on these claims dated 8 July 1862 is an authoritative document.

grant as its absence spoilt the property so much I presume Mr Dilworth finding he was actually excluded by the Act of 1856 did not think it worth while to appeal to me.[38]

With officials of the Crown Lands Office confirming in detail what Bell had said,[39] the petitions committee did not hesitate to turn down Dilworth's prayer. Failure of either Graham or Dilworth to protest at the original Crown grant was regarded as proof that they had 'accepted it in satisfaction of all [their] claims'.[40]

Dilworth was inactive about the reserve over the next few months. He had not capitulated: it was simply that he was abroad on a visit to Britain. Once back he returned to the charge. In an angry letter to the colonial secretary he complained that during his absence the Remuera Road Board had applied to the superintendent for a five-year lease of the reserve, an action that (he submitted) 'could prejudice my just claim to [it]'. His tone was one of a rightful landowner deeply wronged. Rehearsing all the old arguments, he said that his 'repeated' requests in the past had been refused because his case had not been 'properly understood'.

Francis Dillon Bell, the land claims commissioner.
Alexander Turnbull Library

> There is not another land claim in the Colony I believe in the same position as this one. It is a very small piece of land I may say in the centre of my farm: it is not required for public purposes; and it has cost the Government neither money nor trouble. Therefore, why keep it from me or annoy me any longer about it?[41]

But Dilworth's persistence failed once again to budge the land claims commissioner, who wrote, 'it is quite impossible to reopen . . . your claim'.[42]

An irrevocable handing over of the reserve for recreational purposes to the Remuera district board, so much feared by Dilworth, became imminent early in 1878. He protested immediately to the minister of lands, lest 'my righteous claim' be 'shut out' for ever.[43] It was quite unnecessary, he added, to proclaim the land an educational reserve.

> I have always been ready, willing, and indeed anxious—in the event of a satisfactory settlement of my claim—to plant the summit of the Hill in question and to throw it open without any restriction, to be enjoyed by the public generally as a recreation ground. In fact I may state that I have already planted largely the surrounding land.

We need not doubt that given the chance he would have kept his word. He had a good record for tree-planting, for providing right of way through his fields for church-goers and those going about lawful business, and for throwing open his paddocks for sporting functions. But this appeal for a stay of execution to his claim failed. Nevertheless until the very eve of the proclamation of the Mount Hobson reserve as a perpetual recreation ground in February 1880 Dilworth continued to supplicate.[44]

In retrospect Dilworth can be seen as engaging in a battle which, the longer it went on, the less likely he was to win. As Auckland expanded and open spaces dwindled, big suburban landowners were no longer regarded as local heroes. The 1870s and 1880s saw the population of Newmarket, Epsom and northern Remuera grow because of the pressure of population from the inner town; because of improvements in roads, Remuera Road in particular; and because of the subdivision of farmland by James Williamson, Thomas Morrin and others.* The growing settlement needed open public space as 'lungs', in the phrase of the era, to which crowded town dwellers could go 'to breathe'. Brett's *Auckland Almanac* of 1881 accurately enough caught the triumphal mood of the community: 'Mount Hobson has, after a hard fight, been gained for the people, and will be a public reserve for ever'.[45]

In spite of, and perhaps partly because of, losing the summit, Dilworth maintained a deep affection for the western and southern slopes, that part of Mount Hobson which was still in his hands. It was not surprising therefore that this piece of land should have an honoured place in the old man's benefaction upon his death. In his will he directed his trustees to 'set apart . . . not less than twenty-five acres of my land at Remuera . . . known as Graham's Hill' as the site of the buildings and grounds of the Dilworth Ulster Institute.[46]

In the event this was not to be. By the end of the first decade of the twentieth century the Dilworth Trust Board believed that this land was too valuable to be used in that fashion. Dilworth's scheme for educating disadvantaged boys could best be realized, the trustees decided, if the school was built elsewhere and its operations financed through the subdivision and sale of what were now highly-priced residential sites on Graham's Hill. A 1912 Bill passed by parliament authorized this change in the terms of the trust.[47]

But in the following years the Trust Board found that if it wanted to use the hill for housing, it would have a battle on its hands, one far fiercer than Dilworth himself had been engaged in. Many citizens now felt that if the Trust Board no longer needed its twenty-six acres for the site of the Dilworth Institute, it should not convert them into residential allotments but gift them to the city as parkland. C. J. Parr, MP, an ex-mayor for whom creating parks was a consuming passion, went on the attack.[48]† The Trust could afford to give the land. Its estate

---

* Modern Auckland owes much to the doughty Sir James Parr. His 'passion for parks' led to improvements to the Auckland Domain, enlargements to or acquisition of Point Erin Park, Parnell Park, Myers Park (indirectly), the reserve behind Titirangi and other lands in the Waitakere region, Mount Hobson and Lake Waiatarua (indirectly). It has been said 'his monuments are on all sides'.

† The main population growth during this period was taking place, however, in 'Auckland borough', i.e. the inner city, in western districts such as Ponsonby, and in Mount Eden and Devonport which were also growing rapidly. Between 1878 and 1886 the Remuera highway district population grew from 844 to 1,802, though it continued to retain its élite social character.

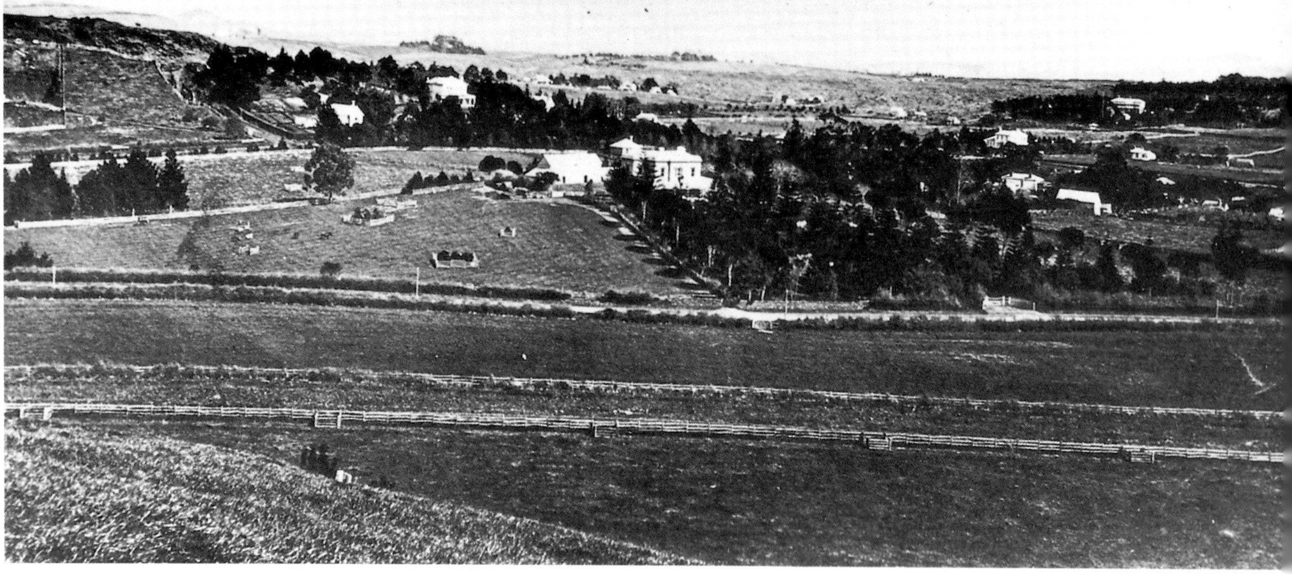

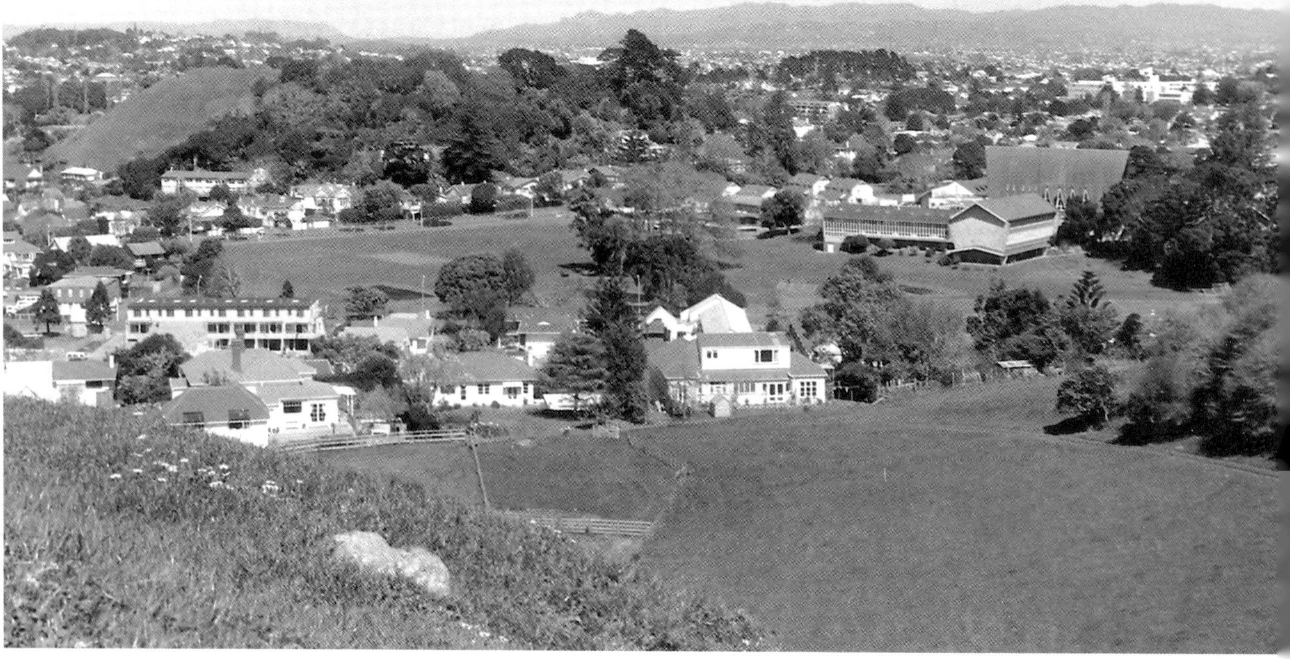

'now drips with the fat of unearned increment',* he declared with characteristic bounce. 'Is it the duty of the trustees to spoil this piece of incomparable landscape in order that they may swell an already fat rent-roll with a few more dollars? Do they owe nothing to the community which has created half the wealth of the Trust?' For its part the Trust Board believed that neither morally nor legally did it have the right to depart from Dilworth's intentions.[49] Further, the Board knew, as Parr did not, that its financial position would not allow it to give away its remaining Mount Hobson land. Far from 'dripping with the fat of unearned increment' the Board was struggling to balance its books; a situation which continued through the war into 1920 when the post-war boom ended. The root of the problem was that war-time inflation had eroded the Trust's real income which was derived from (usually) long-term residential leases taken up at figures based on pre-war land values and purchasing power.

It took five years for the Dilworth Trust and the city council to reach an agreement. In 1921 the Trust Board conveyed to the Auckland City Council the fee simple of something under one-half of the land in question, namely the meadowland of the picturesque upper slopes, conditional upon the council bearing responsibility for roading work (estimated at £4,000) on the lower portion of the property which would be subdivided for housing leases. The roads under discussion were Dilworth Avenue, Mount Hobson Road and Mount Hobson Lane. The council also covenanted to maintain the 'present landscape appearance of the hill'.[50] It was a happy compromise. Travellers moving south from the city today find Mount Hobson's gentle western slope, uncluttered by housing, a source of continuing delight.†

It is the prerogative of the biographer to speculate on how his subject, had he miraculously been granted such foreknowledge, would have felt about what has happened to the hill he once longed to possess. Probably Dilworth would not have been displeased.

---

* 'Unearned increment' is the increase in the value of land or property due not to the action of the owner but to the growth of the community about it. This is a term popularized by the theories of the tax reformer Henry George.

† Because the pre-European Maori did not terrace the western slope, Mount Hobson is exceptional among volcanoes of the region, giving a vivid, visual impression of the unbroken, symmetrical gradient that most of the cones once had before they were modified by man.

Opposite above: *Dilworth's home farm in the 1880s viewed from Mount Hobson. Note how the avenue leading to the house has thickened into a broad band of trees. Note also protective fences around groves of saplings to ward off browsing stock.*
Dilworth School Archives

Opposite below: *The same view in 1994; where the homestead farm was once located is now the senior campus of Dilworth School.*
Kate Stone

CHAPTER TEN

Landed Entrepreneur

A<small>LTHOUGH NEVER ABLE</small> to establish his claim to the summit of Mount Hobson, the piece of land on which his heart had been so set, Dilworth in later life owned property which in value and extent must have far outstripped the most ambitious imaginings of the young Irish immigrant when he first came to Auckland in 1841. This is easily illustrated. For instance, at the time of the 1879 general election, he held a property franchise in eight of the thirteen parliamentary constituencies within the Auckland province.[1] Or look at Sir George Grey's so-called Domesday Survey, *Freeholders of New Zealand, 1882*. The value of his real estate at that point was £81,044; and this a figure which did not take into account the huge Whaiti-Kuranui block (70,169 acres) in the upper Thames Valley, which he jointly owned with Joseph Howard—that land at current valuations would have been worth something approaching £40,000.* What was remarkable in Dilworth's case was that when rural property values fell sheer in the later 1880s, he, unlike most great Auckland landowners but like his Epsom neighbour Logan Campbell, survived with his property substantially intact. One of the concerns of this chapter is to explain why.

Dilworth invested speculatively in land as long as he lived. Because the word 'speculation' has for many a pejorative overtone which is not intended in this account, it must be defined. It is used here simply to denote the buying of land at a low price either to be sold at some later time at a profit, or to be otherwise used and enjoyed as an asset much appreciated in value. Most of Auckland's early settlers who had spare capital of their own, or access to that of others, speculated in land, particularly country land which, in pioneering days, could often be bought for a song. A local historian did not exaggerate when he claimed 'that from 1865 for about the next twenty years land speculation became the great industry of the Auckland province'.[2] In fact this kind of land dealing was in full swing long before 1865. Here

---

* The valuation made by Jackson and Russell, Dilworth's lawyers, as of 25 January 1883, was £48,125, which given the rural downturn was admittedly an optimistic figure (DTBA).

we have much of the explanation for the intense settler interest (which Dilworth shared) in the affairs of the provincial council, especially between its beginnings in 1853 and 5 August 1859 when the Auckland council finally adopted its comprehensive set of land regulations.[3]

It should occasion no surprise, moreover, that Dilworth never lost his habit of land speculation. As one of Auckland's first settlers he quickly learned, as did most who came with a modicum of capital during the early years, that if you bought land while it was plentiful and cheap and hung on to it, the growth of population and improvements in transport would over time greatly enhance its value. For Dilworth land speculation carried fewer risks than for most of his peers. In the last thirty years of his life his position as an investor in land remained strong regardless of any downturn in property values. The two emphases of his property portfolio—investment for generation of income, investment for speculative gains—were, so to speak, in stable equilibrium, the income from the first always sufficient to cover the risks and contingent losses of the second.

By 1870, so remarkable had been the appreciation of land values in the town of Auckland and its inner suburbs that Dilworth became

View from Mount St John towards Dilworth's No. 3 'Dairy Farm'. The diagonal road in foreground is Fountain Road (Mount St John Avenue).
Dilworth School Archives

most averse to selling off any property which he had there, most of all any part of the Remuera estate. (Beyond the grave he was to place the same prohibition upon the trustees of his estate.) By the late 1860s, his investment strategy had become set. His city and suburban properties were to be used to generate necessary income, derived for the most part from leases or rents, or interest earned on mortgage loans on property temporarily conveyed to Dilworth as mortgagee to secure repayment.* Speculative dealing in land, on the other hand, he increasingly conducted in the more remote country areas. Not that investment for income and investment for capital gains in practice fell neatly into well-defined geographical compartments. An obvious area of overlap, most marked in the 1860s, is provided by mortgage advances secured on city and suburban properties, made by Dilworth as a kind of lender of last resort to shaky borrowers. Such a transaction could produce income, but, if the borrower failed, a forced sale could provide Dilworth with what must be regarded as an opportunity for speculative gain.

Success in business, so they say, generally comes from a mixture of skill and good fortune; that the saying has become a commonplace does not make it any the less true. The formula holds good in explaining how Dilworth accumulated his propertied wealth; we note the astuteness with which he managed his stock of capital; but we also recognize the turns of fate which gave him opportunities to exploit. Both were evident between 1844 and 1847 when he acquired Remuera. Both played their part in the 1860s, a decade which saw his position considerably strengthened. The intervening years were not without their achievement, either. The steady rise in property values, 1847–61, made the sale and lease of property so much more profitable. Nor should one overlook how land, now greatly appreciated in value, could be used as security for loans in the early 1860s, as the three newly-formed trading banks competed for custom by offering advances to clients on liberal terms.[4]

An artificial stimulus to the Auckland economy at this juncture, which Dilworth could scarcely have foreseen, in the long run worked to his advantage. Race war, or the threat of it, during 1861–64, in Taranaki, the Waikato and the Bay of Plenty, transformed Auckland into an armed camp, with military expenditure, both by the commissariat and individual soldiers, nourishing the whole economy. The war benefited Dilworth directly. When commissariat demand was at its peak he held a profitable contract supplying troops, in partnership for some of the time, it was later said, with descendants of the Williams family, missionaries in the Bay of Islands.[5] In later 1864, military

---

* Under the deeds system, in operation before the Land Transfer Act 1870, title deeds were conveyed to the mortgagee as security until such time as the borrower (mortgagor), by payment of all due interest and principal, had 'exercised his equity of redemption' and qualified thereby for the return to himself of the original deeds.

expenditure fell away markedly with the ending of the Waikato war and the shifting of troops elsewhere in the North Island. Business morale in Auckland suffered a further blow in the following year when the capital of the colony was shifted to Wellington.

A measure of good fortune saved Dilworth from the disadvantageous consequences of this economic downturn. First, his decision during 1864 not to renew his commissariat contract could not have been more timely, though he seems not to have anticipated that this would be so. And given the withdrawal of troops from Auckland, he was equally fortunate in 1865 to be able to lease his ninety-two-acre (No. 3) dairy farm at Remuera to a group of army meat contractors at the high figure of £900 a year.[6] Second, and equally fortuitous for Dilworth, was the decision made at about the same time by the Auckland and Drury Railway Company to continue its railway through his property. It will be recalled that when the issue of compensation was raised, it was agreed that this was to be assessed in accordance with the price of land as it had stood at February 1865, a formula that enhanced the amount which Dilworth could claim. It should also be borne in mind that a sharp rise in the price of city and suburban land had been associated with the somewhat spurious business boom of the 1861–64 years.[7] Even so late as the crucial February 1865 date, the 'land mania' (as it was described in contemporary newspapers) had not entirely spent itself. In consequence, the compensation paid Dilworth for the severance of his farm was based not on 1866 property valuations, when the bottom had dropped out of the real estate market, but on the inflated figures of the year previously. His position during 1866–67, when he was enriched by compensation money, could be considered analogous to that of gold speculators on the Thames who some months later made their first wonderful windfall strikes and profits just at the time Auckland was still wrapped up in business slump.

After the mid-sixties recession, there were two successive boosts to the Auckland economy. Between 1868 and 1871 the Thames goldfields stimulated the town. And when the mining boom was almost at an end, business in Auckland was refreshed by the inflow of overseas, mainly British, capital entering the colony through public borrowing and by way of trading bank credit.[8] Dilworth reacted positively. He upgraded his commercial buildings in the heart of town to increase his rental income. Taking advantage of Maori defeat in war and the extension of the railway he moved his speculative buying towards the interior of the province.

Always secretive on matters of business, Dilworth seems to have revealed the true extent of his landed estate in later years only to a small inner circle: Isabella, his lawyers Jackson and Russell, his secretary Gerald O'Halloran, and his clerical confidant the Revd George MacMurray. Even to the executors of his estate, the probate copy of his will was probably a revelation. It listed, with a map for each, sixty-four items of real estate, some of them aggregations of smaller parcels.⁹ Whilst his properties were almost entirely confined to the Auckland province, they were widely scattered: in Northland, various parts of the Tamaki isthmus, with odd items on the North Shore of the Waitemata Harbour, the lower and middle valley of the Waikato River, the upper Thames Valley through to Lake Taupo, Raglan on the west coast, the Bay of Plenty and Poverty Bay on the east.

A closer scrutiny of these seemingly disparate properties, however, shows them substantially falling into the two broad categories mentioned earlier, which can be represented in tabular form.

LANDS

Provincial (and speculative)
(a) Northland, between Waitakere and Whangarei
(b) Manukau (later called Franklin) County
(c) Lower Waikato
(d) Upper Thames Valley (Whaiti-Kuranui block)

City and suburban (and income-producing)
(a) Inner city and Parnell
(b) Remuera estate
(c) South-eastern Tamaki isthmus

These groups will now be discussed with the exception of the inner city properties and the Whaiti-Kuranui block, which for contrasting reasons each deserve separate treatment in a chapter of its own.

Apart from the Whaiti-Kuranui speculation, which was a notorious sink of money for Dilworth, his investment in provincial lands was, by the time of his death, a source of neither significant profit nor loss for him. Earnings, save for one or two fortuitous sales, by the mid-eighties barely covered his outlay on property tax and local rates. It is also noteworthy that, when he died, he possessed only two substantial pieces of country land: the 2,000-acre Waitakere farm (current land tax value £2,795) and the 6,000-acre Taupiri estate (£2,769) in the lower Waikato.¹⁰

Much of the credit for the development of the Waitakere farm bought in 1855 must go to Andrew Dilworth. Having his brother resident on the property also helped James in other ways. Although land regulations in Auckland varied considerably after Grey's cheap land proclamation of 16 April 1853, as a general rule the opportunity to buy waste lands on favourable terms depended on the applicant's being resident on or near the land granted.¹¹ Where Waitakere lands were on offer, Andrew was present after January 1861 to fulfil this condition. The Dilworth brothers bought land in this hilly region in all manner of ways. Purchases were made directly from Maori owners (Ngati Whatua).¹² Others were the result of successful bids at Crown

A typical bush homestead like Dilworth's in the Waitakere Ranges.
Auckland Public Library

land auctions[13] and at mortgagee sales of defaulters' property.[14] James also made successful applications for gratuitous grants under the Auckland Waste Lands Act 1858.[15] (His appetite for Waitakere land was never sated; he was still buying it when he was seventy-seven years old.)[16] This does not exhaust the varied kinds of acquisitions; to what effect became apparent when surprised executors first examined Dilworth's will. They found that in the parish of Waitakere alone he had eight allotments, and another five in the adjoining parish of Waipareira.[17]

There was a pattern to this apparently diverse land buying in the Waitakeres. Most of the scattered purchases were small in size, low in value and left undeveloped, having been brought speculatively. The real concern of the Dilworth brothers was to consolidate the Waitakere farm. To this end they made a number of small purchases of allotments contiguous to the farm to straighten boundary lines or to bring in productive pieces. The exception was a 386-acre block taken up at Taupaki, just over two miles north-east of the farm.[18] Bought jointly, in the first instance, by Andrew and Judge Rogan—whom Andrew soon bought out (20 May 1870)—it cost the Dilworths just on £200.[19] Left undeveloped, it was sold by James to a local farmer for £1,000 in 1889 after the construction of the Auckland-Kaipara railway had brought the area within reach of the urban market.[20] (Here was foreshadowed the surge in provincial land values which became much more marked after 1896 when export farming in New Zealand entered a stage of 'take off'. Waitakere land, held in low regard in Dilworth's own time, was to be a lucrative asset for the Dilworth Trust Board in the period after his death.)[21]

Over the last ten years or so of his life, Dilworth allowed the

153

Waitakere estate to slip back,[22] apart from an imaginative and, in the event, prophetic attempt to develop orcharding upon a thirty-acre block close to the main seven-roomed farmhouse.[23] Where he could, in this latter time, he leased out sections of the farm to local settlers for what he could get. He also made his farm buildings available to friends as a holiday retreat.[24] By the time of his death, pasture on the farm, lacking the sustained top-dressing of the past, had deteriorated. Gorse and low tea tree were reappearing, fences were in disrepair. Dilworth in old age had more serious matters on his mind than keeping up the Waitakere farm.

On the Northland peninsula between Waitakere and Whangarei Dilworth had on his hands for many years three unimproved blocks of land: at Mareretu near Maungaturoto (340 acres), at Waikiekie somewhat north of Mareretu (284 acres) and at Grahamtown, a subdivision on the outskirts of Whangarei (fourteen-and-a-half-acres).[25] Originally taken up for speculative reasons, these three properties remained little better than an encumbrance. There was little sign of buyers. In the early 1890s their total value was less than £500.[26]

Not in the northern peninsula, however, but south of the Tamaki isthmus was where the bulk of Dilworth's landed estate in the province lay. His first significant move south he had made as early as 16 April 1853, when he put in a successful bid, under Grey's new land regulations, for 369 acres in the Pukekohe-Ramarama area.[27] This land he subsequently sold. Like almost all of his acquisitions of land between Papakura and Mercer, roughly in the region later to be known as Franklin County, this first purchase had been speculative. As in the north, so in the south of Auckland, his motives were of that sort. The blocks which he bought he picked up, once again, in a variety of ways, and having got them he usually left them in a state of nature. The exceptions were blocks let at low rentals to local improving tenant farmers; this was the case with the Rollett brothers, who held 260 acres of Dilworth's land over two blocks in the vicinity of Papakura. Lessons which he and Andrew had learnt at Waitakere he turned to account here; he was quite prepared to lease unimproved land to bush contractors for kauri milling (Hunua)[28] and to gumdiggers (Papakura).[29]

With the ending of the Waikato war, the tide of European colonization began to flow into the interior of the island. Dilworth's land buying was borne along with it. As an instance of this, he bought 170 acres of confiscated Awhitu land south of the Manukau Heads, subsequently described by a Pakeha valuer as containing 'unimproved poor land',[30] though Maori who had once held the mana whenua over it would surely not have thought so. Again, like many an Auckland capitalist, Dilworth was able to buy up at bargain prices fifty-acre allotments granted to militiamen who either had not taken them up or had abandoned them.³¹ A typical instance is provided by the 1869 deed of conveyance between 'Alexander Finnagan late a private in the first Regiment Waikato Militia but now of Auckland settler, and James Dilworth of Auckland Esquire'. The deed, which records that Dilworth paid a mere £6 5s 0d for his fifty acres at Opotiki, ends thus: 'signed by the said Andrew Finnagan [by a mark] this deed having first been read over and explained to him he being illiterate, in the presence of James B. Graham Clerk Auckland'.³² This allotment multiplied eight times in value over the next twenty years. That was an exceptional increase, however. In most provincial areas where he bought land, and this particularly applied to village allotments and related suburban farm land in 'paper settlements', his investments barely held their value. Even the shrewdest of buyers had not counted on the late nineteenth-century agricultural depression leaving so many enduring rural backwaters.³³ Dilworth was of their number. On balance, by buying into such subdivisions he probably incurred small losses. This was so with Purapura in Waiuku.³⁴ It was also the case with Raglan.³⁵

These scattered parcels did not bulk large in Dilworth's investment schemes, however, representing less than ten per cent by value of the land he held in his own name south of the Tamaki isthmus by the time of his death.³⁶* After the ending of the Anglo-Maori Wars, Auckland capitalists in search of cheap interior lands could get hold of them in two ways. One option was to buy from the Crown any confiscated land on offer, the cheapest of which was swampland available at the low figure of five shillings per acre. Alternatively, as a result of 1862 and 1865 Native Land Acts, Europeans could buy more cheaply than they were able to at Crown land auctions, if they dealt directly with often demoralized Maori owners who had now been put on individualized titles.³⁷ Dilworth acquired large rural estates in each of these ways. The Whaiti-Kuranui blocks his agents bought directly from Maori owners. The 6,000-acre Mangawara estate, our present concern, came from the Crown.

On 4 March 1874 Dilworth and his brother-in-law William Hall were issued with the Crown grant to 5,850 acres of swampland which they were to hold as tenants-in-common.³⁸ No consideration figure was mentioned; it is likely the cost was five shillings an acre. Dilworth called the estate Mangawara after a creek on its eastern boundary of that name, a tributary of the Waikato River which it joined at Taupiri just a few miles away. Dilworth became sole owner in 1877 when he bought out Hall's 'undivided moiety' for £3,050.³⁹ The early 1870s had seemed an opportune time to invest in this lower part of the Waikato Valley. The southern railway had reached Mercer and by 1873

---

* Excluding upper Thames Valley land, the land tax valuation of Dilworth's land in the south of the province in 1894 was £3,043, of which the great component was the Mangawara block, £2,769 [TT3, DTBA].

the government had authorized a survey of the continuation of the line to Ngaruawahia which almost inevitably, and conveniently for Dilworth, would follow a route close to his Mangawara purchase.[40] Like so many prominent Aucklanders—Thomas Russell, James Williamson, Frederick Whitaker, Robert and Every Maclean, among others—Dilworth had decided to follow the will-o'-the-wisp of swampland speculation.[41] His error of judgement (like theirs) was not with regard to the quality of the swampland; when drained it provided a good fertile peaty soil. Rather he underestimated how much would be the cost, in terms of labour and capital, of constructing canals and ditches large enough to drain the swampland and keep seasonal flooding at bay.

Dilworth was still in possession of the Mangawara estate when he died. This had not been his original intention. Like the other swampland speculators he had hoped to unload early and sell at a profit. When provincial farming became depressed in the 1880s, however, even developed farms were a drug on the market. There was no alternative to his being a long-term swamp owner. Typically, he kept financial outlays on the property to a minimum although, once again typically, he was prepared to snap up at bargain prices adjoining allotments either abandoned by military settlers, or put up for auction by the Supreme Court because rate-payers had defaulted.[42]

In the meantime his preference was to lease part or whole of the estate whenever opportunity offered. During the 1880s, for instance, he leased the estate for gumdigging for three years at £500 per annum to that versatile Waikato contractor Isaac Coates, who employed on the job first Maori then Dalmatian diggers.[43] When Coates moved elsewhere, Dilworth permitted two young men to take up the lease to cut flax. The venture failed. When they paid no rent he seized their flax mill and certain other buildings they had put up.[44]

In the later 1880s he veered onto a new tack, accepting as tenant one Louis Hadden who was allowed to run stock on condition that he paid the rates.[45] The arrangement worked, not least because, sensibly, Dilworth paid his tenant wages for any drain-digging he did by way of improvement. By May 1894, the last date at which developmental work is recorded in Dilworth's ledgers, nine-and-a-half miles of drains had been installed. But true development had to wait on machines and large capital outlays. Reports on Mangawara after Dilworth's death concluded that the estate must be regarded as 'practically unimproved',[46] and unsaleable in terms of the existing rural land market.[47] One report depressingly concluded that even the 'reclaimed areas', which had demonstrated that they could sustain good crops of turnips, were nevertheless subject to seasonal floodings with up to ten feet of water.[48] Overall, therefore, the Mangawara estate has to be regarded as a landed investment which, if not costly to maintain, was in the phrase of the time 'a lockup of capital'.

The heart of Dilworth's landed wealth lay in the Tamaki isthmus, in the city itself and in the suburbs. The suburban property was arbitrarily treated in his account books, regardless of its condition, as farmland. Under this heading came the Remuera estate; similarly regarded was a very rocky and rugged five-acre block on the lower slopes of Mount Eden,[49]* as was also a series of holdings which Dilworth thought of as his 'scoria land' located in the south-eastern part of the isthmus. This land, as was often the case with Dilworth, had been acquired at widely differing times and under diverse circumstances.

The largest block was the first bought. On 21 March 1853 Dilworth made a successful bid at a government auction for a block of 357 acres which was going at the upset price of one pound an acre.[50] This property, which had as its southern boundary the shoreline of an upper reach of Manukau Harbour lying between Onehunga and a point near the renowned Maori portage at Otahuhu, extended inland to take in part of those areas known today as Te Papapa and Southdown. The land was strewn with volcanic rock; some parts were swamp; the soil was thin and ungenerous. Demand for such land remained weak in colonial Auckland. Over the next forty years he could unload little of his purchase, and when he did the sale was in small allotments.[51] His most substantial conveyance was in fact to the government, who amply compensated him (£250 15s 0d) for land taken for public works in 1877.[52]

Development of this block was limited; some pasture was sown; the fencing installed consisted mainly of dry-stone walling.[53] Over the years a six-room house was put up together with some miscellaneous farm buildings. Because he had no intention of seriously farming this land himself, Dilworth leased it to others, reimbursing them (according to 'Ulster custom')† for construction work carried out on the property, and paying them for the running of any Dilworth stock entrusted to them. In later years he leased this block and his small neighbouring Mount Smart property for £400 a year to Ambury English & Co., who grazed their town-supply dairy herds there. These two holdings were run in conjunction with the Remuera estate, appearing in Dilworth's financial records as the 'Remuera and Scoria Land Account'. The government valuation for these two scoria farms at that time, 405 acres in all, was only £5,700. But Auckland's population was exploding, and noxious and other industries were beginning to shift

---

* Dilworth procured this Mount Eden block in 1865. He allowed it to remain undeveloped and a wasteland until his death. Its assessed value for death duties was £650; but it was an area of great worth for residential sections in the years to come.

† Unlike in England, where capital improvements were the responsibility of landlords, in Ireland under its early nineteenth-century land law, improvements carried out by tenants reverted to landlords when leases ended. The exception was in certain parts of northern Ireland where tenants were compensated for improvements when leases fell in. This was called the 'Ulster custom'.

into the district. With its frontage to the Great South Road and closeness to rail connection, this scoria land had great potential for subdivision and sale.

This was particularly so in the case of the second property mentioned, the Mount Smart allotment which was fenced and partly in grass, and conveniently close to the Penrose railway junction. How Dilworth came by this Mount Smart land is of particular interest, because it was one of a number of properties which came into his hands because of the failure of the owner to keep up mortgage payments,[54] although in this instance he was not the mortgagee. The original owner, a widow, Mary Tizard, had received a gratuitous grant of eighteen acres in 1863.[55] By 1877 she used her now appreciated property as security for a loan of £170 made by one of Dilworth's brothers-in-law, Edward Hall, sometimes described in the deeds as 'cooper' sometimes as 'farmer'.[56] Mrs Tizard fell behind in her payments, and in April 1882 settled with Hall by surrendering her property to him.[57] Five weeks later Hall conveyed this property and four acres of nearby village allotments to Dilworth for £417 10s.[58]

The third property which Dilworth held in this part of the isthmus appeared originally in his ledgers as 'Lundon's Farm' but later was referred to as the Ellerslie farm. The fact that he acquired it through the power of his wealth and then leased it out for others to work, once again discredits the notion that James Dilworth was a man of the soil, an uncomplicated farmer. The story of this allotment before it came into his hands is also instructive as yet another instance of the incorrigible propensity of early settlers to borrow beyond their ability to repay.

The original owner of this block of 123 acres was an Irish Catholic settler, Patrick Lundon, who shortly after arriving with his family in Auckland bought it from Maori owners under FitzRoy's penny-an-acre proclamation of 10 October 1844.[59] Readers wishing to place this block on a modern map of Auckland should visualize it as having a frontage in Campbell Road, then running diagonally, close to Penrose High School, towards Great South Road, which it met, and had a short frontage upon, at a point close to today's Penrose railway station. On this block Patrick Lundon developed a farm which he called Green Park. Some years later (1857) Patrick's son John, though himself a teetotaller, built and opened the first hotel in the area which he called the Harp of Erin, an inn which stood on a triangular allotment formed by the convergence of the first surveyed roads.[60]* That spot is a modern landmark, still called the Harp of Erin.

Patrick Lundon's efforts as a farmer were dogged from the outset

---

* John Lundon (1830–99) was an able, ambitious colonist. After an early life as farmer, goldminer, trader and soldier, he entered first the provincial council, and then the House of Representatives as a Greyite Liberal. A significant personality in Onehunga, where for a time he was innkeeper of the Railway Terminus Hotel, he was a versatile entrepreneur.

by his lack of working capital. During the 1850s he kept his head above water by borrowing ever more heavily from local capitalists who charged interest at the customary high rate of between fifteen and twenty per cent.[61] Lundon attempted to meet his accumulating interest charges by rolling over his mortgages each time at a higher level. In September 1860 he made an effort to shuffle off his burden of debt by divesting himself of the western (Campbell Road) half of his farm which he sold to a local butcher, William Walters, for £1,440.[62] But relief was only temporary. He then began to raise mortgage loans once again on the remaining half of his property.[63] During the 1865–66 depression his position deteriorated critically. He turned to Dilworth, who advanced him £1,200 at fifteen per cent, with the power of enforced sale in the event of default.[64] On 8 May 1867, just before the first interest payment was due, Lundon died.[65] His two daughters, one a spinster the other a widow, who inherited the farm, were incapable of keeping up interest payments on the mortgage. With £1,200 principal and £170 accrued interest due, a mortgagee sale in the auction mart of Samuel Cochrane in Fort Street resulted. Dilworth's bid of £360 succeeded.[66] So Green Park was his.

Once again Dilworth chose to regard himself as a landlord not a farmer. He leased the farm and its seven-roomed house to tenants, not always very profitably though the property normally paid its way.[67] In the 1890s he leased it to a local farmer, C. Brewster, at a rental of £150 a year; Dilworth also had a bill of sale over Brewster's cattle for £45 bearing annual interest of six per cent.[68] The Ellerslie farm may appear therefore not to have been a particularly good investment for Dilworth. The land was uneven; certainly there was a twenty-acre portion of 'good, ploughable volcanic soil', but thirty acres of the remainder were described as 'very rocky indeed'.[69] The fifty-nine-and-a-half-acre farm at that time carried a government tax valuation of £1,800.[70] But with the prospect of subdivision into housing sites in the not too distant future its value could then become (as the years ahead confirmed) many times the government figure.

It has long been part of the Dilworth mythology that the Remuera estate was the heart of his propertied wealth and that this land he dutifully farmed right to the end. The reality was quite different. About the great worth of his Remuera land there is no dispute. Nor need one question Dilworth's drive, and passionate interest in agricultural affairs, both of which endured into old age. But as early as the mid-1860s he considered himself a proprietor of land rather than a practising farmer. By the 1870s he was regularly farming in his own right at Remuera only the twenty-two acres south of Great South Road which had become a kind of model farm in which the main homestead, orchard and dairy and other farm buildings were located. He still assumed

Looking north-west along Remuera Road from Mount Hobson. Note Dilworth's planting on left-hand side of road. An undated lantern slide.
Dilworth Schoool Archives

Looking north-west from the boundary of Dilworth's farm towards St Mark's in 1890. This photograph shows the 'green belt' Dilworth planted and the post-and-rail fence he had put up.
Auckland Public Library

LANDED ENTREPRENEUR

responsibility for developing the main estate, in which he renovated fences, planted shelter trees, and the fields of which, according to his account books, he regularly top-dressed with bonedust and lime. But otherwise he must be seen as a gentleman farmer, whose main vocation was estate management and property development.

It is interesting to note that although he leased the greater part of this Remuera estate to others he retained full rights over eight acres of land which were designated in his records as 'plantations'.[71] There was a compact block of four acres to the west of Mount Hobson with a Remuera Road frontage, in which he had planted a mixture of native trees and exotics including conifers.* The latter were an unwise introduction, because it was reported after an inspection visit in the 1890s that the pines were killing off the native trees.[72] During the 1880s, he also planted what was called a 'green belt' on the western boundary of his farm along the line where it bordered the grounds of the parish church of St Mark's. Variously described at the time, this belt when inspected through surviving photographs seems to have been a mixture of pinus insignis and macrocarpa. The belt quickly became over-large and had to be felled in 1892. Shortly after, a parish hall (which still survives) was erected where the trees once grew.

* An early Epsom settler has recalled that 'in the early days . . . the eastern and northern aspects of Mt Hobson were covered with native bush. Also the crater' (Edgerley, 'Memoirs'; Barr MS).

Some trees at today's school date back to Dilworth's lifetime.
Kate Stone

Elsewhere on the estate Dilworth continued to plant through the 1870s and 1880s, usually in groves containing a mixture of trees, to give both a variety of shelter from sun, wind and rain for stock, and a variation in shape to please the eye. Two of Eleanor Mossman's sons later recollected how their elderly uncle used to involve them in planting trees, taking the lads with him, spade in hand, to various parts of the Remuera estate. When Dilworth in later years (1889–92) settled farm properties in the back country from Gisborne on these nephews—Willie John and Harry—he made a point of sending shrubs and trees from Remuera for them to plant.[73] The Waerenga-o-kuri block was named The Laurels after trees transplanted from the Remuera nursery. Laurels to this day grow rampantly on that farm.

In keeping with the experimental mood of the 1870s when government and farmers alike sought to diversify the New Zealand economy, Dilworth specially imported two llamas from South America.[74] These he grazed on an eastern flank of Mount Hobson in a field beside the intersection of Remuera and Market Roads. Although these animals aroused much local interest, the experiment—like that of Logan Campbell in introducing wine-grapes and olives into the One Tree Hill estate—came to nothing.

Because farm account books for the last ten years of Dilworth's life have survived, it is possible to see through their pages, as they spell out household and personal expenditure, and as they divide and analyse the components of the Remuera estate, exactly how Dilworth the proprietor managed his affairs there. The information also allows us with some degree of confidence to extrapolate some tentative conclusions back to the years before.

The picture that emerges suggests that from 1883 the whole of the Remuera estate, save for about twenty-two acres with a Great South Road frontage reserved for Dilworth,* was on a long-term lease to Frank Lawry at £1,380 a year. The paths of Dilworth and Lawry had first crossed in 1863 when, shortly after stepping off the *Ulcoates* at the Auckland wharf as a nineteen-year-old farming immigrant, Lawry took up the offer of a job at Remuera.[75] Lawry did not stay long on Dilworth's farm. As ambitious as he was able, he made good during the 1870s as a supplier of dairy produce and meat for the Auckland market. During that decade town-supply farms boomed. Those at Mount Albert alone, said *Brett's Auckland Almanac* in 1878, sent 'about 1,000 tons of oaten and grass hay to market yearly, besides the produce of 100 acres of wheat, large quantities of milk, butter, poultry, eggs etc'.[76]† Lawry made a practice of leasing from others farmland

---

* Part of this area was leased.

† It is often forgotten that the great increase in horse-drawn transport in the late nineteenth century led not only to an explosion of the horse population but also to an extraordinary increase in the demand for fodder. The number of horses in the Auckland provincial district rose from 5,621 in 1861 to 68,449 in 1901.

for his town-supply business. Thus, at one stage he ran stock on James Williamson's Surrey Hills (Grey Lynn) estate. He also had irons in other fires; for many years he was proprietor of the Albert Hotel in Epsom. But Lawry could scarcely have taken up the Remuera lease at a less propitious stage, for the rental was set just at the time the price of suburban land was booming. Dilworth's good fortune was Lawry's misfortune. Lawry persisted with his lease nevertheless, as Auckland was overwhelmed by a slump. In 1890 he chose not to renew his lease, whether because of the adverse turn in the town-supply market, or because he had chosen to throw himself wholeheartedly into the parliamentary arena he had entered in 1887, we cannot say.

With the ending of Lawry's lease on 30 April 1890, two new tenants took over Remuera. The former home farm south of Great South Road, excluding the old Dilworth homestead, was leased with a cottage and milking sheds to W. Sands for £110 a year. Ambury English & Co., at that period the foremost milk and dairy produce suppliers in Auckland, took over the remainder of the estate, 153½ acres containing the old but well-preserved farmhouse once known as Ivy Cottage, a 'men's house'—as the bunkhouse for farmhands was called—'a large milking shed' and stables.[77] The annual rental paid by Ambury's for its five-year lease was £970, but this also included the use of Dilworth's 'scoria land' at Te Papapa. Since the notional split on the books was £500 for Remuera and £470 for Te Papapa,[78] the Remuera estate over 1890–95 was yielding only £610 a year (£500 from Ambury's, £110 from Sands) in contrast to the £1,380 returned by Lawry's lease over each of the previous five years.

Yet Dilworth was probably happy about the new arrangements. When the leases were set in 1890 Auckland was passing through its worst depression ever; bankruptcies were everywhere, land values had collapsed, and prices for farm produce were deeply depressed. Probably Dilworth counted himself lucky to have a financially strong tenant. And he had a further consolation: Remuera had become a farm of great value. It was the largest single piece of flat pastureland in the inner Auckland suburbs. In August 1886, 'Dilworth's paddock' (so-called in the *Herald*) at the corner of Great South and Manukau Roads on the side opposite the Junction Hotel, had been the site of a bitterly contested provincial rugby game* played before a 'dense throng' of 8,000 people.[79] Land so flat and extensive could easily be converted into villa sites. The land-tax valuation of the Remuera estate in 1890 stood at £38,100. Dilworth was astute enough to foresee that, as Auckland continued to grow, the land would be worth much more than

---

* The game between Auckland and a hitherto better-performed Wellington team was won by Auckland, two tries to one. Only after their return to their hometown did the members of the Wellington team reveal their resentment at the 'biased' rulings of the Auckland umpire, A. H. Cotter, who (they claimed) had robbed them of victory. Members of the Poneke Club hanged Cotter in effigy outside their clubrooms.

A horse-tram in Broadway, Newmarket, 1887. Such transport greatly increased the value of Dilworth's farm as a potential site for residential subdivision.
Auckland Public Library

Junction Hotel at the corner of Manukau and Great South Roads in 1878.
Auckland Public Library

that, partly because by the mid-1880s it had become connected with the inner city by horse-drawn trams. Its potential for profitable subdivision was enormous.

It remains only to speak of the Dilworth homestead, not to be regarded in the later nineteenth century as a farm property but as a landed proprietor's residence. How life went on there during Dilworth's later years can be pieced together from two sources: the Dilworth account books, and the contemporary descriptions and recollections of those who knew the house at first hand while James Dilworth lived there.

While it is true that Epsom and Remuera were mainly farming districts until well on in the nineteenth century, as early as the 1860s a migration towards these salubrious suburbs set in among prosperous families from the town. People of mark in commerce, and in the professions of law and banking for instance, began to erect imposing homes in extensive grounds, designed and laid out to give both pleasure to the owners and physical expression to their material success. In the 1860s and 1870s Dilworth gained new neighbours. Close to hand, where the Diocesan Girls' School now stands, the lawyer Edwin Hesketh in 1873 put a large house, which he named St John's Wood, in grounds which over the years he tastefully landscaped. Somewhat earlier, D. L. Murdoch, inspector of the Bank of New Zealand, built a splendid house to the rear of the Dilworths, aptly named Prospect in view of its admirable site on the slopes of Mount St John. Further afield

Prospect, the home of D. L. Murdoch, Inspector of the BNZ.
Auckland Museum Library

other large residences arose.[80] From vantage points within the Dilworth homestead fine houses could be seen: Mr Justice Gillies's Rocklands, Alfred Buckland's Highwic, G. B. Owen's Brightside and J. B. Russell's Marivare, to name a few only. The mood of the time was for owners to surround these houses with a surprising variety of trees and shrubs. So did Dilworth. Not from a spirit of emulation, but through personal inclination, he pressed on with the beautification of the environs of his big house.

The homestead itself, the architect of which is not known, was, as has been earlier noted, impressive but rather lacking in style. It has been referred to as a 'farmhouse mansion', on balance an apt description. The house was approached by way of substantial wrought-iron gates—there is a suspicion of aspiring Irish landlordism here—which opened upon a broad shingle drive rising gently towards the volcanic knoll on which the house stood. A belt of trees, well-established by 1863, as an estate plan drawn at that time makes clear, stood on either side of the drive.[81] Each belt, too substantial to be thought of as an avenue, included but was by no means confined to macrocarpa, radiata pine, pohutukawa, puriri, beech and Norfolk pine. Two Norfolk pines ultimately grew so large that they endangered the house; one of the first duties of the Dilworth Trust Board was to have them felled, a course of action to which the newly-widowed Isabella consented but with voiced reluctance.[82] Clumps and groves which Dilworth planted in the homestead grounds had his usual mixture of natives and exotics: totara, nikau, cordyline (cabbage tree), oaks, planes and Moreton Bay figs—a giant specimen of the last was blown over in a storm as recently as 1991.[83] It is certain he introduced a monkey-puzzle tree and a Queensland kauri. Nevertheless some aged trees and shrubs about the property today, claimed to be of Dilworth's planting, are probably of more recent provenance.[84] The foundation pupils of the school also recalled finely scented roses in beds near the house, and colourful displays of daffodils and dahlias in season. Almost certainly these were put in during Dilworth's lifetime. Those early pupils also spoke of the outbuildings of the old homestead: haylofts, harness sheds and a farm dairy.[85] They further recalled the orchard, and the old freshwater tank which served as the first school baths.

How life was arranged at the Dilworth homestead is best gathered from a complete run of estate accounts covering the period 1886–94 in the Dilworth Trust Archives. The usual number of household servants at that time was about four, two of whom were constant: an outside manservant-cum-farm-manager, one William Bennett, and a female house servant, Mrs Lizzie Firth. Bennett and his family lived in a cottage on the small home farm; his job was to take care of the horses, a small dairy herd and a poultry run; he also fattened a few heifers which, sold to the local livestock agents, Hunter and Nolan or Buckland's, brought in about eighty pounds each year. He was on an

Trees beside the Dilworth homestead drive, now partly covered by the Dilworth School chapel.
Dilworth School Archives

annual wage of seventy-eight pounds a year all found. Mrs Firth, cook and chief indoor servant, was on a monthly wage of £2 8s, also all found. The names of various girls appear in the wages book as Nellie, Jessie and Mary. Sometimes anonymously they appear under the heading of 'servant's wages'. These female servants, presumably housemaids, earned 7s 6d a week. The wages account also refers to temporary workforce. Periodically men were taken on for seasonal or repair work: they were paid at daily rates or employed on contract.[86]

The Personal Expenses Account reveals that James and Isabella spent little on themselves.[87] Life in that big house went on in comfort but without ostentation. Visitors spoke of the tone of the house as severe. The Dilworths were not reclusive in their older years, as rumour has sometime portrayed them; the Coates family of Matakohe, the Cheesemans of Parnell, the Hardy family of Lichfield, Bishop and Mrs Cowie and Isabella's Hall relatives are all known to have visited. But towards the end, socializing in the Dilworth household was limited.

CHAPTER ELEVEN

Proprietor of City Land

WHEN DILWORTH became elderly, people began to speak of his 'enormous wealth'.[1] But whether this was fact, and if so where precisely that wealth came from, they really did not know. Dilworth himself was largely responsible for this ignorance. He always played his cards close to his chest. Onto a natural taciturnity had been grafted, during his early life as a banker, a passion for confidentiality. For the mature Dilworth, discretion was the supreme business virtue. Excessive openness, whether on the part of business associates or relatives, was a matter of great concern to him. Letters he wrote to his nephew Willie John Mossman, who as an adult was an impetuous and loquacious as Dilworth was not, give the clearest insight into Dilworth's own feelings. 'I wish you specially to keep what I write to yourself', he instructed Willie John, 'and I do not want *anybody* to know what I have said to you.'[2] On another occasion, his nephew was told how he was to go about clinching a property deal. 'To carry out this, you must keep your own counsel and let NOBODY know what you intend to do, nor by speaking *to anyone* on the subject, or showing any anxiety, lead *anyone* to suspect you wish to buy.'[3]

Dilworth's advice on this occasion has a particular piquancy, because it relates to a land purchase in which Willie John was only the nominal buyer, acting as an agent for his Uncle James, who was putting up the money, though the property was ultimately given to Willie John. Such dodges on Dilworth's part were not rare. Andrew's 'purchase' of the Waitakere estate in 1861, it will be recalled, was not merely at a fictitiously high figure; it was in fact no purchase at all; James gave the land to his brother.[4] One also encounters deeds of conveyance where Andrew was listed as purchaser but was obviously holding the property in trust for James. (All this had to be hurriedly put right later on by declarations within a will, when Andrew unexpectedly fell mortally ill.)[5] Sometimes properties bought and mortgages advanced by Dilworth were put in the name of relatives or business associates. His Hall brothers-in-law, Robert, William and Edward, all appear to have been used on occasion to conceal Dilworth's own presence in a property transaction. Subterfuges like these (usually covered by declarations of trust) were neither rare nor illegal. Other businessmen resorted to them. But it would be fair to say that, with Dilworth, obfuscation in property matters became almost an art form. Which poses problems for the historian. Even where one has access to Dilworth's registered deeds there can be no guarantee that they tell an unvarnished tale. Particularly does this apply to Dilworth's property transactions in the town.

Given this obsession with secrecy, it is no surprise that Dilworth made no effort to enlighten people about his business affairs, nor to correct the common view that his wealth came mainly from the earnings of his fine Remuera estate and his broad acres scattered through the province. Popular misconception on that score, therefore, was total. The simple truth was that over half of Dilworth's gross income in his later years was derived from two city properties, on opposite corners, at the foot of Queen Street, where it intersected with Customs (then Custom House) Street. Of a total area of less than one acre, these two corners, named after the hotels which stood on them, the Waitemata on the west and the Thames on the east, provided an average annual rental income of £1,987 during the last seven years of Dilworth's life, a period when banks were in crisis and merchant houses rushing into the bankruptcy court.

It is hard to exaggerate the importance of these hitherto largely unregarded inner city properties in accounting for Dilworth's financial success. With their assured income they enabled him to continue to upgrade his commercial buildings in the 1880s, just as they shielded him over the same years against the disastrous losses of the Whaiti-Kuranui speculation. They enabled the old man to ride out, with little hurt, the economic storm that overwhelmed the colony in 1887. Their benefits extended well beyond Dilworth's life. In the early years of the Dilworth Trust Board, they continued to bring, in Pearce's phrase, 'handsome returns'[6]* until the subdivision into long-term leasehold sections of the Remuera and other suburban properties provided an adequate and assured annual revenue to fulfil the intention of Dilworth's will. But for the income derived from those inner city properties it is inconceivable that the Dilworth Ulster Institute would have been able to take in its first boys as early as 1906.

In this biography, something has been made of those strokes of good fortune which Dilworth experienced from time to time to bring him an apparently unintended success in later years. It would be tempting, but mistaken, to say how lucky he was to be able to buy so cheaply in

---

* In 1897, ninety-four per cent of the gross income (£3,560) of the Trust Board came from rentals and leases. Of that figure £1,375 came from the annual rentals of the two hotels leased to The Campbell and Ehrenfried Co. When those leases were renewed in 1902 the rentals rose to £1,950.

Rentals from city properties such as Tyrone Buildings and the Thames Hotel enabled Dilworth School to open in 1906.
Alexander Turnbull Library

Auckland's early days the foreshore land which, in the years ahead, became such valuable real estate in the heart of town. In this instance Dilworth simply actualized the old adage that the businessman who gets on usually makes his own luck.

To understand why this was so in Dilworth's case, one must go back to the beginnings of Auckland. The portion of the block bought from the Ngati Whatua which Governor Hobson marked out as the heart of his new capital in 1840, the immediate hinterland of Commercial Bay and the Horotiu (Queen Street) Valley, suffered from a distinct handicap—a shortage of flat land.[7] To overcome this deficiency, Felton Mathew, the surveyor general, provided, in his first plan, for allotments of reclaimed land to be developed on the tidal flats of Commercial Bay. But reclamation was limited during the first twenty years. First the Crown, then the provincial council, concentrated upon providing wharf and jetty space. The small allotment (1 rood 8 perches) on the eastern side of the foot of Queen Street which Dilworth bought at a Crown auction in 1847 was at the time no more than a tongue of spoil deposited on the shoreline.[8] Further east towards Point Britomart, reclamation had not as yet taken place, as Heaphy's 'Street Plan of

Auckland 1851' confirms, showing Dilworth's as the only occupied section in 'Custom House Street'.[9] The other surveyed allotments in that street still lay beneath the tidal waters of Commercial Bay.

Shortly after his purchase Dilworth sold the non-corner (eastern) half of his allotment.[10] The portion he retained he let lie virtually undeveloped for twenty years. But he had no misgivings about the wisdom of his investment, recognizing that flat land at the centre of settlement would always be at a premium, and his at the point where port and town came together most of all. That is why he was determined to hang on to it, as a journalist later expressed it, 'through thick and thin',[11] always keeping a weather eye on any changes on the waterfront that would increase the value of his allotment. This alone explains why, in 1854, when he was universally regarded as a farmer, he stood (successfully) in a strenuously contested election for the nine-man committee of harbour commissioners set up under the Auckland Harbour Act of 1854.[12]

During Auckland's first twenty years, such prominence as Dilworth's corner allotment had, arose not from what he himself was doing on it but from the activity of others on the foreshore in front of it, beside the first jetty which went up in the 1840s. Here was one of the most favoured spots of the early Maori traders, some of them from tribal areas as far away as the Coromandel Peninsula, who, after beaching canoes or other boats at Commercial or Mechanics' Bay, laid out for sale their plentiful and cheap food usually borne in flax kits: varied vegetables, kumara, peaches, melons, potatoes, onions; and pork, turkey, geese, and fowls also.[13]*

During the 1860s the reclamation of the bed of Commercial Bay accelerated with the filling in of nine acres north of the foreshore between Fore (now Fort) Street and Custom House Street, and east towards Point Britomart.[14] It is known that, although Dilworth did not actually utilize his allotment himself, from the early 1860s it was occupied, almost certainly because he had leased it to others. The records of the newly formed City Board of Commissioners confirm use (or perhaps misuse) of the site.

> 17 July 1863. A report by Drs Philson and Kenderdine was read with reference to a nuisance on a part of the Intake at the Wharf, and the Clerk of the Board [was] ordered to intimate to Mr James Dilworth to remove the nuisance, in terms of the City Board Act 1863.
>
> 24 July 1863. Mr James Dilworth having agreed to remove the nuisance at the Intake, orders were given to take no further action on the matter.[15]

---

* Maori traders were also on the other corner, which in time became Dilworth's as well. The saying that the Maori people victualled Auckland through the 'Three Ps'—pork, peaches and potatoes—is memorable, but understates the range of Maori foods supplied. Maori traders brought much needed firewood, too.

The nuisance was obviously a health hazard, possibly putrescent matter choking drains, with Dilworth acted against as owner of the property and not necessarily as perpetrator of the nuisance.

The reminiscences of an old pioneer in 1925 tell us of how another lessee of Dilworth utilized the site in those times. He recalled that

> In 1865 when I landed, a galvanised shed on high piles occupied the site, and some of my shipmates established in it a marine store, which included amongst its wares second-hand clothing. I am not sure if the tide actually washed around the piles but the water was certainly not far away. I am inclined to think that the section was on one of the tongues of rock* that ran out into the mud. At that time Queen Street at this point was simply an embankment, and the shed in question was reached by planking.[16]

To understand how Dilworth was spurred on to develop his township land, and how he came to acquire further property in the heart of town, the best vantage point to take is the early 1860s. At that time Auckland had a population of barely 12,000, with most of its buildings crudely built of timber, and its main thoroughfare Shortland Crescent (today Street). At the foot of Queen Street, stores, shops and offices, mainly housed in unpainted one- or two-storey weatherboard structures, had sprung up, much more thickly on the western side opposite Dilworth's allotment. On the corner itself was a hotel, the Waitemata, run since 1862 by John Copland.[17] Copland was a popular Auckland character, in later years renowned as a long-serving member of (amongst other yachting groups) the Anniversary Regatta Committee. He was said to have such 'tremendous lung power' that regatta-goers often wondered why he should find it necessary to fire a gun at the beginning and end of races.[18] He also ran a good public house, even if the first Waitemata, though better than the former pioneer grog shops, was, like many of the early Auckland hostelries, not particularly well housed. It was one of the first buildings which H. B. Morton saw as he arrived in Auckland in 1864; it seemed to him 'a primitive-looking wooden building'.[19] It had been built by Hugh Coolahan, who had also put up some stores on his corner section, as had a few of the long-term lessees on the Coolahan allotment.

Hugh Coolahan (1800–72) was an early colonist of some distinction.[20] Like Dilworth, with whom he served on the provincial council in the 1850s as a staunch supporter of John Williamson, he was from Tyrone, but in his case from Strabane, a town on the western border of the county. On arrival in Auckland in 1842, Coolahan set himself up in his home trade as a baker of bread and biscuits in Shortland Street, on a narrow corner section running some distance

---

* Spurs and projections of rock in this area were almost entirely made up of soft Waitemata sandstone.

PROPRIETOR OF CITY LAND

along Fields Lane. Other wooden buildings went up on this allotment, some put up by Coolahan, others by his tenants.* An energetic personality with a speculative cast of mind, Coolahan was much aware of the prospects which gold discoveries would provide for himself and his province. His main speculative activity, however, was concerned with town real estate. In that he bought widely. But his shrewdest and most valuable acquisition, in December 1850, was the irregularly-shaped corner section on which he built the biscuit factory later converted into the Waitemata.[21]† By the 1860s Coolahan had risen to be, like Dilworth, a substantial landed proprietor. His worldly success found expression in the fine seaward-facing home he built beside St George's Bay, Parnell. He was also a good Catholic whose counsel on property matters was often sought by Bishop Pompallier. He was much respected for having donated to the Church the land near today's Richmond Road on part of which St Paul's Marist College now stands.[22]

During 1866 Coolahan suffered a huge set-back when an 'extensive

---

* The tenancy arrangements indicated in the early deeds ran usually like this: with short-term tenancies, say weekly up to annual, the proprietor erected the building; with long-term leases, say ten to twenty-five years, the lessee would as a rule put up the building which, unless specified otherwise in the deed of lease, he would leave behind, when he departed 'peaceably and quietly' at the end of his term.

† On the site he originally opened the 'Commercial Bay Steam Mill, Biscuit Factory and Bakery'; address—'Queen Street Wharf, cnr of Custom-house Street'.

Coolahan's biscuit factory near the Queen Street wharf in 1856.
Alexander Turnbull Library

173

conflagration', the worst for years, laid waste the Waitemata corner.[23] At about ten in the evening of 28 August, a fire which began in the Niccols's ships' chandlery store raged through the five buildings of the area, some of which contained highly inflammable material. In places, flames leaped Queen Street to lick buildings on the far side. So fierce was the blaze that the whole harbour was lit up, illuminating the vessels berthed there. For the 4,000 spectators who gathered at the blaze, all was over in little more than a half-hour; 'eight leading business premises' were destroyed. The total loss was estimated at the time to be £20,000, of which only £12,000 was covered by insurance. The 'two great losers by this calamitous occurrence', as the *Herald* put it, were Copland, the greater part of whose stock was uninsured, and (even more) Coolahan, over whose property—the hotel worth £3,000 and an adjacent building—there was no insurance cover at all.[24]

Guy Scholefield, editor of the first *Dictionary of New Zealand Biography*, has written of this great fire as a cruel twist of fate for Coolahan, which 'destroyed most of his property and his financial prosperity'.[25] But long before 1866 Coolahan's finances were under strain. By the time of the fire they were at breaking point.

At that time, Coolahan's income came from three sources: the earnings of his bakery, speculative profits from land deals and the rents paid for his properties, of which the greater part were on his Shortland Street allotment, the Customs Street West corner and near St Barnabas Point, Parnell, where he had five cottages. Normal trading debts aside, his heaviest outgoing was on mortgage repayment.[26] Almost from the

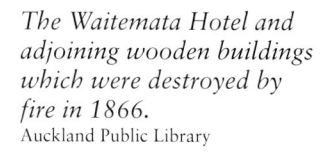

The Waitemata Hotel and adjoining wooden buildings which were destroyed by fire in 1866.
Auckland Public Library

outset, the tenements, stores and offices which he had put up on his properties were financed, not from reinvested profits, but from borrowing. The pattern in the 1850s was for him to raise money by mortgaging his town properties to local capitalists: settlers (J. S. Macfarlane, Logan Campbell, John Pilkington are examples), army officers and men of the cloth.[27] The advances were at rates of between ten and twelve-and-a-half per cent interest, and usually for a year or two, at the end of which Coolahan would seek to roll them over. His mortgage indebtedness beginning at the modest level of £258 10s in 1852[28] had lifted to £1,500 within five years.[29] He seemed unable or unwilling to pull it back.

By 1862 his borrowing reached a new order of magnitude arising out of the financing of buildings on his Customs Street corner. He borrowed £6,000 at ten per cent from the New Zealand Insurance Co. (NZI)[30] of which he had been a founding director three years previously.[31] His cash-flow position deteriorated. Coolahan's inability to meet interest payments saw the NZI, in February 1864, agree to make an overdue £600 a further charge on the loan; but the tone of the new deed was threatening.[32] A year later Dilworth entered the picture. He provided Coolahan with an advance of £2,000 for four years at twelve per cent, secured against a portion of the corner section released by NZI for that purpose, and on the day after (1 April 1865) advanced £1,000 at the same rate, as second mortgage over the lands used by NZI to secure its loan.[33] The language used in the deed of mortgage left the borrower in no doubt that Dilworth was a lender of last resort from whom no mercy was to be expected: in the event of default 'it shall be lawful for the said James Dilworth . . . forthwith or at any time to exercise the power of sale vested in Mortgagees by the 19th clause of the Conveyancing Ordinance, No. 10 . . . after the lapse of three months'.

The fire of 1866 did not destroy Coolahan; it simply pushed him over the brink. But reconstructing the steps between 1866 and 1870 by which Dilworth gained ownership of the properties, which Coolahan had used as security for the first mortgage advance of NZI and the second mortgage put up by Dilworth, is difficult if not impossible. The only known surviving property records for this period are contained in the Deeds Registers in the Auckland Land and Deeds Registry. Two volumes (9M and 23D) once had the relevant mortgages recorded in their pages. Alas, 23D now has pages 568–71 crudely cut out; 9M has pages 838–41 completely extracted. From the documents that are left, however, one is able to infer much of what Dilworth did, even though NZI's role as first mortgagee remains obscure.

What follows is the most likely course of events. Soon after the fire, Coolahan's main creditors, NZI and Dilworth, decided that they would disregard his inability to keep up mortgage payments, and rebuild on his property to keep up their equity in it. An architect,

Richard Keals, was commissioned to design a new Waitemata, to be a three-storey plastered-brick hotel, with a thirty-six-foot frontage on Queen Street, and seventy-five-foot frontage on Customs Street.[34] It reopened, once again with Copland as licensee, in May 1867, a bare nine months after the fire. Keals's design showed a mixture of styles with each storey a distinct order of architecture.[35] Its 'palatial character' was much praised. The *Herald* boasted that it was 'as handsome and imposing a block of buildings as any colonial city could present'.[36]

Whilst Coolahan retained the formal ownership of the land on which the new hotel stood, he had no part in the building's reconstruction, nor, given his financial straits, any prospect at the age of sixty-seven of truly making it once again his own. But he was a man of spirit. He moved on to Shortland (Thames) with the goldminers and opened a bakery there.[37] This business prospered modestly but not in such a way as to enable him to redeem his mortgaged estate in Auckland, on which final payment fell due on 2 March 1869. Dilworth waited a year before approaching the registrar of the Supreme Court, Laughlin O'Brien, to request the right of sale arising out of the default by Coolahan of payment of the £3,144 7s 1d due.[38] When Coolahan did not act within the statutory three months, the registrar directed a public auction to take place at the mart of C. Arthur & Son on 14 June 1870.[39] Coolahan's properties were put under the hammer as a job lot to be entirely paid for in cash. Dilworth's bid of £500 was the highest. He then paid off the first mortgagee, the NZI, who enabled him to do so by advancing him the necessary money. That done, and obviously relieved to have a secure mortgagor at last, the NZI made a conveyance of complete title to Dilworth on 14 July 1870.[40]

The properties which came into Dilworth's possession in 1870 were:

- the corner allotment, Shortland Street (thirty feet), Fields Lane (153 feet), with shops and offices thereon;
- the Waitemata Hotel corner;
- one brick, four wooden houses at St Barnabas Point, Parnell; and
- four allotments in the Parish of Takapuna totalling 202 acres.

By the first three items, Dilworth had almost doubled in value his holding of property in the township and its close environs.

The Waitemata was the second hotel to stand on Dilworth land. By 1870 a new hotel was already up and open on the opposite side of Queen Street, on the allotment at the corner of Customs Street East which Dilworth had left undeveloped for years. He left no record saying why he at last decided to build. Unlike that other great Auckland philanthropist, Logan Campbell, who explained and justified, in two separate autobiographies, every important decision of his life, Dilworth

PROPRIETOR OF CITY LAND

left behind no such authorised version. But in the context of the time it is easy to understand why he made his new departure.

In the winter of 1867, when business spirits in Auckland were at their lowest, wonderful news came through to the town of finds of 'extraordinary richness' on the recently opened Thames goldfields.[41] A boom quickly built up. Thousands of diggers rushed to the Thames, drawing in their wake food, all manner of supplies, and timber and mining equipment—these last two because, unlike the usual alluvial strikes elsewhere, those of the Hauraki fields were an affair of mineshafts and crushing equipment. The mining boom spurred Dilworth into action, though not like the generality of Auckland capitalists, who turned to mining company promotion and speculation in shares. Influenced, no doubt, by the recent rebuilding of the Waitemata, he decided to put his money into bricks and mortar. He was well aware that, for men and goods alike, the main point of departure for the Thames was the Queen Street wharf, on the doorstep of his allotment

Jack Tars bargaining with Maori women for goods in flax kits at the foot of Queen Street in an Illustrated London News *drawing done just before the third storey was added to Tyrone Buildings.*
Alexander Turnbull Library

so to speak. Why not build a diggers' hotel? It was no coincidence that the hotel which went up was called the Thames.

Early in 1868 he made his move, approaching the two with whom he, as a mortgagee, had been most associated in resurrecting the old Waitemata Hotel from the ashes: Richard Keals the architect, and Copland the first licensee of the new Waitemata.[42] Dilworth's first move was to head-hunt Copland to become the licensee of another hotel, the construction of which Copland would undertake on Dilworth's section. Keals was commissioned to design a hotel of two storeys with a forty-foot frontage on Queen Street and seventy-foot frontage on Customs Street. It is not known whether Dilworth agreed to provide Copland with financial assistance in his undertaking. If he did, the fact does not appear on the property records.

In April 1868 Copland applied to the licensing committee for a licence, which shortly after was granted.[43] Keals was prompt in providing a design, this time in a much plainer style, the only distinctive ornamentation being circular-headed windows and openings. The Thames was to be a structure (once again) of plastered brick, standing on a foundation of volcanic bluestone, with an ample basement storey for cellarage. Inevitably it was compared with the recently-completed Waitemata. The view of the press at the time, that, though the exterior of the Thames was not 'so obtrusive', its interior facilities 'surpass[ed] in every respect' those of the Waitemata, seems to be one with which posterity has agreed.[44]

The construction of the Thames, which began in early May 1868, took three months longer than expected, probably because providing satisfactory foundations proved unusually time-consuming. Thirty feet of reclamation spoil and tidal mud had to be penetrated before solid Waitemata sandstone was reached.* As an old man Harry Mossman recalled how 'Uncle Dilworth' on one occasion in 1868 woke the Mossman household at Ellerslie when he 'turned up' on horseback at five in the morning. Harry wrote:

> My mother . . . his favourite sister, was quite concerned, and she said 'What is the matter?'
> He said, 'I have been up all night Eleanor. The tide runs up and down the section I have bought at the bottom of Queen Street, and although it is dark, I will be there every hour while I know they are sinking the piles till I know they have a substantial foundation.'[45]

The piles on which the Thames was to stand, presumably kauri or totara, would have gone down at least thirty feet.[46]†

---

* In later days it was said that the cellars of the Thames would occasionally be flooded by seepage from the harbour.

† The piles on which the Waverley, the hotel built on the opposite (seaward) side of Customs Street, 1883–84, rested were solid kauri spars, forty feet long. When the Waverley was demolished in 1964 to make way for a high-rise successor, the foundations of kauri piles and hand-pressed bricks were found to be well preserved.

The only formal financial assistance known to have been given by Dilworth to Copland was in the form of a mortgage loan of £360—equivalent to the first year's rent—for ten years at ten per cent, secured against the lease.[47] (Copland was to prosper sufficiently in his new hotel to be able to retire this mortgage within thirty months.) The hotel opened on 1 November 1868.[48] Copland's advertisement in the local press read:

>
> NEW RUSH
> OPENING
> of the
> THAMES HOTEL
> JOHN COPLAND
> MONDAY 1ST NOVEMBER
> QUEEN ST WHARF[49]

Just as the Waitemata on the other corner became renowned as the drinking hole, so to say, of yachtsmen, wharf lumpers and overseas seamen, so the Thames began and remained true to its name, as the diggers' hotel. A commemmorative article in the *Herald* a century later explained it thus:

> Adjacent to the Queen St Wharf, the hotel was close to the steamers leaving for and returning from the Thames, and no doubt fortified many a doubtful digger departing for the goldfield and helped solace many of those who returned and whose thirst had not been entirely quenched by the 80 or more hotels which existed at Thames at that time.[50]

Dilworth was so pleased with the results of his first positive venture into urban real estate that he set about building upon the rest of his allotment. Richard Keals was commissioned to prepare plans for a block to be built next to the Thames Hotel and designed to be of a piece with it. Called the Tyrone Buildings, the new two-storey, brick shop and office block, had a similar facade to the Thames and in construction was equally substantial. Not surprisingly the whole block, including the hotel, was at times mistakenly referred to as the Tyrone Buildings.

Problems, probably concerned with laying foundations, caused vexatious delays in the construction of the Tyrone block, and put Dilworth at odds with the City Board of Commissioners. In August 1869 the commissioners instructed its officer of nuisances to order Dilworth to remove a pile of scoria stones he had left lying too long in the street.[51] He removed the nuisance, but progress on the contract remained tardy. In March 1870 the commissioners granted Dilworth 'the space that he presently has' enclosed by hoardings for a further two months, and gave permission for him to erect a fence in Customs Street 'twenty feet from his building for three months'.[52] When at the end of that time Dilworth asked for a further extension of time to keep up his hoardings, the commissioners, whose ears were ringing with the complaints of neighbouring shopkeepers, lost all patience with the applicant and resolved that 'Mr Dilworth be written to and requested to remove the nuisance, in terms of the Auckland Municipal Police Act'.[53]

Since commissioners' reports recorded no further complaints it can be assumed the block was finished soon after. This was, however, simply the first stage in Dilworth's building programme, which in the event extended over twenty years, not just for the hotels but the adjoining buildings as well. In 1883 a third storey was added to the Thames and Tyrone Buildings, to the design of the architect Edward Mahoney. A modern architectural historian has lavished high praise on the Mahoney additions which, as he puts it, 'transformed this [hotel] into a splendid hostelry at vast expense'.[54] As was customary with long-term urban leases of that era, the exterior alterations were the responsibility of the proprietor (Dilworth) while the cost of interior refurbishment fell upon the lessee, at that date R. Whitson & Sons, brewers. In 1889 Mahoney was called upon once again to extend the Waitemata Hotel, mainly a matter of carrying out a long overdue upgrading of the interior, and of improving the associated stores and offices. Dilworth was wise to continue this investment in his city

The Thames Hotel and Tyrone Buildings; an undated (1884?) sketch just after the third story had been added.
Alexander Turnbull Library

properties. During the 1891 financial year the return on leases and rentals for the two corners was over fifty-one per cent of his earnings from all sources.[55]

With hindsight wisdom it can be seen that when Dilworth in the later 1860s began to shift the chief emphasis of his investment away from farming and rural land speculation towards city real estate, he made the most astute business move of the second half of his life. (His massive speculation in upper Thames Valley lands ten years later was an aberration, therefore; he departed from economic good sense and was punished.) Between 1871 and 1885 the value of city and suburban land in Auckland multiplied many times over.[56] The reason is not hard to find. In 1871, Auckland like the colony at large was on the threshold of a period of great growth. Within twenty years the population of Auckland city and suburbs rose to over 50,000, an increase of 150 per cent.[57] More significantly, the city began to assume its modern function as the main entrepôt of the whole country. Its mercantile character was expressed in the transformation of the foreshore and the wharves. Much was done by the new harbour board on money borrowed abroad. The Queen Street wharf was extended and additional tees were attached to create (in Brett's view) a 'magnificent wharf, which is unequalled in the Australasian colonies'.[58] On either side of the Queen Street wharf, reclamation of the seabed went on apace. As the city boomed under expansionist policies, urban land values rose extraordinarily. Reclaimed land on the western side of the main wharf put up for leasehold auction in 1878 realized bids at a level usually associated with freehold. The 'unearned increment' produced by city growth—so popular with controversialists of that era—was making Dilworth's two corners very valuable indeed.

During the 1880s the foot of Queen Street became, more than ever, a point of convergence for traffic. In 1884 the new City of Auckland Tramways Company placed its terminus there for the horse-tram service running to Ponsonby and Parnell. In the following year, on 26 October, the chief railway depot for the province, hitherto at Point Britomart, was shifted to a point in Queen Street, a minute's stroll from Dilworth's two hotels.[59]* The Dilworth properties were now at the gateway to the city and remained so for over half a century. They were regarded as landmarks; 'Meet you at the Thames [or Waitemata] corner!' was to be a parting cry heard on Auckland streets for decades.

This Dilworth would not have known when he launched himself as a rentier of city real estate. Having seen so many settlers (Lundon and Coolahan among them) come to grief through inability to service their loans, the cautious Dilworth must have been conscious of the

---

* The fill from the demolition of Point Britomart was utilized for further waterfront reclamation.

risks as well as the rewards of a move which, for the first time in his life, made him a long-term borrower. But borrow he must. Consider the financial liabilities he undertook over a short period of time.

FINANCIAL OBLIGATIONS INCURRED BY DILWORTH, 1868–70, ARISING OUT OF URBAN AND SUBURBAN PROPERTY DEALS

Date	Sum	Obligation incurred	Remarks
23/6/68	£1,560	Lundon's Farm (Ellerslie) assigned in lieu of payment of principal (£1,200) and accrued interest (£360)	Deed No. 37702 in LTO. See also DI 3A: 2082
1868–70	Say £2,000	Estimate of capital put up by Dilworth for building of Thames Hotel and Tyrone Buildings	Figures not available. Value of buildings based on 1892 land tax returns
14/6/70	£500	Successful bid by Dilworth at registrar's sale of Coolahan's mortgaged properties	Properties on Waitemata corner, Shortland Street, Parnell and Takapuna
On or about 14/6/70	£9,850	Dilworth takes over from Coolahan his indebtedness to NZI, giving as security for payment, properties bought in at 14 June 1870 auction	Deed No. 41922 in LTO; 25D:503; Deeds Index 4R:456. Sum borrowed equivalent to principal and accumulated interest
7/7/70	£3,144 7s 1d	Sum forfeited in principal and interest due when Dilworth requested registrar's sale re Coolahan's default of second mortgage	Deed No. 41920 in LTO. See 25D:28

Dilworth's city properties viewed, in 1885, from the Queen Street entrance of the new railway station (today's Queen Elizabeth Square).
Alexander Turnbull Library

To put things bluntly, Dilworth, like so many settlers who had made money in the early years, had become restlessly acquisitive; accumulating greater possessions seems to have become, at this stage of his life, an end in itself. In economic terms, the case for borrowing to achieve such a goal was very strong: land values were rising; loan money was freely available; and profits arising from speculative sale of property on a rising market could well fund interest payments. In any case, the quantity of land which Dilworth still left unencumbered was his guarantee of survival. At that time it was thought, as it is today, no more than sound business practice to use one's asset strength to fund growth by borrowing.

The years ahead were to show that Dilworth's move into city properties was a shrewd one. When hard times came in the mid-1880s he survived; more, he prospered. Auckland men of mark supposed to be grander and wiser than he—James Williamson, Thomas Morrin, J. C. Firth, Frederick Whitaker and others—were unable to do either.

DILWORTH'S MORTGAGE BORROWING, 1870–87

Deed no.	Date	Where recorded at LTO	Mortgagee	Terms	Security provided	Date retired
41922	12/7/70	16M: 503	NZI	£9,850 at 8% for 4 years	Coolahan's properties bought in 14/6/70	20/12/72 13M: 791
46409	21/12/72	17M: 290	South British Insurance	£4,000 at 6.5% for 10 years	Thames Hotel corner	7/8/77 24M: 267
46410	21/12/72	17M: 293	South British Insurance	£6,000 at 6.5% for 10 years	Waitemata corner	5/6/77 22M: 726
36785	5/6/77	23M: 260	Edward Costley	£6,000 at 7% for 10 years	Tyrone Buildings	5/2/84
57790	5/10/77	27M: 15	J. C. & W. F. Buckland	£4,000 at 6% for 4 years	Thames Hotel	28/2/83 R3: 536
64736	6/5/80	29M: 410	NZ Loan & Merc. Agency Co.	£15,000 at 8% for 4 years	Taupiri Estate Pt Remera, etc	28/10/80 F4: 693
67101	19/10/80	29M: 644	Edward Costley	£8,000 plus £2,000 at 6.5% for 10 years	Waitemata Hotel corner	5/2/84 R10: 139
46410	21/12/82	17M: 293	South British Insurance	£6,000 at 6.5% for 2 years	Customs St W shops	
87420	21/5/84	R11: 273	Conveyance Costley excrs to C of E Trust	£6,000 at 6.5%; term indefinite	Tyrone Buildings and Thames	
87568	4/6/84	R10: 407	J. M. Clark, G. Harper, W. A. Waddell. Trustees?	£7,000 at 7% for 5 years	Customs St W shops	
90958	25/11/84	R7: 699	G. P. Pierce, R. Walker, M. Rawlings. Trustees?	£3,000 at 7% for 7 years	Thames Hotel corner	

When farming was depressed, and large unsaleable Waikato estates a nightmare for those lumbered with them, Dilworth had what many fellow-businessmen hadn't: a sustained cash flow. His town properties, because money-spinners, proved to be his salvation.

Some early settlers who prospered used their land to raise loans which they applied simultaneously to sustain a high life style and to branch out into speculative enterprises. Dilworth was not of their number. He did not believe that it was possible (so to speak) to take milk and meat from the same beast. Anyway, on balance he was a lender of money not a borrower; a saver not a spender. He usually funded further properties bought, or fresh investments made, by ploughing back accumulated profits. That he and Isabella lived frugally also helped.[60] During his fifty-three years in New Zealand he departed twice only from this regime of prudence and economy: between 1848 and 1853 when he invested heavily in the Remuera estate, and between 1870 and 1887, the years now particularly under review.

Before turning to this later period, two cautionary points should be made. First, from the time Dilworth established himself in the mid-1850s, he continued to advance money on mortgage without intermission, even during those years when he himself was borrowing heavily. His asset strength and steady cash flow permitted this. A sign of his great financial strength right to the end was given in 1892 when the colony's banks were in crisis and savagely cutting back their advances; in that year he made, with comfort, a £1,500 mortgage loan to the owners of the Exchange Hotel building at the corner of Queen and Wyndham Streets.[61] At the time of his death Dilworth held seven mortgages totalling just on £5,000. Because his properties were spread far and wide and most were small, only the main borrowing is dealt with here.

Heavy financial commitments Dilworth entered into between 1868 and 1870 drove him into borrowing for the first time in thirteen years; these commitments included the final assignment by the Lundon family of the Ellerslie farm, the purchase of the Coolahan properties and erecting buildings on the Thames corner. There was a level of expenditure beyond the reach of his accumulated reserves, even though that fund had been added to recently by the railway compensation. The mortgage accommodation provided by the New Zealand Insurance Company was timely, though no doubt the insurance company for its part, much embarrassed by the protracted lock-up of funds in the Coolahan mortgage, was happy to substitute so strong a mortgagor as Dilworth for one so frail as Coolahan. In December 1872 Dilworth retired the NZI mortgage short of its full term, as the deed allowed, replacing it by an advance provided at a lower rate by the newly-formed South British Insurance Company. The £10,000 put up by the South British must have represented almost all the premium funds available for investment at that time.[62] Knowing each member of the board personally and having one (Joseph Howard) as a close friend probably helped Dilworth's cause and could help to explain why directors looked with favour on his application. However that may be, the board would have considered an advance to a sturdy borrower like Dilworth was liquid and therefore highly proper.[63]

In spite of a growing rental income from his new properties, Dilworth chose not to pay back his loan to South British as early as the agreement allowed.[64] The need to outlay over £3,800 for the Mangawara (Taupiri) Swamp—£750 for Dilworth's share of the initial 1872 purchase, and then £3,050 in 1877 to buy out William Hall's 'moiety'—is part of the explanation.[65]

Having decided that his borrowing would have to continue indefinitely, Dilworth was greatly assisted by his trusted attorney, Samuel Jackson, who arranged for Edward Costley, a long-term client of Jackson and Russell to put up a ten-year mortgage for him in 1876.[66] Costley was something of an Auckland eccentric. He was a denizen of Queen Street, often to be seen lounging about there, an elderly man with a flowing beard, humbly dressed—like a Jack Tar from a man-of-war—broad brimmed straw hat, check shirt thrown open to the waist and moleskin trousers. Appearances deceived, as did Queen Street chatter that he was a miser living on eighteen pence a day. On his death he was to be revealed as one of the wealthiest men in Auckland, and the shrewdest of businessmen, earning £1,600 a year from rents and £2,488 from interest on mortgage loans. By providing Dilworth with a £6,000 mortgage for ten years, Costley enabled his fellow-Irishman to retire his South British advance.[67] Jackson was also successful four months later in arranging for Dilworth another private mortgage, from the Otago Bucklands of Tumoi.[68] It was this second loan which obviously enabled Dilworth to settle his Mangawara account.

By 1880 Dilworth's finances came under further strain because of purchases of land negotiated with Maori tribes of the upper Thames Valley. Once again Costley came to the rescue with an £8,000 advance, extendable to £10,000 at Dilworth's request.[69] But because Dilworth had become hostage to a mortgage debt of upwards of £14,000, Costley's sudden death in 1883 was a considerable embarrassment to him. He was in the midst of the costly alterations to the Thames and Tyrone Buildings, a difficulty compounded by quarrels between two provincial land syndicates, to one of which he belonged, which had driven him into a large bank overdraft until the litigation was settled, and by a delay in payment for the lands by an English company.* Furthermore, the peculiar requirements of Costley's will meant that its executors had quickly to realise on his deceased estate.[70] It was fortunate that Samuel Jackson was Dilworth's solicitor as well as a trustee of the Costley will. Jackson was able to treat Dilworth

---

* See Chapter Twelve.

with consideration, coming to the rescue with alternative mortgage advances from Jackson and Russell clients,[71] one of whom happened, conveniently, to be a trust board of the Anglican diocese of which Dilworth himself was a long-term member.[72]

By 1887 Dilworth's period of borrowing was drawing to a close. He had lost heavily on his Whaiti-Kuranui speculations, but that failed business venture was behind him at last, and so the haemorrhage of payments to banks, syndicate accounts and lawyers was at an end. Financial adversity buffeted him on a number of fronts. He would never get his money back on the companies he had invested in.* His loss on what were once thought to be rock-solid shares in the BNZ was great and would continue. The collapse of property values which set in in 1885 was to carry on for years and wiped tens of thousands of pounds from his estate by the time of his death.

But the paradox was that in the period after 1887 when so many of Auckland's capitalists were ruined, Dilworth's position became unassailable. His asset strength, his freedom from crushing debt, the cash flow from the leases and rentals of his city and suburban properties, had put him in a sounder financial position than he had been in for years. Nor did he lose faith in Auckland land. It had made his fortune as a young man. He believed it would not let him down in his old age.

In 1889, when Dilworth was seventy-four, his young Irish friend the Revd George MacMurray came to Auckland on a visit, in response to an urgent invitation from Dilworth. During the 1930s slump MacMurray looked back upon his impressions of Auckland at the time of that visit forty-six years before:

> I was tremendously impressed on my arrival by the greatness of the economic depression, hardly believable now. I do not think there was a single carriage and pair owned in Auckland then. Mr Dilworth told me that it was never worse than it was then. But he had no doubts about the future of Auckland, and advised me that I could not make a mistake if I invested in Auckland property with my eyes closed.[73]

But to invest in property, however profitably, with eyes closed or open, the buyer must have money. 'Unfortunately', said MacMurray ruefully, 'I had none to invest'.

In giving this advice, Dilworth was reiterating the age-old adage of shrewd investors: 'Buy in gloom and sell in boom'. His long experience in the colony and his confidence in Auckland gave him no reason to doubt the instruction. His two greatest coups, buying Remuera in 1844 and getting his toehold on the Waitemata corner in 1866, had been achieved in times of slump. The business collapse of the 1880s should be looked on, he believed, not as an unrelieved

---

* These companies included: Colonial Bank, BNZ, Auckland Fibre, Auckland Tug, Union Sash & Door, NZ Freezing, NZ Woollen, Thames Valley & Rotorua Railway, New Moanatairi Goldmining, Maraitai Land and NZ Thames Valley Land Companies.

Wooden cottages in lower Parnell similar to those near St Barnabas Point that Dilworth took over from Coolahan.
Alexander Turnbull Library

disaster, but as an intermission which gave opportunity to those with the wit and the means, to buy cheaply into property on which they would reap a speculative harvest in the years ahead. Time proved his prediction right. But there were few others at that time with his financial resources to put this buying policy into practice.

This chapter ends with an attempt to answer the question with which it began: how wealthy was Dilworth? Stating correctly what his true financial position was over the last years of his life is not easy. Book valuations of his lands had to be revised downwards year by year. His share portfolio, which fortunately for him was relatively small, was devastated; and this applied to holdings in large concerns once thought soundly based and the rentiers' favourites, like the Bank of New Zealand and South British Insurance. A general picture of Dilworth's financial position in his last years is provided by three main sources:

- the estate ledgers covering 1887–94;
- the taxation returns provided by Dilworth after the passage of the Liberal Government's Land and Income Assessment Bill 1891; and
- the statement by the administrators of Dilworth's estate upon his real and personal property, acting upon probate, dated 1 February 1895.

What now follows is a statement drawn from the estate ledgers for 1892.[74]

J. DILWORTH'S ASSETS 30 APRIL 1892*

Real Estate	£	£
Freehold land	101,663	
Thames Valley Land Co.	7,296	
Maraitai Land Co.	5,381	
Tauranga land	2,081	
Gisborne land	1,305	
		117,726
Farm Improvements		1,838
Mortgages		
John Brown	300	
Patrick Heath	1,116	
James Henry	251	
Thomas Hall	750	
Thomas Paton	500	
		2,917
Joint Stock Companies		
South British Insurance	200	
Auckland Fibre	25	
Colonial Bank	1,115	
Bank of New Zealand	1,211	
Cambria G.M. Co.	45	
Moanatairi G.M. Co.	36	
		2,632
Sundry Debtors		2,884
Deposit Account in BNZ		3,000
		130,997
Less Sundry Creditors		141
Total Assets as at 30 April 1892		£130,856

Any statement of Dilworth's assets in these last years freezes what was an essentially fluid situation. Changing the image, attrition of those assets was constant through the early 1890s. That was why the administrators of the Dilworth estate in the year following his death returned a figure of £100,651 11s 10d as their estimate of its worth in terms of the Estates Duties Act. A fall in value of the assets of about twenty-three per cent in three years reflected drastic downward revaluations of rural land, a significant if less marked decline in suburban land values, and a continued slaughtering of the worth of Dilworth's company investment. But stocks and shares had not been crucial to his financial well-being at the end. He was essentially a landed proprietor.

*Figures are rounded to the nearest pound.

But even to dwell on the fall in value of Dilworth's landed assets distorts the picture. Provincial land prices had been fictitiously high in the early 1880s. The 1890s were, in a sense, simply a return to reality. In that environment the value of the Remuera estate and the city properties held up remarkably well. A much more effective measure of Dilworth's financial sources over the last years is provided by the profit and loss accounts, such as the 1891/92 returns.[75]

PROFIT AND LOSS ACCOUNT FOR THE YEAR ENDING 30 APRIL 1892*

Expenditure	£	Income	£
House expenses	367	Taupiri farm earnings	97
Personal expenses	265	Interest: bank & loans	357
Commission to agents	38	Rents	
Insurance	68	City properties	1,897
Rates and taxes	522	Parnell cottages	70
		Remuera & Te Papapa	1,056
		Lundon's farm	84
Charges—legal, accounting, administrative	160	Company dividends	138
Annuity to Mrs A. Dilworth	120		
Annuity to Mrs Eleanor Mossman	100		
	1,640		
Net profit	2,059		
	£3,699		£3,699

There are some notable features here. Although a return of £2,059 may not seem a high yield on a capital outlay of about £100,000, in the setting of 1891/92, which is usually regarded as the trough of the long depression, mere survival was a notable achievement. So many of the Auckland capitalists who were going under were (using the argot of the modern business world) 'asset rich but cash flow poor'. There would have been few in this era who would not have envied Dilworth's ability to pass on about £2,000 to his reserve of accumulated profits. Even more significant was that the account for the year ended 30 April 1892 was in no way exceptional. During the seven depression years recorded in the Dilworth ledgers (1888–94 inclusive) the profit and loss accounts had average annual outgoings of £1,651 compared with an average annual income of £3,913. This meant that net profits available for appropriation over the period were £15,833. In the financial context of the times this was an 'embarrassment of riches'. What is also significant is that out of the total earnings from those

---

*Figures are rounded to the nearest pound.

years, £27,393, over half, £13,910 came from the Waitemata and Thames corners.* As income from other sources fell away the earnings of those two corners (appearing in Dilworth's records as 'Town Rents') had lifted to fifty-seven per cent of his total income.

Regarded by the world at large as a quintessential man of the land, James Dilworth, unobserved, ended his days as a rentier of city real estate. His town properties were his salvation.

Queen Street looking southwards, from the Waitemata corner, in the late 1880s. A pioneer city transformed.
Auckland Public Library

---

* On the Customs Street East corner were the Thames and Tyrone Buildings which had five shops and stores. On the Customs Street West corner was the Waitemata, with three shops or stores, two with a Queen Street frontage (TT3, DTB).

CHAPTER TWELVE

Whaiti Kuranui

> When you shall these unlucky deeds relate,
> Speak of me as I am; nothing extenuate,
> Nor set down aught in malice.
> —Shakespeare, *Othello*

About 1870 Dilworth became friends with Joseph Howard, a tall, self-confident Auckland businessman somewhat younger than himself.[1] Like Dilworth, Howard was Irish, Anglican and prosperous. Unlike Dilworth he was impetuous. In time they entered a joint speculation in provincial land. Acting in partnership was something new for Dilworth who until then had been solitary in matters of business. The association was to harm the fortunes of both.

Born in 1832, the son of a Dublin merchant, Howard entered banking at the age of eighteen.[2] For eight years he remained in the service of the Provincial Bank of Ireland, holding positions in various parts of the province of Munster. Like many ambitious young Irishmen of that era, he decided to emigrate.[3] His chance to do so came in 1860 when the London office of the Union Bank of Australia appointed him to a post in Melbourne, where it was intended that he should serve for five years on an annual salary of £250.[4] He did not remain long in Australia. In 1861 he was shifted by the Union Bank to New Zealand where there was a surge of banking business arising out of the Otago gold discoveries, and the need for the Union to protect itself against the challenge of two new trading banks. Posted to Auckland, Howard rose to be accountant, the second most important officer of the branch there.

Shortly after the gold rush to the Thames began in 1867, a visitor named William Hunt dropped into Howard's office in Queen Street to seek help. He explained that he was one of a syndicate of four prospectors who had discovered gold on their claim beside the Kuranui Stream in the Thames 'but had no money to work it'.[5] Hunt then went on to offer Howard a tenth-share as a sleeping partner in this mine (which had been named the 'Shotover' after the fabled gold-rich South

Island river) if he would 'grubstake' the claim by putting up £100.*
A speculator at heart, Howard agreed. During lunch, friends told
Howard he had been a fool and should go down to the wharf and
retrieve his money straight away.[6] He went down but was too late, the
ship having already left for the Thames with Hunt aboard. For Howard
this was a lucky miss. With Howard's £100, and a similar amount from
H. F. Christie, BNZ manager at the Thames, Hunt's syndicate was
able to work the 'Shotover' mine until it made a fabulous strike. 'The
extraordinary yields from this property', according to one account,
'in a comparatively brief space of time raised the shareholders from
poverty to affluence.'[7] For their respective £100 grubstake Howard
and Christie each got back £20,000. On 19 August 1869 Howard
resigned from the Union Bank. His inspector reported it as 'an
unfriendly parting'.[8]

---

* 'Grubstakes' in miners' slang stood for 'food supply'. Grubstaking came to be applied to the practice of a syndicate of miners taking in sleeping partners to provide it with working capital to tide over the group during the period of tunnelling and shafting before returns came in. The practice was well-developed in the Thames by June 1868. (For the semantic origins of 'grubstake' see Partridge, *Smaller Slang Dictionary*, London, 1963, p. 64.)

Hunt's Shotover Mine which Joseph Howard grubstaked.
Alexander Turnbull Library

Hauraki mines required capital for machinery and for digging shafts.
Auckland Public Library

At the age of thirty-seven Howard had a competence and could live as an independent gentleman and entrepreneur. He married without delay, and settled with his wife Isabella Armstrong in a new house on a double-allotment in fashionable Wynyard Street.[9]* Not surprisingly, he continued to invest in gold mining companies.[10] But he also became a property investor in the Thames where he erected, in the boom settlement of Grahamstown, an imposing wooden hotel which he called the Pacific, locating it on the seafront opposite the main passenger jetty.[11] He built as an attachment to this hotel a theatre, naming it the Academy of Music. Hotel and theatre became a famous social centre, occasionally the resort of the famous. (During his visit to New Zealand, in 1869–70, Prince Alfred, Duke of Edinburgh, second son of Queen Victoria, stayed for a while with his entourage at the Pacific.)

In the 1870s Howard, who began listing his occupation as 'gentleman' or 'commission agent', diversified his portfolio.[12] He took shares in companies and particularly in three generally assumed to be copper-bottomed: the Bank of New Zealand, the Union Steam Saw Moulding Sash and Door Company ('Sash and Door'), and the South British Insurance Company of which he was a founder in 1872. He became a

---

* The Howard home a century later began to house the University of Auckland crèche.

long-standing director of both the Sash and Door and the South British, and was noted at their shareholders' meetings for his impassioned advocacy of expansionist policies.[13] Between 1874 and 1878 he was also owner of sawmills on the northern shore of the Manukau Harbour at Whatipu, Huia and Pararaha, and of small steamers and cutters servicing the mills.[14] Because timber markets even in those boom years were highly competitive, profit margins were slender. He was relieved therefore to be able to sell out his timber interest on the Manukau to Guthrie and Larnach & Co. Ltd late in 1878.[15]*

Howard had not been chastened by his experience of the risks of the timber industry. Incurably sanguine, he increased his holding in the Sash and Door Company, although, as a director, he must have known that the mammoth firm was beginning to stagger under a heavy burden of debt. Yet, in the critical 1881–83 period, he was one of the board which agreed to further borrowing for machinery and forests knowing that bank loans would be at a higher rate of interest than the projected rate of profit on shareholders' funds.[16] The historian is left with two perplexing questions. How could a former banker like Howard with first-hand experience of the perils of the timber trade become an advocate of so disastrous a gearing policy? And why did Dilworth, whose caution was already a byword in Auckland, allow his landed investments to be entangled with those of this impulsive businessman?

In the late 1870s the two men developed their joint speculative interest in a block of about 78,000 acres called Te Whaiti Kuranui, located for the most part within the newly (1877) created Piako County.† Whaiti Kuranui was itself part of a huge corridor of land running from the Firth of Thames in the north, almost to Lake Taupo in the south, flanked on either side by confiscated blocks, the one to the west made up of land taken from Waikato tribes, the other to the east, in the Bay of Plenty about Tauranga, of land taken mainly from the Ngati Rangi tribe.[17] Associated with these confiscations had been the ending of Crown pre-emption in 1865, thus enabling European settlers to buy lands not confiscated directly from Maori owners. To facilitate such sales a Native Land Court was set up to determine which among contending Maori claimants to any given block had the legal right to have their names entered on the title. Over the years the court sittings at Cambridge, Rotorua and elsewhere aroused scandalized comment in the Pakeha press.[18] Preliminary negotiations outside and judgments inside the court were bedevilled by chicanery; and Maori people, obliged

---

* This was an unwise buy by W. J. M. Larnach, chief proprietor of Guthrie and Larnach, and added to the financial problems that ultimately overwhelmed the Dunedin businessman.
† *Freeholders of New Zealand, 1882*, listed the Kuranui Land Society as owning 77,980 acres valued at £96,225.

to attend prolonged sittings far from home kainga, were impoverished by the fees of lawyers and the accounts of local storekeepers.

By 1873 tension between sellers and non-sellers in the upper Thames Valley, particularly within the ranks of Ngati Haua and Ngati Raukawa, had built up to the point where one T. Sullivan, a European employee of Edwin Barnes Walker, a Pakeha buyer, was murdered while trespassing on disputed ground. Thoroughly alarmed, the government of the day issued a proclamation placing an embargo on land sales over a large area of about 300,000 acres that became known as 'Patetere'.[19] After taking steps to compensate speculators for what they had already outlaid in 'purchases' within the now proclaimed region, the Crown indicated that henceforth it alone would be responsible for land negotiations with Maori there.[20] But over the next four years government negotiations for Patetere land were conducted in a half-hearted and desultory fashion.

This situation changed spectacularly in October 1877 when a new ministry under the radical premier, Sir George Grey, came to power. Grey was anxious that the Crown should use its pre-emptive monopoly over Patetere to build up a landed estate which could then be made available for the settlement of hundreds of humble, land-hungry settlers drawn from places like Thames. Over 1878–79 he and his allegedly dissolute lieutenant, the native minister John Sheehan, initiated surveys and land negotiations. But the Crown agents working in Patetere soon became aware that they did not have the field to themselves. Private speculators, in defiance of the proclamation, had arranged for surveys to be carried out (in Grey's phrase) 'by stealth' so that titles of certain select blocks could be determined at imminent sittings of the Native Land Court.[21] Some took the further step of making advances of money to probable Maori owners in the hope that a change of government would see an end to pre-emption and the validation of the purchases which they had irregularly made. Two syndicates were foremost in this activity: one was the Patetere Land Association, the other the Whaiti-Kuranui Association of Dilworth and Howard.

The story of these two syndicates is so complex as to require, if it were to be adequately told, much more than the single chapter which can be spared here. But that story must be covered, even if perfunctorily, in a book that claims to be an objective account of Dilworth's life, of which most historians would consider the Whaiti-Kuranui affair to be the least creditable part. For in order to buy these lands he and Howard perforce became entangled in the sometimes disreputable activities surrounding the nineteenth-century Native Land Court, and so made their contribution to the demoralizing process (so destructive of Maori society) by which the native peoples became separated from their ancestral lands.[22] Victorians claimed to believe that those who touched pitch could not avoid being defiled by it.[23] Howard and Dilworth cannot escape that censure. The Whaiti-Kuranui venture must be seen, therefore, as diminishing the reputation of James Dilworth.

Dilworth's posthumous defence must rest on his right to have his actions seen in context. The *mentalité* of the settler society of which he was part was quite unlike that of today; the buying of Maori land (with scant regard for the effect on the aboriginal sellers) was regarded as a legitimate activity by Pakeha in most walks of life, above all among businessmen. The seeming sanction of nineteenth-century society mitigates Dilworth's offence, but does no more than that. As was true of Logan Campbell and many another venerated pioneer, trading in Maori land was Dilworth's foot of clay.

The hopes of the two syndicates seeking to buy lands within the Patetere block were realized to the letter over 1879–81; the Grey government fell, and its successor in time revoked the Crown's pre-emptive proclamation over the block. On 29 July 1879 the Grey government was defeated by a vote of no-confidence in the House.[24] The new administration, under John Hall, progressively withdrew during 1880 from buying Maori land. Committed to a policy of retrenchment, it asserted that it simply did not have the money available to continue buying from Maori owners at Patetere.[25] In any event, the declared priority of the new native minister John Bryce was not to purchase Maori land for settlement but to subdue Te Whiti at Parihaka in Taranaki. The government also agreed, in May 1880, to allow individual blocks of land within the proclaimed region to pass through the Cambridge native land court to determine ownership,[26] thereby giving the Patetere syndicates which had carried out illicit surveys an advantage over fellow colonists wanting to buy, but late in the field.[27]

On 10 March 1881 the Hall government brought its Patetere policy to a predictable conclusion by announcing in the *Gazette* that the Crown had surrendered its interest in Patetere and removed its pre-emptive right over it.[28] This abdication outraged government opponents and popular elements of the press alike, who bitterly complained that speculative syndicates ('land rings' they were called at the time) acting outside the law would now be allowed to bear away the spoils.[29] Such too has been the received view of historians, but one which must now be called into question. The business records of James Dilworth, and those of the two Auckland law firms with closest dealings with the syndicates, namely Jackson and Russell and Hesketh and Richmond, tell a different story.[30]* The speculators' triumph was much less complete and the movement of blocks into their hands slower and costlier than have been recognized.

The two syndicates were differently constituted. The affairs of the Whaiti-Kuranui Association (WKA) were organized informally; all

---

* Jackson and Russell were lawyers for the Whaiti-Kuranui syndicate; Whitaker [F. A.] and Sheehan, Waikato-based, for the Patetere syndicate. Hesketh and Richmond (today Hesketh Henry) have records of the continuing quarrels of the two groups, 1880–86, because Edwin Hesketh was the nominated arbitrator.

between Dilworth and Howard was conducted, it seems, as a gentleman's agreement. If the Patetere group had also began that way, this was soon changed. When it became obvious that the government was withdrawing from the Patetere purchase, eight syndicate members formally reconstituted themselves on 8 April 1880 as the Patetere Land and Settlement Company (PL&S Co.), taking up, in total, seventy-three shares of £500 each.[31] Although shareholders varied over the years ahead, the main and constant figures were E. B. Walker, Major John Wilson, W. L .C. Williams (all of Cambridge, the first two supposedly well-to-do), F. D. Rich, an Otago runholder, and J. E. Pounds, manager of the Union Bank in Auckland. Originally it had been intended to convert this association into a registered joint stock company, but that further step was never taken.[32] The large sum subscribed was justified, according to a memorandum circulated among members, by the need to expend funds in 'paying agents, advances for food and other expenses to natives, and in making advances to natives on a/c of agreements they have made to sell all lands they own as declared by the Native Lands Court at Cambridge but for which they have not yet received Crown Grants'.[33] Expenses of the WKA were of a similar nature.

Operating in adjoining blocks and loosely associated with each other, the two syndicates inevitably shared the services of those facilitators of Maori land buying needed to make the Native Land Court work: lawyers, agents, surveyors, shopkeepers who provided the 'ground bait', and so forth. Meeting the charges of these people created endless problems. When there had to be a periodical settlement of accounts the two syndicates tended to fall out over the perennial question of what share of the combined costs should be borne by each.[34] Often negotiations ended in deadlock and outside arbitrators like R. C. Barstow, a retired magistrate, and Edwin Hesketh, a much respected senior lawyer, had to be called on to enforce a settlement.

Because of his age and business ties in Auckland, Dilworth himself spent little time in the Waikato over the 1880–83 period when the Whaiti-Kuranui blocks were being acquired. During sessions of the Native Land Court in Cambridge when WKA titles were under investigation Howard was usually in attendance. If he could not be there then James Russell of Jackson and Russell, feed at four guineas a day, was generally instructed to act. Others figuring frequently in WKA accounts were Whitaker and Sheehan (Waikato lawyers), W. L .C. Williams (native land agent) and Oliver Creagh (surveyor).

Increasingly Dilworth relied on the services of Gerald O'Halloran,*

---

* Gerald Richard O'Halloran (1844–1925) was born in Cushendall, County Antrim, northern Ireland. He came to New Zealand in 1861 with his brother George by way of the Victorian goldfields. Both brothers served in the Anglo-Maori Wars of the 1860s. After the wars O'Halloran worked at the Thames before running a store at Te Aroha. Dilworth's secretary at the time of his death, he became the first secretary of the Dilworth Trust Board. On his retirement, his son Gerald O'Halloran junior succeeded him.

a land agent who in mid-1880 came to Auckland from the Waikato, where he had been latterly associated with the Patetere land syndicate led by E. B. Walker. There was much about O'Halloran (yet another Ulster Anglican) to make an appeal to Dilworth. He was business-like, spoke Maori fluently, had personal knowledge of Maori land buying and was familiar with the whole Patetere area between the east bank of the Waikato and the Tauranga watershed. Though now settled in Auckland he spent much time during the early 1880s acting on behalf of Dilworth and Howard in the Cambridge and Oxford (Tirau) areas.[35] Over those years he usually recorded his occupation as land agent. But he had a wider competence than that. He was an efficient company secretary and by 1880 had acquired sufficient on-the-job skills as a double-entry bookkeeper to put out his shingle in Shortland Street as an accountant. At first Dilworth made only an occasional call on O'Halloran's services; by 1885 such was his usefulness he had become the Remuera landowner's factotum.

During 1881 the PL&S Co. and the WKA made two important decisions: they would combine in selling their blocks, and they would dispose of them not in New Zealand but in Britain.[36] Believing British capitalists to be 'on the feed' for colonial land companies at this time, the syndicates sent two separate agents, A. W. F. Halcombe and Francis Dyer Rich, to London.[37] Halcombe was an experienced emigration agent having already acted for nine years on behalf of the Emigrant and Colonist's Aid Corporation in the settlement of the 100,000-acre Manchester block in the Manawatu.[38] His role now was primarily that of publicist. Rich had excellent farming credentials. He was the son of a pioneer farmer from Somerset, George Rich, who in the 1840s had introduced a number of stud merino sheep into Auckland. Currently the owner of Bushey Park, a showpiece run three miles out of Palmerston (North Otago), F. D. Rich had been a runholder in Auckland, Otago and Canterbury. His brief in England, however, was chiefly financial. The syndicates conferred on him a power of attorney which they had already given to Falconer Larkworthy, manager of the Bank of New Zealand in London, and Frederick Augustus du Croz of the merchant firm of Dalgety Du Croz and Co. of the same city. Rich was empowered to act with either one or both of these two Londoners on behalf of his New Zealand principals to sell 'at a price of not less than One pound twelve shillings and six pence per acre' all lands 'the Proprietors' had put at his disposal.[39]

After his arrival in England Halcombe arranged for the publication of a booklet *Reports on the Selwyn Block with Map*, which contained enthusiastic reports on the Whaiti-Kuranui and Patetere lands and a statement provided by the proprietors for prospective buyers about the organized way in which it was proposed to settle the area.[40] By calling the block on offer Selwyn and its chief town Lichfield, names with an ecclesiastical ring to them, the promoters tried to give their

'When I first put this uniform on!' (G. S. Gilbert) —Gerald O'Halloran (1844–1925). This photograph was taken October 1918.
Supplied by Mr G. M. O'Halloran

J. C. Firth, a land speculator of the upper Thames Valley.
Auckland Institute and Museum

enterprise respectability and credibility.[41]* Certainly credibility was needed. Lichfield, although eventually planned to be over 640 acres in area, had as yet an existence only on paper. An essential part of the project, which took shape after the Halcombe booklet was published, was the construction of a branch railway to link Lichfield with Morrinsville, a junction giving access to the Auckland-Waikato railway system. As a press article observed soon after, 'settlers whom it is hoped to induce to come from England would not be disposed to live the secluded half-barbarous life of those who are removed from all means of communication'.[42] The Patetere syndicates, like the other chief promoters of this railway (Thomas Morrin, J. C. Firth and the proprietors of the Auckland Agricultural Company) were anxious to provide easy access to their Thames Valley estates so that they could subdivide and sell them.[43] After an inaugural meeting to promote the Thames Valley and Rotorua Railway Company in September 1881, the company was registered in January of the following year. Dilworth took up a large share-holding, as did Howard, who also became a board member to protect their joint investment in the concern.

On 7 July 1882, after weeks of strenuous negotiation, the New Zealand Thames Valley Land Company (NZTVL Co.)[44] was formed to give effect to agreements reached privately between the promoters in London, and Halcombe and Rich, the agents of New Zealand syndicates.[45] The vendors undertook to supply to the company within two years 250,000 acres of land, which possessed clear titles under the Land Transfer Act 1870, and were available for immediate settlement. The purchase price settled on was £1 12s 6d an acre, the bare reserve figure that had been set in Auckland.

The company's nominal capital was £500,000 made up of 50,000 ten pound shares. As was customary with most Australian and New Zealand companies formed in London in the late nineteenth century, the NZTVL Co. held share registers in Britain and in the colony, and provided for a London board with overall authority and a colonial board to whom precisely defined powers and responsibilities were delegated. By the end of the first year of the company's existence, 48,000 shares had been taken up, each carrying an initial call of three pounds.

Little of the £144,000 so raised found its way, however, to the vendors. It had been agreed that the consideration of £1 12s 6d an acre would be paid over in four instalments; 8s 1½d in cash, 8s 1½d in twelve months, 8s 1½d in two years and 8s 1½d in the form of company shares.[46] Because the vendors were obliged by the terms of incorporation to subscribe one-fourth of the total share capital,[47] they found that much of their initial payment of 8s 1½d an acre had to be

---

* Projected settlements in the Selwyn block were given the names of towns and villages in the vicinity of England's Lichfield, e.g. Tamworth and Trentham.

in effect reconverted into vendors' shares. The syndicates had other expenses. There was the need, for instance, to subscribe heavily to support the district railway company which would open up their lands.

Then late in 1882 they were caught up in yet another financial obligation. The London board had cabled the alarming news that applications for shares in London were lagging so badly that the fledgling company was likely to fail unless a heavy application for shares on the colonial register, which was about to be opened in Auckland, gave a clear signal that the venture had the support of informed capitalists in the colony.[48] Here was a real difficulty; the truth was that most knowledgeable New Zealanders had little confidence in the Patetere lands. Discussing the NZTVL Co. prospectus with his old colleague John Hall, the Canterbury politician Edward Wakefield remarked: 'I hear that most of the land is wretched and that the settlers will find it hard to obtain a *modus vivendi*'.[49] Since this was a commonly held opinion in the colony, few local capitalists were likely to subscribe for shares. Fortunately for the company, the BNZ, which had already made substantial loans to the PL&S Co., 'rather than see the company fail at the last moment' advanced money to the vendors so that they could prop up the local register.[50] This advance enabled six of the vendors (who included Howard but not Dilworth) to apply for 8,000 shares in the names of thirteen prominent Auckland businessmen who had agreed to hold those shares in trust for the vendors. For 'allowing their names to be made use of as the registered owners of the shares' these nominee shareholders were entitled to any profits from the conveyance of the shares which they held in trust, whilst being indemnified against any losses.[51] The real New Zealand owners of these shares were of course the members of the two Patetere syndicates (already heavily in debt to the BNZ and the Union Bank) who now had their overdraft at the BNZ increased by a further £24,000.[52] (This advance by the BNZ involved it in a heavy loss in the years ahead.)

By this time, for most of the members of the two vending syndicates, the burden of debt and of interest repayments was becoming intolerable. Little wonder that, as limited sums of money were disbursed by the parent company over 1883–84 in payment for land, the syndicates should have quarrelled so bitterly over allocations.

The scheme by which the NZTVL Co. attempted to sell off its lands under its first estate manager A. W. F. Halcombe was imaginative, and on paper at least had distinct merit.[53] The company proposed to begin its operations by selling individual blocks ranging from 200 to 800 acres at four pounds an acre[54] to young capitalist farmers from England who would be brought out to the Selwyn estate and instructed in colonial farming before they cultivated their selections full-time.[55] A club-house was built for these cadets near Lichfield to act as a social centre softening the rigours of a solitary backblocks life. But few cadets

Thomas Morrin, a dummy shareholder in the Thames Valley Land Company.
Alexander Turnbull Library

from Britain took up land, and in spite of persistent advertising little land was sold to New Zealand settlers either.

The Thames Valley venture was a failure from the outset. It was born out of season; 1882 was an inauspicious time to sell rural land in New Zealand, Auckland provincial land perhaps most of all. The bottom had dropped out of the rural property market. Values went right down and stayed down until the mid-1890s when intensive farming based on supplying overseas markets with refrigerated produce became an economic proposition. For the few who had settled on NZTVL Co. lands a completely unexpected obstacle appeared. The company promoters had advertised their property, in good faith, as 'good grazing land'. Most of it was pumice land which in a state of nature had been covered by tussock and scattered scrub, and which after early manuring had produced luxuriant clover.[56] But for those who settled on the Selwyn lands this fertility was short-lived. After the first year or so, sheep and cattle suffered from what was called 'bush sickness'; they lost their appetite and wasted; many died.* Bush sick lands completed the undoing of the Selwyn settlement. They were the 'badlands' of colonial New Zealand, heartbreaking to farm, impossible to sell.

By the time the NZTVL Co. held its second annual meeting in London in July 1884 the company had manifestly failed. The London board was deeply aggrieved, blaming the vendors for shilly-shallying over constructing the district railway and, more importantly, for misrepresenting the incompleteness of land purchases from Maori owners at the time of incorporation, and, as they often reiterated, for 'laches' thereafter—the term they used for the neglect of the vendors to perform their contracted obligations.

Differences came to a head in July 1884 when the vendors claimed their final payment on land conveyed to the company, submitting titles for 268,000 acres as a fulfilment of their undertaking to supply within two years a minimum of 250,000 acres with titles registered under the Land Transfer Act. The London board jibbed, dismissing as unsatisfactory the titles attached to tens of thousands of acres. Noting that many blocks had only provisional titles, they cited various defects: instances of challenges to ownership by Maori, of erroneous boundaries cut, and of overstatement of quantities of bush in certain blocks.† As a measure of their disquiet, in October 1884 they sent instructions by cable to Jackson and Russell, the land company's solicitors in Auckland, to place an immediate requisition on the titles

---

* Not until 1935 was the discovery made that minute or 'trace' deficiencies of cobalt in the soil were responsible for lands being 'bush sick'. The condition is remediable today by including trace elements of cobalt in fertilizer used.

† The initial prospectus of the company had made the availability of large stands of native bush an important selling point in their approach to subscribers.

WHAITI KURANUI

of land the vendors claimed to have conveyed.[57]* This had the effect of stopping any payment by the local board to the vending syndicates out of the £100,000 they had previously lodged in the Union Bank for that purpose. Jackson and Russell and the local board, rallying to act as the mouthpiece of the local syndicates on this issue, protested. Jackson and Russell maintained that under New Zealand conditions provisional titles were regarded as defensible 'against all the world', and that these titles which London had questioned would in time be converted into full certificates of title once the land transfer office had caught up on its backlog of work.

---

* Requisitions on title are written inquiries by a purchaser's solicitor addressed to a vendor's solicitor asking him to explain or remove any impediments in the title to the land.

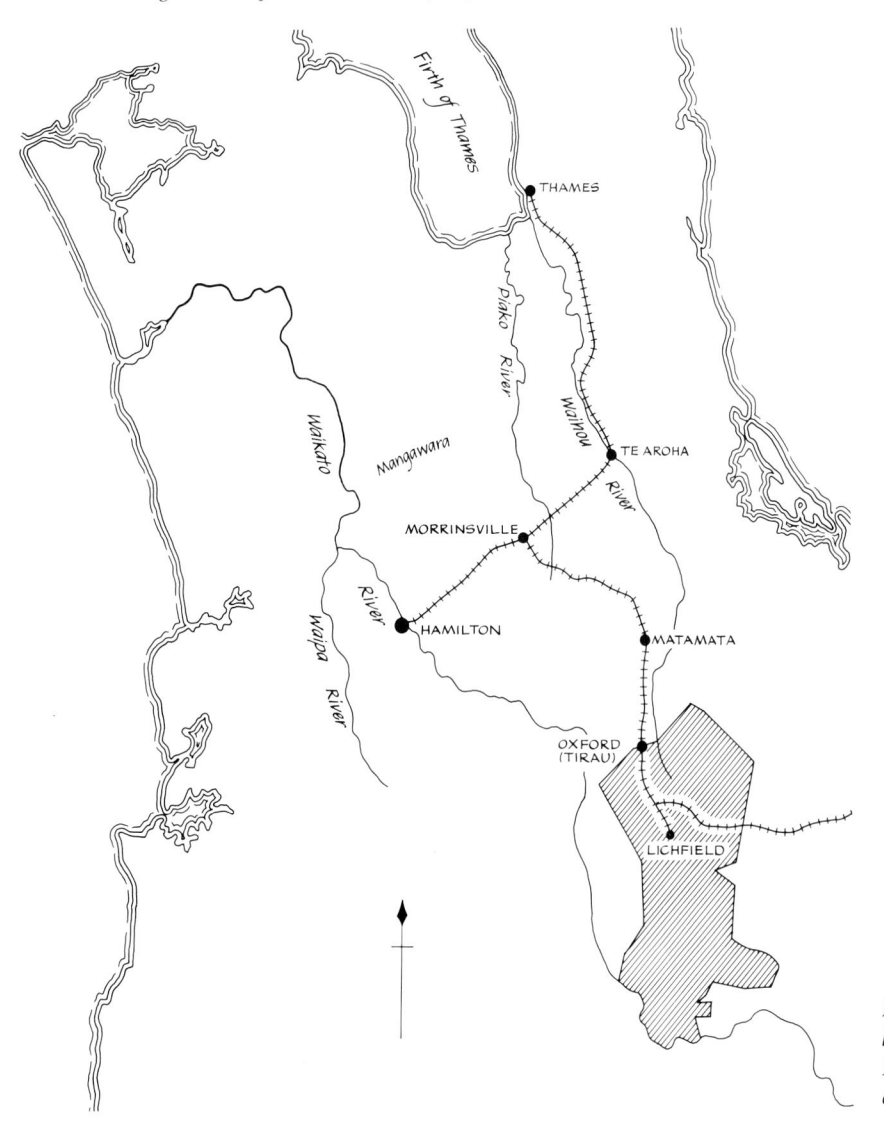

Dilworth's main provincial land interests in the 1880s: Mangawara, and the Patetere estate centred on Lichfield.

203

The London board was unconvinced, and the moratorium on payments to the vendors remained. All the New Zealand speculators save Dilworth were desperate for money to service their debts, but the London directors of the company would not budge. This was the state of apparent deadlock when early in 1885 an alarming cable arrived in Auckland to the effect that the London board proposed to go to law and contest the 1882 contracts in the Court of Chancery. Fearful of the consequences of this recourse to litigation, which held for the vendors the appalling prospect that they could have reconveyed to them all the land they had considered sold and could have the cognate obligation to return to the company the £179,000 which they had already received in part payment for that land, the two syndicates decided to form an immediate deputation to go to London and make terms. Walker, Pound and Rich were appointed by the PL&S Co. and Dilworth by the WKA.[58] Dilworth would not have been willing to absent himself from Auckland for almost six months had he not believed that he now had in O'Halloran an agent in whose hands the management of his properties could confidently be left. On 12 March 1885 he and Mrs Dilworth sailed from Auckland to Lyttelton where they boarded the *Ruapehu* for London. In early June Dilworth joined the other members of the deputation to take part in negotiations with the London board subsequently described as 'long and arduous' before an agreement was reached.[59] The settlement arrived at was referred to as a 'compromise'. It was scarcely that. The disputants were unequally matched; the colonial deputation was virtually confronted with an ultimatum; they conceded much and gained little. A new contract was signed which varied the provisions of the 4 September 1882 contract under which the affairs of the company had previously been conducted.[60] Under the new heads of agreement the signatories arranged for:

- 105,000 acres of the less valuable land (the Tokoroa, Maraitai and Whakamaru blocks) to be conveyed back to the vendors;
- the vendors to guarantee completion of the conveyance of 162,500 acres of specified land with indefeasible titles by 31 March 1886 (with harsh penalties provided for non-fulfilment); and
- a final cash settlement of £12,700 to be made once the lands were completely conveyed to the company.*

When news of the agreement was received back in Auckland local newspapers spoke of it as an even-handed compromise (which it certainly was not) and, in a similar flight from reason, spoke of the dawn of a wonderful future for the Selwyn settlement. The quarrel which had left 'the whole place almost at a standstill'[61] was ended,

---

* The indenture also provided for a payment of £8,000 (face value) of company debentures, maturing in five years, should certain other smaller nominated blocks be conveyed.

and 'the work of settlement . . . of this valuable tract of land can now be pushed forward with expedition'.[62] This was sheer whistling in the dark; the intractable problems of agricultural depression and bush sickness were years away from being solved. A year later Sir William Fox informed Halcombe that, in spite of months of strenuous advertising and promotion, the company 'have not as yet sold 50 acres and of course in the present [depressed] state of affairs are not likely to'.[63] His pessimistic prognosticaton was well founded.

Dilworth was too hardheaded, too knowledgeable about the land market in New Zealand, to delude himself with spurious optimism. All that the deputation of which he was part had been able to do in London was to salvage what little they could from the shipwreck of their speculation. Personally, he had been involved in the greatest business failure of his life; had had a setback which but for the accumulated wealth of many pioneer years and the continuing income of his city properties in Auckland would have been as ruinous for him as it was for Howard, and for Walker and his fellow-Patetere speculators. It was as a man much sobered by his losses that Dilworth waited in England and Ireland for his return to New Zealand in August 1885.

On his arrival back in Auckland in early October Dilworth anticipated that working out the final financial settlement between the WKA and PL&S Co. would be awkward. The reality proved far worse than that. Howard was now seriously ill and so, in spite of Dilworth's advanced years, the burden of acting for the WKA fell on his shoulders. But with whom was he to negotiate? The Patetere syndicate no longer spoke with a united voice; it was riven by the quarrelling of members, some of whom were beside themselves with their losses. Early in January 1886, Dilworth, while confined to bed by bronchitis—'your illness is a terrible misfortune for us' remarked Howard by telegram[64]— wrote to Howard outlining his strategy. Given the rifts within the Patetere group the WKA partners (Dilworth believed) must insist that 'anything short of the entire submission to arbitration of all matters in dispute between both sides' would not be satisfactory.[65]

Dilworth's view prevailed and a neutral lawyer in Auckland, H. Shera, was commissioned to draw up a 'deed of submission' which all members of both syndicates signed undertaking to put 'all longstanding claims and differences' in the hands of three arbitrators, J. A. Connell, John Chambers and Charles Alexander, whose ruling was to be accepted as final.[66] There were seven matters in dispute, four of which were the more significant:

- the claims of 'one group against another';
- the distribution of money paid by the company in the past or to be paid in the future;
- the allotment of paid-up shares in the company (Maraitai Land Co.)

James Dilworth, an undated photograph, c. 1885.
Dilworth School Archives

Edwin Hesketh (1843–98) who mediated between the Patetere syndicates.
Auckland Public Library

- to be formed to hold the land reconveyed from the NZTVL Co.; and
- the disposition of the final sum of £12,700 paid over by the company.

The arbitrators made their awards on 16 April and 16 June 1886;[67] but it was symptomatic of the intransigent quarrelling within the Patetere syndicate that one of its members, the extraordinarily disputatious bank manager J. E. Pounds, should apply to the Banco (Civil) Division of the Supreme Court to have these awards set aside.[68] Mr Justice Gillies then ruled that the arbitrators had technically gone beyond their terms of reference and returned the matters to arbitration once more.

Desperate for a settlement at last, all syndicate members accepted the revised awards which the arbitrators made shortly after. When the final payments from the NZTVL Co. were allocated, the two associations asked Connell (an accountant) to act as liquidator for each of the syndicates, whose members were sick unto death of their speculation. As the Auckland *Star* primly observed, the chief beneficiaries of 'several months' of quarrelling among 'the Patetere proprietors *inter se*', and between the two syndicates, were the legal firms who had been employed at 'very considerable expense'.[69] When the winding up of the PL&S Co. was completed on 30 April 1887, Connell found that assets carrying a book value of £67,834 had a realized value of £2,787.[70] The unrealized portion included 39,000 shares in the Maraitai Land Co. which now held the lands returned by the NZTVL Co. These had to be assigned by the Patetere syndicate to the BNZ, as part of the foreclosed securities taken over by the bank.

The speculation from which it had been imagined, in 1880, that great fortunes would be made had had a disastrous outcome for the members of the two syndicates. When Major John Wilson was asked at this time by Sir William Fox 'what his prospects were, he answered "Simply ruin" '.[71] Fox went on to remark 'I hear he stands to lose about £20,000 and has dismissed his gardener etc.'. Williams and Walker did equally badly. Halcombe, who lost heavily, went to live out his later years modestly in Taranaki. F. D. Rich, his successor as farm manager, had been forced to sell up Bushey Park and came to live permanently in Lichfield.[72] J. E. Pounds coolly cut his losses, went to Melbourne, borrowed from his bank the Union and plunged into the urban land boom there; he bankrupted himself once again.[73]

Connell completed his final liquidation of the Whaiti-Kuranui Association on 1 October 1887.[74] The association had made heavy losses but unlike the PL&S Co. was solvent at the end. Out of £4,000 of realized assets £3,192 was taken up in debt and interest payments to the BNZ. Howard was impoverished by the speculation. Dilworth easily survived, though he probably lost over £30,000. He even decided

J. M. Clark, local director of the New Zealand Thames Valley Land Company, who was later ruined by the 1880s business collapse.
Auckland Public Library

to hang on to his 14,349 Maraitai Land Co. shares though these had little money value. Between them, he and the BNZ held over 80,000 of the 90,000 shares of that company.[75]

Dilworth did not leave for posterity any written record which tells how he reacted to the bitter ending of the Whaiti-Kuranui speculation, the great failure of his later years. We can only draw inferences from his subsequent behaviour. There is little doubt that the trip to Britain he was compelled to make in 1885 and the harsh treatment meted out to the vendors' deputation of which he was part affected him deeply and provoked soul-searching on his journey home. That year was the watershed of his later life. Until then success in business was the ultimate satisfaction. It was no longer so. The use to which his wealth would be put once he died became the preoccupation of his remaining years.

CHAPTER THIRTEEN

Wills and Inheritance

It is a view widely held that chief among the residual pleasures of old age are will-making and will-shaking. However that may be, once the childless Mr Dilworth reached his declining years, just how he intended to make his will became a matter of inquisitive speculation, and this among people beyond the ranks of Mossman and Hall relatives who, with reason, had expectations of some sort. This wider curiosity broke into print in 1881 when the new Auckland 'society paper' the *Observer*, a mildly scandalous weekly, posed the question in this way:

> Old Jimmy who has been money grubbing in this province for about forty years has made a will, and left almost all of his wealth to trustees, for the erection of a monument to his memory, which will be put up in Belfast, his native town. Alas! for Auckland, and poor relations.[1]

It is not unlikely that Dilworth had recently made a will, though no evidence of one of that date remains today. Even so, the gossipy item was well off the mark with most of its information. Apart from the fact that Dilworth had not come from Belfast, the idea of his wanting to put up a monument to himself was preposterous. Vainglory of any kind he could not stand. Some of his generation certainly believed him 'money grubbing' or 'tightfisted' and (as it was later reported) obsessive about 'the accumulation of money'.[2]

Those most closely acquainted with him were aware of another side, spoke of an innate kindliness and of generous giving mostly in secret. Two things are undisputed. First, unlike a number of colonists— James Farmer, J. T. Mackelvie, William Brown and others—who won a fortune then returned to Britain to live out their days in comfort and style, Dilworth was unencumbered with such ambitions. Second (a consequence of the first), for many years the disposition of his estate on death concerned him greatly. The officiating vicar at his funeral remarked that he 'habitually and consistently looked on all that he had ... as a gift or trust'.[3] This high-flown rhetoric should not conceal the fact that for the greater part of his life Dilworth considered—as had cousin Anne before him—that wealth was accumulated not for personal indulgence but to be held in trust for one's family.*

Yet as the *Observer* article implied, by 1881 Dilworth was rethinking his trusteeship, most of all because the Mossmans, for reasons unknown to us today, had fallen from favour. Possibly he felt he had helped them enough. There is evidence that once they had come to New Zealand, Dilworth gave financial assistance to the family by paying regular money to Eleanor, a practice that gave him some misgiving because trying to help her, he later complained, was 'like putting something in a bottomless bucket'.[4] Perhaps this private income also helps to explain why, once Mr and Mrs Mossman began to live in New Zealand, Eleanor always seemed to 'hold the cheque book'. But although the relationship had soured, Dilworth cut off neither Eleanor nor her sons completely. His invariable practice near the end of his life was to pay Eleanor (apart from occasional gifts of money) £100 each year.[5] In his last will he directed the trustees to pay her an annuity of the same figure for life.[6]

The Mossman nephews, at one stage Dilworth's chief heirs, are not mentioned at all in that final will. But some short time before he died he provided for them, too, by financing Eleanor's two surviving sons in New Zealand onto Poverty Bay land which, though broken, was good sheep country. Willie John was given the Waerenga-o-kuri block some twenty miles west of Gisborne, later known as The Laurels, and Harry a farm further up country at Hangaroa which, it was agreed, would be called Dunsirk.[7] That name was a revealing one.

At no point does it appear that James Dilworth ever contemplated making his younger brother Andrew his heir. One assumes that James felt that by having already given Andrew his Waitakere farm he had provided adequately for him. In any case, by the end his brother was not available to be made heir.

Late at night on 25 May 1881 Andrew Dilworth suffered a frightful injury. After returning from Auckland where he had been attending a meeting of the Waitemata County Council, he collected his chestnut horse which had been stabled at the hotel in Henderson and began to make his way home.[8] Two miles out from Henderson, while passing over a portion of the road, constructed upon tea tree fascines, that had been much torn up by government navvies putting through the railway to the Kaipara,[9] Andrew's normally surefooted horse stumbled, first throwing its rider then dragging him for some distance until his face was dashed against a protruding stump. Andrew suffered severe head injuries particularly about the nose. He lay unconscious and

---

* Dilworth's aspirations towards the Anglo-Irish landed tradition—that property and its attendant status should move on intact within a family, passing from generation to generation—was shared by another northern Irishman, James Williamson. That is why the loss of The Pah, Williamson's home estate, as a result of his impoverishment by the financial collapse of the mid-1880s was such a bitter blow to him.

bleeding until dawn. A man of fortitude, and physically hardy despite his fifty-eight years, Andrew then dragged himself though in great pain to the cottage of a nearby settler who transported him to Andrew's own Waitakere farm. Dr J. H. Hooper,[10]* Auckland's senior surgeon, made a special trip out to the farm to treat the injured man. Only with great difficulty was the doctor able to bring separated portions of skull bone together.

On hearing of his brother's plight, James Dilworth went to Waitakere with a friend in a two-horse wagonette. He bore Andrew carefully back to town to lodge him at the Auckland hotel, close to Dr Hooper's Hobson Street surgery. A week after the accident, James shifted Andrew once again, this time to the Remuera farm where Dr Hooper could continue to treat him while he was receiving, according to press reports, 'careful and assiduous nursing'. The outlook, however, was not good. With such severe facial injuries it was feared erysipelas would intervene. Andrew's friends at that stage, it was said, had 'slight hopes of his recovery'.[11] But sturdy Andrew defied this gloomy prognosis. By July he was able to return to his farm on the hills. Within a month of his return he was attending a meeting of the Waitakere highway district council,[12] where he was elected chairman. It was reported that one of his first resolutions was to call on the government to make good the ravaged road on which his accident had occurred.

But the recovery was delusory. On 11 September he suffered a stroke, almost certainly as a consequence of his accident.[13]† James brought Andrew and his wife Mary Jane back to Remuera once more. Four days later Andrew made a will, in which, after making a small bequest to his wife and also passing on certain personal effects to her, he 'devised and bequeathed' the rest of his estate to James, contingent upon that brother's binding himself to guarantee an annuity to Mary Jane as long as she lived. In his will Andrew carefully explained why he had arranged things in this way.

> The fact my said brother James Dilworth gratuitously presented me with my property at Waitakere which was the foundation of my success in life will fully account for my having made my said brother (after providing for my wife) my sole heir.[14]

On 21 September Andrew died. Two days after, his body was borne on a hearse from the Remuera homestead, followed by a cortege of twenty-three carriages and numerous people on foot, to St Mark's

---

* Dr Hooper, in private practice in Auckland, and a member of the first surgical staff of the public hospital there, had been in New Zealand since 1861. His experience as a field surgeon during the land wars of the 1860s gave him particular skill in dealing with severe trauma.

† The death certificate listed 'serous apoplexy 10 days' (Dr T. M. Philson). A retrospective diagnosis based on available evidence made by a modern specialist has, as the probable cause of death, the effusion and pressure on the brain of serum issuing from a subdural haematoma.

where the funeral service took place.[15] He was then interred in the parish graveyard. When James himself died thirteen years later he was buried beside Andrew.

After Andrew's death his wife, Mary Jane, did not remain long in New Zealand. A trust fund of £2,000 was duly set up in the following year and Dilworth signed a deed in which he testified that he regarded himself as 'held and firmly bound' under a penalty for breach of £4,000 to provide Mary Jane with an annuity of £120 for the rest of her life.[16]* She then left for San Francisco where she lived until her death in 1901 at the age of seventy-three.

Andrew's death distressed Dilworth. Theirs had been a close brotherly relationship. And inevitably the older brother was reminded of his own mortality, an awareness reinforced by Dilworth's part in the making of Andrew's will and his assumption of an obligation of trust towards Andrew's widow. But no hard evidence survives to indicate that Dilworth was contemplating drawing up a will with beneficiaries outside the family before he went abroad in 1885. On the other hand one of the executors of Dilworth's final will (15 November 1894) claimed that the old man had been pondering 'for many years' (by implication as far back as the early 1880s) how his wealth could be used to benefit the wider community.[17]

Dilworth also had in Samuel Jackson, his trusted attorney, a remembrancer (as it were) standing at his shoulder, ever likely to encourage in him thoughts of public benefaction. A persistent nineteenth-century rumour, coyly confirmed in Jackson Russell's *Scrapbook History*,[18] had Jackson virtually writing the highly philanthropic will of Edward Costley when the old man was moribund.[19] Certainly the loose wording of that will is suggestive of a document put together in haste when the testator was at death's door. The beneficiaries of the will, by common consent at the time, were nevertheless all seven deserving Auckland institutions, and Jackson, a principled lawyer, would scarcely have taken the liberty of making the testator a public benefactor had he not been apprised by Costley at some earlier stage of his general intentions with regard to his deceased estate.

Jackson would have had little difficulty in directing Dilworth's thoughts as well into philanthropic channels. They were already there. Dilworth's interest in charitable and church organisations had grown with age. Bishop W. G. Cowie praised him in 1887 as his 'warm-hearted sympathising friend' on the Diocesan General Trust Board whose 'valued advice' had long been at the disposal of the trust. The year before, Dilworth had rejoined the board of the Auckland Savings Bank and stayed there as its senior trustee until he died. Increasingly his

Samuel Jackson, Dilworth's trusted solicitor and remembrancer.
Jackson Russell Dignan Armstrong

---

* The annuity of £120 p.a. (payable half-yearly) was calculated on the presumption that six per cent was a reasonable annual return on an investment of the £2,000. After Dilworth's death the Trust Board regarded itself as fully bound to continue the annuity.

interests were concentrated on the young, particularly their educational and social needs. He was one of the founders of the kindergarten movement in Auckland during 1886–87, and remained a foremost financial supporter.* Mindful of Dilworth's interest in education and aware of how useful his financial skills would be to the youthful Auckland University College, his friends the parliamentarian G. M. O'Rorke and Bishop Cowie encouraged him in 1890 to join them on its governing council.[20] It was quite in character that one of the the last public meetings he attended was of the finance committee of the council held five days before his death.[21]

But back in the early 1880s not good works but pressing private business matters were in the forefront of his thinking. Costley's death in April 1883, it will be recalled, came at a most inconvenient juncture for Dilworth. The executors of Costley's will had to realize quickly on his investments, and this meant Dilworth was obliged to pay back mortgage loans from Costley at the very time he was over-extended financially. And not only was 1883 the year of expensive additions to the Thames Hotel and Tyrone Buildings, but it was also a time when the Whaiti-Kuranui partnership was caught up in moving 7,000 acres of land which it wanted to buy from Maori owners through the Native Land Court. It will be recalled, too, that 1883–84 were years of bitter wrangles between the two vending syndicates mixed up in the NZTVL Co. speculation. But what drove Dilworth to Britain in 1885 was the even more serious threat of the London board of the NZTVL Co. to liquidate the company and return the land to the syndicates. Dilworth and Howard by that time were racked with worry; the landed speculation they had hoped to enrich them was proving a nightmare. Although Dilworth was not chosen initially as one of the representatives of the Auckland vendors to go to London, he and Howard agreed that he must go and participate in the negotiations to safeguard the interests of their partnership and to keep its losses to a minimum.

This brief catalogue of Dilworth's financial concerns between 1881 and 1885 serves to remind us how much the miscarriage of his speculation in the upper Thames Valley worried and distracted him. Chroniclers of his life, over the years, have made much (and rightly so) of the extent to which the collapse in rural land values and the failure of Thames Valley Land Company reduced the value of the estate he was able to pass down to posterity. The continued worry and cost of the Whaiti-Kuranui venture may also have delayed the framing of his famous bequest by some years.

Even though Dilworth's journey to Britain in 1885 was essentially one of business, once again, as in 1873, he and Isabella were able to

---

* The moving spirit behind the Jubilee Kindergarten Association was Mrs Dudley Ward. 'Jubilee' in the title commemorated the founding date of the body, 1887, the fiftieth year of Queen Victoria's reign. Dilworth gave the kindergarten £200 in its first year, and £100 each subsequent year.

include in their itinerary a pilgrimage to County Tyrone. On this occasion they stayed with another cousin, Mrs Annie Watt, whose husband William farmed Dunseark, the townland where James had been born. The visit was an emotional one. It was then that the Watt family took their guests on the excursion to Donaghmore where James broke down at the sight of the lost family farm of Mullaghcreevy. And there were other more general changes in Tyrone to upset him. By 1885 the Home Rule agitation in British politics, and the associated rise of Irish nationalism with Catholic overtones, had aroused a new level of apprehension among Ulster Protestants.[22] It is also likely he became aware of the poison of sectarian warfare seeping into County Tyrone from Belfast;[23] but that we can only surmise. What is certain is that he became conscious of a new level of deprivation in his homeland. Although the north had fared better economically than the south in the later nineteenth century, a flight from diminished opportunities and poverty had led to a depletion of the youthful age cohorts in the counties of Tyrone, Fermanagh and Down.[24] Recognition of privation among the young lay behind the special provision of places in the Dilworth Ulster Institute, which Dilworth later founded, for destitute Ulster boys, with preference given 'to boys resident in or near the town of Dungannon'.[25]

In spite of being by habit and temperament the least impressionable of men, when on 13 August 1885 Dilworth boarded the ship that was to take him back from London to the Antipodes he was in an unusually susceptible state of mind. For this his recent Irish experience was by no means mainly responsible. Also boarding the S.S. *Arawa* was a

S.S. Arawa carried Dilworth and MacMurray on her maiden voyage, 1885.
Alexander Turnbull Library

Church of Ireland clergyman, the Revd George MacMurray, setting out for Australia to take up a curacy in Ararat, Victoria. The meeting of these two men was to be momentous for each of them. The date remained vivid in MacMurray's mind. He turned thirty that day. Two days out at sea Dilworth also had a birthday, attaining his biblical lifespan of three score years and ten, an anniversary in his culture and time almost equivalent to a rite of passage, when one made a stocktaking of one's life, and, in the phrase of the period, began 'putting one's house in order'. Almost certainly this also contributed to Dilworth's susceptibility.

Despite a disparity in ages of forty years, the stocky and emphatic young clergyman and the tall taciturn colonist became (as MacMurray later represented it) 'great friends on board ship'.[26] Personal life-stories and confidences were exchanged. They had much more in common than their shared staccato mid-Ulster speech—though from Donegal, MacMurray's home town of Lifford was just over the border from Tyrone.* Both had attended the Royal School of Dungannon. The dynamic young headmaster of Dilworth's last years there, Dr Darley, had, in 1878, as a venerable and aged bishop, priested MacMurray in the little county cathedral of Kilmore. Ship-board confidences revealed that both were committed orthodox low churchmen. So strongly did the young clergyman appeal to Dilworth that (as MacMurray later told it) 'when approaching Cape Town he asked me to allow him to cable to Bishop Cowie suggesting I should be appointed Vicar of Saint Marks which was then vacant. . . . I definitely declined as I was under engagement to a parish in Australia.'[27] Even this refusal commended the young curate all the more to Dilworth. Here was the kind of man he admired, one who if he had given his word would not be diverted from his bounden duty to keep it. And for Dilworth, as MacMurray was later to appreciate, 'Duty was the watchword of his life'.[28]

If, after taking leave of MacMurray in Australia, Dilworth imagined he would be able to return home to work out some philanthropic purpose for his estate he was quickly disabused. The Auckland he had left in March 1885, in spite of stagnation in farming and sluggish prices for rural land, had been reasonably prosperous. Six months later it was no longer so. And conditions quickly worsened. By 1886 a slump overwhelmed Auckland from which the city did not finally escape for ten years. The only encouraging feature for Dilworth on his return from abroad was the competence with which his agent Gerald O'Halloran

---

* George MacMurray was born in Lifford, County Donegal, 13 August 1855. After gaining his MA at Trinity College, Dublin, he was ordained on 22 December 1878. He was curate of two Irish parishes and rector of a third before emigrating to Australia, where he was curate at Ararat, Victoria, 1885–86, and rector of St Paul's, Ballarat, 1887–92. In New Zealand MacMurray was vicar of St Mary's, Auckland, 1892–1919, and Archdeacon of Auckland, 1914–28. A member of the Dilworth Trust Board from its foundation in 1894 until his death in 1941, he was chairman for the last twenty years of his life.

had administered his business affairs. All appeared shipshape and to the old man's satisfaction.

Any thought Dilworth had, however, of delegating responsibility to his partner Joseph Howard for their shared landed investment had to be dropped out of hand. On his return Dilworth found Howard broken in health, demoralized in spirit, and financially troubled. While Dilworth had been sailing back to the colony Howard had suffered an 'apoplectic seizure' which for days had left him in a 'precarious condition'.[29] Howard survived the stroke, but never fully recovered his health.[30] Over recent years he had become a big man, reaching a weight of nineteen stone. Doubtless his physical condition predisposed him to the onset of a stroke. But business anxieties played their part, too. Even while he convalesced, troubles vexing the Thames Valley Land Company had resurrected themselves, though in a different form. Further, lacking the financial resources of Dilworth, Howard was now submerged by a rising tide of private debt. As the depression deepened over 1886–88 his financial situation became much worse. Dividends from companies and institutions which he had relied on for survival were greatly reduced, had even disappeared (he had been a heavy investor in, among other companies, the NZTVL Co., the Union Steam Saw Moulding Sash and Door Company, Auckland's Frozen Meat Company, the Bank of New Zealand and South British Insurance). As a board director he was discredited completely. Outraged shareholders who remembered his irrepressible optimism and his policies of borrowing in the expansionist early 1880s now denounced him.[31] By 1886 the stuffing had been knocked out of Howard. Dilworth was forced to shoulder responsibilities for a partnership he had once hoped to leave to the younger man.

Many years after MacMurray sailed on the *Arawa* to Australia, he came to the conclusion that even during this voyage Dilworth had been turning over in his mind how he might use his property in a beneficent way.[32] This being so, the changing attitude on social questions which Dilworth would have found back in the colony must have given his ruminations greater focus. As the depression bit more deeply over 1886–87 the needs of the destitute became a constant concern in the city of Auckland. This was in contrast to the pioneer years. Then, compassion had tended to be a scarce commodity; the orthodoxy among those in authority had been that charitable assistance to the needy should be sparing lest the lower orders lose their habit of self-reliance. The slump destroyed this complacency once and for all. As conditions worsened destitution became widespread. Old social abuses such as employing children of under twelve in factories, or boys as teamsters driving drays—simply because their labour was cheap— began to get out of hand.[33] So did the desertion of families by workless husbands (often with the collusion of wives) in order that those left behind might receive rations and become a charge upon the state.[34]

JAMES DILWORTH

Under the weight of demand without precedent, the rudimentary welfare system broke down. The Auckland Charitable Aid Board set up in 1885 with the responsibility of providing assistance for the needy soon ran out of funds.

Institutions with a special concern for indigent children proved as deficient in expertise as they were in funds. The standard practice at that time was to send neglected or deserted children to 'industrial schools' located in places like Kohimarama[35] where they were haphazardly housed with young delinquents convicted by the courts.[36] In industrial schools and orphanages alike it was customary in the 1880s and 1890s for wards as they grew older to be sent to live and work on the farms of settlers in the hope that they would be incorporated into family life.[37] But all too often foster homes were not rigorously inspected; as late as 1900 there were complaints that children in some such 'homes' were overworked, neglected or ill-clad.[38]

Conditions in orphanages of the day were severe. As a member of the General Trust Board of the diocese, Dilworth would have learnt at first hand about the regime of the St Stephen's Orphan Home in Parnell, an institution to which destitute and abandoned children as well as orphans were sent.[39] Even before bad times came in the later 1880s the demand for places had quite outstripped existing accommodation. The reminiscences of a certain James Williamson, an orphan boy who was resident there in the 1880s, tell a piteous story of an existence characterized by overcrowding, harsh discipline, and food in short supply ('we were always hungry', he recalled).[40] His stay there terminated, as it did for many boys, when he was apprenticed—'bound down' was the term used—to a local suburban farmer at an

Parnell Orphanage, 1870s.
Revd John Kinder, Alexander Turnbull Library

early age on a wage of 2s 6d a week.* In effect the boy's formal education was at an end. Unhappily, conditions in most orphanages were equally unsatisfactory. Those in industrial schools were generally worse, although practices there had marginally improved after 1882 when control passed from the Department of Justice to the Department of Education.

Constant publicity on this social issue obviously shaped how Dilworth began to think on the question of institutional care of disadvantaged boys which had now begun to interest him. The principles that informed his thinking are well known, partly because he spelt them out in some detail in his will; partly because MacMurray in later years frequently provided a gloss on Dilworth's original intentions. Of his compassionate concern there can be no doubt. But the temptation to regard him as a progressive educationist born out of season must be resisted. He was very much a man of his time, with a Victorian enthusiasm for self-reliance, discipline, earnestness and hard work.[41] The enlightened aspect of his thinking lay in the emphasis he placed on education in the promotion of the best interests of boys who had been placed in institutional care. In spite of his English and Anglican background he had the ingrained Scots-Presbyterian respect for education that was part of Ulster culture. What he grasped was that boys from deprived backgrounds were in danger (in modern educational parlance) of 'under-achieving'. Only education, provided as long as a boy could benefit from it, could break the iron ring of disadvantage and poverty that could otherwise entrap the less well off and pass from generation to generation.

This, in general terms, was the stage that Dilworth's thinking had reached in 1888 when he went with Isabella on a visit to Australia. While there he took the opportunity of dropping in on MacMurray; though for so calculating a person as Dilworth the remeeting could well have been the main purpose of his trip to Australia.[42] The year before, MacMurray had been appointed to the parish of St Paul's, Ballarat, and so it was at the rectory there that the Dilworths were the guests of MacMurray and his wife. For Dilworth this was no simple social occasion, although certainly the friendship was further strengthened. But Dilworth had come, as MacMurray came to recognize subsequently, in order to weigh him up and see whether he was the man needed to bring to fruition (as Dilworth was later wont to phrase it) his version of Christ's Hospital in Auckland. Nevertheless, while at the rectory at Ballarat, Dilworth seems not to have spoken at all about his scheme. Yet it is clear that before he left he was in no doubt that MacMurray was the man he wanted to have beside him in

---

* The farmer, Captain Hawes of Kohimarama, paid the boy 2s 6d a week 'and found', for which he had 'to milk the cow . . . look after the garden, help the maid wash up and clean all the pots etc. and do all the odd jobs about the place' (Williamson, 'Recollections', pp. 3–4).

Auckland. 'With some eagerness' he insisted that the MacMurrays should, next year, make a return visit to New Zealand.

This visit the MacMurrays duly made in 1889, staying with the Dilworths in their Remuera home. Dilworth spoke of business, the depression and the buying of property. More importantly, he opened up for the first time about his dream; he confided in his guest that

> as he and his wife had no children, they intended to leave their property in trust for the benefit of sons of good character and in straitened circumstances, boys who were to be trained and educated to be good and useful citizens.[43]

MacMurray later admitted that when he heard Dilworth's proposal 'I was very interested in the idea. But I had no thought that I should be connected with it'.[44]

There the matter slept until 1892; slept for MacMurray but not for Dilworth. The depression continued to deepen. Distress had spread through all walks of life confirming in Dilworth his belief that his scheme to provide education for boys in straitened circumstances was more needed than ever. Guided by Jackson, he prepared drafts of his will. Privately, and with great care, he began to mark out those who should be his trustees, people who knew his mind and would respect his intentions. Frustrated perhaps by the infirmity of age, he decided he must now also have beside him someone who was youthful and determined like MacMurray, a man to help give the will its final form and to see it executed when he was gone. But MacMurray was left in the dark about this.

Consequently when two important letters from Auckland arrived at his Ballarat rectory, he was much surprised. The first was from Dilworth warning MacMurray that a further letter from the nominators for the parish of St Mary's, Parnell, was about to arrive inviting him to be vicar.[45] In his letter Dilworth went on to plead with MacMurray to accept both that invitation and one which he himself was now also offering MacMurray to be a trustee under his will setting up an institute for boys. Dilworth argued that it had become essential for him to have MacMurray in Auckland to help with the detailed drafting of the will. So determined was he to ensure that MacMurray answered yes that he ended his letter with a touch of moral blackmail: 'he held a pistol at my head', said MacMurray, 'telling me that he was an old man, and that if he did not have my assistance he would be inclined to drop the whole idea' [of a Dilworth Trust].[46] The second letter duly arrived from the diocese offering St Mary's. Dilworth's influential hand was obvious in all this. As for himself, confessed MacMurray, he 'was reluctant to leave Australia'; he had a satisfactory parish in Ballarat and had recently been elected a canon of the cathedral there.[47] But, as he long after explained, his sense of duty to generations of boys yet unborn no less than 'the pressure exerted by Mr Dilworth' left him, he felt, no option.⁴⁸ He accepted. He came to Auckland and there remained for the rest of a very long life.

Dilworth had only two-and-a-half years to live after MacMurray settled in Auckland in June 1892. During that time the men were often closeted together, having, under the guidance of Sam Jackson, 'many conversations about the will' as they mulled over its principles and refined its details.⁴⁹ In consequence, said MacMurray, 'I got to know him very intimately'.⁵⁰ Much that has been written about the personality of the elderly Dilworth is derived from the observations made by MacMurray during those final years. Dilworth struck him (he later stated) as a person 'somewhat brusque in manner, in business matters very keen and shrewd which created in many minds the idea of hardness'.⁵¹ But he also emphasized that he was more than just a stereotype Ulsterman, despite his having most of the virtues and many of the limitations of that cultural group; for beneath that 'rough exterior he had a very kindly heart'.

MacMurray first began to appreciate this secret side to Dilworth when he saw the generous spirit his old friend brought to his will-making. Obviously, Dilworth's sympathy for boys deprived of opportunity permeated the whole document. Nor was this some newly acquired enthusiasm. The provision he made for grants to go to the kindergarten movement simply continued his long-standing practice of giving privately to that cause.⁵² Nor did he forget those who had loyally served him. In both the 1873 and 1894 wills, bequests were made to employees. Thus in the 1894 a bequest was made to William Bennett who ran the homestead farm; nor were Bennett's three children forgotten—each received twenty-five pounds. A further bequest in this last will of fifty pounds 'unto Bernard Foy of Pukekohe, an old faithful servant of mine' remained mysterious for many years until the researches of David Sherratt in the mid-1950s led to the appearance of a letter from J. J. McKinney of Pukekohe which explained all:

Robert Hall (1832–1920) Dilworth's brother-in-law, long-standing friend and foundation member of the Trust Board.
Dilworth Trust Board Archives

> Previous to coming to Pukekohe, Mr Barney Foy worked for James Dilworth at Remuera. One day, a bulldog sprang at J.D. and got him on the throat, when Bernard Foy came on the scene. He promptly got the dog by the throat with both hands and choked him off. He was given a sum of £100 for the rescue; soon afterwards he came to Pukekohe and bought ten acres of land with the money. Bernard Foy was a really good Irishman and a good Roman Catholic.⁵³

The reference to Foy's Catholicism is pertinent here. In view of the distinct Anglican coloration that the will imparted to the Dilworth Trust, the question inevitably arises: how far was Dilworth himself imbued with sectarian prejudice? A quick answer can be given—very little. When I solicited the public for information on forebears who had worked on the Dilworth estate a number of people of Catholic Irish extraction came forward. They told me that Dilworth had

JAMES DILWORTH

employed their ancestors as workers usually on the ground that they were Irish (some he even recruited on arrival at port). That they were also Catholic seemed not to trouble him. Some time after Andrew's death, part of the Waitakere farm, with a residence upon it, was leased to Henry Edwards and his family who were Catholic.[54] When, in the hard times of the late 1880s, Edwards fell behind in his rent Dilworth did not evict.[55]

In his selection of those who would be the executors of his will and the trustees of his residuary estate, however, Dilworth gave full rein to his essential Protestant clannishness. The six he chose, all close to him, were his wife Isabella, Robert Hall, his brother-in-law and manager of Logan Campbell's One Tree Hill farm, the Revd William Beatty, warden of St John's College, William Gardner, settler, of Epsom,* the Revd George MacMurray and Sir George Maurice O'Rorke, Speaker of the House of Representatives. All were Protestant Irish (four from the province of Ulster itself), all had Protestant ascendancy antecedents though none had emigrated as particularly well-to-do.

Three of the six had unimpeachable Irish university backgrounds.† Each was chosen for some personal talent apart from an intimacy with Dilworth. Isabella, his wife, he trusted as one who knew his mind from far back. Hall and Gardner were shrewd judges of suburban farm land and skilled property managers. O'Rorke was discerned by Dilworth as having a particular usefulness in his scheme for the education of boys. A superb Speaker of the House, O'Rorke stood high in the national regard, and his common law training meant he would be an excellent in-house counsel for the Trust. His long service on the Auckland Education Board and the college council gave him an extraordinary breadth of educational experience.[56] What commended the two Anglican ministers as trustees to Dilworth was, among other considerations, their relative youthfulness—Beatty was thirty-eight and MacMurray thirty-nine at the time of Dilworth's death. Their ability to serve for many years, Dilworth believed, would give continuity to the running of the Institute, just as their clerical vocation would ensure that it would keep the religious character he wished to impart to it.

Dilworth completed the final version of his will on 15 November 1894, less than six weeks before his death, although as Isabella later stated neither she nor he had any inkling at that time that the end was near.[57] Since the provisions of this lengthy (5,500 words) will are as important today as when it was executed, a summary is provided at the end of this book. Only its chief items are discussed here.[58]

Revd William Beatty (1856–1928).
Dilworth Trust Board Archives

Hon. Sir George Maurice O'Rorke, executor of Dilworth's will and member of the Trust Board.
Dilworth Trust Board Archives

---

* William Gardner was an executor of Dilworth's will until his death in February 1899, but never a member of the Trust Board because he elected not to sign the required declaration that he was a member of the Church of England.

† MacMurray had an MA and O'Rorke a BA (Hons) from Trinity College, Dublin; William Beatty an MA from both Trinity College and Queen's University of Belfast.

220

WILLS AND INHERITANCE

The six executors were designated also as trustees of the Dilworth Ulster Institute (DUI). In his will Dilworth provided for Isabella, 'my beloved wife', a life tenancy of the Dilworth homestead and its surrounding twenty-two-acre farm with all livestock and dead-stock, while within the house she was to be given all furnishings and pictures with a few named exceptions. Trustees were directed to pay Isabella an annuity of £500 for life. Small bequests were made to eleven people, past and present workers, friends and relatives. Bequests were made to the YMCA and Institute for the Blind in the form of trust funds for investment. Apart from the annuity for Isabella, the trustees were directed to pay annual sums of £100 to Dilworth's sister Eleanor, to her daughter Isabella Stubbs, to the Jubilee Kindergarten and to the diocese of Auckland to augment the stipends of needy clergy in rural parishes.

After providing these annual sums Dilworth moved on to make an important declaration:

> And whereas I have now to the satisfaction of my own conscience provided for all persons who I think have any moral claims upon me and being convinced that I can in no way better dispose of the possessions with which it has pleased God to endow me than by making a further charitable disposition of my property I have determined to establish an Institution to be called the Dilworth Ulster Institute with the object of affording to boys of the classes hereinafter mentioned such maintenance education and training as will enable them to become good and useful members of society.

Isabella Dilworth photographed after James's death. Note that she is wearing the traditional white widow's cap.
Dilworth Trust Board Archives

In consequence he called on his trustees to use his remaining property (real and personal) as a trust to promote that Institute and 'to form a reserve fund' to repair and build his properties in the City of Auckland and Parnell to generate income from leases and rents. He directed them to 'reserve twenty-five acres of my land' at Mount Hobson as the site for the buildings of the Dilworth Ulster Institute, and to set apart certain other land in Waitakere for Institute use. Apart from this property, all other lands could be leased but subject to certain restrictions according to a graduated scale of distance from the general post office. But he enjoined upon his trustees caution in their investment and building programme lest 'the net income derivable from my estate should fall below five thousand pounds'. Dilworth further instructed his trustees that, when the net income was stabilized at £5,000 and the reserve fund was no less than £10,000, they were to erect the first 'substantial buildings' for the DUI on that portion of the slope of 'Graham's Hill' which he had designated for this purpose. On completion of 'the first buildings', trustees must then, with all speed

> select so many boys of sound bodily and mental health being orphans or sons of persons of good character and of any race as in the opinion of the said Trustees that portion of the income available for the

purpose will be sufficient from time to time to support train and educate and the boys to be so selected shall be either destitute orphans or children of parents in straitened circumstances resident in the Provincial District of Auckland or in the Province of Ulster in Ireland.

The boys from Auckland had to be between three and five years of age and those from Ulster between four and eight. Thereafter the boys were to be 'maintained' and

clothed in a suitable uniform dress and shall be brought up and educated in the tenets of the Church . . . of the Province of New Zealand commonly called the Church of England and shall be instructed in such branches of learning and industry as shall be considered likely to make them good and useful members of society.

The somewhat low-church Anglican character of the Institute was further entrenched by Dilworth's instruction that no chaplain, teacher or officer was to be appointed 'until he shall have signed a Declaration that he is a member of the . . . Church of England and that he accepts and maintains the principles of the Reformation accomplished in the Church of England in the Sixteenth Century of the Christian era'.

Dilworth laid it down that students must leave the Institute on reaching fifteen years, which, it should be recognized, was an age at which few pupils at that time were still at school. But the liberal character of the Trust went further. Any student who had demonstrated at the age of fifteen that he had 'knowledge, industry and natural talents' that would enable him to benefit from 'studies in any university in New Zealand or . . . Dublin or . . . in any college near the City of Belfast' was to be supported within the institute until he moved on to take up that further stage in his education.*

The remainder of the will was concerned with the duties of trustees and is not relevant here.

But some brief appraisal of the will and the Trust which it set up is called for. A particular virtue of the will is that, although some matters bearing on property and finances were precisely defined and were, therefore, particularly binding upon trustees, Dilworth presented the purposes of his Institute in so generous and open-ended a way that trustees, in later years, were able, while adhering to the intention of the will, to make pragmatic changes to the nature of their trust. This explains why trustees have been able to respond so realistically to the changing needs of boys entering the school in the twentieth century. Of course, like most trusts, the Dilworth board has been obliged over the years to seek alteration to the terms of its trust by means of private Bills passed by the Legislature. The process began early. A 1902 Bill, for instance, was needed to empower the board to sell land more than

Opposite: *A view of the central portion of the Dilworth senior school, 1994.*
Kate Stone

An aerial view of the junior campus of Dilworth School, 1994.
Dilworth School Archives

---

* Every boy proceeding to tertiary education from Dilworth School today receives a grant of $500 to launch him on his studies. In special cases old boys have had their university education subsidized throughout.

WILLS AND INHERITANCE

fifteen miles from the city for reinvestment closer to Auckland.[59] The Trust also successfully sought changes concerned with the sale, subdivision and lease of its property. This was just as well. The transformation of the property market in Auckland, the fastest growing city in New Zealand, in the twenty years following Dilworth's death was so sweeping that even so farsighted an investor as he could scarcely have foreseen it.

Some provisions in the will were shown to be impracticable long before the school opened in 1906. The age of entry for Auckland boys (three to five) was far too low and, as the trustees later phrased it, would virtually convert the Institute into a nursing home.[60] As a result the upper age of entry for boys from Auckland and Ulster alike was lifted to nine.[61] Nor was the scheme for recruiting boys from Ulster ever effectively realized. (Between 1906 and 1932—when the last lads came—only twelve came out from Ireland.) It quickly became apparent that Irish parents and relatives with deprived boys in their care could not bear to be parted from them. There is, however, a County Tyrone component in the Dilworth School system today. It is in a form which Dilworth himself did not envisage but of which, had he been granted foreknowledge, he would certainly have approved.*

If the will has, as I believe, a marked Protestant-Anglican inclination, that owed more to MacMurray than to Dilworth. To be sure, Dilworth was an unregenerate low churchman, reflecting the influence of the Church of Ireland in which he was raised, a province which was puritanical upon matters of liturgy, vestments and ritual. This was the religious outlook he brought with him to New Zealand, and which he never lost.[62] Not surprisingly, when the choir of St Mark's Remuera donned surplices in the later 1880s Dilworth was among those denouncing that 'Popish practice'.[63] But he was not extreme. Bishop Cowie observed that crosses, vestments and ritual scandalized large numbers of the diocese during his episcopate.[64] So Dilworth was not unusual. And, as has been already been mentioned, when dealing with fellow-Irishmen he demonstrated no anti-Catholic rancour.

MacMurray was otherwise. A self-confessed patriot and imperialist, he came from Ireland in an era when Protestants felt themselves beleaguered in a way they never had during Dilworth's years there. The Ulster which MacMurray had left was one in which Catholicism had become closely linked to revived Irish nationalism. As a boy in Donegal he was raised in a region of Fenian insurgency.[65] As rector of Killukin he saw 'Land Leaguers' being whipped up by C. S. Parnell and J. G. Biggar who were 'flying about in a jaunting car'.

---

* Since 1987 selected seventh-form scholars (at first two a year, and since 1992 three a year) from the Royal School of Dungannon have been awarded 'Dilworth Scholarships' to come as tutors for one year to Dilworth School in Auckland. Fares and a living allowance are paid in return for part-time hostel duties. Almost all of the scholars on their return go to university or polytechnical colleges in Ireland or Britain.

Farm buildings of the Dilworth homestead became the classrooms of the Dilworth School which opened in 1906.
Dilworth School Archives

Earlier he had been a curate of Cavan when the Boycott land strikes were at a peak in central Ireland. MacMurray was the man more likely to have given the Orange hue to the will.

But long before the school opened its doors, a Privy Council ruling, and taxation advantages from being interdenominational, gave the trustees of the Institute every incentive to tone down the emphatic Anglicanism of the will. From the outset recruitment of entrants was on the basis of the school's being an interdenominational charity. Through the school's career, boys have indeed been exposed to the 'tenets of Anglicanism' as Dilworth had stipulated. But proselytism has been unknown. This compromise has worked, and is likely to continue.

One could almost say that nothing so much became the life of James Dilworth as the last will and testament with which it ended.

CHAPTER FOURTEEN

Last Things

THE LAST YEARS of Dilworth's life were of more leisurely pace. Upon his return to the colony in 1885 he began progressively to turn over more of his day-by-day business to Gerald O'Halloran who during his absence had proved a faithful steward. Though O'Halloran continued thereafter to practise as an accountant out of his office in Shortland Street, he spent much time at Dilworth's own home and was on constant call. Originally on an annual retainer of £100, he found his growing worth to his elderly client recognized in 1890 by an increase in this figure to £150, a revision which was markedly contrary to the downward trend of almost all remuneration in those difficult times.[1]

Financial records of the Remuera estate after 1885 were entirely written by O'Halloran. Similarly all of Dilworth's outward correspondence from that time was in O'Halloran's clerkly copperplate, occasionally with an appended note that the letter was dictated by Dilworth. Such an annotation was not necessary. The economical turn of phrase and the asperity with which folly or imagined incompetence was assailed leave no doubt that here was a verbatim transcription.

Dilworth's use of an amanuensis during his latter years raises a question of health to which there is no sure answer. Twenty years before his death Dilworth's writing became tremulous, the deterioration being most marked in his somewhat florid signature.[2] The presumption is that difficulties with writing rather than mere convenience had led to his employment of O'Halloran as scribe. What remains unclear is whether Dilworth had developed some pathological condition or whether he was simply subject to a benign, so-called 'essential tremor' accentuated by old age. The only direct evidence is provided by the reminiscences of a Mrs Hardy who, sixty years after, recalled a visit she made as a girl of eight to the Remuera homestead in the last year of Dilworth's life.

> My Aunty [Mrs Mary Cheeseman of Parnell] took me visiting with her to see Mr and Mrs Dilworth in their beautiful home, which is now Dilworth School. Poor old Mr Dilworth suffered from palsey [sic] and it was pitiful to see him sitting there, shaking all the time.

James Dilworth's signature.
Top: *1891.* Bottom: *1841.*

They had a pony carriage made very low especially for him and Mrs Dilworth, so that he could get in and out easily, and Mrs Dilworth used to take him driving every day.[3]*

Until quite modern times, 'palsy' was the term to denote what is now known as Parkinsonism, and that complaint could have caused the tremor discernible to this girl. But there is no reference elsewhere to his being physically impaired in this way; in fact the only other medical complaint referred to in Dilworth's correspondence is an occasional bout of bronchitis.[4] And to the end he carried out, for a man in his late seventies, an exacting round of public duties. Death when it came therefore was something of a shock. 'My husband', observed Isabella, 'was suddenly called away.'[5] The death certificate made up by Dr E. D. MacKellar makes no reference to any chronic complaint as a contributory cause of death.[6]

The weight of evidence suggests that whatever the nature of Dilworth's neurological condition it did not noticeably impair his physical and mental abilities. His reduced participation in active business seems therefore to have resulted from a choice natural in a person of advancing years rather than from any medical disability.

Life in the Dilworth household in these latter years continued on its habitual quiet tenor. For Isabella and James (as for most elderly people) traits of personality remained as they had ever been except that they became, as it were, even more so. Researching in the 1950s into the life of Dilworth, David Sherratt spoke to people yet living who, sixty or more years before, had visited the Dilworth household and knew its owners at first hand. From these informants he learned that the Dilworths, never ardent socializers, entertained little towards the end. To this practice there was one exception; old whist-playing friends were welcome, providing they played the game in the same uncompromising spirit as Lamb's Sarah Battle.† A Hall descendant related how

> I used to visit the house in those days and it was one of the customs of [Dilworth] to play whist with his old friends. The game was pursued with some skill and there was little tolerance of poor play. I was conscripted on one occasion, and recall coming in for a great deal of comment and some impatient criticism from the other players, and in particular from my host.[7]

The impression of the elderly Dilworths that Sherratt gained from his informants was that 'both were rather typical of their age; rather strict and somewhat formal in manner, with a devotion to routine, a strong

---

* Probably the carriage referred to here was the jaunting car which had been in use for over thirty years and if so had not been constructed because of any infirmity of James Dilworth.

† Sarah Battle 'was none of your luke-warm gamesters, your half and half players. . . . She loved a thorough-paced partner, a determined enemy' ('Mrs Battle's Opinions on Whist' in Charles Lamb, *The Essays of Elia*).

sense of respectability and the "rightness of things"'.[8] Sherratt, like MacMurray and other people who knew Dilworth personally, spoke of him as a tall man. Photographs confirm that he remained lean, and that, fully bewhiskered in the fashion of the day, as his hair whitened with age he took on a distinctly patriarchal look. Physically Dilworth seems to have had no other impact upon his contemporaries, being unremarkable Sherratt said 'for any ostentation in dress and manner'. But emphatically he was 'a Protestant of the first water'.[9]

During these depression years there was little comfort in the world outside Remuera. General hardship was everywhere, giving greater urgency to his scheme to educate the boys of families fallen on hard times. With his own affairs quietly prospering, Dilworth was spared the anguish of many of his fellow-businessmen. Together with Logan Campbell he was one of the few survivors of the old order. So many others who had once been looked on as unassailably prosperous had gone under or were living in much reduced circumstances. In 1889 his old friend Joseph Howard died in his Wynyard Street home of a heart complaint.[10] He had never recovered from his stroke of four years before, and for several months before death had been in 'a delicate state of health', obviously harassed by continuing business worries.[11] Once envied as an independent gentleman with a handsome competence, Howard left behind a widow and seven children in unaccustomed indigence. And some of Dilworth's friends or acquaintances from even further back had fared equally badly; in 1887 James Williamson died penniless.[12] One-time wealthy expatriates like James Farmer and William Brown, caught by the collapse of the BNZ and other financial institutions, were facing an old age of privation. James McCosh Clark, former mayor of Auckland, whose fine house The Tower stood on the opposite side of Remuera Road from Dilworth's eastern ('Dairy') farm, was forced by his losses in 1889 to leave the country. J. C. Firth and T. Morrin like Dilworth were encumbered by great unsaleable provincial estates but, unlike him, as mammoth borrowers were ruined by those lands. Debt also ruined Sir Frederick Whitaker, Dilworth's old colleague of provincial government days. Whitaker's last years brought him little joy; his favourite son, F. A. Whitaker, depressed by losses, had committed suicide in 1887; and threatening penury kept Sir Frederick himself chained to his office desk, at which he died working in 1891.[13]

Williamson, McCosh Clark, Morrin, Firth, Whitaker and other prominent Aucklanders were not only stripped of their wealth; they had also lost their good name. The 'Limited Circle' grouped around Dilworth's Mount St John neighbour, the banker D. L. Murdoch, after the findings of an audit committee of the Bank of New Zealand in 1888, was vilified by press and public for having brought great harm to that Auckland-based bank.

Public affairs in these tense times were no distraction for Dilworth.

The meetings of the diocesan general trust board in the late 1880s and 1890s were far from being a peaceful Trollopean backwater. Quarrels associated with St John's College, its staffing, location, trust funds and scholarships—though constitutionally the concern of general synod—brought bitterness into the meetings of the local diocesan trust board, too. The panic run on the Auckland Savings Bank (totally unjustified in the event) which took place in August 1893 must have seemed to Dilworth as senior trustee as being all of a piece with his impression of a once prosperous colonial society in danger of falling apart.[14] Nor was Dilworth's term on the council of the university college restful. This was a strenuous commitment, for his financial skills were in much demand as the slump put the budget of the infant college under much strain.[15] The university's historian, Sir Keith Sinclair, wrote of the early 1890s as a time of rancour and great unpleasantness in council politics as well.[16] Intermittent friction between professors and council, present almost from the college's formation, came to a head with what Sir Keith

THE SCAPEGOAT.
(See Leviticus, chapter XVI., verses 21, 22, 23, 24.)

An 1888 cartoon by 'Blo' (William Blomfield) in the Observer, *in which D. L. Murdoch, head of the Bank of New Zealand, has been sent into the wilderness to 'bear upon him all the iniquities of the children of Israel'. Note that among the 'Bad Investments' of the Bank is the skeleton of the 'Pate[tere] Co.'*
Alexander Turnbull Library

JAMES DILWORTH

called the 'contrived dismissal' of Professor William Steadman Aldis, *bête noire* of the council chairman Sir Maurice O'Rorke—an extreme action which the university historian considered 'discreditable' and almost certainly unjustified.[17] Here was a murky quarrel, so labyrinthine in character it cannot be discussed here. Suffice it to say, it brought out the worst in the normally punctilious O'Rorke, who had been blinkered by a sense of loyalty to his somewhat spoilt polo-playing son Teddy.[18]* Voting figures of the Council imply that on this issue Dilworth was torn between his desire to back up his Irish friend

---

* Teddy O'Rorke was for a time tenant of Williamson's Pah when it passed into the hands of the Bank of New Zealand Estates Co. He converted the large flat field beside the mansion into a polo field. Teams of horses pulling mowers or rollers were shod with leather lest their hooves damage the sward.

'Waiting for the doors to open': the panic run on the Queen Street branch of the ASB, 1 September 1893. The rumour of insolvency was quite unfounded.
Auckland Public Library

O'Rorke and his deep-rooted sense of natural justice—Aldis had the backing of almost all of Auckland's leading ministers of every denomination.[19]

    Thus it was, in the setting of the personal tragedies of old friends like Howard and Whitaker, the factional disputes of college councils and trust boards, and the overall gloom and panic of a prolonged depression, that Dilworth immersed himself in will-making. But the task was not an anodyne for the pain of a world with which he had become increasingly out of sympathy. Nor was it a simple matter of 'putting of one's house in order'. The will had an existence, a rationale of its own; had become a final attempt to give a pattern and purpose to a life which hitherto, ignobly perhaps, had been preoccupied with worldly things. The will speaks, however, of a conscience at rest at last. His accumulated wealth had become sanctioned, he believed, by the new obligation he had taken on towards the wider community.

    One also remarks the central place given in his will to land on the flank of Graham's Hill, the summit of which he had ardently but fruitlessly pursued for over thirty years. A twenty-five-acre portion, carefully drawn on an accompanying plan, was expressly excluded from lease and sale so that it could be set apart for ever for the buildings

The Auckland University College Council, 1894. In the centre front is the Anglican triumvirate of Bishop W. G. Cowie (long white beard), Sir Maurice O'Rorke and Dilworth.
Dilworth Trust Board Archives

W. Gardner, executor of Dilworth's will who chose not to attest that he was an Anglican.
Dilworth Trust Board Archives

and activities of the Institute. The placing of the school beside the hill had a deep significance for Dilworth.

Dilworth's life ended suddenly. For some weeks he had been busy with meetings, particularly those (it was reported) concerned with putting the finances of the Auckland college council 'on a sounder footing'.[20] During the week in which he last took to his bed he had attended meetings in town on Monday, Tuesday (the diocesan general trust board) and Thursday. On the evening of his last meeting he came home complaining of feeling tired and unwell. Overnight his condition worsened, and his family doctor of long standing, Dr E. D. MacKellar, was summoned. He diagnosed peritonitis.[21] On the next day, Saturday, Dilworth lost consciousness. The following day, Sunday (23 December 1894), he died at three in the afternoon.

The funeral took place on the afternoon of Christmas Day. At three o'clock a cortege left Dilworth's Remuera residence and crossed to St Mark's, the church of which Dilworth had been a foundation parishioner.[22] The mourners were met at the gate of the churchyard by the Revd George MacMurray, and the Revd William Beatty, who was now vicar-elect of the parish. The church within was crowded with friends and relatives and prominent citizens, among whom were many civic, educational and church dignitaries. In his funeral oration Beatty praised Dilworth as 'a good man and a great citizen' whose days a merciful God had 'lengthened sufficiently' so that he might mature his plans 'for the benefit of future generations'. (The foreshadowed philanthropy would have been no surprise to the congregation; obituaries in the press had spoken of a large educational bequest to be made to the city.)

On the completion of the address the body was committed to a grave 'lined with ever greens' beside that of Andrew.

Two days later the will was published in summary in the local newspapers. Citizens were astonished at the extent of Mr Dilworth's munificence. But what of Dilworth himself? Would a modest anticipation of community gratitude have been his sole reward? Probably not. One wonders whether the bequest had a further purpose, the making of amends by expunging the stain of the loss, long ago, of Mullaghcreevy for which Dilworth, however unwittingly, believed he bore some responsibility. He who had been unable to retain the family home standing beside a Celtic ring-fort in County Tyrone, was now to provide beside the Maori pa of Remuwera an inalienable home for future generations of boys. If ending life rightly gives peace, then Dilworth is likely to have earned his ease at last.

APPENDIX A

Summary of the Will of James Dilworth Dated 15 November 1894

Date of death   23 December 1894

1. Executors and Trustees: Isabella Dilworth, Robert Hall, Revd William Beatty, William Gardner, Revd George MacMurray, Sir George Maurice O'Rorke.
2. Devise of property to wife; homestead and twenty-two acres of land.
3. Bequests: Rebecca Wall £50; Bernard Foy £50; William Bennett senior £50; May, William and Ellen Bennett each £25; Jane Kidd £100; Annie Hall £100; Isabella Paton £100; Annie Watt (Dungannon) £100.
4. Trusts: YMCA £500; Institute for Blind £500.
5. Annuities: Isabella Dilworth £500; Eleanor Mossman £100; Jubilee Kindergarten £100; Auckland Anglican Diocese £100 (to augment clergy stipends).
6. 'And whereas I have now to the satisfaction of my own conscience provided for all persons who I think have any moral claims upon me and being convinced that I can in no way better dispose of the possessions with which it has pleased God to endow me than by making a further charitable disposition of my property I have determined to establish an Institution to be called the Dilworth Ulster Institute with the object of affording to boys of the classes hereinafter mentioned such maintenance education and training as will enable them to become good and useful members of Society. Now therefore in exercise of every power and authority enabling me I devise bequeath and appoint unto the said Trustees the whole of the residue of the real and personal estate which at the time of my death I shall have power to dispose of by Will . . . .'
7. Trustees empowered to 'repair, enlarge or renew' buildings and houses on 'my land situate in the City of Auckland or in the Borough of Parnell'.
8. Trustees directed 'at their discretion' to let land as the will allows.
9. 'And I direct that the said Trustees shall set apart and reserve from lease for the purpose hereinafter mentioned not less than twenty-five acres of my land at Remuera aforesaid known as Graham's Hill as per plan or tracing annexed hereto showing the position in which the buildings hereinafter directed to be constructed shall be placed.'

10. Trustees are directed to lease land subject to the following conditions:

   (a) 'The said Trustees may let any portion of my lands situate in the City of Auckland and the Borough of Parnell and the houses thereon for any term not exceeding ten years.

   (b) Any land situate outside of the said City of Auckland but within the distance of four miles as the crow flies from the General Post Office in the said City of Auckland except the before mentioned Twenty-five acres and subject to the before mentioned devise may be let in portions not exceeding three acres each and in all not more than twelve acres in any one year for a term not exceeding twenty-five years, on condition that each such Lessee shall covenant to erect a substantial wooden building. . . .

   (c) Any of my land situate beyond the distance of four miles but within the distance of eight miles as the crow flies from the said General Post Office may be let in the same manner as directed in the next preceding clause and on the same conditions as to building except that the area to be included in any lease may be of any extent not exceeding ten acres and the aggregate of the land so let in one year shall not exceed fifty acres. . . .

   (d) Any of my land situate beyond the distance of eight miles but within the distance of thirty miles as the crow flies from the said General Post Office in the said City of Auckland may be let by the said Trustees to be used for any purpose and without restriction of area for any term not exceeding fifteen years. . . .

   (e) Any of my lands situate beyond the distance of thirty miles as the crow flies from the said General Post Office may be let by the said Trustees to be used for any purpose and without restriction of area for any term not exceeding twenty-five years. . . .'

11. Trustees are directed that in addition to investing in real estate they consider investing funds on 'fixed deposit in any Bank carrying on business in Auckland', or on first mortgage of freehold estate, or in Public Stocks and securities.

12. 'And I direct that whenever the net annual income of my said estate shall amount to not less than Five thousand pounds and the moneys in the hands of the said Trustees shall amount to not less than Ten thousand pounds' designs are to be sought for 'a substantial building' to go on allotment Number Two of Section Number Eleven of the Suburbs of Auckland known as Graham's Hill 'as per plan of tracing annexed hereto with all the outbuildings walls fences and other appurtenances which in the opinion of the said Trustees shall be necessary for the purposes hereinafter expressed. And I direct that as soon as the first of the buildings hereinbefore directed to be built shall have been completed and all liabilities incurred in the erection thereof shall have been discharged the said Trustees shall as soon as conveniently may be select so many boys of sound bodily and mental health being orphans or sons of persons of good character and of any race as in the opinion of the said Trustees that portion of the income available for the purpose will

be sufficient from time to time to support train and educate and the boys to be so selected shall be either destitute orphans or children of parents in straitened circumstances resident in the Provincial District of Auckland or in the Province of Ulster in Ireland And I direct that in the selection of boys resident in Ulster a preference shall be given *ceteris paribus* to boys resident in or near the town of Dungannon in the County of Tyrone in the said Province of Ulster And I direct that the boys to be so selected in the said Provincial District of Auckland shall not be under the age of three years nor over the age of five years and that the boys to be so selected in the said Province of Ulster shall not be under the age of four years nor over the age of eight years.'

This section goes on to give guidance on how boys are to be recruited and selected in Ulster.

13. 'I direct that all boys however selected or nominated as Pupils of the said Institute shall be maintained in the buildings of the said Institute and clothed in a suitable uniform dress and shall be brought up and educated in the tenets of the said Church of the said Province of New Zealand commonly called the Church of England and shall be instructed in such branches of learning and industry as shall be considered likely to make them good and useful members of society.'

14. 'Suitable curricula of studies' to be determined by Trustees and awards to be made for 'proficiency and diligence'.

15. 'I authorise the said Trustees from time to time to appoint all such Chaplains Secretaries Officers Servants and other persons as they shall think necessary for the purpose of carrying on the business of the said Institute and to pay to them a suitable remuneration for their services and from time to time to dismiss any of them without being obliged to give any reason therefor But no person shall be appointed Chaplain Secretary Master Teacher or other officer of the said Institute until he shall have signed Declaration that he is a member of the Church of the Province of New Zealand commonly called the Church of England and that he accepts and maintains the principles of the Reformation accomplished in the Church of England in the Sixteenth Century of the Christian era . . .'

16. 'No pupil . . . be allowed to remain in the said Institute after he shall have attained the age of Fifteen years And I authorise the said Trustees whenever any pupil of the said Institute shall have attained the age of Fifteen years to apprentice him to any trade business calling or profession And if they shall think that any pupil having attained the age of Fifteen years shall by his knowledge industry and natural talents be likely to distinguish himself they may make arrangements for his maintenance and the prosecution of his studies in any University in New Zealand or in the City of Dublin in Ireland or in any College situate in or near the City of Belfast in Ireland and in the meantime he may be allowed to remain a resident of the said Institute.'

17. Directions to build up a reserve fund.

18. Authority given to Trustees, when buildings have been erected 'on Graham's Hill', 'to erect a gymnasium and to form cricket and play grounds on the said Twenty-five acres of land so directed to be reserved from leases as aforesaid for the use of the pupils of the said Institute and they may form plantations of trees shrubs and flowers thereon and otherwise improve and ornament the same and do all such other things as they may think necessary for the health recreation and education of the said pupils.'

19. (a) Trustees directed to 'pay all my just debts', carry out all building and maintenance requirements.
    (b) Payment of Trustees for their services.
    (c) Form of resignation, and reappointment of Trustees.
    (d) Disqualification and appointment of Trustees.
    (e) Trustees required to declare they are Anglicans.
    (f) Rules for conduct of Board meetings.

20. 'I direct that so soon as the said Dilworth Ulster Institute shall be in operation by having inmates as pupils the Bishop of the Diocese of Auckland hereinbefore mentioned shall be invited by the said Trustees to be Visitor of the said Institute and as such shall be empowered from time to time at his discretion to visit and inspect the said Institute and to enter such remarks as he may think fitting in a book which shall be kept for that purpose and shall be called The Episcopal Visitor's Book and to make annually a Report respecting the work and condition of the Institute. . . .

In witness whereof I have to each sheet of this my will contained in nineteen pages of paper set my hand this Fifteenth day of November One thousand eight hundred and ninety-four.

J. DILWORTH

Signed by the said Testator James Dilworth as and for his last Will and Testament in the presence of us present at the same time who in his presence at his request and in the presence of each other have hereunto subscribed our names as witnesses.

GRAVES AICKIN,
Chemist, Auckland.

Wm. S. COCHRANE,
Land Agent, Auckland.'

APPENDIX B

The Dilworth Trust in 1995

For 100 years a succession of Trustees has been charged with the responsibility of investing the capital from the Residuary Estate of James Dilworth in a way that realizes his wish to help boys from families in straitened circumstances.

Each time a boy is accepted for Dilworth School the Trustees take on a commitment to care for that boy for up to nine further years. This is a costly obligation. The expense of running the school on its two campuses is reflected in an annual budget of $6 million. Because of this, and in order to follow the express directions of Mr Dilworth in his will, the Board has sought to be conservative in its investment decisions. Further, out of respect for James Dilworth's business acumen the Board has also followed his policy of investing in property. His influence on the Dilworth Trust Board, therefore, continues to this day in that the Board remains essentially a property investor, while adhering to his further investment principle that in diversity lies safety. Much of James Dilworth's original Remuera land remains in Trust hands and both the senior school in Great South Road and the junior school in Omahu Road are part of the original estate. The rest of the Remuera land was progressively subdivided by the Trustees into residential and commercial sections and leased in perpetuity with twenty-one-year rent reviews. The residential lessees have, at times, been offered the right to freehold their leasehold sections, and probably fifty per cent of the residential land bounded by Great South Road, Remuera Road, St Marks Road and Omahu Road has been freeholded in this way. In 1993 the residential lessees were given the right to freehold their leasehold land at any time and it seems inevitable that eventually all of the residential leasehold land will become freeholded.

Conscious of the need to retain its property investment portfolio, the Board has reinvested funds in normal commercial property. This policy of reinvestment in commercial property has progressed to the stage where over fifty per cent of the Board's income is derived from standard commercial rentals whereas only thirty per cent comes from ground rental leases. Commercial properties owned vary from office blocks to vehicle franchises to industrial developments. The commercial properties are located in areas as diverse as Takapuna, Epsom, Remuera, Newmarket, Penrose and Hamilton.

By following James Dilworth's lead the Board has progressed to the stage where it can look after 520 boys in the junior and senior schools, and Dilworth School is the largest boarding school in New Zealand.

Clark Thomas
Secretary-manager

APPENDIX C

Dilworth School Today

Although the Dilworth Trust Board came into being in 1894 the school itself did not open its doors to its first eight boys until twelve years later. The opening day, 12 March 1906, was no doubt a source of great satisfaction to the Trustees after the initial frustrations, but even they must have wondered what would become of the fledgling institution with its tiny complement of small boys, one teacher and a collection of wooden farm buildings. Even the most optimistic and farsighted of them could not have envisaged the developments which would take place over the next nine decades until in 1994 Dilworth School lays claim to being the largest full boarding school in the country.

James Dilworth was an extraordinarily shrewd judge of future trends in land values in various parts of Auckland, the settlement of his choice. Thanks to his prophetic insights, the Trust which bears his name was able to build on the original landed investment and bring it to the point where today it supports a school of significant size on two separate campuses.

It is a matter of record that for almost ninety of the hundred years we celebrate at this time the school has operated on the same site, the very land farmed by Mr Dilworth, and that many generations of boys from the Auckland provincial district have benefited from what it offers. The founder's bequest and the talents of successive trustees have ensured the continuity of the financial foundation required to sustain an educational institution which provides every requirement to those fortunate enough to be selected for entry. In effect, the Dilworth Trust Board annually makes available over 400 full boarding and tuition scholarships, and, with the planned roll increases over the next four years, that number will increase to around 550 by 1998, of whom some 50 to 60 will be seventh formers. It would be difficult to imagine any other institution anywhere able to offer without cost so much to so many for their education.

In 1993 the Trust Board realized a significant goal when it opened the new junior school on the Hobson Park campus. While the whole school still functions as a unit, a degree of autonomy has been bestowed on the junior school enabling it to develop its own character within the framework of the total organization. Simultaneously, the Board has been able to make significant improvements on the senior campus. None of the original wooden buildings remains as all have been progressively replaced by modern facilities.

At the time of this publication a new boarding hostel has been completed, along with a new swimming pool and a series of townhouses for resident staff. The recent arrival on the site of the Dilworth Centennial Cross, commissioned by the Old Boys Association, marks the culmination of years of planning. It is a spectacular work of art which symbolises the Christian ethic that Dilworth believed should lie at the heart of the school, and is at the same time a fitting tribute from the old boys to the founder and to his Irish origins. Still on the drawing board is a series of new facilities: a hostel for seventh form students, a centre for science and technology, a redeveloped library and administrative area, a sports complex and expanded playing fields. These developments will be brought to fruition in the next five years.

For almost ninety years Dilworth has benefited from a succession of dedicated teachers and other staff who have guided and directed the school and have ensured a rich heritage for present generations to enjoy. Much of the school's success can be attributed to a growing number of teachers who have devoted a working lifetime to supporting the Dilworth philosophy and carrying out the aims of the founder. A school thrives with such continuity of service and the stability it provides.

In the final analysis we look to the students of our school to see whether the aims of the founder are being fulfilled. Following the years of expansion, Dilworth School has reached a size and maturity which were unthinkable in earlier times. It is the belief of staff and trustees, confirmed by unsolicited outside comment as well as by the achievements of individual students, that Dilworth boys are in general well groomed, well trained, sensitive to the needs of others and well prepared to take their place in society.

Finally, the old boys of Dilworth carry the good name of their school into the workplace and into the community. We observe with pride the achievements of so many of our ex-students, from time to time basking in the reflected glory of a 'superstar' singer or a governor general, a national sportsman or a cabinet minister, yet deriving equal pleasure from the majority who give their best in every endeavour. The founder's confidence in a young and developing nation inspired him to invest heavily in its educational future. A century later we can safely say that his confidence was well-placed and that his dream has been realized.

M. T. Wilton
Headmaster

REFERENCES

Abbreviations

AES	*Auckland Evening Star*
AHB	Auckland Harbour Board
AJHR	Appendices to the Journals of the House of Representatives
AI and ML (or AR)	Auckland Institute and Museum Library
Ak.	Auckland
APC	Votes and Proceedings of the Auckland Provincial Council
APL	Auckland Public Library
Arch.	Archives
ASB	Auckland Savings Bank
ATL	Alexander Turnbull Library
AWN	*Auckland Weekly News*
BNZ	Bank of New Zealand
C of T	Certificate of title
DI	Deeds Index
DNZB	*Dictionary of New Zealand Biography*
DSC (or SC)	*Daily Southern Cross*
DTB	Dilworth Trust Board
DTBA	Dilworth Trust Board Archives
DTBMB	Dilworth Trust Board Minutebook
DTBSB	Dilworth Trust Board Scrapbook
Hist. Journ. of Ak. and Waik.	*Historical Journal of Auckland and Waikato*
IA	Internal Affairs Department
Inform.	Information (supplied by)
LTO	Land Transfer Office
NArch	National Archives (Wellington)
NARC	National Archives Record Centre (Auckland)
NZGG	*New Zealand Government Gazette*
NZH	*New Zealand Herald*
NZI	New Zealand Insurance Company
NZJH	*New Zealand Journal of History*
NZPD	*New Zealand Parliamentary Debates*
obit.	obituary
OLC	Old Land Claims files, National Archives, Wellington
P	Papers
PRO	Public Record Office (London)
Wn	Wellington

Chapter One

1. Virginia Bushman, *Genealogy of the Dilworth Families in America, 1550–1970*, Salt Lake City, private publication, 1970, p. vii.
2. Emeritus Professor F. S. Scott offering an informal opinion.
3. *Dilworth Newsletter*, No. 2, 1987, Walthamstow, pp. 1–2, copy DTB.
4. *Victoria History of the Counties of England: a History of the County of Lancashire, Cumbria and North Wales*, reprinted and edited Phillimore, Chichester, 1978, p. 201.
5. *Dilworth Newsletter*, No. 4, 1988, p. 3.
6. Philip S. Robinson, *The Plantation of Ulster: British Settlement in an Irish*

REFERENCES

Landscape, 1600–1670, Dublin, 1984, pp. 1–2.
7. Gilbert Camblin, *The Town in Ulster*, Belfast, 1971, p. 17.
8. Robinson, *Plantation*, pp. 63–64.
9. Mary Rogers, *Prospect of Tyrone*, Enniskillen, 1988, p. 69.
10. *Dilworth Newsletter*, No. 5, 1988.
11. Copy in possession of John Dilworth, Dungannon. For information on townlands see: *Irish Genealogy: a Record Finder*, ed. Donal F. Begley, Dublin, 1981, pp. 46–48; and *Heather Peat and Stone: the Parishes and Townlands of Tyrone*, ed. William O'Kane, Dungannon, 1992, pp. 58–63.
12. *O.S. Memoirs of Ireland, Parishes of County Tyrone II*, Vol. 20, Belfast, 1993, pp. 66–68.
13. *Dilworth Newsletter*, No. 5, 1988.
14. Robinson, *Plantation of Ulster*, pp. 105–6.
15. Cit. William O'Kane, in *Heather Peat and Stone*, p. viii.
16. G. L. Pearce, *A Heritage in Trust*, Auckland, 1986, p. 16.
17. R. F. Foster in *The Oxford Illustrated History of Ireland*, Oxford, 1991, pp. 192–93.
18. 'Notes and Reminiscences of James Brown of Donaghmore', 1904–1905, typescript, p. 2. Copy with DTB.
19. Donaghmore Heritage Centre, database records.
20. The author is grateful for the assistance of Mr Norman Cardwell of the Royal School of Dungannon who acted as co-worker in research on County Tyrone and particularly Dungannon. Staff of 'Irish World' of Dungannon were also helpful.
21. John McEvoy, *County of Tyrone, 1802: a Statistical Survey*, reprinted and edited, Belfast, 1991, pp. 69, 135,158.
22. Ibid, pp. 133,158.
23. *O.S. Memoirs*, report of Lt G. Dalton, Jul. 1834, p. 40.
24. McEvoy, p. 69.
25. Gearoid O'Tuathaigh, *Ireland Before the Famine, 1798–1848*, Dublin, 1972, p. 129.
26. McEvoy, pp. 168–70.
27. Proinsias O'Conluain, 'Benburb and the Powerscourts' in *Duiche Neill*, Benburb, 1987, pp. 61–62.
28. See e.g. James Dilworth to W. J. Mossman, 18 Jul. 1891, Mossman P, DTB.
29. *O.S. Memoirs*, report of Lt Dalton, pp. 43–44; McEvoy, pp. 105, 111, 200.
30. McEvoy, p. 19.
31. See e.g. Pearce, p. 30.
32. McEvoy, pp. 108, 193.
33. Reminiscences of Esther Ann Evans née Dilworth, Mossman P.
34. Lease cited in marriage settlement, James Dilworth upon Sarah Dilworth Moorhead, ? Feb. 1777; also Lease Thomas Verner to Mary Dilworth, 1 Nov. 1759, cit. Memo Wilfred Dilworth, 14 Jan. 1994. DTB. For information on respective rights of landlords and tenants, see A. P. W. Malcolmson, *The Pursuit of the Heiress, 1750–1820*, Antrim, 1982, passim.
35. Pearce, p. 16.
36. Foster in *Oxford Illustrated History*, p. 174.
37. O'Tuathaigh, pp. 128, 133, 135.
38. Some of the more important material has been photocopied in Ireland and is now deposited in Dilworth Trust Board Archives, Auckland. In tracing James Dilworth's family and early life I owe an immense debt to the findings of John Dilworth and his son Wilfred, both of Derrybuoy near Dungannon. A research visit I paid to County Tyrone in 1993 was made much more fruitful because of their guidance.
39. Marriage settlement, ? Feb. 1777, in which James Dilworth settled on Sarah his daughter a sublease of twenty acres of Mullaghcreevy to the Owens family dated 17 Oct. 1770, DTB.
40. Tithe applotment, 1822–37. Donaghmore Heritage Centre database, DTB.
41. See e.g. lease of Garvagh by Anne Dilworth to John and William Davis, 29 Apr. 1822, DTB.
42. See e.g. assignment by Anne of mortgage over Aghareany to Andrew Dilworth, 13 May 1831; bond of William Henderson to Anne Dilworth for £33 6s 8d dated 25 Nov. 1816, DTB.
43. Report of R. Oram, Environment Service of Northern Ireland, 9 Feb. 1994: 'The Dilworth House, Donaghmore', DTB.
44. Memo, Wilfred Dilworth, 14 Jan. 1994.
45. Copy of deed of lease, DTB.
46. Inf. Mr Ian Wilson, Dilworth School.

47. This para based on W. Dilworth memo, 14 Jan. 1994.
48. Ibid.
49. *Irish Genealogy*, p. 159.
50. Ibid, p. 157.
51. W. Dilworth memo, 14 Jan. 1994, p. 7.
52. For information on the RSD I am much indebted to a present teacher at the School, Mr Norman Cardwell. A useful comment on the school at the time Dilworth attended is provided in O.S. . . . *Parishes of County Tyrone*, p. 41.
53. Marion Mossman to Lillian Evans, 9 Feb. 1937, 19 May 1937, Mossman, P; W. G. Cowie, *Our Last Year in New Zealand*, London, 1888, pp. 72, 234.
54. *Cyclopedia of New Zealand*, Vol. II, p. 191.
55. Foster in *Oxford Illustrated History*, p. 196.
56. Rory Fitzpatrick, *God's Frontiersmen. The Scots-Irish Epic*, London, 1989, p. 159.
57. O'Tuathaigh, pp. 142–45.
58. Fitzpatrick, p. 232.

Chapter Two
1. *Lloyd's Register*, 1840.
2. *New Zealand Gazette*, London, 17 Jul. 1841, p. 173; 'Emigration from Sydney to New Zealand'.
3. *Cyclopedia of New Zealand*, Vol. II, p. 191.
4. NZH, 24 Dec. 1894.
5. *Cyclopedia of New Zealand*, Vol. II, p. 191.
6. S. M. D. Martin, *New Zealand in a Series of Letters*, London, 1845, p. 128; see also Charles Terry, *New Zealand*, London, 1842, pp. 155–56, and R. A. A. Sherrin and J. H. Wallace, *Early History of New Zealand*, Auckland, 1890, pp. 552–54.
7. NZH & AG, 4 Sept. 1841.
8. Ibid, 25 Sept. 1841.
9. George Graham, Diary, 3–7 Sept. 1841, MS 119, AR.
10. Dilworth to Andrew Sinclair, 20 Nov. 1846, OLC 1055–58, N. Arch; Wn.
11. MacMurray's Introduction to *1927 School List*.
12. MacMurray, gramophone record, 29 Sept. 1932.
13. David Rough, *Early Days of Auckland*, Auckland, 1896, np.
14. J. L. Campbell, *Poenamo*, London, 1881, p. 109.
15. J. L. Campbell, 'Reminiscences', Auckland, 1875-6, pp. 112–13, AR.
16. MacMurray, 29 Sept. 1932.
17. *Cyclopedia*, 1902, p. 191.
18. Sherrin and Wallace, p. 552; see also Stone, *Young Logan Campbell*, Auckland, 1982, p. 95, and P. H. Curson, 'Auckland in 1842', *New Zealand Geographer*, Vol. 30 (1974), pp. 107–28. Citation of Swainson from J. P. Kalaugher, *Gleanings from Early New Zealand History*, Auckland, 1950, p. 19.
19. Martin McLean, *Auckland 1842–1845*, Auckland, 1989, p. 5.
20. IA I, 12/2, N.Arch, Wn.
21. Peter Adams, *Fatal Necessity*, Auckland, 1977, pp. 161–62.
22. IA I 41/922.
23. B. A. Moore and J. S. Barton, *Banking in New Zealand*, Wellington, 1935, p. 6.
24. S. J. Butlin, *Australia and New Zealand Bank*, Sydney, 1961, p. 155.
25. Moore and Barton, p. 7.
26. Ibid, p. 5.
27. NZH & AG, 14 Aug. 1841.
28. *Auckland Standard*, 25 Apr. 1842.
29. Ibid.
30. Edward Ashworth, Journal, 25 Oct. 1842, AT.
31. Stone, *Young Logan Campbell*, p. 113.
32. J. J. Craig (comp.), *Historical Record of Jubilee Reunion (1892)*, Auckland, 1893, p. 13.
33. Ibid.
34. Sect. 2, No. 13, Suburbs of Auckland; Bk IG : p. 511, Crown Grant No.18, 18 Apr. 1843, LTO, Auckland.
35. Bk IG : p. 717, C.G. No.1581a, 2ac, 1r. 16p; A81a of S. 1, Suburbs of Auck; LTO.
36. Martin McLean, *Auckland 1842–1845*, Auckland, 1989, p. 44.
37. Cit. J. P. Kalaugher, *Gleanings from Early New Zealand History*, Auckland, 1950, p. 19.
38. Moore and Barton, p. 7.
39. Ibid.
40. A. Kennedy to J. Dilworth, 23 Apr. 1844, Barr P; AP.
41. J. L. Campbell, 'Reminiscences', p. 306; tense of citation changed.
42. Mary FitzRoy to Fanny Rice Trebor, 16 Sept. 1844, FitzRoy P; MS 805, AT.
43. Campbell, 'Reminiscences', p. 306.
44. SC, 4 May 1844; Stone, *Young Logan*

REFERENCES

    Campbell, p. 119.
45. *SC*, 4 May 1844, p. 2. See also J. B. Condliffe, *A Short History of New Zealand*, Christchurch, 1925, p. 63.
46. Ibid, 25 May 1844, p. 1, cols 3–4.
47. See e.g. *SC*, 1 Jun. 1844, p. 2, col. 1, arrival of Dilworth on the *Dolphin*.
48. *SC*, 7 Dec. 1844.
49. Moore and Barton, p. 7.
50. Manager of Bank of Australasia, Sydney, to J. Dilworth, Russell, per *Terror*, 19 Jul. 1844, Barr P, AP.

Chapter Three

1. To this dearth of research there are two honourable exceptions; the work of Professor Alan Ward and Mr Maurice Alemann. Alemann's 'Early Land Transactions in the Ngati Whatua Tribal Area', an unpublished MA thesis, University of Auckland, 1992 is cited in several of the notes that follow. Professor Ward's investigations on behalf of government departments are generally written in confidential, as yet unpublished reports. Though I cannot cite them directly I here acknowledge how deeply those reports have influenced and informed this chapter.
2. The following authorities who have shaped my work on Tamaki-makau-rau have their work listed in full in the Bibliography: F. D. Fenton, 1869; George Graham in Barr, 1922; K. M. Holloway, 1962; L. G. Kelly, 1949; F. L. Phillips, 1989; S. Percy Smith, 1897; John Waititi, 1969. *Report of the Waitangi Tribunal on the Orakei Claim (Wai-9)*, Nov. 1987, is a helpful source as well.
3. John Waititi, 'An Outline of Auckland's Maori History', *J. of Ak. Hist. Soc.*, Oct. 1963, p. 9.
4. F. D. Fenton, Judgment (Dec. 1869) *Important Judgments . . . 1866–1879*, Wellington, 1879, p. 95. (Hereafter 'Fenton's Judgment').
5. Ibid, p. 75.
6. Ibid.
7. H. H. Turton, *Maori Deeds*, 1877, Deed No. 206.
8. Ibid, Deed No. 207, 28 May 1841.
9. Ibid, Deed No. 208, 29 Jun. 1841, (pp. 270–71).
10. Ibid, Deed No. 209, 'Land situate on the Manukau Road' (200 acres); Deed No. 211, 'Remuera Block (Epiha Putini's Claims)', which is discussed later in this chapter.
11. J. L. Campbell, *Poenamo*, London, 1881, p. 102.
12. *Orakei Report*, Wai-9, 1987, p. 17; Stone, *Young Logan Campbell*, 1982, p. 59.
13. *Report of the Agricultural and Horticultural Society of Auckland*, Auckland, 1843, p. 9.
14. Stone, *Young Logan Campbell*, pp. 94–95.
15. Ian Wards, *DNZB*, Wellington, 1990, p. 131.
16. *Statistics of New Zealand for Crown Colony Period*, Table 49, Auckland, 1954.
17. *SC*, 1 Jul. 1843, p. 2.
18. Stone in *Provincial Perspectives*, Christchurch, 1980, p. 29.
19. T. Bunbury, *Reminiscences of a Veteran*, London, 1861, Vol. 3, pp. 179, 184.
20. Alemann, pp. 126–27; Turton, Deed No. 234.
21. Lot 4, Sect. 13, Suburbs of Auckland, 'Kohiraunui Block'; Turton, Deed No. 48.
22. Fenton's Judgment, p. 83.
23. Bunbury to Lord Stanley, 12 Feb. 1844, cit. Bunbury, Vol. 3, p. 184.
24. *SC*, 28 Oct. 1843, p. 2.
25. Alemann, p. 114.
26. *Brett's Auckland Almanac*, 1874, p. 94.
27. J. B. Condliffe, *A Short History of New Zealand*, Christchurch, 1925, p. 63.
28. Ian Wards, *DNZB*, Wellington, 1990, p. 131.
29. Mary FitzRoy to Mrs F. R. Trebor, 8 Jan. 1844, FitzRoy P, Nat. Lib, Wn, MS 805.
30. *SC*, 6 Jan. 1844, pp. 2–3.
31. Bunbury, p. 182.
32. Ibid, p. 183.
33. Ibid, p. 185.
34. Later to be Sect. 11, No. 10, Suburbs of Auckland; Turton, 1883, Deed No. 15, p. 443.
35. OLC, 1050, Nat. Arch. Wn.
36. Turton, 1882, Enclosure to Deed No. 15, pp. 443–44.
37. CG. 3770 in 4G:113; 3D: 505; LTO, Ak.
38. Turton, 1882, Deed No. 14, p. 442.
39. Paul Tuhaere to George Clarke, 10 Feb. 1844, cit. Bunbury, Vol.3, p. 187.
40. Apihai Te Kawau to George Clarke, 10 Feb. 1844, ibid. See also Report of

Select Committee for New Zealand, *GBPP*, 1844, Appendix, p. 492.
41. Bunbury, p 188.
42. FitzRoy to Lord Stanley, 25 May 1844, *GBPP* (NZ), Vol. 4, p. 8.
43. Sherrin and Wallace, *Early History of New Zealand*, p. 686.
44. FitzRoy to Stanley, 25 May 1844, loc. cit.
45. Turton, 1877, Deed No. 211, p. 273; for Putini's private sales see, e.g. Turton, 1882, Deeds Nos 27, 46.
46. *SC*, 30 Mar. 1844, leader.
47. A. W. Shrimpton and Alan E. Mulgan, *Maori and Pakeha*, Christchurch, 1922, p. 109.
48. Figures based on Turton, 1882.
49. Alan Ward, private information.
50. 'Report of Mr. Commissioner F. Dillon Bell, 8 Jul. 1862', Turton, 1882, p. 626.
51. OLC 1055–58, notes on Turton's Deed No. 74.
52. 'Report of Mr. Commissioner F. Dillon Bell, 8 Jul. 1862', Turton, 1882, p. 626.
53. Alemann, p. 122.
54. See e.g. Deed No. 23, Turton, 1882, p. 448.
55. George Grey to Earl Grey, 15 May 1848, Turton, *Epitome*, 1883, p. 49.
56. Grey to Lord Stanley, 10 Dec. 1845, *GBPP* (NZ), Vol. 5, p. 358.
57. DTB Arch. TTI.
58. Una Platts, *Nineteenth Century New Zealand Artists*, Christchurch, 1980, p. 168.
59. FitzRoy to Lord Stanley, 25 May 1844, *GBPP* (NZ), Vol. 4, p. 9. The account of the feast is based mainly on this despatch and the article 'Native Feast' in *SC*, 18 May 1844, p. 2.
60. Ann Parsonson, 'The Pursuit of Mana', in *Oxford History of New Zealand*, Wellington, 1981, p. 140.
61. Lesley G. Kelly, *Tainui*, 1949, p. 428.
62. Ibid.

Chapter Four
1. 'Report of Mr. Commissioner F. Dillon Bell, 8th Jul. 1862', Turton, 1882, p. 627.
2. Dilworth to Col. Sec., 24 Nov. 1846, OLC 1055–58, N. Arch., Wn.
3. Turton, 1882, p. 455 (Deed No. 32); receipt for £17.
4. Ibid, pp. 483–84 (Deed No. 73); receipt for £52.
5. Dilworth to Col. Sec., 6 Jun. 1844, OLC 1055–58.
6. Ibid, 19 Jun. 1844.
7. Minutes of Land Commissioner's Court, 1 Feb. 1847, OLC 1055–58.
8. Turton, 1882, pp. 484–85 (Deed No. 74); receipt for £107.
9. Ibid, 'Report', 8 Jul. 1862, p. 626.
10. Dilworth to Col. Sec., 4 Nov. 1845, OLC 1055–58.
11. Alemann, 'Early Land Transactions', pp. 64–67.
12. Lot 74, CG No. 8829 in 3G: 1302, dated 1 Feb. 1845; 19ac. 2r. 35p.; price £75; LTO.
13. Lot 92, 21D:664, dated 1 Feb. 1845; 126ac. 3r. 2p.; price £126 15s 3d; LTO.
14. 23D: 273; dated 6 Sept. 1845.
15. 6D: 121; 2 Nov. 1855.
16. Lord Stanley to Acting-Governor, 16 Jan. 1843, cit. *NZGG*, 26 Mar. 1844, p. 67.
17. *SC*, 23 Dec. 1843, p. 2; see also *NZGG*, 1844, pp. 26–28, 99.
18. Bell, Turton, 1882, p. 627.
19. *NZGG*, 25 Oct. 1844, p. 144.
20. 3G: 246; LTO.
21. Stone, *Makers of Fortune*, p. 182.
22. Turton, 1882, p. 628.
23. Charles Heaphy, 'Plan of the Town of Auckland, 1851', Rare Book Room, APL.
24. IG: 717, Deed No. 1581a, dated 3 Nov. 1846, Sect. 1, No. 81a, Suburbs of Ak., 2ac. 0r 16p.
25. 2D: 1089, Deed No. 1590a, dated 9 Apr. 1849.
26. Sect. 2, A. 5, City of Auckland; IG:679, Deed No. 1474a, dated 8 Nov. 1847, 1r. 8p.
27. Dilworth to James Simms, 29 Dec. 1847, 2D: 104.
28. Cit. Sherrin and Wallace, *Early History of New Zealand*, p. 692.
29. *Rep. of Ag. & Hort. Soc.*, 1843, pp. 12–13.
30. Ibid, p. 10.
31. Sherrin and Wallace, p. 692.
32. *AJHR*, 1948, G8, p. 68, which cites report of 1856 Domett Committee.
33. Dilworth to Col. Sec., 24 Nov. 1846, OLC 1055–58.
34. Land Commissioner's Court, Case 1, 1 Feb. 1847, Ibid.
35. Ibid.
36. 4G:39; 4G:69, LTO, Ak.
37. Turton, 1882, p. 466; 4G: 71, LTO; OLC 1095.
38. Turton, 1882, p. 443; OLC 1050; 4G: 113, 2D: 1306, LTO.
39. 3D: 505 dated 21 Dec. 1847, LTO.

40. Turton, 1882, pp. 451, 457–58; OLC 1067–69; TT10, DTB; 2D: 836, LTO.
41. DM: 187 (dated 7 Jul. 1848), LTO.
42. 2D: 1005 (dated 31 Aug. 1848); Stone, *Young Logan Campbell*, pp. 192–93.
43. Turton, 1882, p. 444; 4G: 31, LTO; OLC 1075.
44. *NZH*, 11 Aug. 1884, p. 5 (obit.).
45. Commission Court hearing, 15 Mar. 1847, OLC 1075.
46. *NZGG*, 1848, result of 16 Sept. auction.
47. Sect. 12, No. 1 (Dilworth); Sect. 12, No. 2 (Shepherd); for Shepherd, OLC 1123.
48. Former reserve was No. 1a; 23M: 539 (dated 24 Apr. 1849), LTO.
49. Sect. 11, No. 6; Turton, 1882, pp. 449–50; OLC 1100, 4G: 49, LTO.
50. D2: 1132, LTO.
51. Sect. 11, Nos 3 and 5.
52. *New-Zealander*, 6 Mar. 1852, p. 1.
53. 2D: 1089, LTO.
54. 1DM: 360–61, 601; 3M: 729.
55. 1DM: 391.
56. 2M: 231.
57. 2M: 232 (dated 20 Jul. 1853).
58. 4M: 484.

Chapter Five

1. W. Macdonald, *Recollections 1850–1920*, Remuera, 1982, p. 11. See also Berry, p. 9; Pearce, p. 25.
2. *DSC*, 14 Mar. 1866, p. 6.
3. Sherrin and Wallace, *Early History of New Zealand*, p 692.
4. *NZH*, 20 Jul. 1929.
5. *New-Zealander*, 6 Mar. 1852, p. 1. See also Macdonald, p. 9.
6. DTBMB, 21 May 1895, p. 23.
7. *New-Zealander*, 6 Mar. 1852, p. 1.
8. H. F. Reid, *St Mark's Remuera: 1847–1981*, Auckland, 1982, p. 17, citing parishioner.
9. *Rep. of Ag. & Hort. Soc.*, 1843, p. 15.
10. Fitzpatrick, *God's Frontiersmen*, p. 245.
11. Reid, pp. 15, 19.
12. David Sherratt, 'James Dilworth, His Life and Times', Auckland, 1958. (typescript), p. 17.
13. Photographs, AI & ML.
14. Macdonald, p. 8.
15. John Edgerley, 'Reminiscences', Barr MS 415, APL.
16. *DSC*, 14 Mar. 1866, p. 6.
17. N. G. Butlin, *Investment in Australian Economic Development 1861–1900*, Cambridge, 1964, p. 79.
18. *Rep. of Ag. & Hort. Soc.*, 1843, p. 22.
19. *Auckland Chronicle*, 17 Jan. 1844; see also David Rough, 'Early Days of Auckland', Auckland, 1896.
20. J. H. Rose, *Some Houses in Ohinerau*, 1984, p. 11.
21. J. K. Davis, *History of St John's College*, Auckland, 1911, p. 16.
22. *New-Zealander*, 4 Sept. 1847, p. 3.
23. *NZGG*, 1842, pp. 58, 78, 274, 279–80; 1844, p. 102.
24. See e.g. 'Public Notice' in *NZGG*, 1843, p. 101.
25. *New-Zealander*, 4 Sept. 1847, p. 3.
26. *SC*, 7 Aug. 1847, p. 4.
27. *New-Zealander*, 4 Sept. 1847.
28. Ibid, 31 Mar. 1849, p. 3.
29. Ibid, 7 Apr. 1849, pp. 3–4.
30. Sherrin and Wallace, p. 674.
31. G. MacMurray, address, 12 Mar. 1927, DTBA.
32. Sherrin and Wallace, pp. 691–92.
33. Lady Martin, *Our Maoris*, London, 1884, p. 54; Kalaugher, *Gleanings from Early New Zealand History*, pp. 30–32, 36.
34. *New-Zealander*, 24 Nov. 1847.
35. *Stats of NZ*, AUC, 1954, Table 31.
36. Ibid, Table 32.
37. Ibid, Table 36; Kalaugher, p. 32.
38. W. Swainson, *Auckland, the Capital of New Zealand*, London, 1853, pp. 37–38.
39. Ibid, p. iv.
40. *Stats of NZ*, AUC, 1954, Table 1.
41. *New-Zealander*, 12 Jul. 1851, p. 2.
42. OLC 1055–58, Mins of Case 1, heard by Maj. Matson, 1 Feb. 1847.
43. *Rep. of Ag. & Hort. Soc.*, 1843, p. 1l.
44. *New-Zealander*, 6 Mar. 1852, p. 1.
45. Ibid.
46. *New-Zealander*, 12 Mar. 1853, p. 5.
47. *DSC*, 14 Mar. 1866, p. 6.
48. Pearce, *A Heritage in Trust*, p. 26.
49. *DSC*, 14 Mar. 1866, p. 6.
50. Sherratt, p. 17.
51. Report of G. O'Halloran, 20 Aug. 1895, DTBMB.
52. G. Graham to Col. Sec., 16 Oct. 1847, OLC 1067–69.
53. F. D. Bell, Report in Turton, 1882, p. 628.
54. Stone, *Makers of Fortune*, p. 122.
55. *DSC*, 14 Mar. 1866, p. 6.
56. Marriage Certificate, DTBA.
57. *NZH*, 24 May 1920, obit. Robert Hall.
58. Passenger lists, APL.
59. *Govt Gaz. for Auckland & New Ulster*, 1848, p. 19.

60. *A Century of Progress*, Otahuhu, 1948, pp. 7–8.
61. Inform. supplied by Hall family descendants, especially Mrs Marion Young of Warkworth, and Mr Derek Hall of Waerenga.
62. Kalaugher, p. 53.
63. Stone, *Father and his Gift*, Auckland, 1987, p. 116.
64. Isabella Dilworth to Trustees, ? Sept. 1896, DTBA.
65. Mossman P., passim.
66. M. Mossman to L. Evans, 28 Feb., 19 May 1937; L. Evans, 'Reminiscences', n.d., p. 1; J. E. Crawford to 'My Mossman Cousins', 17 Apr. 1960; Mossman P.
67. Cit. Sherratt, p. 24.
68. Kalaugher, p. 58.
69. *DSC*, 24 Aug. 1872, p. 2, obit.; J. Mogford, *The Onehunga Heritage*, Onehunga, 1989, pp. 27, 91.
70. Sherratt, p. 21, citing MacMurray.
71. Ibid, p. 22.
72. Card index on Dilworth, APL.
73. Pearce, p. 28.

Chapter Six
1. Alf McCreary, *By All Accounts*, Antrim, 1991, pp. vii, 11–12.
2. *Auckland Savings Bank Centenary 1847–1947*, Auckland, 1947, p. 7.
3. Ibid, p. 13.
4. *New-Zealander*, 2 Jun. 1847, p. 4.
5. Moore and Barton, *Banking in New Zealand*, p. 114.
6. *NZGG*, 1848, p. 67.
7. See e.g. *New-Zealander*, 9 Jun. 1847, p. 2.
8. Ibid, 2 Jun. 1847, p. 2.
9. *ASB Centenary*, pp. 21–22.
10. Ibid, pp. 23.
11. Moore and Barton, pp. 115–16.
12. *Cyclopedia of New Zealand*, Vol. 2, pp. 294–95.
13. *ASB Centenary*, p. 56.
14. Ibid, p. 127.
15. See *First Annual Report of the Agricultural and Horticultural Society of Auckland*, Auckland, 1843.
16. Erik Olssen, 'Towards a New Society', *Oxford History of New Zealand*, 2nd ed., p. 262.
17. *NZH*, 31 Jul. 1929. Series 'Makers of Auckland'.
18. *New-Zealander*, 29 Dec. 1847, cit. Kalaugher, *Gleanings from Early New Zealand History*, p. 51.
19. *New-Zealander*, 13 Dec. 1848, p. 2.
20. Kalaugher, p. 52.
21. *NZH*, 13 Jul. 1929.
22. Kalaugher, p. 62.
23. Sherratt, 'James Dilworth', p. 19.
24. Kalaugher, p. 64.
25. *Auckland Standard*, 25 Apr. 1842.
26. *New-Zealander*, 20 Jul. 1853, p. 2.
27. G. H. Scholefield (ed.), *New Zealand Parliamentary Record 1840–1949*, Wellington, 1950, p. 183.
28. See e.g. APC, I, p. 39A; ix, pp. 44–46.
29. APC I, p. 98 (2 Feb. 1854); viii, p. 75 (20 Jan. 1858).
30. Stone, 'Auckland Party Politics . . . 1853–58', *NZJH*, Vol. 14 (Oct. 1980), pp. 155–59.
31. Stone, *Young Logan Campbell*, pp. 212–14.
32. APC, ix, p. 1 (4 Oct. 1858, comment by J. Williamson).
33. *Cyclopedia of New Zealand*, Vol. 2, p. 35.
34. APC, ix, p. 1 (4 Oct. 1858).
35. Ibid, ix, p. 15.
36. See e.g., ibid, viii, A1.
37. Ibid., I, pp. 8, 32; ii, p. 46; vii, pp. 171–78; ix, p. 13.
38. Ibid, Session vii.
39. Ibid, pp. 36–38.
40. Stone, *Young Logan Campbell*, p. 220.

Chapter Seven
1. L. P. Moch, *Moving Europeans*, Bloomington, 1992, p. 17.
2. David Fitzpatrick, 'Irish Emigration to Nineteenth-Century Australia', in *Australia and Ireland, 1788–1988*, ed. Colm Kiernan, Dublin, 1986, p. 138.
3. Oliver MacDonagh, 'Emigration from Ireland to Australia: An Overview', in Kiernan, p. 122.
4. Keith Sinclair, *A History of New Zealand*, London, 1959, p. 100.
5. W. P. Morrell, *The Provincial System in New Zealand, 1852–76*, 2nd ed., Christchurch, 1964, pp. 105, 142.
6. Lillian Evans, 'Reminiscences', n.d., p. 1, Mossman P, DTBA.
7. James Dilworth to Col. Sec., 18 Nov. 1846, OLC 1055–58, N. Arch.
8. Evans, 'Reminiscences', p. 1.
9. Mormon Church Records, Belfast.
10. John Dilworth, Dungannon, Inform. 1993.
11. Wilfred Dilworth, memo., 15 Apr. 1994, p. 2; will of James Dilworth, 20 Sept. 1873; both DTBA.
12. Ibid, 27 Jan. 1994, p. 3, DTBA.
13. Ibid, 16 Feb. 1994, p. 8, DTBA.

14. Geoffrey Blainey, *The Tyranny of Distance*, Melbourne, 1968, *passim*.
15. Wilfred Dilworth, memo. 14 Feb. 1994, p. 8.
16. Pearce, *A Heritage in Trust*, p. 35.
17. Marion Mossman to Lillian Evans, 19 May 1937, Mossman P, DTBA.
18. *New-Zealander*, 26 Nov. 1859, p. 1.
19. See e.g. 2K:1; 2J: 5; LTO.
20. Lot 17, parish of Waipareira; 9A: 265; LTO.
21. See e.g. 6D: 785; 14D:617; R32: 826; 6G: 1227; LTO.
22. Aitken Report to DTB, 29 Apr. 1897, TT3, DTB.
23. Cowie, *Our Last Year in New Zealand*, p. 235.
24. J. T. Diamond, *Once the Wilderness*, Auckland, 1977, pp. 164–71.
25. Diamond, copy 1989 lecture notes.
26. *Southern Cross*, 24 Aug. 1860, p. 2.
27. Inform. J. T. Diamond.
28. Part of Lot 17, parish of Waipareira, and part of Lot 15, parish of Waitakere; deed 17532 in 6D:783; LTO.
29. Deed 73676 in 34M:726; LTO.
30. *Henderson School Jubilee Booklet*, Henderson, 1933, p. 92; Inform. J. T. Diamond.
31. Ibid, p. 93.
32. J. T. Diamond, 'Lecture on Prior's Landing', 1989, p. 2.
33. *Henderson School Jubilee*, p. 71.
34. Marion Mossman to Lillian Evans, 19 May 1937; Mossman P.
35. June Evans Crawford, memo, 17 Apr. 1960, ibid.
36. Diamond, 1989 lecture, p. 3.
37. *Henderson School Jubilee*, p. 7.
38. Ian B. Madden, *Riverhead, the Kaipara Gateway*, Auckland, 1966, p. 136.
39. J. T. Diamond, *Once the Wilderness*, p. 46.
40. Ibid.
41. *NZH*, 24 Sept. 1881, p. 4.
42. Marion Mossman to Lillian Evans, 28 Feb. 1937.
43. *Daily Telegraph*, Napier, 26 Aug. 1899, obit. T. W. Mossman.
44. M. Mossman to L. Evans, 19 May 1937.
45. Catherine Bradley, cit. ibid, 28 Feb. 1937.
46. Ibid, p. 3.
47. Thomas Webb of Aratapu, cit. Brett and Hook, *The Albertlanders*, Auckland, 1927, p. 208.
48. Theophilus Cooper Snr, cit. ibid, p. 125.
49. *DSC*, 11 Feb. 1863, p. 3.
50. Ibid, 9 Feb. 1863, p. 3.
51. M. Mossman to L. Evans, 28 Feb. 1937, p. 3.
52. Inform. Mrs E. D. Mossman, 9 Dec. 1992.
53. M. Mossman to L. Evans, 28 Feb. 1937, p. 4, also will of James Dilworth, 20 Sept. 1873; both DTBA.
54. Ibid, p. 5.
55. Information on Irish background of Dilworth of Portadown provided by Wilfred Dilworth in memos, 18 Mar., 31 Mar., 15 Apr., and 21 Apr. 1994. DTBA.
56. Pearce, p. 25.
57. *AJHR*, 1864–5, D3, pp. 10–12.
58. Ibid, pp. 13–14, citing *Cork Herald* of 3 Nov. 1864.
59. *DSC*, 15 Feb. 1865, p. 4.
60. Ibid.
61. Nona Morris, *Early Days in Franklin*, Auckland, 1965, pp. 148–50.
62. Ibid, p. 153.
63. Tuakau North, Sect. 361, applications, Micro.90, APL. 6.
64. Morris, pp. 162–67.
65. Pearce, p. 27.
66. Morris, Appendix A, p. 196.
67. Electoral Rolls of G.A. for Franklin South, 1881, 1887.
68. Symonds St Cemetery Burial Records, 1882–85, APL.
69. See e.g. *NZH*, 2 Apr. 1883, p. 3.
70. This section rests heavily on the Reminiscences of Lillian Evans, n.d., Mossman P, DTBA.
71. Reminiscences of Jeanne Brown Nelius, Mossman P.
72. June Evans Crawford to 'My Mossman Cousins', 17 Apr. 1960. DTBA.
73. *DSC*, 25 Mar. 1865, p. 4.
74. The next three paras based on J. E. Crawford, 17 Apr. 1960.
75. Reminiscences of Esther Ann Evans related by Lillian Evans, n.d., Mossman P, DTBA.
76. J. E. Crawford, 17 Apr. 1960.
77. M. Mossman to L. Evans, 19 May 1937, Mossman P.
78. *Daily Telegraph*, Napier, 26 Aug. 1899, obit. of T. W. Mossman.
79. *DSC*, 20 Oct. 1866, p. 4.
80. P. J. Gibbons, *Astride the River*, Hamilton, 1977, p. 65; H. C. M. Norris, *Armed Settlers*, Hamilton, 1963, p. 150.

81. Gibbons, p. 47.
82. Crown Land Grants, Micro.90, APL.
83. See will of James Dilworth, 20 Sept. 1873, and Deeds associated with DI 3A:2082.
84. This para. is based on correspondence of W.J.'s second wife Marion Mossman and the reminiscences passed on orally 1992–94 by his daughter-in-law Mrs E. D. Mossman, now (1994) ninety-nine years of age.
85. M. Mossman to L. Evans, 28 Feb. 1937.
86. James Dilworth to W. J. Mossman, 6 Nov. 1890, Mossman P, DTBA.
87. Ibid, 18 Jul. 1891.
88. Ibid, 15 Apr. 1890.
89. Ibid, 14 Oct. 1891.
90. Will of James Dilworth, 20 Sept. 1873, DTBA.
91. For remainder of para., M. Mossman to L. Evans, 10 May 1937, Mossman P.

Chapter Eight

1. R. S. Fletcher, *Single Track: The Construction of the North Island Main Trunk Railway*, Auckland, 1978, p. 17. Fletcher is the best secondary source for this topic. The main archival source for this chapter is the DTB Archives TT9.
2. G. C. Dunstall, 'Colonial Merchant', unpublished thesis, University of Auckland, pp. 188–89.
3. Les Kermode, 'Ferdinand von Hochstetter' in *The German Connection*, ed. J. Northcote-Bade, Auckland, 1993, pp. 152–61.
4. Kermode, interview.
5. Dunstall, p. 186.
6. Fletcher, pp. 18, 20–21.
7. Ibid, pp. 23–24.
8. *Statutes of NZ*, 1863, 'Local and Personal' No. 2.
9. *NZGG*, 1863, p. 429 (17 Sept. 1863).
10. Ibid, 1864, pp. 407–8 (11 Nov. 1864).
11. See Fletcher, Fig.5, p. 22.
12. *DSC*, 16 Feb. 1865, p. 4; ed. 'Turning the First Sod'.
13. Ibid, 17 Feb. 1865, pp. 5–6.
14. Robert Graham to J. Dilworth, 18 Feb. 1865, TT9.
15. Fletcher, p. 21.
16. *DSC*, 19 Jan. 1866, p. 6.
17. Newspaper clipping, DTB, TT9.
18. This paragraph on the Village of Mount St John speculation (Suburbs of Auckland; Sec.11, No. 11) is based on material in the Auckland Land and Deeds Registry; see Deeds Index 3A:2056 and 9A:891.
19. *DNZB* I, pp. 598–99.
20. 8D: 461, LTO. Deed 14883 dated 22 Jul. 1859.
21. 8D:462, Deed 14884 dated 3 Sept. 1859; see also 14D:925.
22. Stone, *Father and his Gift*, Auckland, 1987, pp. 49–50.
23. Fletcher, p. 31.
24. E. J. Seale, *Auckland City of Volcanoes*, Auckland, 1964, pp. 70–71; see also Searle, 'Volcanic Risk in the Auckland Metropolitan District', *NZ Journal of Geology and Geophysics*, Vol. 7, no. 1 (Feb. 1964), p. 8. See also F. Hochstetter, *The Geology of New Zealand*, Auckland, 1864, pp. 39–40.
25. New Zealand Land Inventory: 'Whangaparaoa Auckland Map', n.d.; compiled by L. O. Kermode; also Kermode, inform.
26. *DSC*, 16 Mar. 1866, pp. 5–6.
27. Pearce, *A Heritage in Trust*, p. 27.
28. Thomas Cheeseman to J. Dilworth, 12 Aug. 1865. TT9 (as is subsequent correspondence on this issue).
29. Dilworth to Cheeseman, 24 Aug. 1865.
30. Ibid, 31 Aug. 1865.
31. Dep. Sup. to Dilworth, 31 Aug. 1865.
32. *DSC*, 14 Mar. 1866. The arbitration hearing began 24 Nov. 1865.
33. Dep. Sup. to Dilworth, 31 Aug. 1865.
34. *DSC*, 17 Mar. 1866, p. 6.
35. Ibid, 14 Mar. 1866, p. 6.
36. Ibid, 17 Mar. 1866, p. 6.
37. Ibid.
38. Ibid, 14 Mar. 1866, p. 6.
39. Ibid, 17 Mar. 1866, p. 6.
40. See land agents' and valuators' reports to Dilworth in TT9.
41. *Brett's Auckland Almanac*, 1874, p. 95.
42. *DSC*, 19 Jan. 1866, p. 6. (But see 19D:16, Deed 27953, dated 16 Dec. 1864, which suggests the price paid was lower.)
43. Ibid. (tense changed).
44. Ibid, 17 Mar. 1866, p. 6.
45. Ibid, 19 Jan. 1866, p. 6.
46. Henry Wrigg's report in TT9.
47. *DSC*, 17 Mar. 1866, p. 6.
48. Ibid.
49. These terms are given as recited in Deed 32932 dated 25 Jun. 1866 in 20D:117, LTO.
50. Instructions under seal by Beckham

and Thornton, JPs, to Thomas Cheeseman, dated 2 May 1866.
51. *DSC*, 15 Mar. 1866; report of proceedings of the Auckland Provincial Council.
52. Dunstall, pp. 81–91.
53. Cheeseman to Dilworth, 12 May 1866, TT9.
54. Ibid.
55. Dilworth to Superintendent, 29 May 1866.
56. Cheeseman to Dilworth, 12 Jun. 1866.
57. Dilworth to Superintendent, n.d.
58. Ibid, 26 Jun. 1866.
59. Superintendent to Dilworth, 13 Aug. 1866.
60. Ibid, 25 Feb. 1867; Dilworth to Superintendent, 5 Mar. 1867.
61. Fletcher, p. 35.
62. Ibid, p. 38.
63. Ibid, p. 45.
64. *NZH*, 22 Dec. 1873.

Chapter Nine
1. E. J. Searle, 'Studies in the Auckland Volcanic Field', Auckland, 1961, Auckland University Geology Department Library; E. J. Searle, 'Volcanic Risk in the Auckland Metropolitan District', *New Zealand Journal of Geology and Geophysics*, Vol. VII, No. 1, pp. 94–100. Also L. J. Kermode, interview.
2. E. J. Searle and Janet Davidson, *A Picture Guide to the Volcanic Cones of Auckland*, Auckland, 1973, pp. 2–3, 13.
3. David Simmons, *Maori Auckland*, Auckland, 1987, p. 47.
4. F. von Hochstetter, *The Geology of New Zealand*, Auckland, 1864, p. 40; see also essay on Hochstetter by L. Kermode in *The German Connection* (ed. J. N. Bade), Auckland, 1993.
5. E. J. Searle, *Auckland City of Volcanoes*, Auckland, 1964, p. 73.
6. I Kings, 21:1–14.
7. Proceedings of Court of Major Henry Matson, Commissioner, 27 Mar. 1847, OLC 1067–69, N. Arch., Wn.
8. H. H. Turton, *Maori Deeds of Old Private Land Purchases . . . .*, Wellington, 1882, Deeds Nos 27 and 35, pp. 451, 457, 458.
9. Sherrin and Wallace, *Early History of New Zealand*, p. 692.
10. Evidence before Matson, 27 Mar. 1847, OLC 1067–69.
11. Graham to Sinclair, 18 Oct. 1847, OLC 1067–69.
12. Memo. Grey to Sinclair, 20 Oct. 1847, OLC 1067–69.
13. 4G:15, C.G. No. 1170a, LTO, Ak.
14. Sect. 11, No. 2, Suburbs of Auckland, 1DM:187, LTO, Ak.
15. 2D:923, No.1278a, 9 Sept. 1848; J. King Davis, *History of St John's College*, Auckland, 1911, p. 43; Hilary F. Reid, *St Mark's Remuera 1847–1981*, Auckland, 1982, p. 1.
16. Graham to Dilworth, 7 Jul. 1848, OLC 1067–69.
17. Ibid, 13 May 1848.
18. Dilworth to Agent of Gen. Govt, 24 Aug. 1865, OLC 1067–69.
19. Pollen to Domett, 4 Sept. 1865, OLC 1067–69.
20. Domett, minute, 4 Sept. 1865.
21. Dilworth to W. Gisborne, 19 Jun. 1867.
22. J. C. Prendergast, Opinion, 14 Dec. 1868.
23. Gisborne to Dilworth, 19 Sept. 1867.
24. Dilworth to Col. Secty, 2 Jul. 1868.
25. Gisborne (Under-Secretary) to Dilworth, 14 Nov. 1868, TT10, DTB.
26. Domett, memo., 10 Nov. 1868, OLC 1067–69.
27. J. C. Prendergast, Opinion, 10 Nov. 1868.
28. Domett, memo., 10 Nov. 1868.
29. Pollen, minute (nd) on Dilworth's letter of 2 Jul. 1868.
30. *Auckland Provincial Government Gazette*, 24 Oct. 1868.
31. Pollen to Col. Secty, 2 Dec. 1868.
32. Dilworth to Col. Secty, 30 Nov. 1868.
33. Pollen to Col. Secty, 2 Dec. 1868.
34. *Cyclopedia of New Zealand*, Vol. II, p. 42.
35. Minute initialled 'T. B. G.' (n.d.), OLC 1067–69.
36. Copy of petition with amendments, TT10, DTB.
37. Ibid.
38. Notes of evidence dated 15 Oct. 1872, OLC 1067–69.
39. Evidence of Herbert Edward Leadam, 16 Oct. 1872, which summarized the CLO's findings.
40. Thomas Kelly, chairman of G.A.'s Public Petitions Committee to Dilworth, 24 Oct. 1872, TT10, DTB.
41. Dilworth to Col. Secty, 22 Dec. 1873, OLC 1067–69.
42. H. A. Atkinson to Dilworth, 26 Oct. 1874, TT10.

43. Dilworth to Minister of Lands, 7 Jan. 1878, OLC 1067–69.
44. Dilworth to Crown Lands Office, 14 Jan. 1880, 23 Jan. 1880, 4 Feb. 1880, TT10, DTB.
45. *Brett's Auckland Almanac*, 1881, p. 92.
46. TT1, DTB.
47. Pearce, *A Heritage in Trust*, p. 60.
48. *AES*, 28 Apr. 1916. See also DTB Scrapbook, *passim*; DTB Minutebooks Vols 7–9, covering 1916–21, which are full of material on Mount Hobson reserve.
49. C. J. Parr, Letter to Editor, *AES*, 4 May 1916.
50. *NZH*, 1 Apr. 1921; DTB Minutebook, Vol. 9, pp. 20, 37.

Chapter Ten
1. General Assembly Electoral Rolls, 1879–80, APL.
2. J. H. Rose, *Scrapbook History of Jackson Russell*, Auckland 1983, p. 19.
3. *NZGG*, Proclamation by Governor, 26 Aug. 1859.
4. Sinclair and Mandle, *Open Account*, pp. 44–55; Dunstall, 'Colonial Merchant', Auckland, 1970, p. 23.
5. *NZH*, 24 Dec. 1894.
6. *DSC*, 14 Mar. 1886, p. 6.
7. Dunstall, pp. 82–83.
8. Stone, *Makers of Fortune*, pp. 11–14.
9. TT1, TT1A, DTBA.
10. TT3, DTBA.
11. See e.g. *Land Regulations . . . Province of Auckland, 1859*, London, 1866.
12. DI 13A:421; 21D:511, dated 12 Feb. 1868, Lots 41–44 Taupaki, 386ac., LTO.
13. DI 9A: 278; IG:3094, dated 7 Jul. 1857, LTO.
14. DI 12A:29; 21D:293, dated 5 Oct. 1867.
15. DI 13A: 59, 60; 6G: 1227.
16. DI 7A:83; R39:96, dated 21 Dec. 1892.
17. TT1A, DTBA.
18. 21D:511, dated 12 Feb. 1868, LTO.
19. 25D:511, dated 20 May 1870.
20. R32:826, dated 14 May 1889, Dilworth to James Cottle, farmer, Taupaki.
21. See report of Hall and O'Halloran, dated 26 Feb. 1895, TT3, DTBA.
22. Based on ibid, and report of W. Aitken, dated 29 Apr. 1897, TT5, DTBA.
23. *NZH*, 5 Apr. 1884, p. 5.
24. Cowie, *Our Last Year in New Zealand*, pp. 234–35.
25. Parcels, in turn: DI 3B:942, B3:517; DI 4B:464, B5:642; DI 7B:109, R45A.
26. TT3, 5, DTBA.
27. Sherratt, 'James Dilworth', p. 26.
28. 12A:846, R20:434; report TT5.
29. Aitken report, TT5.
30. Ibid.
31. Stone, *Makers of Fortune*, p. 10.
32. DI 10:283, 01:135, No. 133 Parish of Waioeka, LTO.
33. See e.g. Village of Drury, Section 7, DI 8A:467.
34. DI 13A:55, 1G:3213 dated 4 Mar. 1857.
35. DI IG:624, GI:84 (Parish of Whaingaroa), dated 3 Jan. 1863.
36. Reports TT3, 5, DTBA.
37. Dunstall, p. 170.
38. DI 2F:589 8GF:171. (Though the Crown grant was issued on 4 Mar. 1874, Hall and Dilworth had a title 'granted to them as tenants-in-common, not joint tenants', as early as 25 Apr. 1872.)
39. F3:825 dated 26 Oct. 1877.
40. Fletcher, *Single Track*, p. 43.
41. Stone, *Makers of Fortune*, p. 177.
42. See e.g. DI IF:414, R22: 574.
43. Isaac Coates, *On Record*, Hamilton, 1962, pp. 134–36.
44. Hall and O'Halloran report, 26 Feb. 1895, TT3, DTBA.
45. 1887–94 Dilworth Account Book, pp. 114–15, DTBA.
46. Hall and O'Halloran report, TT3.
47. Aitken Report, TT5.
48. O. F. Creagh Report, 25 Apr. 1904, TT5.
49. Sect. 12, Nos 5, 69, 70, 80, Suburbs of Auckland, DI 13A:63, 7G: 41, purchase dated 9 Sept. 1865, LTO.
50. Sect. 17, As 5–7, Suburbs of Auck. 3G Vol. 3: 1558, 1559, consideration £373 15s 9d.
51. See e.g. 26D:11, dated 31 Dec. 1867.
52. 22M: 388, 3 Jan. 1877. Land taken 4ac. 1r. 25p.
53. This para. largely based on TT3, and Dilworth Account Book (1887–94).
54. See e.g. DI 16A: 761 Subdivision of As 1–3, S.17, Suburbs of Auck., R36:820, dated 26 May 1891.
55. DI 11A:58, 6G: 944, dated 8 May 1863.
56. 23M: 325, 326.
57. R2: 11.
58. C2: 611; the additional property was

No.47, a subdivision of lots 1, 2, 3 and 4, S.7, No. 2 Suburbs of Auck.
59. S.12, No. 15, Suburbs of Auck., OLC 1176–77, N.Arch., Wn.
60. For John Lundon, *AWN*, 10 Feb. 1899, p. 21; David Routledge, *DNZB*, Vol. II; G. H. Scholefield, *New Zealand Parliamentary Record 1840–1949*, p. 183.
61. DI 3A:2082. See e.g. 1DM: 620; 2M861.
62. 11D: 202, dated 13 Sept. 1860.
63. 12M: 229.
64. 11M: 230, dated 11 May 1866.
65. *DSC*, 9 May 1867.
66. 20D: 719, Deed No. 37702, dated 23 Jun. 1868.
67. Dilworth Account Book, 1887–94.
68. Hall and O'Halloran report, TT3.
69. Aitken report, 23 Apr. 1897, TT5.
70. TT3.
71. Ibid. The phrase used is 'reserved from above [leases]'.
72. DTBMB, 20 Aug. 1895, p. 41.
73. Inform. Miss Georgina Mossman, 20 Jul. 1994.
74. Pearce, *A Heritage in Trust*, p. 150.
75. *Cyclopedia of New Zealand*, Vol. II, p. 98.
76. *Brett's Auckland Almanac, 1878*, p. 95.
77. Hall and O'Halloran report, TT3.
78. DTBMB, 21 May 1895, p. 23.
79. *NZH*, 12, 14, 20 Aug. 1886.
80. See J. M. Stacpoole, *Houses of the Merchant Princes*, Auckland, 1989, pp. 4–8.
81. Pearce, p. 28.
82. DTBMB, 12 Jun. 1895, p. 31.
83. *NZH*, 6 Nov. 1991, p. 3.
84. Cf. Pearce, p. 29.
85. See also details of will, TT1.
86. 'House Expenses', also accounts for 'Horses', 'Home Cattle', 'Sheep', Dilworth Estate Accounts 1887–94, pp. 1–13.
87. 'Personal Expenses Account', 'Furniture Account', ibid, pp. 14–19.

Chapter Eleven

1. See e.g. *Observer*, 5 Mar. 1881.
2. Dilworth to W. J. Mossman, 12 Sept. 1890, Mossman P.
3. Ibid, 15 Jul. 1891.
4. DI 9A: 265, C2:528.
5. 34M: 726, Deed No. 73676.
6. Pearce, *A Heritage in Trust*, p. 46.
7. Platts, *The Lively Capital*, pp. 213.
8. IGv2: 679; CG 1474a.
9. Rare Book Room, APL.
10. 2D: 1034.
11. C. W. Carrick, *New Zealand Observer*, 11 Feb. 1935, p. 6.
12. Barr, *Ports of Auckland*, pp. 41–43.
13. W. Macdonald, *Auckland Yesterday and Today*, 1957, p. 10.
14. Barr, *Ports of Auckland*, pp. 45–47.
15. *Commissioners Reports*, Vol. I, p. 9; entries for 2 Jun., 17, 24 Jul. 1863; APL.
16. *NZH*, 10 Aug. 1925; DTBSB, p. 81.
17. *SC*, 18 Apr. 1862, p. 4.
18. *NZH*, 10 Aug. 1925.
19. H. B. Morton, *Recollections of Early New Zealand*, Auckland, 1925, p. 18.
20. *NZH*, 26 Jun. 1872, obit.; *DNZB*, 1940, Vol. I, p. 174.
21. Part of Nos 11–13, Sect. 17, Town of Auckland. DI 4A: 314, 3 Dec. 1850; 3D: 20, 29 Oct. 1851 for later addition.
22. Material provided by B. C. Bollard, archivist, Catholic diocese of Auckland.
23. Description of fire in *NZH*, 29 Aug. 1866, p. 3; 30 Aug. 1866, p. 4; *DSC*, 29 Aug. 1866, p. 4.
24. *NZH*, 29 Aug. 1866, p. 4.
25. *DNZB*, 1940, Vol. I, p. 174.
26. DI 1A: 127; 3A:2031; 4A: 314.
27. 6M: 56, 257; 10D: 790; 1DM:564.
28. 1DM: 716, dated 25 Jun. 1852.
29. 4M: 617, dated 22 Sept. 1857 (Henry Harkness).
30. 8M: 422, Deed No. 24469, dated 8 Oct. 1862.
31. *Bold Century*, 1959, p. 12.
32. 8M: 518, Deed No. 24935, dated 1 Feb. 1864,
33. 9M: 422, 30 Mar. 1865; 9M:424, 1 Apr. 1865.
34. *NZH*, 17 Oct. 1866, p. 1.
35. Ibid, 15 May 1867, p. 5.
36. Ibid.
37. Ibid, 26 Jun. 1872, p. 2.
38. DI 4A: 456; 25D: 28, Deed No. 41920, dated 7 Jul. 1870.
39. *NZH*, 14 Jun. 1870, p. 3.
40. 25D: 28.
41. *Cyclopedia of New Zealand*, Vol. II, p. 859.
42. *NZH*, 10 May 1868, p. 3.
43. Ibid, 22 Apr. 1868, p. 3.
44. Ibid, 20 May 1868, p. 3.
45. Cit. Sherratt, 'James Dilworth', p. 24.
46. For the Waverley see *NZH*, 3 Oct. 1883, p. 5; 5 Jun. 1884, pp. 3–4; Ak. Scrapbook at APL, Oct. 1964, p. 57.
47. 15M:114, Deed No. 38536 dated 5 Dec. 1868.

48. 14M:545, dated 21 Jan. 1871.
49. *DSC*, 1 Nov. 1868, p. 1; 3 Nov. 1868, p. 3.
50. *NZH*, 5 Aug. 1967, Magazine sect., p. 3.
51. *Commissioners' Reports*, Vol. VII, p. 8, 2 Aug. 1869.
52. Ibid, p. 31 (7 Mar. 1870), p. 32 (10 Mar. 1870).
53. Ibid, 28 Jun. 1870.
54. T. Hodgson, *Heart of Colonial Auckland*, Auckland, 1992, p. 16.
55. Dilworth Account Book (1887–94), pp. 516–17.
56. Stone, *Makers of Fortune*, pp. 112–14.
57. *NZOYB*, 1896, p. 88.
58. *Brett's Auckland Almanac*, 1879, pp. 108.
59. Barr, *City of Auckland*, 1922, pp. 103–4.
60. Dilworth Account Book (1887–94), pp. 14–22.
61. DI 16A: 855; R43:248, Deed No. 121800, dated 13 Sept. 1892.
62. C. W. Vennell, *Risks and Rewards*, Auckland, 1972, pp. 17–18.
63. 17M: 270, Deed No. 46049, dated 21 Dec. 1872.
64. Dilworth had right of termination without penalty as from 1 Jun. 1874.
65. DI 2F: 589; 8F: 171; F3: 825.
66. For Costley: *NZH*, 19 Apr., 23 Apr., 25 Apr., 15 Jun., 18 Jun., 11 Oct. 1883; *Observer*, 23 Jun. 1883, p. 210.
67. 23M:260, Deed No. 56785, dated 5 Jun. 1877; 24M: 267, dated 7 Aug. 1877.
68. 27M: 15, Deed No. 57790, dated 5 Oct. 1877.
69. DI 4A: 456, 29M:664, Deed No. 67101, dated 19 Oct. 1880.
70. Dilworth Account Book (1887–94), p. 133, Dilworth's explanatory memo.
71. See R7:699, Dilworth conveyance to Pierce and others, 25 Nov. 1884.
72. R11: 273, Jackson and Hean conveyance to Bishop W. G. Cowie and others, 21 May 1884.
73. Cit. Sherratt, p. 33. MacMurray told this story on a number of occasions.
74. Dilworth Account Book (1887–94), pp. 516–17.
75. Ibid, p. 517.

Chapter Twelve
1. Information on Joseph Howard (1832–89) provided by his grandson Mr Joe Howard of Taupo who also made available the Joe Howard Papers (Howard P).
2. *NZH*, 9 Sept. 1889, obit.
3. Testimonial written by Thomas Stewart, banker, Tralee, 10 Aug. 1858, Howard P.
4. Memo. of agreement between Joseph Howard and Union Bank of Australia, Broad St, London, 22 Sept. 1860, Howard P.
5. Copy of letter sent by Howard's son, Effingham Howard, to *AWN*, 1935, Howard P.
6. Inform. J. T. Diamond repeating oral reminiscence of Effingham Howard.
7. *Cyclopedia of New Zealand*, Vol. 2, p. 462.
8. Report of Inspector to Gen. Man. Union Bank, 6 Sept. 1869, Howard P. Howard was asked to resign presumably for having conducted private business while serving as an officer of the bank.
9. The house was a substantial one, insured on 24 Jul. 1873 with South British Insurance Co. for £1,200.
10. Jackson and Russell letterbooks, *passim*.
11. Notes on Pacific hotel compiled by Alistair M. Isdale, Thames, ? Sept. 1991, Howard P.
12. Electoral Rolls, G.A. Lib., Wn.
13. See e.g. C. W. Vennell, *Risks and Rewards*, Auckland, 1972, p. 39; Stone, *Makers of Fortune*, p. 36.
14. Inform. and research notes, J. T. Diamond.
15. Ibid.
16. Stone, 'Auckland Business . . . in the 1880s', PhD thesis, AU, 1969, p. 353.
17. For general background to Patetere see *AJHR*, 1880, G-1.
18. See e.g. *NZH*, 2 Mar., 6 Mar., 17 May 1883; *Wanganui Herald*, 19 Mar. 1883, p. 3; *Observer*, Auckland, 10 Mar. 1883, p. 403. Most of these comments are on the adjudication over the Te Whetu block.
19. *NZGG*, 31 Jul. 1873, p. 443; 21 Jul. 1873, pp. 475–76; 17 Sept. 1874, p. 635.
20. See M. P. K. Sorrenson, 'The Purchase of Maori Lands, 1865–92', MA thesis, Auckland University, 1955, pp. 138–44.
21. Grey to Sheehan, telegram, 20 Jun. 1879, *AJHR*, 1880, G-1, p. 2.
22. See e.g. *Waikato Times*, 8 Jan. 1883, p. 2.
23. *Ecclesiasticus*, 13, 1 (*Old Testament Apocrypha*).

24. Stone, 'The Maori Land Question and the Fall of the Grey government 1879', *NZJH*, Vol. I, No. 1 (1967), pp. 57–64.
25. H. A. Atkinson to J. C. Sharland, 9 Feb. 1881, Atkinson P, Vol. 43.
26. J. Bryce to F. D. Fenton, 8 May 1880, *AJHR*, 1880, G-1, p. 31.
27. See e.g. H. Roche to ed. *AWN*, 2 Jul. 1880, p. 19; *NZPD*, Vol. 36 (21 Jul. 1880), J. A. Tole; Grey, *AJHR*, 1881, G-13, p. 17.
28. *NZGG*, 1881, Vol. 1, p. 309; *AJHR*, 1881, G-13, p. 15 (No. 39).
29. *Lyttelton Times*, 16 Mar. 1881, p. 4; *Observer*, Auckland, 21 May 1881.
30. For Jackson and Russell material, TT11, DTBA; for Hesketh and Richmond, Hesketh P, APL.
31. Agreement, 8 Apr. 1880, drawn up by Hesketh and Richmond, TT11, DTBA.
32. Ibid, Article 22.
33. Memo. written by J. E. Pounds, 23 Jun. 1880, TT11, DTBA.
34. See e.g. 'Settlement of Accounts between Whaiti-Kuranui Proprietors and Patetere Proprietors', 18 Aug. 1883; *NZH*, 6 Aug. 1884, p. 4; 11 Oct. 1884, p. 3.
35. See e.g. Samuel Jackson to G. O'Halloran, 11 Jan. 1883, Jackson and Russell Letterbook, Aug. 1882–Mar. 1883, p. 761. Mr G. M. O'Halloran of Papakura has passed on to me much oral history about his grandfather, also the manuscript 'Autobiography of G. S. O'Halloran', the memoirs of G. R. O'Halloran's brother.
36. Agreement 'between Dilworth and another and Walker and others', 10 Oct. 1881, TT11.
37. For Rich's role see *NZH*, 13 May 1893, article 'Old Identities'.
38. G. M. Swainson, *DNZB*, Vol. 2, 1993, pp. 184–85.
39. Agreement, 10 Oct. 1881, TT11.
40. *Reports on the Selwyn Block with Map*, London, 1882, copy ATL.
41. *NZH*, 31 Mar. 1883, p. 4, comments on the 'saintly' names chosen by the speculators.
42. Ibid, 29 Oct. 1883, p. 6.
43. Stone, 'The Thames Valley and Rotorua Railway Company Limited, 1882–9'. *NZJH*, Vol. 8, No. 1 (Apr. 1974), pp. 22–43.
44. Records of NZTVL Co. are in PRO, London. Reference: PRO 107 BT31 3016 17040C.
45. Deed of Agreement confirming contract, 4 Sept. 1882, between James Dilworth and others and NZTVL Co., TT11, DTBA.
46. *NZH*, 2 Mar. 1882, p. 5.
47. *Times*, London, 4 Nov. 1882, p. 11, 'Money Market and City Intelligence'.
48. For prospectus published in New Zealand, *NZH*, 29 Mar. 1883, p. 5.
49. Edward Wakefield to John Hall, 13 Feb. 1883, Box 19, Hall P, Nat. Lib.; cf. William Rolleston to F. D. Bell, 10 Sept. 1882, Box 6, Rolleston P, Nat. Lib.
50. *AJHR*, 1896, I-6, p. 16.
51. Deeds of Agreement 'between E. B. Walker and others and Samuel Jackson and others', dated 4 Dec. 1882 and 11 Jan. 1883, TT11.
52. *NZH*, 1 Jan. 1883, Supp. p. 3; Stone, *Makers of Fortune*, pp. 85–86.
53. See *Reports on the Selwyn Block*, *passim*; *NZH*, 23 Aug. 1882, p. 5; 30 Oct. 1883, p. 6; *Waikato Times*, 30 Jan. 1883, p. 2.
54. *NZH*, 29 Mar. 1883, p. 5.
55. Ibid, 5 Oct. 1883, p. 6.
56. Ibid, 5 Oct. 1883, p. 6; 12 Apr. 1886, p. 6.
57. Opinion, Jackson and Russell to local directors, 30 Oct. 1884; report by local directors to London Board, 31 Oct. 1884; both TT11.
58. *NZH*, 27 Feb. 1885, p. 4; 2 Mar. 1885, p. 2; 12 Mar. 1885, p. 4.
59. Ibid, 28 Jul. 1885, p. 6.
60. Ibid, 18 Jul. 1885, p. 6; 29 Jul. 1885, p. 6; 20 Aug. 1885, p. 4; also Indenture, 'Agreement of Compromise between New Zealand Thames Valley Land Co. and the Vendors', 29 Jul. 1885, TT11; agreement confirmed at extraordinary general meeting of company, 22 Jul. 1885, PRO file.
61. *NZH*, 20 Aug. 1885, p. 4.
62. *Waikato Times*, 16 Jun. 1885, p. 2.
63. Fox to Halcombe, 20 Aug. 1886, Halcombe P, ATL.
64. Howard to Dilworth, 6 Jan. 1886, Dilworth P, TT11.
65. Dilworth to Howard, 7 Jan. 1886, Howard P.
66. Deeds of Agreement, 'between J. Dilworth and another and E. B. Walker and others', 20 Jan. and 19 Feb. 1886, TT11, DTBA.
67. Deed of Settlement drawn up by Russell and Campbell, 5 Jul. 1886,

TT11.
68. *NZH*, 12 Aug. 1886, p. 3.
69. *AES*, 2 Sept. 1886, p. 4.
70. Statement of liquidator of PL&S Co., 30 Apr. 1887, TT11.
71. Fox to Halcombe, 20 Aug. 1886, Halcombe P, ATL.
72. L. M. Hardy, 'Out of the Past', n.d., p. 84, AI and ML.
73. Michael Cannon, *The Land Boomers*, Melbourne, 1966, pp. 83–84.
74. Statement of Liquidator of Kuranui Land Society, 1 Oct. 1887, TT11.
75. Maraitai Land Co., Deed Co. file No. 335, NARC, Ak.

Chapter Thirteen
1. *Observer*, Mar. 1881, 'Brief Mention'.
2. C. W. Carrick, *NZ Observer*, 11 Jul. 1935, p. 5.
3. Main Scrapbook, Vol. XIV, p. 170, AI and ML.
4. M. Mossman to L. Evans, 19 May 1937, Mossman P.
5. Financial accounts (1887–94), p. 202.
6. TTI, DTBA.
7. Memo, Georgina Mossman, 20 Jul. 1994.
8. *AWN*, 4 Jun. 1881, p. 20; Diamond, *Once the Wilderness*, pp. 164–66.
9. *AWN*, 6 Aug. 1881, p. 15.
10. *Cyclopedia of New Zealand*, Vol. II, p. 284.
11. *AWN*, 2 Jul. 1881, p. 13.
12. Ibid, 6 Aug. 1881, p. 15.
13. Death certificate supplied by *DNZB*, Ref. 1881/1417. Cause of death 'serous apoplexy'.
14. Deed No. 73676 in 34M : 726, probate of will, LTO.
15. *AWN*, 1 Oct. 1881, p. 13.
16. Bond dated 29 Mar. 1882, TT1, DTBA.
17. G. MacMurray, in *NZH*, 29 Dec. 1894.
18. Rose, *Scrapbook History of Jackson Russell*, p. 23.
19. Cowie, *Our Last Year in New Zealand*, p. 89.
20. Keith Sinclair, *A History of the University of Auckland*, Auckland, 1983, pp. 51–53.
21. *NZH*, 24 Dec. 1894.
22. Patrick Buckland, *Irish Unionism*, London, 1973, pp. 9–11.
23. Rory Fitzpatrick, *God's Frontiersmen*, p. 201.
24. *Oxford Illustrated History of Ireland*, p. 215.
25. Copy of Will, TTI, DTBA.
26. MacMurray statement, 29 Sept. 1932, DTBA.
27. MacMurray address, 12 Mar. 1927, DTBA.
28. Ibid.
29. *NZH*, 20 Aug. 1885, p. 4.
30. *AES*, 9 Sept. 1889.
31. Stone, *Makers of Fortune*, p. 203
32. MacMurray, 12 Mar. 1927.
33. *NZH*, 13 Feb. 1885, p. 5.
34. Ibid, 12 Dec. 1883, p. 5, and 22 Aug. 1884, p. 5 give early instances of this.
35. *Brett's Auckland Almanac*, 1873, p. 75; 1875, p. 47.
36. J. Beagle, 'Children of the State', MA thesis, The University of Auckland, 1974, p. 37.
37. *NZH*, 12 Mar. 1885, p. 4.
38. Beagle, pp. 145–52.
39. Cowie, pp. 92, 164, 382.
40. 'Recollections of James Williamson', MS, AI and ML, pp. 1–2.
41. MacMurray, 12 Mar. 1927.
42. C. W. Carrick, *NZ Observer*, 11 Jul. 1935, p. 5.
43. This excerpt is a conflation of MacMurray's statements of 12 Mar. 1927 and 29 Sept. 1932.
44. MacMurray, 12 Mar. 1927.
45. Ibid.
46. *NZ Observer*, 11 Jul. 1935.
47. Ibid.
48. *NZH*, 22 Nov. 1928.
49. MacMurray, 29 Sept. 1932.
50. Ibid.
51. Ibid.
52. Financial accounts (1887–94), pp. 14–19.
53. Cit. Sherratt, 'James Dilworth', p. 42.
54. Cowie, p. 235.
55. Financial accounts (1887–94), p. 226.
56. *NZH*, 26 Aug. 1916, Obit.; *DNZB*, Vol. II, 1993, pp. 368–69.
57. Isabella Dilworth to Trust Board, ? Sept. 1896, DTBA.
58. DTBA TT1 has full will, and TT1A, documents pertaining to will.
59. Pearce, *A Heritage in Trust*, p. 45.
60. Ibid, p. 46.
61. Ibid, p. 48.
62. Sherratt, pp. 35–36.
63. Reid, *St Mark's*, p. 22.
64. Cowie, pp. 113–15, 197, 254–55.
65. *NZH*, 22 Nov. 1928.

Chapter Fourteen
1. Financial accounts (1887–94), pp. 223–24, DTBA.
2. See e.g. J. Dilworth's will,

20 Sept. 1873, DTBA.
3. L. M. Hardy, 'Out of the Past', Auckland, n.d. (1953?), pp. 85–86, AML.
4. See e.g. J. Dilworth to Joseph Howard, 7 Jan. 1886, Joe Howard P.
5. Isabella Dilworth to DTB, ? Sept. 1896, TT1A, DTBA.
6. Death cert dated 23 Dec. 1894, 1894/1823, *DNZB*.
7. Cit. Sherratt, 'James Dilworth', p. 35. (Extract converted from reported to direct speech.)
8. Ibid.
9. Ibid, pp. 35–36.
10. Death cert. dated 9 Sept. 1889, age 57, 1889/1061, *DNZB*.
11. *AES*, 9 Sept. 1889.
12. Stone, *Makers of Fortune*, *passim*, for Aucklanders mentioned in this para.
13. *DNZB*, Vol. I, 1990, pp. 586–87.
14. *Auckland Savings Bank Centenary, 1847–1947*, pp. 62–69.
15. *NZH*, 24 Dec. 1894.
16. Sinclair, *University of Auckland*, ch. 3.
17. Ibid, pp. 50–51.
18. For more on Denis O'Rorke see G. G. M. Mitchell, 'The Pah Farm Story', *HJAW*, No. 4, Apr. 1964, pp. 31–33; John Stacpoole, *The Northern Club*, 1994, p. 43.
19. Sinclair, pp. 51–53.
20. *NZH*, 24 Dec. 1894 (Obit.).
21. Death cert. 1894/1823, *DNZB*.
22. *NZH*, 27 Dec. 1894.

BIBLIOGRAPHY

I PRIMARY SOURCES

A Manuscript Sources

1. Dilworth Trust Board Archives

The bulk of these archives are in folders in two japanned tin trunks which I have labelled for convenience TT. The folders are

1. Probate of the will of James Dilworth.
1A. Matters arising out of the will of James Dilworth.
2. Death certificate; old property valuations; interpretations of Dilworth's will.
3. Report on inspection of Dilworth's Property 1895.
4. 1895–96 Payments of Board arising out of James Dilworth's will.
5. Reports on Dilworth's properties, 1897 onwards.
6. Dilworth Trustee Act, 1902.
7. 1903–09 Letters and rulings arising out of James Dilworth's will.
8. Copies of original Crown Grants surrendered.
9. Dilworth's claims and litigation re compensation over severance of his estate by Auckland and Drury Railway Company.
10. Dilworth's claims for recovery of the Mount Hobson reserve.
11. New Zealand Thames Valley Land Co. and associated speculation.
12. Appeal to Privy Council over James Dilworth's will.
13. Miscellaneous receipts.
14. Miscellaneous letters.
15. Dilworth Trust Board, early balance sheets.
16. Dilworth Trust Board, miscellaneous business.
17. Appointment of early staff.
18. Archdeacon MacMurray; reminiscences.

Also of value:

Ledger, Financial Accounts, 1887–94.
Dilworth Trust Board Minutebooks, 1895–.
Dilworth Trust Board Letterbooks, 1895–.
Dilworth Trust Board Scrapbook.

2. Government and Public Archives

Auckland City Council Records and Archives Division.
Companies Office.
Department of Survey and Land Information. (Historical map resources very valuable.)
Lands and Deeds Registry.
Northern Archives and Record Centre; important for nineteenth-century discharged mortgages and dead companies file.
National Archives, Wellington, with special reference to Old Land Claims (OLC) files.

3. General Manuscript Sources

Anglican Church: Archives of the Anglican Archives of Auckland.
Ashworth: Edward Ashworth Journals 1841–45, Alexander Turnbull Library, MS 1841–45P.
Atkinson: H. A. Atkinson, Inward Correspondence, Richmond Atkinson Papers, Alexander Turnbull Library.
Brown: 'Notes and Reminiscences of James Brown of Donaghmore, Co. Tyrone 1904–05', Photocopy, Dilworth Trust Board Archives.

Campbell: Sir John Logan Campbell Papers, Auckland Institute and Museum Library, MS 51.
Diamond: J. T. Diamond, memos and notes on James and Andrew Dilworth, Dilworth Trust Board Archives.
Edgerley: John Edgerley, 'Memoirs', Auckland, n.d., Barr Papers, Auckland Public Library, MS 415. Barr Papers are also of general value.
FitzRoy: Correspondence of the family of Governor Robert FitzRoy, Alexander Turnbull Library , MS 80.
Graham: George Graham, Diary, Auckland Institute and Museum, Library, MS 119.
Halcombe: A. W. F. Halcombe Papers, Alexander Turnbull Library.
Hall: Sir John Hall. Private and Official Letters and Telegrams 1870–90. Alexander Turnbull Library, MS 1784.
Howard: Joseph Howard Papers in the possession of his grandson, Joe Howard of Taupo. The collection is small in bulk but valuable.
Lush: *The Auckland Journals of Vicesimus Lush 1850–63*, (ed. Alison Drummond), Christchurch, 1971.
Mossman: The Mossman Papers have two elements: photocopies of correspondence and memoirs of descendants of James Dilworth's sister Eleanor Mossman, also correspondence between James Dilworth and W. J. Mossman, 1890–93. (Copy in Dilworth Trust Board Archives.)
Rolleston: William Rolleston Papers, 1861–1894, Acc. 77–248, Alexander Turnbull Library.
Rough: Captain David Rough, 'Early Days in Auckland', book of cuttings from *New Zealand Herald*, Auckland Public Library.
Shipping Lists: Names of Arrivals, Auckland Public Library.

4. *Business, Professional, and Family Papers*

Hardy, L. M. 'Out of the Past', Auckland, n.d. (1953?), Auckland Institute and Museum Library. Memoirs of a girl reared on the Selwyn estate.
Hesketh: Edwin Hesketh papers deposited in the Auckland Public Library.
Jackson and Russell Letterbooks, 1879–94, Auckland Institute and Museum Library.
New Zealand Loan and Mercantile Agency Company Limited Papers, 1865–93, Alexander Turnbull Library.
O'Halloran: 'Manuscript Autobiography of G. S. O'Halloran, Captain of New Zealand Militia', Sydney, Nov. 1894. (Copy in Dilworth Trust Board Archives.)
Rose, J. H., *Jackson Russell: A Scrapbook History*, Auckland, 1983, photocopied and bound.
Russell McVeagh McKenzie Bartleet & Co. Archives. Has material on the Patetere and Whaiti-Kuranui syndicates.
Thames Valley and Rotoura Railway Company Minutebooks. When used these were in the hands of the late D. C. O'Halloran, public accountant.
Williams: W. L. C. Williams Letterbook 1879–93. When used this was in the possession of the late Mr John Main of Cambridge.

B. Oral Evidence

Ireland and England

Norman Cardwell of Dungannon; John Dilworth and Wilfred Dilworth both of Derrybuoy, Dungannon; W. J. (Bill) Dilworth of Walthamstow, London; Eion Kerr of 'Irish World', Dungannon; Bertie McLean of Donaghmore.

New Zealand

J. T. (Jack) Diamond of Blockhouse Bay; Derek Hall of Waerenga; Joe Howard of Taupo; Les Kermode of Auckland; Mrs E. D. Mossman, Dilworth Mossman, Georgina Mossman, all of Taupo; Bishop G. R. Monteith of Auckland (on MacMurray); Hon. W. J. (Jack) Scott of Stanley Bay; J. M. Stacpoole of Remuera.

C. Official printed papers

Appendices to the Journals of the House of Representatives.
Auckland City Board of Commissioners. Reports of Proceedings, 1863–71.
Auckland Provincial Council. Votes and Proceedings, 1853–61.
Electoral Rolls for the General Assembly, Auckland Public Library.
Great Britain: *British Parliamentary Papers: Colonies: Papers Relating to New Zealand*,

Vols 1–5, Irish University Press reprint, 1968–71.
Land Regulations in the Province of Auckland adopted by the Provincial Council on the 5th Day of August, 1859, London, 1966.
McLean, Martin, *Auckland 1842–45*, Auckland, 1989. This is a demographic study based on the first police censuses.
Native Land Court: *Important Judgments Delivered in the Compensation Court and the Native Land Court, 1866–79*, Wellington, 1879. Fenton's Orakei Judgment is on pp. 53–96.
New Zealand Government Gazette.
New Zealand Parliamentary Debates.
New Zealand Statutes.
The Province of Auckland: The Acts of the Superintendent and the Provincial Council of the Province of New Zealand, Auckland, 1866.
Results of a Census of New Zealand, 1858–96.
A Return of the Freeholders of New Zealand, 1882, Wellington, 1884.
Scholefield, G. H., *New Zealand Parliamentary Record 1840–1949*.
Statistics of New Zealand, Wellington.
Statistics of New Zealand for the Crown Colony Period 1840–52, Department of Economics, Auckland University College, 1954.
Turton, H. Hanson, *Maori Deeds of Land Purchases in the North Island of New Zealand, Vol. I, Province of Auckland*, Wellington, 1877.
Turton, H. Hanson, *Plans of Land Purchases in the North Island of New Zealand, Vol. I, Province of Auckland*, Wellington, 1877.
Turton, H. Hanson, *Maori Deeds of Old Private Land Purchases in New Zealand, from the year 1815 to 1840, with Pre-emptive and Other Claims . . . and the Report of Mr Commissioner F. Dillon Bell*, Wellington, 1882.
Turton, H. Hanson, *An Epitome of Official Documents Relative to Native Affairs and Land Purchases in the North Island of New Zealand*, Wellington, 1883.

D. Newspapers and Periodicals

Auckland [Evening] Star, Auckland.
Auckland Weekly News, Auckland.
Australasian Insurance and Banking Record, Melbourne.
Brett's Auckland Almanac, Auckland.
[Daily] Southern Cross, Auckland.
Dilworth Newsletter, Walthamstow, United Kingdom.
Historical Journal of Auckland and Waikato, Auckland.
New Zealand Herald, Auckland.
New Zealand Herald and Auckland Gazette, Auckland.
[New Zealand] Observer, Auckland.
New-Zealander, Auckland.
Times, London.
Waikato Times, Hamilton.

II SECONDARY SOURCES

A. Published Books and Articles

The Irish Existence

Begley, Donal F. (ed.), *Irish Genealogy: A Record Finder*, Dublin, 1981.
Buckland, Patrick, *Irish Unionism 1885–1922*, London, 1973.
Bushman, Virginia, *Genealogy of the Dilworth Families in America, 1550-1970*, Salt Lake City, private publication, 1970.
Camblin, Gilbert, *The Town in Ulster*, Belfast, 1971.
Fitzpatrick, David, 'Irish Emigration to Nineteenth-century Australia', in *Australia and Ireland, 1788–1988*, ed. Colm Kiernan, Dublin, 1986.
Fitzpatrick, Rory, *God's Frontiersmen. The Scots-Irish Epic*, London, 1989.
Foster, R. F. (ed.), *The Oxford Illustrated History of Ireland*, Oxford, 1991.
Hayward, Richard, *In Praise of Ulster*, Belfast, 1938.
MacDonagh, Oliver, 'Emigration from Ireland to Australia: An Overview', in *Australia and*

Ireland: Bicentenary Essays, ed. Colm Kiernan, Dublin, 1986.
McCreary, Alf, *By All Accounts. A History of Trustee Savings Banks in Northern Ireland*, Antrim, 1991.
McEvoy, John, *County of Tyrone 1802: A Statistical Survey*, Dublin, 1802. Facsimile reprint, Belfast, 1991, with introduction by W.H. Crawford.
Malcolmson, A. P. W., *The Pursuit of the Heiress: Aristocratic Marriage in Ireland 1750–1820*, Antrim, 1982.
Moch, Leslie Page, *Moving Europeans. Migration in Western Europe since 1650*, Bloomington, 1992.
O'Conluain, Proinsias, 'Benburb and the Powerscourts', *Duiche Neill*, Benburb, 1987.
O'Doibhlin, Eamon, *Domnach Mor*, Dungannon, 1968.
O'Kane, William (ed.), *Heather Peat and Stone: The Parishes and Townlands of Tyrone*, Dungannon, 1992.
O'Kane, William (ed.), *You Don't Say: The Tyrone Crystal Book of Ulster Dialect*, Dungannon, 1991.
Ordnance Survey Memoirs of County Tyrone, 1825, 1833–5, 1840, Mid and East Tyrone, ed. Angélique Day and Patrick McWilliams, Belfast, 1993.
O'Tuathaigh, Gearoid, *Ireland Before the Famine, 1798–1848*, Vol. IX in *The Gill History of Ireland*, Dublin, 1972.
Robinson, Philip S., *The Plantation of Ulster: British Settlement in an Irish Landscape, 1600–1700*, Dublin, 1984.
Rogers, Mary, *The Prospect of Tyrone*, Enniskillen, 1988.

The New Zealand Existence

Adams, Peter, *Fatal Necessity: British Intervention in New Zealand 1830–1847*, Auckland, 1977.
Alison, E. W., *A New Zealander Looks Back*, Auckland, 1947.
Auckland Savings Bank Centenary, 1847–1947, Auckland, 1947.
Barr, John, *The City of Auckland, New Zealand, 1840–1920*, Auckland, 1922.
Barr, John, *The Ports of Auckland*, Auckland, 1926.
Bartlett, Jean (ed.), *Takapuna: People and Places*, Takapuna, 1989.
Blainey, Geoffrey, *The Tyranny of Distance: How Distance Shaped Australia's History*, Melbourne, 1968.
Bold Century, pub. New Zealand Insurance Company, Auckland, 1959.
Brett, H. and H. Hook, *The Albertlanders*, Auckland, 1927.
Brown, William, *New Zealand and its Aborigines: Being on Account of the Aborigines, Trade and Resources of the Colony: And the Advantages it now Presents as a Field for Emigration and the Investment of Capital*, London, 1845.
Bunbury, J., *Reminiscences of a Veteran*, (3 vols), London, 1861.
Burn, R. Scott, *Landed Estates Management*, London, 1877.
Butlin, N. G., *Investment in Australian Economic Development 1861–1900*, Cambridge, 1964.
Butlin, S. J., *Australia and the New Zealand Bank*, Sydney, 1961.
Campbell, John Logan, *Poenamo: Sketches of the Early Days in New Zealand*, London, 1881.
Cannon, Michael, *The Land Boomers*, Melbourne, 1966.
Carrick, C. W., 'Pioneer's Legacy to New Zealand Boys', *New Zealand Observer*, 11 Jul. 1935.
Chappell, N. M., *New Zealand Banker's Hundred*, Wellington, 1961.
Coates, Isaac, *On Record*, Hamilton, 1962.
Cowie, W. G., *Our Last Year in New Zealand*, London, 1888.
Craig, J. J. (comp.), *Historical Record of the Jubilee Reunion (1892)*, Auckland, 1893.
Curson, P. H., 'Auckland in 1842', *New Zealand Geographer*, Vol. XXX (1974).
Cyclopedia of New Zealand, Vol. II, Christchurch, 1902.
Daly, G. T., 'The Grasslands of New Zealand' in *Pastures: Their Ecology and Management*, ed. R. H. M. Langer, Auckland, 1992.
Davidson, Allan K., *Selwyn's Legacy. The College of St John the Evangelist, Te Waimate and Auckland, 1843–1992. A History*, Auckland, 1993.
Davis, Eliot, *A Link with the Past*, Auckland, 1949.
Davis, John King, *History of St John's College, Tamaki, Auckland, New Zealand*, Auckland, 1911.

Diamond, John T., *Once the Wilderness*, 2nd ed., Auckland, 1977.
Dictionary of New Zealand Biography, Vol. I, 1769–1869, ed. W. H. Oliver, Wellington, 1990; Vol. II, 1870–1900, ed. Claudia Orange, Wellington, 1993.
Familton, A. S., 'Animal Disorders Arising from the Consumption of Pasture', in *Pastures: Their Ecology and Management*, ed. R. H. M. Langer, Auckland, 1992.
Fletcher, R. S., *Single Track: The Construction of the North Island Main Trunk Railway*, Auckland, 1978.
F. W. W., 'Makers of Auckland', series of articles in *New Zealand Herald*, 8 Jul. 1929 to 21 Aug. 1929, bound and paged in Auckland Public Library.
Gibbons, P. J., *Astride the River. A History of Hamilton*, Hamilton, 1977.
Green, R.B., *Auckland to Onehunga Railway Centennial, 1873–1973*, Auckland, 1973.
Hochstetter, F., *The Geology of New Zealand*, Auckland, 1964.
Hodgson, Terence, *The Heart of Colonial Auckland 1865–1910*, Auckland, 1992.
Holloway, K. M., *Maungarei. An Outline History of the Mount Wellington, Panmure and Tamaki Districts*, Auckland, 1992.
Holmes, C. O., 'James Dilworth: Some Early Land Dealings', *Journal of the Auckland Historical Society*, Vol. I, No. 1 (Oct. 1962).
Kalaugher, J. P., *Gleanings from Early New Zealand History*, Auckland, 1950.
Kelly, L. G., *Tainui*, Wellington, 1949.
Kemp, H. T., *Revised Narrative of Incidents and Events in the Early Colonizing History of New Zealand from 1840 to 1880*, Auckland, 1901.
Kermode, Les, 'Ferdinand von Hochstetter', in *The German Connection: New Zealand and German-speaking Europe in the Nineteenth Century*, Auckland, 1993.
Kissling, T. G., *The Parish of St Mary Parnell, Auckland, New Zealand 1860–1960*, Auckland, 1960.
Langridge, W. B., *Descriptive Handbook of the Waikato: Its Condition and Resources*, Hamilton, 1880.
Lowe, D., *Tracks Across the Isthmus: A Centennial History of the Building of Auckland's First Railway*, Auckland, 1973.
Macdonald, Winifred, *Auckland Yesterday and Today*, Auckland, 1957.
Macdonald, Winifred, *Recollections 1850–1920: A Sketch History of Early Remuera*, Remuera, 1984.
Macky, N. L., *The Macky Family in New Zealand 1845–69*, Auckland, 1969.
McLintock, A. H., *Crown Colony Government in New Zealand*, Wellington, 1958.
Madden, Ian B., *Riverhead: the Kaipara Gateway*, Auckland, 1966.
Martin, Lady [Mary Ann], *Our Maoris*, London, 1884.
Martin, S. M. D., *New Zealand in 1842, or the Effects of a Bad Government on a Good Country. In a Letter to the Right Honourable Lord Stanley, Principal Secretary of State for the Colonies*, Auckland, 1842.
Martin, S. M. D., *New Zealand in a Series of Letters*, London, 1845.
Mogford, Janice, *The Onehunga Heritage*, Onehunga, 1989.
Moore, B. A. and J. S. Barton, *Banking in New Zealand*, Wellington, 1935.
Morris, Nona, *Early Days in Franklin: A Centennial Volume*, Auckland, 1965.
Morton, H. B., *Recollections of Early New Zealand*, Auckland, 1925.
[Otahuhu Borough Council], *A Century of Progress 1848–1948*, Otahuhu, 1948.
Oxford History of New Zealand, ed. W. H. Oliver, 1st edn, Wellington, 1981; 2nd edn, Auckland, 1992, ed. Geoffrey W. Rice.
Pearce, G. L., *A Heritage in Trust: James Dilworth and his School*, Auckland, 1986.
Phillips, P. L., *Landmarks of Tainui*, Otorohanga, 1989.
Platts, Una, *The Lively Capital. Auckland 1840–1865*, Christchurch, 1971.
Reid, Hilary F., *St Mark's Anglican Church Remuera: The Story of a Parish 1847–1981*, Auckland, 1982.
Report of the Agricultural and Horticultural Society of Auckland, Auckland, 1843.
Reports on the Selwyn Block with Map, (ed. A. W. F. Halcombe), London, 1882.
Rose, J. H., *Some Houses in Ohinerau*, Auckland, 1984.
Rutherford, J., *Sir George Grey, KCB, 1812–98: A Study in Colonial Government*, London, 1961.
Ryburn, E.K., 'Remuera: Some Notes on its Beginnings and Early Land Purchases', *Journal of the Auckland Historical Society*, Vol. I, No. 1 (Oct. 1962).
Salmon, J. H. M., *A History of Goldmining in New Zealand*, Wellington, 1963.

Scholefield, G. H., *Captain William Hobson: First Governor of New Zealand*, London, 1934.
Scholefield, G. H., *Dictionary of New Zealand Biography*, Wellington, 1940.
Searle, E. J., *Auckland: City of Volcanoes*, Auckland, 1964.
Searle, E. J. and Janet Davidson, *A Picture Guide to the Volcanic Cones of Auckland*, Auckland, 1973.
Sherrin, R. A. A. and J. H. Wallace, *Early History of New Zealand*, Auckland, 1890.
Simmons, David, *Maori Auckland*, Auckland, 1987.
Smith, Norman, *Native Custom and Law Affecting Native Land*, Wellington, 1942.
Smith, S. Percy, 'The Peopling of the North', Appendix to *Journals of the Polynesian Society*, Vol. VI, Wellington, 1897. (Also published as a separate volume.)
Sorrenson, M. P. K., 'The Maori People and the History of Auckland', *Te Ao Hou*, No. 27 (Jun. 1959).
The Souvenir of the Henderson School and Diamond Jubilee Booklet, 1873-1938, (comp. A.W. Hepburn), Henderson, 1933.
Stacpoole, John, *The Houses of the Merchant Princes*, Auckland, 1989.
Stacpoole, John, *The Northern Club 1869-1994*, Auckland, 1994.
Stone, R. C. J., 'Auckland's Political Opposition in the Crown Colony Period, 1841–53,', in *Provincial Perspectives*, eds Len Richardson and W. David McIntyre, Christchurch, 1980.
Stone, R. C. J., 'Auckland Party Politics in the Early Years of the Provincial System, 1853–58', *New Zealand Journal of History*, Vol. XIV, No. 2 (Oct. 1980).
Stone, R. C. J., *Makers of Fortune: A Colonial Business Community and its Fall*, Auckland, 1973.
Stone, R. C. J., 'The Maori Land Question and the Fall of the Grey Government, 1879', *New Zealand Journal of History*, Vol. I, No. 1 (Apr. 1967).
Stone, R. C. J., 'The New Zealand Frozen Meat and Storage Company', *New Zealand Journal of History*, Vol. V, No. 2 (Oct. 1971).
Stone, R. C. J., 'The Thames Valley and Rotorua Railway Company Limited, 1882–9', *New Zealand Journal of History*, Vol. VIII, No. 1 (Apr. 1974).
Stone, R. C. J., *Young Logan Campbell*, Auckland, 1982.
Swainson, William, *Auckland, the Capital of New Zealand, and the Country Adjacent*, London, 1853.
Terry, Charles, *New Zealand, Its Advantages and Prospects as a British Colony, With a Full Account of the Land Claims, Sales of Crown Lands, Aborigines etc., etc.*, London, 1842.
Vennell, C. W., *Risks and Rewards: A Policy of Enterprise 1872–1972*, Auckland, 1972.
Waititi, John, 'An Outline of Auckland's Maori History', *Journal of the Auckland Historical Society*, Vol. II, No. 1 (Oct. 1963).

B. Unpublished Theses

Alemann, Maurice, 'Early Land Transactions in the Ngatiwhatua Tribal Area', MA thesis, University of Auckland, 1992.
Beagle, Jan, 'Children of the State: A Study of the New Zealand Industrial School System', MA thesis, University of Auckland, 1974.
Dunstall, G. C., 'Colonial Merchant: J. T. Mackelvie, Brown Campbell & Co., and the Business Community of Auckland, 1865–71', Auckland, 1970.
McGarvey, R. D., 'Local Politics in the Auckland Province, 1853–62', MA thesis, University of Auckland, 1954.
Sherratt, David, 'James Dilworth, His Life and Times', assignment for Auckland Teachers' College, 1958. Copy lodged with the Dilworth Trust Board.
Sorrenson, M. P. K., 'The Purchase of Maori Lands, 1865–92', MA thesis, University of Auckland, 1955.
Stone, R. C. J., 'Auckland Business and Auckland Businessmen in the 1880's', PhD thesis, University of Auckland, 1969.

INDEX

Abbreviations

See p. 240, and

JD   James Dilworth
DUI   Dilworth Ulster Institute
NZTVL Co.   New Zealand Thames Valley Land Company
RSD   Royal School of Dungannon

Agricultural and Pastoral Society, 88–90
Alemann, Maurice, 42, 243
Ambury English & Co., 163–64
Anglo-Maori Wars, 119–20, 121
Arawa, SS, 213, **213**, 214
Auckland, purchase, 35–37; sparse early settlement, 25; short of flat land, 170; early depression, 30; Crown land sales in, 23, 37–38; appreciation of values, 53, 149; poor early roads, 74–75; numbers of people and livestock, 78; ferocious politics, 92–94; 1860s—much land, little capital, 118; harbour reclamations, 171; a wooden city, 171, 172; population growth in 1880s, 145, 145n; horse population, 162n; scope for subdivision, 165; stimulated by gold discoveries, 177; post-1871 growth, 181; 1880s depression ruins its élite, 187, 228; 1880s depression overwhelms, 214; child destitution, 215; a 'falling apart' of society in 1890s, 229
Auckland and Drury Railway Co., coal discovered at Waihoihoi, 119; Railway Bill, 120; 'first sod' turned, 121; compulsory purchasing power, 122; construction problems, 124; JD's compensation claim, 124–28; award of £6,343 to JD; quarrel over crossings, 130–31; resumption of construction, 132; line to Onehunga completed, 133
Auckland Savings Bank, 86–88; 87n, 229, **230**

Beatty, Revd William, 220, 220n.
Bell, Francis Dillon (land claims commissioner), 53, 57, 141, 143n, 143–44, **144**

Brookfield, F.M.P. (lawyer), 125, 126–28
Brown, William (merchant), 61–63, **62**, 92, 228
Buckland, Alfred, 125
Bunbury, Major Thomas, 39, 41, 45
'Bush sickness', 202, 202n, 205

Campbell, Dr John Logan (merchant), 24, 27n, 29, 39, 82, 86–88, 89–90, **90**, 93, 95, 134, 176
Chain migration, 96, 99–114
Child destitution, 215, 216–17
Clark, James McCosh (mayor), **207**, 228
Confiscations (Ireland), 2–3
Coolahan, Hugh (baker and landowner), 172, 173, 173n, **173**, 174, **174**, 175–76
Copland, John (hotel-keeper), 172, 176, 178–79
Costley, Edward (landlord), 184, 186–87, 211
Cowie, Bishop W.G., 101, 211, 212, 224, **231**

Daldy, Captain William Crush (pioneer), 27, **27**, 88
Darley, Dr John Richard (headmaster and bishop),18, **214**
Deserters (army), 75–76
Diamond, J. (Jack) T., 102n, 103
Dilworth, family in Dungannon, 1–6, 8, 9, **10**, 20, 96–99, **98**
Dilworth, Andrew b.1823 (brother), comes to Auckland, 99; given Waitakere farm, 100–02; marries, 102; skilful farmer, 103; 'likeable', 104; frightful accident and death, 209–11
Dilworth, Anne b.1789 (second-cousin), 12, 13, 15, 20–21, 99
Dilworth, Isabella b.1828 (wife), comes to NZ, 81; settles in Otahuhu, 82; portrait, **82**; able, 83; JD's confidant, 151; trustee, 220; portrait, **121**; annuity, 233
Dilworth, James b.1842 of Portadown and Pukekohe, 108–11

Dilworth, James b.1815

LIFE AND BUSINESS: born Dunseark, 13–14; moves to Mullaghcreevy, 15; attends Donaghmore school, 16; at RSD, 18; enters banking, 19–20; emigrates to Australia, 20–21; on to Auckland, 22; settles in Auckland, 24–25; government clerk, 27–28, career in NZ Banking Co., 27–32; early land buying, 30–31, 33, 53–54; buys with pre-emption waivers, 55–58; buys at Takapuna with scrip, 58–60; buys at Parnell and Customs Street, 60–61, **61**; farms at Remuera and erects cottage, 63; commissioner approves claim, 64–65; continues to buy and sell land, 68–69; rationalizes his finances, 69–70; Irish influences on farm, 71–72; hedges, fences and drains, 71–72; terrorized by deserters, 75–76; gives farm pastoral bias, 77–78; attempts to lease and sell, 79–80; becomes wealthy, 81; marries Isabella Hall 81–82; buys jaunting car; builds homestead, 84–85; helps found ASB, 86–87; takes first deposit, 87; 'Father of ASB', 88; gives leadership in A&P Society, 89–90; on first provincial council, 91; political concerns are practical, 92–94; becomes a political veteran, 94; advocates Auckland's separation from colony, 95; loses taste for politics, 95; starts chain migration of family, 96; family tensions in Dungannon, 97–98; loss of Mullaghcreevy and Dunseark, 99; invites Andrew to colony, 100; and gives Waitakere farm to him, 101–02; invites Jimmy Mossman to be heir, 105–06; experiment fails, 107–08; stays aloof from JD of Portadown, 108–11; invites out family of sister Esther, 111–12; experiment fails, 113; invites sister Eleanor and family, 113; settles Mossmans at Auckland and employs nephews, 114; makes three Mossman nephews heirs, 115–16; revokes 1873 will, 117; enriched by railway compensation, 118–19, 151; estate severed by railway, 120; 'first sod' turned on Remuera, 121–22; JD buys Mount St John land, 123; arbitration hearing in Banco Court, 125–28; JD awarded £6,343; quarrels over bridges etc., 130–31; railway completed, 132; always wanted Graham's Hill, 136; buys Mount Hobson, 138; claims Mount Hobson reserve, 1865, 139; 1867 resurrects claim, 140; quarrels with superintendents over reserve, 141–42; Gillies resists his claim, 143; JD continues his agitation, 144; loses out by 1881, 145; substantial landowner by 1882, 148; invested in land lifelong, 149; lucky and astute, 150; his provincial land less important, 152; Waitakere important until 1881, 153; buys Waikato land after wars, 154–5; Mangawara disappoints, 156; his 'scoria' lands, 157–8; acquires Tizard and Lundon farms, 158–59; plants on Remuera and introduces llamas, 161–62; leases Remuera to F. Lawry then Ambury & Co., 163–64; essentially a landed proprietor, 165; household servants, 166; limited socializing, 167; main income from city properties, 169; made his own luck, 170; buys Customs Street allotment, 170; creates a nuisance, 171–72; lends to Coolahan, 175; takes over Waitemata hotel, 176; builds Thames hotel, 178; puts up Tyrone block, 179; adds third storey, 180; upgrades the Waitemata in 1889, 180; becomes a heavy borrower, 1882, 184–85; has South British and Costly as main mortgagees, 1886; by 1887 borrowing at end, 187; wealth little eroded by depression, 188–90; importance of city properties, 191; befriends Howard, 192; but a puzzling relationship, 195; forms Whaiti-Kuranui Association, 197; rarely in Waikato himself, 198; increasingly relies on O'Halloran, 199; large holding in TV & RR Co., 200; goes to London, 204, 213; returns much chastened, 205; syndicate quarrels resolved, 206; turns to will-making, 207; gives farms to nephews, 209; brings injured Andrew to Auckland, 209–10; on his death gives annuity to wife, 211; meets MacMurray on turning seventy, 214; Howard incapacitated, 215; destitution in Auckland in 1880s, 216; plans educational trust, 217; visits MacMurray, 217; host to MacMurray and invites him to Auckland, 217–18; works with MacMurray on will, 219; selects trustees, 220; not markedly sectarian, 223–24; tremulous but otherwise healthy, 226–27; plays whist, 227; depression tensions in Auckland, 228; strain of college council work, 229–30; dies, 231; buried at St Mark's, 232

APPEARANCE, CHARACTER AND PERSONALITY: pictures of, **82**, **205**, **231**; secretive and

JAMES DILWORTH

hard in negotiations, 7, 22; dour and devoted to hard work, 18; gruff and unbending, 21; aloof and shy but not reclusive, 71; extraordinarily single-minded, 77; good horseman, 83; unobtrusive and self-effacing, 86; well developed sense of duty, 88; has drive like an Ulster Scot, 97; bitter at loss of Mullaghcreevy, 99; lacks Andrew's sociability, 103–04; reserved, 104; childlessness 'a grief' to him, 105; severe, 113; dogged in negotiation, 140–42; has few confidants, 151; opposed to excessive openness in business, 168; used 'dummies' in deals, 168–69; leaves nothing to chance, 178; becomes acquisitive, 183; repute diminished by Patetere, 197; much sobered by NZTVL Co. failure, 205, 207; combined hardness with kindness, 208; strong sense of duty, 214; shakes as an old man, 226; sturdy to the end, 227; uncompromising whist player, 227, 227n; unostentatious manner, patriarchal appearance, 228

ATTITUDES AND OPINIONS: deep sense of Irish nationhood, 4; agitates for self-government, 29; stern on crime and punishment, 76–77; belief in self-help, 88; encourages backblocks settlement, 88; A&P enthusiast, 89; not a 'political animal', 91; a watching brief in provincial affairs, 92; finds factionalism distasteful, 92–93, 95; temporarily a separatist, 93–94; stern disciplinarian, 113; hard headed, 115; has respect for legality, 129; can alternate obstinacy with conciliation, 130–31; regards Mount Hobson as another Mullaghcreevy?, 136; enduring affection for Mount Hobson, 145; abhorred vanity, 208; growing interest in social issues, 211; concern for disadvantaged boys, 217; not obviously anti-Catholic, 219–20; yet has Protestant clannishness, 220; provides in will for 'straitened' boys, 221–22; low Church Anglican, 222; 'Protestant of the first water', 228

FARMING PRACTICES AND INTERESTS: enthusiasm for manuring, 8, 72; disclaimed being a 'practical farmer', 62, 71; his first fences, 62; efficient, with many Irish practices, 71; has famed hawthorn hedges, 72; ditch-and-hurdle, and post-and-rail fences, 73; drainage and irrigation, 73–74; moves towards pastoralism, 77–78; proprietor rather than farmer, 72 79; ardent arborist and weed controller, 80; champion of A&P, 88; helps to buy showgrounds, 89; president of A&P, 90; wants increased settlement and pest control, 91–94; deliberately chose volcanic soil, 135; plantations on Remuera estate, 161

PROPERTIES AND FINANCES: model of 'man of property', 34, 191; buys Parnell property, 30–31; buys Remuera, 33; astute financier though young, 33, 53; buys land shrewdly, 53; plan of Remuera estate, 56; uses scrip to buy Takapuna land, 58; never a simple farmer, 60; invests in urban real estate, 61; acquires Remuera, chapter 4; caution over borrowing, 66; position strengthened by railway compensation, 118, 129, 151; used property to secure borrowing, 119; largest claim for compensation from railway, 122; thinks of subdividing Remuera, 127–28; major landholder by 1880, 148; city growth pushes up value of JD's properties, 149, 157–58; two kinds of property investment, 149–50; becomes lender of last resort, 150, 175–76; extended city real estate 1868–71, 151; Waitakere important, 153; invests in Waikato after the land wars, 154–55; Mangawara unproductive, 155–56; Tamaki isthmus the centre of investment, 157; 'Scoria farms', 158–59; Remuera leased, not farmed by self, 160–63; homestead a 'farmhouse mansion', 164–67; cash flow from city properties, 169, 181, 191; Customs Street properties crucial, 171; money put into bricks and mortar, 177, 179–80; borrowing brings risks, 182, 184; money used for investment rather than consumption, 185–86; end of borrowing, 1887, 188–90; sound financial position in old age, 188–90

WILL-MAKING AND PHILANTHROPY: makes Jimmy Mossman his heir, 106; 1873, makes an entail will, 115; H. A. Mossman main beneficiary, 116; 1873 will revoked, 117; includes Mount Hobson in will, 145; public curiosity about Dilworth's intentions, 208; by 1880s Mossmans out of favour, 209; Sam Jackson's influence on will, 211; returns from UK ready to make will, 213; depression hardship for children, 215–17; discloses intentions to MacMurray, 218; Dilworth, MacMurray and Jackson plan will, 219; chooses

trustees, 220; chief features of 1894 will, 221–22, 223; will has Anglican but not sectarian flavour, 224; influence of MacMurray, 225; 1894 will in summary, Appendix A
Dilworth, John b.1785 (father), 11, 13, 97–99
Dilworth, Mary Ann b.1789 (mother), 11, 13, 97–98
Dilworth, Mary Jane née Daniels (sister-in-law), 102, 104, 112, 209–10, 211
Dilworth, W.J. (Bill), 1–2
'Dilworth Scholars' from RSD, 224
Donaghmore, 16–17, **17**
Dungannon, 3, 18–19, 67, 78, **112**
Dunseark, 12–13, **14**, 97–99

Evans, Mrs Esther Ann b.1826 (sister), cares for mother, 97; goes to USA, 97; JD invites to Auckland, 111; stays with Andrew, 111; quarrels with JD over discipline, 112–13; returns to USA, 113

Farmer, James, 119, 228
Fenton, Francis Dart (Chief Judge of Native Land Court), 35
Firth, Josiah Clifton (miller and speculator), 183, 200, **200**, 228
FitzRoy, Governor Robert, Treasury empty, 32; portrait, **43**; colony in turmoil, 42–43; makes proclamation waiving pre-emption, 47; proclamation disadvantages Ngati Whatua, 48; influenced by Remuera Feast, 50–52
Fox, Sir William (politician), 205, 206
Foy, Bernard of Pukekohe, 219

Ganges (clipper), 109–10, **110**
Gardner, William, 220, 220n, **232**
Gillies, Thomas Bannatyne (lawyer, superintendent, judge), 89, 126–28, 142, 166, 206
Graham, George (government engineer), land speculations, 23–24; Remuera farmer, 63; grows wheat, 77; has orchard, 80; sells Graham's Hill to JD with mortgage, 67; biographical note, 136; constructions as clerk of works, 136–37; had bought land by stealth, 137; circumstances of sale to JD, 138
Graham, Robert (superintendent and landowner), 89, 121, 132–33, 141
Grey, Governor George (KCB 1848), restores Crown pre-emption, 48; approves of ASB, 87; attends A&P show, 79; president of A&P, 138; premier 1877 at time of Patetere troubles, 196; thwarted over Patetere, 197
Grubstaking, 192–93

Halcombe, Arthur William Follett (emigration agent), 199, 200–01, 205–06
Hall, Isabella, see Isabella Dilworth
Hall, John (brother-in-law), 81–82
Hall, Robert (brother-in-law), comes to Auckland, 81; JD befriends, 82; named trustee in 1873 will, 116; trustee in 1894 will, 220
Hall, William (brother-in-law), 81–82
Hardington, Henry (land agent), 124
Hardy, Mrs L.M., 226
Henry, Thomas (farmer of One Tree Hill), 67–68, 68n, 76, 78, 91
Hesketh, Edwin (lawyer), 165, 197, **205**
Hobson, Mount, beautiful aspect, 134; doubt over Maori name, 135; appearance from Mount Eden, **139**; view to south-west from, **142**; to be site of Institute, 211, 231–32
Hobson, William (governor), 34–36, 38–39
Hochstetter, Ferdinand von (geologist), 119, 135
Howard, Joseph (businessmen), friend of JD, 186; Irish background, 192; grubstakes Shotover claim, 193; becomes entrepreneur, 194; impetuous and sanguine, 195; joins JD in Whaiti-Kuranui speculation, 195; shareholder in NZTVL Co., 200; has stroke, 205; impoverished, 206; ill and demoralized, 215; dies poor, 228
Hunt, William (goldminer), 192–93, **193**

Jackson, Samuel (solicitor), 151, 186, 187, 197, 197n, **211**
Jackson and Russell (JD's lawyers), 151, 186–87, 197n, 202–03
Jaunting car, 84, 227n

Keals, Richard (architect), 176, 178, 179
Kennedy, Alexander (banker), 28–29, 31, 86

Lawry, Frank, (JD's tenant), 162–63
Lundon, Patrick and John, 158–59

MacMurray, Revd George, JD confided in, 151; on 1889 depression, 187; meets JD on the *Arawa*, 213–14; biography, 214n, JD visits, 217; visits JD in Auckland, 218;

JD asks him to help with Trust, 219; works with JD on will, 219; chosen as trustee, 220; influence on Anglicanism of DUI, 224–25

Mangawara, 155, 156, 184–85
Maraitai Land Co., 187, 189, 204–05, 207
Martin, Sir William (chief justice), 76
Matson, Major Henry (land commissioner), 64–65
Merrett, Joseph Jenner (artist and speculator), 50–52, 55, 135
Meurant, Edward (interpreter), 46, 46n, 57, 64
Moffitt, Charles Henry, 43–45
Montefiore, John Israel (pioneer), 29, 76–77, 87, **87**
Morrin, Thomas, 145, 183, 200, **201**, 228
Mossman, Mrs Eleanor (sister), marries T.W. Mossman, 97; emigrates to Canada, 105; JD 'begs' her to come to NZ, 113; portrait, **114**; is given an annuity in 1873 will, 115; shifts to Waikato and Hawke's Bay, 117; JD gives money frequently, 209; given annuity under 1894 will
Mossman, Henry ('Harry') Albert (nephew), works at Remuera, 114; major beneficiary in 1873 will, 116; had JD's business drive, 117; tells of JD on a visit, 178; JD gives him Hangaroa farm, 209
Mossman, James ('Jimmy') Dilworth (nephew) chosen as heir, 105; arrives in NZ, 106; talented but solitary, 107; turns his back on the inheritance, 107–08; disinherited, 115
Mossman, William John (WJ) (nephew), works on Remuera estate, 114; JD instructs on business, 115; but no businessman, 117; JD tells to be secretive, 168; is given farm at Waerenga-o-kuri, 209
Mullaghcreevy, 9, 11, 14, 99, 232
Murdoch, Dalvid Limond (banker), 127, 165, **165**, 228, **229**

Nathan, David (merchant), 28, 76–77
New Zealand Banking Company, opens Auckland branch, 27; crisis develops, 31, 43; undermined by governor's debentures, 32; ceases operations in Feb. 1845, 35
New Zealand Thames Valley Land Company, 199, 200, 201–2, 203–04, 205–07

O'Halloran, Gerald Richard (agent), JD's confidant, 151; biography, 198n; becomes JD's factotum 199, **199**; worthy steward, 214; increasing use by JD, 226
O'Rorke, Sir George Maurice (politician), 220, 220n, **220**, 230–31, 230n

Paora, Tuhaere (Ngati Whatua chief), 45–46, **46**
Parr, C.J. (MP), 145, 147, 145n
Patetere, 195–97
Patetere Land and Settlement Company, 198–201, 207
Plantations in Ireland, 2
Pollen, Dr Daniel, 139n, 139–40
Pounds, Joseph Elam (banker), 198, 204, 206
Provincial politics of Auckland, 91–95

Remuera estate: chapter 5; has 'Green Road', 71; fences and hawthorn hedges, 72–73; drainage and irrigation, 72–74; new pastoral emphasis, 77–78; up for lease or sale, 79; really three farms, 80; tree planting, 80; the homestead, 84–85; spoilt by railway severance, 122–28; bridges and crossings, 129; Graham's farm added, 138; JD retreats to homestead farm, 159; contemporary views, **160**, trees survive today, 161, **160**, **161**; plantations, 162; llamas, 162; decorative planting, 166, **167**, dairy farm, 149
Remuera Feast (or Paremata), 41–42, **50–51**, 49–52
Rich, Francis Dyer (farmer), 198, 199, 204
Roads, 74–75
Royal School of Dungannon (RSD), 18–19, **19**, 224
Russell, Hon. Thomas, 115, 115n, **115**, 118, 120

Saint John's College, 72, 74–75, 229
Saint Mark's Church (Remuera), 138, 138n
'Scoria farms', 157–59; see also Remuera estate
Scrip, government land, 54, 58–59
Selwyn Bishop G.A., 30, 72, 74

Tamaki-makau-rau, 34–35, 134–35
Taylor, Allan Kerr, 85
Taylor, William Innes, 90
Te Kawau, Apihai, 35, **35**, 37, 46
Te Wherowhero, Potatau, 39, 46, 49–52, 56.
Thames hotel, JD purchases site, 170–71; left undeveloped, 172; hotel constructed during gold rush, 178; construction difficulties, 178n; 179; adds third storey, 180; Auckland landmark, 181; JD uses as

security for borrowing, 184–86; great money spinner, 181, 191; pictures of, **170, 177, 180, 183**

Thames Valley and Rotorua Railway Co., 187, 200

Tyrone Buildings, constructed, 179; construction creates nuisance, 178–79; pictures of **170, 177, 180**

Ulster, 2–3, 6, 7–9, 20, 213, 222

Waikato tribe, 35, 39–41, 48–52, 57

Waitakere farm, bought, 100; access to, 101, **101**, given to Andrew, 101–02; heavily fertilized, 103; used for holidays, 104; seriously farmed, 152–54; pictures of access, **101, 104**; typical homestead, **153**

Walker, Edward Barnes (Waikato speculator), 196, 198–99, 204, 206

Waitemata hotel, opened under Copland, 172; appearance, **173, 174, 183**; destroyed by fire, 174; rebuilt in brick, 175; upgraded by Mahoney, 180; JD borrows upon, 184–85; great money spinner, 181, 187, 191

Ward, Professor Alan, 48, 243

Wetere, Wiremu (Te Kauae), 64–65, 68

Whaiti-Kuranui Land Association, 195–200, 202, 204–06, 212

Whitaker, Sir Frederick (lawyer, businessman, politician), 76–77, **94**, 118, 141, 163

Williamson, James (businessman), 118, 122n, 122–24, 145, 228

Williamson, John (newspaper proprietor and superintendent), 89, 92–93, 92n

Wilson, Major John (Waikato speculator), 198, 206

269